Samuel G. Beatty, J. W Johnson

The Canadian Accountant

A practical system of book-keeping - containing a complete elucidation of the science of accounts by the latest and most approved methods. Eighth Edition

Samuel G. Beatty, J. W Johnson

The Canadian Accountant

A practical system of book-keeping - containing a complete elucidation of the science of accounts by the latest and most approved methods. Eighth Edition

ISBN/EAN: 9783337188726

Printed in Europe, USA, Canada, Australia, Japan

Cover: Foto ©Andreas Hilbeck / pixelio.de

More available books at **www.hansebooks.com**

THE CANADIAN ACCOUNTANT,

A PRACTICAL SYSTEM OF

BOOK-KEEPING,

CONTAINING

A COMPLETE ELUCIDATION OF THE SCIENCE OF ACCOUNTS BY
THE LATEST AND MOST APPROVED METHODS, BUSINESS
CORRESPONDENCE, MERCANTILE FORMS, AND
OTHER VALUABLE INFORMATION.

DESIGNED FOR THE USE OF

COUNTING HOUSES, BUSINESS COLLEGES, ACADEMIES
AND HIGH SCHOOLS.

BY

S. G. BEATTY AND J. W. JOHNSON, F.C.A.

THE FORMER FOUNDER, AND THE LATTER ONE OF THE PRINCIPALS OF ONTARIO BUSINESS COLLEGE, BELLEVILLE, ONT.; A MEMBER OF THE COUNCIL OF THE INSTITUTE OF CHARTERED ACCOUNTANTS OF ONTARIO, AND AUTHOR OF "JOHNSON'S JOINT STOCK CO. BOOK-KEEPING."

Eighth Edition. Revised and Enlarged.

PUBLISHED BY THE COLLEGE.

PRICE $2.00.

BELLEVILLE: PRINTED FOR THE PUBLISHERS.

1889.

ENTERED ACCORDING TO ACT OF THE PARLIAMENT OF CANADA,
IN THE YEAR ONE THOUSAND EIGHT HUNDRED AND SEVENTY-FOUR, BY S. G. BEATTY,
AND IN THE YEAR ONE THOUSAND EIGHT HUNDRED AND SEVENTY-NINE,
BY S. G. BEATTY, AND J. W. JOHNSON,
AT THE DEPARTMENT OF AGRICULTURE.

WARNING.

The appropriating for other books of the matter herein contained, without authority and acknowledgment, will be, as it has been, severely dealt with.

PREFACE.

The study and practice of Book-keeping are now recognized not only as a Science but equally so as an Art, and, while the *science* remains permanent, the *art* is almost as variable as the different methods of conducting business. They are intimately connected with the principles upon which most men have to depend for success in the business of life, and appeal strongly to the judgment of all as essentially necessary in the education of the people.

No sensible man now disputes their paramount importance. The time has long since gone by when a hap-hazard system of recording business transactions will answer the requirements of men engaged in trade and commerce. The magnitude and variety of these engagements are such that no dependence upon mere memoranda, or an unsystematic method of keeping accounts, will enable an individual to calculate with accuracy his gains and losses, and so order his affairs that he may know at any time how he stands with his debtors and creditors. There must be a system, and that system must be reduced to an exact science, as invariable in its results as the problems of Euclid. Is such a thing possible in the theory and practice of Book-keeping? It is possible, and its possibility is not only thoroughly established in the commercial world, but it is made imperative in the qualification of those who expect to compete in the great struggle of business life. This view is now so universally acknowledged and acted upon, that attention is being called to the necessity that exists for a more thorough and practical course of business training even in our public schools.

In the present work the authors have aimed at a combination of the most practical modes of keeping accounts, adapted to various departments of business, and have brought to bear upon it the experience gained as practical accountants, in connection with some of the most extensive business houses, joint stock companies, and manufacturing concerns in Canada, and as teachers of the subject for many years in the largest and most successful Business College in the Dominion.

The arrangement is such that the divisions of the subject are presented in a naturally progressive order, and the student is led by easy transitions from simple transactions to the most intricate exercises to be met with in business, and is able without difficulty to trace the connecting links that make the whole science one harmonious system of definite and accurate business record. The work is, as the name implies, something more than a mere treatise on Book-keeping. It deals not only with the *science* as applied to accounts, but explains and elucidates the *art* by which these accounts and all other forms of dealing and communication are applied to every-day transactions.

It is divided into three parts, each distinct in its own special design, but so arranged that the student can trace the mutual dependence of one upon the other, and follow the progressive steps that lead to the final result.

Part I. Contains a complete and comprehensive course of Book-keeping, illustrated by means of examples of sufficient variety to make it easy of comprehension.

Part II. is intended as a business course for advanced pupils, and comprehends the most practical forms of keeping accounts, according to the methods adopted by the best business houses. It includes Wholesale and Retail Merchandising, Manufacturing, Settlement of Estates, Steamboating, Municipal Book-keeping, Warehousing, Banking, Farm Accounts, Church Accounts, Practical office work, Joint Stock Companies, &c.

Part III. contains a comprehensive summary of Ontario Law, forms of business papers in general use, and the principal laws which govern them, full instructions on Commercial Correspondence, with a great variety of Model Business Letters, short practical methods of computing Interest, Percentage, Partial Payments, Partnership Settlements, &c., besides valuable rules for Lumbermen, Mechanics and Farmers, illustrated by examples.

Many thanks are here tendered business men and mechanics, who most courteously responded to questions presented to them, and furnished valuable and reliable information respecting particular departments of business.

PREFACE TO FOURTH EDITION.

To the present edition has been added a set of Farm Accounts, originally prepared by J. W. Johnson, at the suggestion of the Honorable the Provincial Treasurer of Ontario, for the Royal Commission appointed to take evidence on Agricultural matters in the year 1880, and which is recommended by the Commissioners, and printed by them, along with the author's evidence, in their report.

The present edition is thoroughly revised, and the work is again enlarged, much valuable and practical matter being added.

The authors are determined that the "CANADIAN ACCOUNTANT" shall always be in the front rank as a text book, and they will continue to add, as they have in this and former editions, whatever in their own experience, or the experience of others, they may find valuable in accounts, and worthy of a place in such a work.

PREFACE TO FIFTH EDITION.

The last edition of this book was published in 1881, and in 1882 another is called for.

We have in this, as in all former editions, added a large amount of original and valuable matter, and notably a set of accounts illustrating a double entry method of keeping the books of a church or other public institution. Other subjects, pertaining to practical accounting and office work, which had already a place in the book, have been enlarged upon, and more fully illustrated and explained.

Since the fourth edition was published, the law imposing duties upon Promissory Notes and Bills of Exchange has been repealed, and the necessary changes, consequent on this, have been made throughout the various portions of the work.

PREFACE TO EIGHTH EDITION.

A large amount of new and valuable matter has been added to the last two editions; notably the chapter on Law, prepared by Mr. W. N. Ponton, M. A., barrister, of Belleville, and lecturer on Commercial Law at Ontario Business College. High Schools and Business Colleges, with which the "Canadian Accountant" is so popular as a text book, will find this new feature of the work most valuable to their pupils.

The chapters on Banking and Joint Stock Companies that we have added will also, we venture to say, be found worthy of a place in the book.

The demand for the "Accountant," for use in High Schools, Business Colleges and offices, now extends throughout all the provinces of Canada, and many orders are received from the United States and the West Indies.

S. G. BEATTY.
J. W. JOHNSON.

Ontario Business College,
    Belleville, 1889.

INDEX TO SUBJECTS.

Subject	PAGE
Abbreviations used in the Work	9
Account Sales	60
Accommodation Note	66, 178
Acceptance of a Draft	63, 230
Addition	272
Administrator's Form	120
Advice of Shipment	267
Agreement for Building a House	245
Alteration of Notes	227
Application for a Situation	269
Arithmetical Signs	10
Articles of Co-Partnership	244
Assets and Liabilities Statement	173
Assessment	154
Assignment of Lease	235
Assignment of Mortgage	237
Average of Accounts	283
Average of Account Sales	288
Balancing Accounts	42
Balance Sheet	91
Banking	137
Bank Pass Book	138
Bank Check Book	139, 143
Bank Draft	142
Bill Book	54, 55
Bills and Invoices	56
Bill for Services	59
Bills of Exchange	224
Bills of Lading	232, 242
Bills Payable	20
Bills Receivable	20
Board Measure	294
Bonds and Mortgages Payable	2
Bonds and Mortgages Receivable	21
Bond	236
Bricklayers' Work	290
Books as Evidence in Court	176
Books used in Double Entry	16
Book-Keeping for Churches and Public Institutions	199
Business Forms	56
Business Letters	261
Business Series	49
Business Statements	90
Cash Account	19
Cash Book	71, 86, 109
Cancellation	276
Carpenters' Work	296
Cattle Weight by Measurement	304
Charges Account	21
Changing Single to Double Entry	82
Changing Double to Single Entry	84
Cheese Factory Milk Book	134
Circular Letter	270
Classified Statements	37
Classification of Accounts	39
Clearing House	141
Closing the Ledger	43
Combined Statement	76
Commercial Papers	232
Commercial Law	216
Compound Partnership	309
Condensed System of Book-keeping for Retail Business	122
Consignments Explained	67
Cost Mark, Set of Characters for	198
Coupons	232, 250
Correspondence	253
Correction of Errors	48, 136
Credit Note	59
Cross Entries	136
Day Book	16, 28
Day Book Index	123
Dealings with Banks	138
Detection of Errors	47, 135
Deposit Slip	142
Debentures	156, 232, 250
Debenture Register	156
Debtor and Creditor	16
Deeds	243
Delivery Order	181
Dividend on Shares	72
Distribution of Gains and Losses in Partnership	80
Distinction between Single and Double Entry	15, 81
Discharge of Mortgage	238
Discounting Bills and Invoices	305
Discounting Notes and Entries	178
Dissolution of Partnership Notice	311
Divisors for Circular Figures	302
Double Entry	15, 23
Double Equation of Accounts	285
Drafts	62, 67
Due Bills	64
Dunning Letters	263
Easy Method of Addition	273
Entries for Renewals of Notes	176
Equation of Accounts	283
Estimates Municipal Book-keeping	154
Etiquette of Letter Writing	259
Exercises in Ledger Accounts	18
Exercises in Journalizing Shipments and Consignments	68
Expense Account	21
Example of Single Entry	81
Explanations and Forms of Business Papers	224
Examples of Punctuation	256
Filing Business Papers	73
Farm Accounts	186
Form of a Bond	235
Form of a Letter	255
Forms of Endorsements	228
Forms of Business Papers	224
Freight Book	144, 148
Fuel Book	144
Glaziers' Work	301
Gauging Casks	303
Good Will	77
Hands' Register	144, 146
Hay, Figuring Cost of	291
How to put Cheques through the Cash Book	88
How to Mark Cost and Retail Price on Goods	198
Insurance Account	21
Interest and Discount Account	21
Index to the Ledger	32
Invoices	58
Invoice Book	107, 108
Indorsements	228
Interest by Cancellation	277
Interest (various methods)	277
Interest on Notes	231
Inventory of Stock	29
Journal	17, 30
Journalizing	24
Journal Day Book	85, 105, 130
Journalizing Shipment Co.'s and Merchandise Co.'s	94
Joint Notes	227
Joint Stock Companies	207

	PAGE
Ledger	17, 32, 45
Leases	234, 235
Letter inclosing Account Sales	268
Letter of Recommendation	268
Letter Answering an Advertisement	268
Letter of Authority to Sign Business Papers	271
Letter Acknowledging Receipt of Shipment	271
Letter of Credit	224
Letters of Introduction	261
Logs Reduced to Board Measure	294
Lost Bill or Note	232
Manufacturing Business	125
Manifest	242
Mason's Work	298
Mercantile Terms	10
Merchandise Account	19
Merchandise Companies	92
Measurement of Lumber	293
Measurement of Corn in Crib	303
Measurement of Grain	304
Measurement of Wood	291
Measuring Land	304
Mechanics Work	296
Method of Writing off Bad Debts	179
Method of keeping Bank Acct. in Cash Book	109
Millers' Rule for Weighing Wheat	292
Monthly Trial Balance	116
Monthly Journal	124
Mortgage	236
Monthly Statement	57
Municipal Accounts	154
Multiplication	274
Non-Resident Tax Book	156
Notes and Bills	51, 65, 225
Notice of Protest	241
Obligations of Parties	228
Observations on Books	147
Opening Ledgers under various circumstances	183
Order of Closing Accounts	42
Orders	64
Order for Goods	265
Partial Payments	282
Painters' Work	298
Partnership	308
Partners' Capital and Partners' Current Acct	185
Partnership Settlements	310
Passage Book	144, 146
Parties to a Bill or Note	226
Pay Roll	133
Paying a Note before Maturity	179
Payment of Notes	231
Personal Accounts	21
Plasterers' Work	298
Plant Account	129
Power of Attorney	247
Promissory Notes	65, 225
Private Ledger	175
Protests	238
Practical Computations	272
Profit and Loss	281
Problems in Partnership Settlements	312
Punctuation	255
Questions for Review, Chap. I	23
Questions for Review, Chap. II	38
Questions for Review, Chap. III	48
Questions for Review, Chap. IV	66
Questions for Review, Chap. V	88
Questions for Review Business Papers	252
Quit Claim Deed	243
Rapid Process of Marking Goods	275
Results of Exercises in Ledger Accts	22
Remarks on Notes and Bills	51

	PAGE
Remittance Blank and Receipt	233
Renewals of Notes	54, 70
Receipts	61, 233
Recommendations in favor party seeking a situation	269
Reduction of Dollars and Cents to Sterling Money	324
Reduction of Sterling Money to Dollars and Cents	324
Requisites of a Bill or Note	225
Retail Mark, Set of Letters for	198
Rule for Journalizing	25
Rules for Journalizing Drafts	67
Rules for Cancellation	276
Sales Book	117
Set I	27
Set II	49
Set III	50
Set IV	53
Set V	69
Set VI	74
Set VII	76
Set VIII	79
Set IX	83
Set X	96
Set XI	103
Set XII	120
Set XIII	125
Shares Bought	69
Shipments Explained	67
Shipment Companies	92
Simple Deed	242
Single Entry	78
Six Column Journal	96, 100
Simple Partnership	308
Sinking Fund, How to Levy	156
Slating Measurement	297
Specimen Ledger Closed	45
Statement of Losses and Gains	37
Statement of Resources and Liabilities	38
Steamboating Set	144
Stock Exchange	211, 214
Storage	290
Stock or Inventory Book	99
Subsidiary Ledger	190, 204
Suggestions to Depositors in Banks	139
Suggestions for Drawing Checks	130
Summary of Ontario Law	216
Sundry Debtors Account	99
Superscription, Form of	260
Table for marking articles bought by the dozen	270
Time and Wages Register	131
Titles of Respect in Correspondence	257
Tiling Measurement	297
To close a Single Entry Ledger	82
To show Settlements in Ledger Accounts without ruling	180
To find the Cubical Contents of Round Timber	295
To find the Cubical Contents of Square Timber	295
Trial Balance	36, 172
Trade and Cash Discounts	196
Transfer of Notes and Bills	229
Transferring Accts. from an old Ledger to a new one	186
Useful Contractions	274
Waiving Protest	238
Warehousing Set of Books	181
Warehouse Receipt	181
Warrant Book	156
Weekly Time and Wages Register	132
Will	246

TO THE STUDENT.

The course of study comprehended in this work is of the most useful and practical nature. It is not designed simply for the merchant, but so arranged as to be of incalculable advantage to all classes of the community—the farmer as well as the merchant, the mechanic as well as the professional man.

As you commence these studies, remember they are worthy of your best energies, and require persevering application to thoroughly master them. You enter upon them for the purpose of acquiring an education that will fit you to transact business systematically. You bring to bear in connection with your labors such heart and brain as it pleased the Almighty to give you. You should let it be a settled rule with you never to proceed onward while anything remains unconquered behind.

The implied compact between you and your teachers pledges both parties to a faithful performance of duty. It is, therefore, of the first importance that you should enter upon your labors with a thorough appreciation of your privileges and obligations.

In the first place you require to apply yourself systematically and faithfully or the best instruction will avail you but little. Your teacher is merely your guide. He can locate your difficulty, and point out the path you are to pursue, but learning is the result of thinking, and no teacher can either think for you or endow you with thought.

Do not be ashamed to confess your ignorance, or pretend to understand that which you do not, for assumption of knowledge is the greatest stumbling-block to progress; it becomes a perpetual rock of offence to those who would gladly aid you, if the way were clear.

Do not ask for aid until you need it, which will be when, after faithful trial, you have failed in the attainment of the desired result. A teacher who will aid you sooner than this may mean to be kind, but is unthinking, and in fact doing you an injury.

This book contains the work assigned for the Theoretical Course in Ontario Business College, and is calculated to impress upon your mind the principles of the science of accounts, and to prepare you for work of a more difficult and varied nature which will be presented hereafter. Your success in the more advanced departments will depend to a great extent upon the thoroughness of your understanding of the work you are about to commence; therefore, do not measure your attainment from time to time by the number of pages over which you pass, but by the perfectness of your mastery over them. Do not under any consideration pass from one set to another without fully understanding the subject both in its general and special application.

Your labor will not be purely and only intellectual. The accountant requires a neat, legible, rapid style of penmanship. The intrinsic value of this accomplishment is beyond computation, and should receive the attention its importance demands. A good, expeditious hand-writing is one of the strongest elements of promotion and success, and carries with it an indisputable reference.

The collateral studies of Arithmetic, Correspondence, etc., which you will pursue in connection herewith, are essential to a fair understanding of your duties, as well as to the symmetry of your course of training, and should not be under-rated.

Make every arithmetical calculation yourself, as you proceed. Rely upon no result stated in the book, until you have first made the computation on which it depends; otherwise you will gain little from its perusal. What is worth doing at all is worth doing well.

In solving the Examples for practice, exercise your *own common sense* in determining how each transaction is to be entered.

Make yourself familiar with the most concise and business-like form of expression, in recording your transactions, and in your correspondence.

Spell all words correctly. Pay the strictest attention to punctuality, neatness, accuracy and order.

Accuracy in accounts is a cardinal virtue. It is less difficult to fall into errors than to *correct* them. Therefore,

Exercise all diligence to keep your Account Books neat, legible, promptly written up, and free from errors.

VOCABULARY

OF

ABBREVIATIONS AND MERCANTILE TERMS

ABBREVIATIONS.

Adv.	Adventure.	Ent.	Entry.
Ac't.	Account.	Ex.	Example.
Amer.	American.	Exch.	Exchange.
Am't.	Amount.	Exp's.	Expenses.
Ans.	Answer.		
Apr.	April.	Fav.	Favor.
Ass'd, or As'd.	Assorted.	Feb.	February.
Aug.	August.	Fig'd.	Figured.
		Fol.	Folio.
Bal.	Balance.	Forw'd.	Forward.
B.-B.	Bill Book, Bank Book.	Fr.	From.
Bbl.	Barrel.	Fr't.	Freight.
Bills Pay. or B.P.	Bills Payable.	F. O. B.	Free on Board.
Bills Rec. or B.R.	Bills Receivable.	F. O. C.	Free on Cars.
B'k.	Bank.		
Bl'k.	Black.	Gal.	Gallon.
Bo't.	Bought.	Guar.	Guarantee.
Bro't.	Brought.		
		Hhd.	Hogshead.
Cap.	Capital, Chapter.		
C.-B.	Cash Book.	I.-B.	Invoice Book.
Co.	Company.	I. E.	(Id est.) That is.
Col'd.	Colored.	Ins.	Insurance.
Com.	Commission, Commerce	Insol.	Insolvency.
Consg't.	Consignment.	Inst.	(Instant) The present month.
Cr.	Creditor or Credit.		
C. O. D.	Collect on Delivery.	Int.	Interest.
D.-B.	Day Book.	Inv't.	Inventory.
Dec.	December.		
Dep.	Deposited.	Jan.	January.
D'ft.	Draft.	Jour.	Journal.
Dis.	Discount.	J. F.	Journal Folio.
Div.	Dividend.		
Do.	(Ditto) The same.	Lab.	Labor.
Doz.	Dozen.	Lbs.	Pounds.
Dr.	Debtor or Debit.	Led.	Ledger.
Dray.	Drayage.	L. F.	Ledger Folio.
D'ys.	Days.	L. & G.	Loss and Gain.
Ea.	Each.	Mar.	March.
E. E.	Errors Excepted.	Mdse.	Merchandise.
E. & O. E.	Errors and Omissions Excepted.	M. or Mo.	Month.
		Mols.	Molasses.
Eng.	English.	Mut.	Mutual.

N. B.	(Nota Bene.) Take notice.	St'b't.	Steamboat.
No.	Number.	Stor.	Storage.
Nov.	November.	Sund's.	Sundries.
		Super. or S.F.	Superfine.
Oct.	October.		
O. I. B.	Outward Invoice Book.	Ult.	(Ultimo.) The last.
P.	Page.	Viz.	(Videlicet.) To wit, namely.
Par.	Face Value.	Vs.	(Versus.) Against.
Pay't.	Payment.		
P.-C.-B.	Petty Cash Book.	Weigh.	Weighing.
P'd.	Paid.		
P'k'g's.	Packages.	Y'ds.	Yards.
Per.	Personal.	Yr.	Year.
Pr.	(Per) By.		
Pr. ct.	(Per centum.) By the hundred.	@	At.
Prem.	Premium.	%	(Per centum.) By the hundred.
Prof.	Profit.		
Prox.	(Proximo.) The next month.	+	Sign of Addition.
Ps.	Pieces.	−	" Subtraction.
Rec'd.	Received.	×	" Multiplication.
R.-R.	Railroad.	÷	" Division.
		=	" Equality.
S. B.	Sales-Book.	"	(Ditto.) The same.
Sept.	September.	1¼	One and one-quarter.
Sh.	Share.	1½	One and one-half.
Ship't.	Shipment.	1¾	One and three-quarters.

MERCANTILE AND LEGAL TERMS.

Abatement—A deduction of discount for damages on goods, or for payment of demands before due, etc.

Acceptance—1st. The receiving of a draft or order, in such a way as to bind the acceptor to payment. It consists in the acceptor writing across the face of the bill "accepted," and signing his name. If drawn payable at a certain number of days' sight, the date of acceptance should also be given. 2nd. A draft accepted.

Accommodation—A loan of money. When applied to bills of exchange, it is where the drawee lends his name for the use of the drawer.

Account Current—An exhibit in detail of a running account between two or more parties.

Account Sales—An exhibit of the sales of goods disposed of on commission, with the charges incurred thereon.

Ad Valorem—According to value. An ad valorem duty is a certain percentage on the first cost or invoice price.

Advance—Additional price; profit; premium. Money paid on property or goods accepted, or on goods held in possession for security.

Adventure—Goods sent to a distance to be sold on commission.

Advice—Mercantile intelligence.

Alias—Otherwise.

Annuity—A sum of money payable periodically, usually yearly.

Ante-date—To date before the present time; to date beforehand.

Arbitration—The hearing and determination of a cause between parties in a controversy, by a person or persons chosen for the purpose. A hearing before arbitrators, though they make no award.

Assets—Available means for payment of debts; goods, estate, and indebtedness of others.

Assignee—One to whom an assignment is made. One appointed or deputed for some specific purpose.

Assignment—Conditional transfer of property to another. The property so transferred.

Assignor—One who makes an assignment.

Attachment—A claim on property legally executed.

Aune—A French cloth measure, one yard and a quarter.

Average—Sums allowed for losses at sea. A medium time found by equation.

Balance—To close an account in the Ledger. Difference between the debits and credits. An account in the Ledger, into which all balances are closed.

Bankrupt—Insolvent. One unable to pay his debts.

Bill, or Bill of Parcels—A statement in detail of goods bought or sold.

Bills—A term applied to drafts, notes, etc.

Bill of Entry—A list of goods entered at the Custom-house.

Bill of Exchange—An order for the payment of money; usually applied to drafts on persons in another country from the drawer.

Bill of Lading—A written account of goods shipped, having the signature of the master, agent or purser of the vessel on which shipped.

Bill of Sale—A contract under seal for the sale of goods.

Bill of Store—A Custom-house Licence for carrying to sea ship-stores and provisions free of duty.

Blank Credit—Permission granted by one house to another to draw on it at pleasure to a specified amount.

Bona fide—In good faith.

Bond—A note. An obligation or deed by which a person binds himself, his heirs, executors and administrators, or a company, or corporation bind themselves to pay a certain sum on or before a certain day.

Bonded Goods—Those for the duties on which bonds are given at the Custom-house.

Bottomry Bonds—A mortgage or lien upon a vessel.

Brace— A measure of $\frac{5}{8}$ of a yard.

Broker—A money or stock trader. Factor; agent.

Brokerage—A percentage for the purchase and sale of money and stocks.

Capital—Stock in trade.

Capias—A writ to authorize the seizure of a defendant's person.

Cargo—The lading or freight of a vessel.

Catty—A Chinese weight of $1\frac{3}{4}$ lbs. Avoirdupoids.

Carrying Trade—The transportation of goods by a vessel from country to country.

Charter Party—A written agreement between the owner of a vessel and the person to whom she is chartered.

Circular Letter—A printed notice issued by a house, relative to its business.

Clearing a Vessel—Entering at the Custom-house all particulars relating to her when she is ready to sail, and paying clearance charges.

Clearance—A certificate from a Custom-house that a vessel has been cleared.

Closing an Account—Making an entry to balance it, and drawing lines underneath to indicate that it is closed.

Cocket—A Custom-house warrant to show that goods have been entered.

Commission—A percentage allowed for the sale of goods.

Compound—To settle with a creditor by agreement, and discharge a debt by paying part of its amount.

Compromise—An adjustment of difference by mutual concession.

Consignee—One to whom goods or wares are consigned.

Consignment—Goods sent to an agent to be sold for the consignor.

Consignor—The person making a consignment.

Contraband Goods—Articles prohibited by the law to be imported or exported.

Contra—On the other side; opposite.

Convoy—Ships of war sailing with other vessels as a protection.

Co-partnership—The union of two or more persons for purposes of trade.

Counter order—A revocation of a former order.

Credit—That side of the account which shows the amount due to the person or thing represented. The amount of confidence reposed in another.

Custom-house—The House where vessels are entered and cleared, and where the duties on goods are paid.

Days of Grace—The days allowed for the payment of a bill after it becomes due. In the United States and in Great Britain and her dependencies, the number of days of grace is three; but it varies very much in other commercial states, reaching thirty days in Genoa, there being none allowed at Leghorn. Bills drawn at sight are usually paid when presented, without grace.

Debenture—A writing ackowledging a debt, a Bond on which Companies or Municipalities borrow money.
Debit—That side of an account which shows the indebtedness of the person or thing represented.
Defalcation—Deduction; diminution. That which is deducted or cut off.
Demurrage—Forfeit money for detaining a vessel beyond the time specified in her Charter-party.
Depot—A place where goods are deposited; a depository; a magazine.
Deviation—The voluntary departure of a vessel without necessity, from the regular and usual course of the specific voyages insured, which frees the underwriters from obligation.
Discount—Any deduction from the stipulated price of goods, or from a sum due or to be due at a future time.
Dividend—Gains on stock, shares in trade, etc.
Dock—A place to build, repair or lodge vessels.
Draft—An order from one person on another for the payment of money; a bill of exchange.
Drawer—The one who draws a bill or draft on another. The maker of a note.
Drawee—The person on whom a bill is drawn.
Drawback—Amount paid back. Any loss of advantage, or deduction from profit.
Duplicate—A copy.
Duty—A government tax on exported or imported goods.
E. G. Exempli gratia—For the sake of example.
Effects—Money, property on hand, and debts due.
Ell—Flemish (E. Fl.)—A measure of ¾ of a yard.
Embargo.—A restraint on ships by Government; or prohibition of sailing either out of port, or into port, or both.
Emporium—A mart. A town or city of trade; particularly a commercial city.
Endorse—To write one's name on the back of a bill; to become security for its payment.
Entry—A record made in an account book. The depositing of a ship's papers at the Custom-house to procure license to land goods.
Engross—To monopolize; to purchase the whole or large quantities of commodities in market, so as to enhance the price.
Equity of Redemption—The advantage allowed to a mortgagor, of a reasonable time to redeem lands mortgaged.
Ex-officio—By virtue of his office.
Exchange—The giving of one commodity for another. The place where the merchants, bankers and brokers meet, at certain hours, to transact business. Discount and premium arising from the purchase and sale of bills and money.
Ex-parte—On one part.
Face—The amount for which a bill is drawn.
Fac simile—An exact copy.
Factor—An agent employed by merchants to buy and sell, or transact business on their account.
Failure—A breaking or becoming insolvent.
Favor—A bill is said to be drawn in favor of the person to whom it is payable.
Finance, or Finances—Revenue; funds in the public treasury. The resources or income of individuals.
Financier—One skilled in money matters. A revenue officer.
Firm—The name or title under which a company transacts business; a partnership, or house.
Flat—Low (as in the prices of goods); or dull (as to sales).
Foreclose—To foreclose a mortgage is to cut a mortgagor off from his equity of redemption.
Folio—Page of an account book; both the right and left hand pages expressed by the same figure.
Freight—Lading; that which is carried by carriers. Sums charged by a vessel for the transportation of goods.
Good Will—Bonus paid for a business.
Guarantee, or Guaranty—Indemnity or security against loss; a pledge for the fulfilment of stipulations; one who binds himself to see the stipulations of another performed.
Gratis—For nothing.
Habeas Corpus—(a writ in law) you may have the body.
Honor—As applied to drafts, means to accept and pay when due.
Hypothecate—To pledge, to give as security.
Hypothecated—Pledged, as security for money borrowed.
H. C. J.—High Court of Justice.

Importation—The bringing of goods from another country to one's own country. The commodities imported.
Insurance—Security against loss. The premium paid for insuring property or life.
Insolvent—Not having money, goods, or estate sufficient to pay all debts. A debtor unable to pay his debts.
Instalment—A part of a sum of money paid, or to be paid, at a particular period.
Interest—A percentage paid for the use of money.
International—Relating to the mutual intercourse between different nations.
Inventory—An account in detail of property.
Invoice—See Inventory. Inventory is generally applied to a catalogue of goods on hand; Invoice to goods purchased, received from abroad, or about to be shipped.
Ipse dixit—He himself said it.
Labor Omnia Vincit—Labor conquers everything.
Landing Waiter—A Custom-house officer whose duty is to wait or attend on the landing of goods.
Lease—A contract granting possession of property for a stipulated time.
Letter of Attorney—A writing by which one person authorizes another to act in his stead.
Letter of Credit—A letter authorizing one person to receive funds on the credit of another.
Letter of Licence—A written permission for a person under embarrassment to conduct his business for a time without molestation.
(L.S.) Locus Sigilli—the place of the seal.
Letter of Marque—A written commission or authority given by Government to private vessels, to make reprisals on the vessels of another nation.
Liabilities—Debts of an individual, or claims against him.
Licence—A legal permit to sell certain articles of merchandise.
Lien—Legal claim, as a lien upon land, houses, etc.
Lighter—A craft used to lighten vessels in shoal water.
Lighterage—A charge for carrying goods to and from a vessel in a lighter.
Liquidation—The act of adjusting and paying debts. Winding up a business.
Locum tenens—A deputy or substitute.
Manifest—An exhibit of a vessel's cargo.
Mandamus—We order; a law writ.
Mart—A place of public sale and traffic.
Maturity—The time when a bill falls due.
Maximum—The highest price of an article.
Merchandise—The usual articles of trade.
Metre—A measure of 11-12 yards.
Minimum—The lowest price of an article.
Minutiæ—Trifles; minute parts.
Mint—A place where money is coined.
Mortgage—The grant of an estate in fee, as security for the payment of money.
Mortgagor—The person who grants or pledges property for security of debt.
Mortgagee—The person to whom an estate is mortgaged.
Nem. con.—Abbreviation for nemine contradicente—Without opposition.
Net proceeds—The remainder after deducting all charges from the amount of gross sales.
Net weight—The weight of a commodity after deducting tare and all other allowances.
Nolle prosequi—To be unwilling to proceed.
Non-claim—A failure to claim within the time limited by law. Omission of claim.
Notary, or Notary Public—A person legally authorized to attest contracts or writings of any kind; also to take note of the non-payment of bills, promissory notes, etc., which is called protesting.
Note—A written obligation to pay money; a memorandum.
Obligation—Indebtedness. A bond with a consideration annexed, and a penalty for non-fulfilment.
Obligee—The person to whom another is bound.
Obligator—The person who binds himself, or gives a bond to another.
Order—A request to deliver or pay to a person certain moneys or goods. Any request made of another in writing.
Par of Exchange—The intrinsic value of money, when compared with that of other countries, both in weight and fineness. The nominal value of a pound sterling.
Partnership—See Co-partnership.

Payee—The person to whom money is to be paid.
Per Annum—By the year.
Per Pro—Per Procuration.
Per Se—By itself.
Policy, or Policy of Insurance—The writing, or instrument by which a contract of indemnity to the insured is effected between him and the insurer.
Portage—The incidental sums paid by a Captain in running his vessel.
Postdate—To date after the real time.
Posting—Transferring the Journal entries into the Ledger.
Power of Attorney—Written authority given to a person to act for another.
Premium—Beyond the face value.
Price Current—A list of various articles of merchandise, with their market values.
Prima Facie—On the first view, or appearance. Presumptive evidence.
Principal—The chief of a commercial house or firm. Capital sum due, lent or owed, in contradistinction to interest.
Primage—A percentage allowed to the master of a vessel on the amount of freight transported.
Procuration—The act of procuring. The instrument by which a person is empowered to transact business for another.
Pro Tempore—For the time.
Pro Forma—According to form. Thus a pro forma Account Sales is an imaginary Account Sales, made out in form of a real one, to send to parties abroad, to give information of prices, charges, commission, etc.
Promissory Note—A writing which contains a promise for the payment of money unconditionally.
Protest—A Notary's document, declaring that a bill was not accepted when presented, or was not paid when it fell due.
Quantum—How much.
Quarantine—Restraint of intercourse to which a ship is subjected, for a limited term, on the presumption that she may be infected with a malignant contagious disease.
Quid pro quo—What for what.
Quo warranto?—By what warrant? (a legal writ.)
Rate of Exchange—The percentage above or below the par value of a Bill of Exchange.
Rebate or Rebatement—Abatement of price; deduction for prompt payment.
Receipt—A writing acknowledging the receipt of money or goods.
Remittance—Bills or money sent from one house to another. The act of sending the same.
Renewal of a Bill—Prolonging the time of payment, by making a new bill.
Resources—Funds, money, or that which may be converted into supplies. See Assets.
R. S. O.—Revised Statutes of Ontario.
Salvage—A reward allowed for saving property from loss at sea or by fire.
Schedule—A piece of paper or parchment containing an inventory of goods.
Sea-worthy—Fitted in every respect for a voyage.
Seize—To take possession by virtue of a warrant, or legal authority.
Set of Exchange—A number of Bills of Exchange (usually three), drawn of the same tenor and date. Each Bill is forwarded by a different conveyance, to prevent failures, and one of them being paid the remainder are of no value.
Shipment—Goods on board a vessel. The goods shipped.
Sight or at Sight—The time when a bill is presented to the drawee.
Signature—The name of a person written or subscribed by himself.
Sine die—Without fixing the day.
Sine qua non—Without which a thing cannot be; hence an indispensable condition.
Smuggling—Passing goods into a country clandestinely, without paying duties.
Solidity—The estimate a mercantile house bears as to property.
Solvent—Able to pay all debts.
Staple Goods—The principal products of a country. Goods not liable to perish.
Stock—Capital invested in trade. Goods on hand. The name of a person in business.
Subpœna—Under a penalty. A writ summoning a witness.
Surety—Security against loss or damage. One bound for payment of another's debts; bondsman; bail.
Tare—An allowance for the weight of boxes, barrels, etc., in which merchandise is put up.
Tariff—A list or table of duties or customs on Mdse., imported or exported.
Teller—An officer of a bank employed to receive deposits or pay money on cheques.
Tide Waiters—Officers who watch the lading and unlading of a vessel, to secure duties, as a check on contraband trade, etc.
Tonnage—The weight or measurement of goods carried in a vessel, or the capacity of a vessel.
Transfer—To carry from one account to another. To make over; to convey from one to another.
Trustee—A person to whom anything is committed in trust.
Underwriters—Persons who insure property against loss.
Usury—Formerly interest; in present usage, illegal interest.
Vice-Versa—The terms being exchanged.
Voucher—A book, paper or document, which serves to vouch the truth of accounts; a receipt.
Wharfage—Money paid for the use of a wharf.

BOOK-KEEPING.

CHAPTER I.

BOOK-KEEPING is the science of recording business transactions in such a manner that a clear and accurate statement of affairs is always shown. Every person engaged in the ordinary pursuits of life should keep a book of some kind in which to record his business transactions. The farmer, the mechanic, and the day laborer, as well as the merchant, should keep an account with every person with whom they deal, and not trust transactions of a pecuniary nature to memory alone.

There are two methods of Bookkeeping; the one is termed *Single Entry*, and the other *Double Entry*.

In Single Entry each transaction is entered but once in the Ledger, to the *debit* or *credit* side of an account; while in Double Entry each transaction is entered twice in the Ledger, to the *debit* side of one account and the *credit* side of some other account; that is, Single Entry consists of but one *debit* or one *credit*; while Double Entry contains both a *debit* and a *credit*. A fuller explanation of the principle will be found at page 26.

DOUBLE ENTRY.

The origin of the science of Double Entry Book-keeping has been a matter of much speculation by different writers on the subject, but nothing definite can be ascertained respecting it. It is said to have been first practised in Venice, Genoa, and other towns of Italy, where trade was conducted on an extensive scale, at a much earlier date than in England, France, or other parts of Europe. To whomsoever the credit belongs, the Italians have pretty generally received it, and the system shown in the explanatory set given here is usually denominated the Italian method.

The system of keeping books by Double Entry is much to be preferred, on account of its greater accuracy. It not only affords a proof of its own correctness, but in addition to showing the condition of business, gives also, with mathematical exactness, an indication of the particular channels through which gains and losses accrue. In Double Entry, all the results, including resources, liabilities, gains and losses, are shown in the Ledger, while in Single Entry the results attainable are partially gathered from auxiliary books, such as the Cash Book, Bill Book, &c.

The main distinction between the two systems is that, while in Single Entry a record is kept of RESOURCES and LIABILITIES shown in accounts with persons only; in Double Entry a similar and additional record is kept of all resources and liabilities, and of special GAINS and LOSSES. This great feature of Double Entry should commend it at once to all prudent business men; for, while it may properly be regarded as affording a true indication of the comparative merits of the various schemes of profit, it also, in a great measure, guards against errors and omissions which might pass undetected in Single Entry. Another important consideration in this connection is, that an individual or firm may engage in various kinds of business, or may divide a large business into various departments, and in the same set of books, by Double Entry, tell what each gains or loses. This knowledge could not be obtained by Single Entry.

The leading feature of Double Entry is the theory of equal debits and credits, that is: every DEBIT must have a CREDIT of equal amount, and every CREDIT a DEBIT of equal amount.

DEBTOR AND CREDITOR.

One of the great difficulties that besets the student on commencing the study of accounts is a proper knowledge of the meaning of the terms "Debit and Credit." A simple meaning of debit is to *charge*, and of credit to *trust*.

Whenever one person receives anything from another, which he does not pay for at the time, he is said to *go in debt* for it, and is called a DEBTOR. A person who sells property without receiving his pay at the time is said to *give credit*, and is called a CREDITOR. In other words, the *receiver* is always the DEBTOR, and the *giver* the CREDITOR. In keeping accounts it is customary and more convenient to abridge and write Dr. for Debtor, and Cr. for Creditor.

A business transaction consists in the exchange of one thing for another. In every transaction there must be both a *buyer* and a *seller*. When the property which exchanges hands is not paid for at the time of the transfer, the buyer becomes a Debtor, and the seller a Creditor. The following will serve as an illustration of the correct use of the terms already employed:

TRANSACTION.—*John Smith buys of Thomas Jones one suit of clothes, for which he agrees to pay him hereafter twenty dollars.* In this transaction John Smith is the debtor, or *receiver;* and Thomas Jones the creditor, or *giver*.

BOOKS USED IN DOUBLE ENTRY.

The old Italian method of keeping books by Double Entry has been adopted in the first sets of this Work, because it is the basis of all other forms, and therefore the best from which to learn the first principles of the science. The main books of entry are, Day-Book, Journal and Ledger. Other books are introduced further on.

DAY-BOOK.

The Day-book, in the Italian method, is a plain history of business transactions, written in the date and order of their occurrence. It is necessary to open the Day-Book by giving therein a statement of your effects at the commencement of business, and also what debts you owe. Afterward record in detail every transaction that occurs in the course of business, making the entry in as few words as possible; but having it complete. Every entry should embrace the following particulars: 1st, the date; 2nd, the person or account; 3rd, what you have bought or sold, paid or received; 4th, the terms of payment; 5th, the articles, quantities, prices and amounts.

In writing this book, everything should be clearly expressed in as uniform a style as possible, and the use of ambiguous words and phrases carefully avoided.

JOURNAL.

The Journal is used for arranging under Ledger titles the entries of the Day-Book, and for affixing to each Ledger title the correct amount of debit or credit, which is called journalizing. This is done that the accounts may with ease be collected under their proper heads in the Ledger.

LEDGER.

The transferring of accounts from the Journal to the Ledger is called posting.

The Ledger may be appropriately termed the *grand réservoir* of accounts, into which all records in the other books flow as naturally as streams into the ocean. Its principal use is to collect under one head all sums belonging to the same account.

The advantages of having the items of accounts thus collected are, that, by looking at any person's account in the Ledger you can see at a glance your whole dealings with that person, and also the balance which is due him or you, which you could not find without much trouble and great liability to error, if the amounts of debit and credit were all left standing scattered through the Day Book.

The following examples of these separate books, showing their characteristic record of the same transaction, will indicate their use:—

1. DAY-BOOK.

Belleville, January 1, 1889.

Journal Page.	Date.	Dollars.	Cents.
	Bought of JAMES SMITH, on account, 500 bbls. Flour at $8	$4000	
	2		
	Sold STEPHEN BROWN, for cash, 100 bbls. Flour at $8.50	850	

2. JOURNAL.

Belleville, January 1, 1889.

                                                           Dr.   *Cr.*

Ledger Page.			Date.	Day Book Page.	Dollars.	Cents.	Dollars.	Cents.
	1 2	Merchandise, Dr .... To James Smith			$4000		$4000	
		2						
	3 1	Cash, Dr .... To Merchandise			850		850	
	Ledger Titles—Dr.	Ledger Titles—Cr.						

NOTE.—Knowing from experience the advantage to be derived from adopting the direct address in teaching, the authors have made use of pronouns of the first and second person, instead of the third, and are confident that those who peruse with a desire to obtain information will be pleased that all formality has been laid aside, and the conversational style adopted instead. To those whose sole object is criticism, it need only be said, the book was not written for their pleasure.

3. LEDGER.

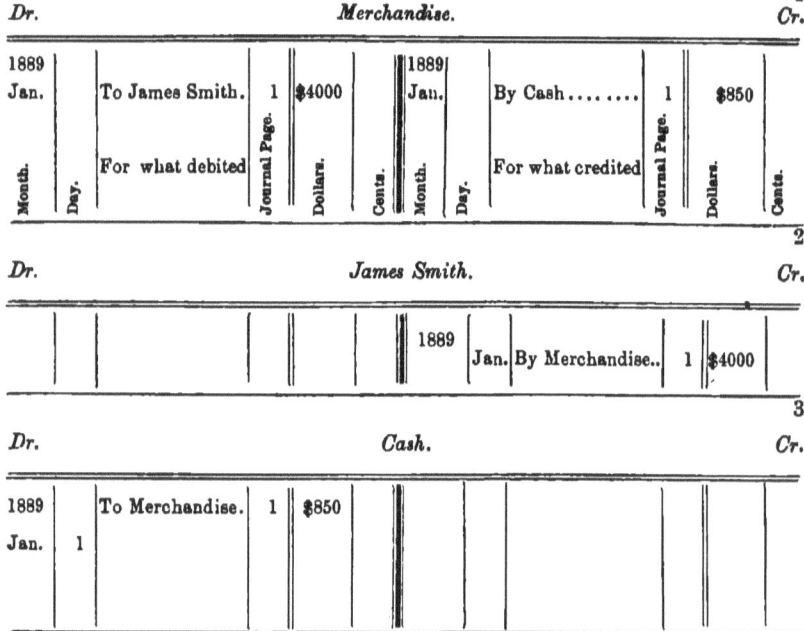

LEDGER ACCOUNTS AND EXERCISES THEREON.

In Book-keeping we name our goods *Merchandise*, we call our money *Cash*, a house and lot *Real Estate;* these terms used as ledger titles are called *accounts*.

The purpose of the exercises, in connection with the following explanation of the various accounts which occur in the most simple business operations, is to elucidate the initial difficulties of the science.

We have found by experience that it is almost impossible to make a pupil who has no knowledge of the subject understand the Journal, until he is made acquainted with the nature and disposition of the accounts in the Ledger. How, for instance, can we explain to a beginner such an expression as "Cash Dr. to Stock," but by taking him to the Ledger, and there explaining to him the Cash and Stock Accounts, the manner of keeping them, and the object for which they are kept? Until he has the Ledger explained to him in some way, the language of the Journal must remain unintelligible to him; and to this may be ascribed the ill-success in teaching Book-keeping from some of the most popular treatises in use in our public schools; in which, after bewildering the pupil with rules and lectures upon journalizing, they conclude with what ought to be first explained—the Ledger.

A faithful adherence to the instructions given on the following Ledger Accounts will enable the learner to record, readily and correctly, the exercise in connection with each; which should be written on a Skeleton Ledger, ruled by the pupil himself, similar to the following form :

CASH EXERCISE.—Commenced business with a cash capital of $8,500. Bought merchandise and gave in payment cash $1,500. Borrowed of A. B. $300. Paid rent of store $250. Lent W. Snow $300. Sold for cash a bill of goods amounting to $1,000.

Required, The amount of cash on hand?

Dr.	Cash.	Cr.
$8500 300 1000		$1500 250 300 Bal. on hand 7750
9800		9800

CASH ACCOUNT.

This account is kept to show the amount of cash received, the amount paid out, and the balance on hand at any time. All amounts of cash received are placed on the *debit* (left hand) side of this account, and all amounts paid out on the *credit* (right hand) side; consequently the *debit* side shows the amount received, and the *credit* side the amount parted with.

THE BALANCE ON HAND is ascertained by deducting the total credit from the total debit. The debit side is always the larger as long as there is any cash on hand, since cash must be received before it can be paid out. This account is closed "*By Balance.*"

EXERCISE—CASH ACCOUNT.

Cash invested $12,000. Paid for rent $400. Borrowed of George Sherry $175. Paid for merchandise $6,500. Received for merchandise $400. Received from George Sherry $100. Paid on our note $250. Received on B. Canniff's note $400. Lent W. Ross $200. Paid George Sherry $275. Lost $100. Received from W. Ross $100. Found $250. Paid for coal $40.

Required, The amount of cash on hand?

MERCHANDISE AND OTHER SIMILAR ACCOUNTS.

The Merchandise account is kept to show the cost and proceeds of merchandise, and, as a consequence, the gains or losses thereon. Merchandise is *debited* with the amount on hand on commencing business and with the cost of all purchases. It is *credited* with all sales of merchandise; consequently, the *debit* side shows its cost, and the *credit* side its *proceeds*. When all is sold the difference between the two sides will be a gain or loss. If a portion of goods remains unsold, the account must be credited with this balance, prior to closing, as an off-set thus far against its cost. If the *debit* side is the larger it is closed "By Loss and Gain;" if the *credit* side is the larger it is closed "To Loss and Gain." Real Estate, Bank Stock, Railroad Stock, Steamboat Stock, Shipment Accounts, and all other speculating property accounts are kept for the same purpose, and treated in the same manner as Merchandise account.

EXERCISE—MERCHANDISE ACCOUNT.

Have on hand merchandise valued at $19,000. Sold for cash, as per sales book, $2,300. Sold for note a bill amounting to $3,000. Bought on account bill of cotton $400. Sold A. B. on account bill amounting to $1,500. Sold R. S. on his acceptance a bill amounting to $2,000. Bought, as per invoice, broadcloth at $1,500. Sold for cash a bill of goods at $3,100.

Value of unsold merchandise $8,450.25.

Required, The gain or loss on merchandise?

NOTE.—The results of the Exercises are given at page 22.

BILLS RECEIVABLE.

By this title is meant all written obligations, of whatever form, in your possession, for which a certain specified amount is to be *received*.

They may be:

1st. A note in your possession, drawn by another person, payable to you, or bearer, or order.

2nd. A note drawn by another person, purchased by you, although not originally made payable to you.

3rd. A draft or bill of exchange drawn by one party on a second, and coming into your possession as a third party, whether accepted or not.

4th. Your draft on another, accepted by him and retained in your possession.

The object in keeping this account is, that you may know the amount of other persons' notes received, the amount that has been disposed of, and the notes in hand. This account is debited with the amount received, and credited with the amount of notes disposed of; therefore, the debit side shows the amount of notes received and the credit side the amount parted with. The debit side is always the larger, if either, and the excess shows the balance of notes in hand. When all the notes received have been disposed of, this account closes itself; but, if any remain unpaid, it is closed "By Balance."

Exercise—BILLS RECEIVABLE.

Have on hand the following Bills Receivable:—R. Gordon's note for $740; J. Dixon's for $800; S. G. Beatty's for $950. Sold A. Wilson on his note merchandise $580. Received of W. Diamond his note, in full of account, $450. R. Gordon pays cash for his note $740. Sold W. Barber merchandise, and received in payment his draft on A. Foster for $400. S. G. Beatty redeems his note for $950. Had A. Wilson's note discounted at the Merchants' Bank, face of note $580. Bought merchandise and gave in payment J. Dixon's note $800.

Required, The amount of notes on hand?

BILLS PAYABLE.

Bills Payable is a name given to your written obligations or promises to pay, and by which you keep an account with your own notes.

They may be:—

1st. Your note payable to another person.

2nd. A draft or bill of exchange on you and accepted by you.

3rd. Any bond or obligation in contract, with your signature and requiring payment of you.

This account is kept that you may know the amount of your notes issued, the amount taken up or redeemed, and the balance still outstanding against you. On the credit side are entered all notes issued, and on the debit side all notes redeemed; hence the *credit* footing shows the amount of notes issued, and the *debit* footing the amount of notes redeemed. The *credit* side is always the larger, if either, and the excess shows the balance of notes outstanding unpaid. When all the notes issued are paid, this account closes itself; but if any remain unpaid, it is closed "To Balance."

Exercise—BILLS PAYABLE.

Have the following notes outstanding: One in favor of H. Card for $425. One in favor of P. Grass for $500. An accepted draft favor of N. Day for $250. Bought on our note merchandise amounting to $750. Sold merchandise and received in payment our note favor of H. Card $425. Paid cash for our note favor of P. Grass $500. Gave Peter Mann our note in settlement of account $375.

Required, The amount of our outstanding Bills?

BONDS AND MORTGAGES RECEIVABLE are a class of Bills Receivable, and might be kept under that head, but a separate account is often opened for them, which is treated precisely like Bills Receivable.

BONDS AND MORTGAGES PAYABLE are a class of Bills Payable, and treated precisely like them.

BANK.—When a bank account is kept it is similar in its treatment to Cash and Bills Receivable, the *debit* side showing the amount of value deposited in bank, and *credit* side the amount checked out; consequently the difference is a balance in bank; it is closed " By Balance."

EXPENSE, INSURANCE, CHARGES, INTEREST AND DISCOUNT, and similar accounts, are kept to ascertain what they cost you, what they produce you, and, as a consequence, whether you gain or lose thereon. Excess of *debit* shows a larger amount of cost than proceeds, and a consequent loss upon the account; while excess of *credit* shows a larger amount of proceeds than cost, and a consequent gain. These accounts are closed "To" or "By Loss and Gain." Expense account must always close "By Loss and Gain," as it can only show a loss.

EXERCISE—EXPENSE.

Paid for clerk's salary $425. Paid gas bill, $30. Paid rent, $200. Paid for postage, $7; Paid for stationery, $40. Paid freight, $15.

Required, The loss on incidental expenses?

PERSONAL ACCOUNTS.

Accounts are kept with persons to show your business dealings with them. A person is debited when he receives value from you; in other words, when he costs you value, and he is credited when he produces you value in any way. Therefore, whenever you do a job of work for any person, or sell him anything, or pay him money, or he in any other manner becomes indebted to you, he must be charged (or debited) with the same to show that *he owes you*. And whenever any person sells you anything, pays you money, or does work for you, or you in any other manner become indebted to him, he must be credited with the same to show that *you owe him*. The *debit* side of a Personal account shows the amount of your account against the person, and the *credit* side shows the amount of his account against you. The difference shows the balance either due you or due him. These accounts are closed either " To Balance," or " By Balance."

EXERCISE—PERSONAL ACCOUNTS.

Open an account with each person interested, viz.: Robert Jones, A. Brown, James Smith and Thomas Graves.

Robert Jones owes us $5,000. Received on account of Robert Jones, $300. Sold merchandise to A. Brown, on account, $1,500. Lent James Smith $750. Borrowed of Thomas Graves $800. Sold merchandise to Robert Jones, on account, $3,000. Received on Robert Jones' account his note for $1,500. Received of A. Brown, on account, cash $700. Received of J. Smith, cash $750. Received on Robert Jones' account, John Jones' note for $2,000. Drew a draft on Robert Jones for balance of his indebtedness, $———

Required, The standing of each of the personal accounts named?

Stock, as a Ledger title, means simply the proprietor of the business. It is your representative when conducting business without a partner, and is used instead of your own name. The Stock account exhibits the proprietor's personal dealings with his own business, or his relation to it.

Debts at starting, sums drawn out during the continuance of business, and net loss at closing, are placed upon the *debit* side of Stock. Effects invested at starting, sums invested during the business, and net gain at closing, are placed upon the *credit* side. After receiving the net gain or net loss, if the credit side of this account is the larger, the difference or excess is your *net Capital*. If the debit side is the larger, the excess is your *net insolvency*. It is closed "To," or "By Balance."

Where more than one proprietor is represented, an account is opened for each, and the net investment or insolvency of each proprietor is shown in the same manner under his proper name.

INVESTMENT—SINGLE PROPRIETORSHIP.—Invested in business, $9,000. Assumed to pay from the business a private debt of $450. Drew out for private expenses, $675. The Gains during the year amount to $8,000, which are retained in the business.

Required, The proprietor's net worth at the end of the year?

INVESTMENT—PARTNERSHIP.—A. and B. are partners. A. invests in cash $6,000, B. in stock, fixtures, etc., $8,500. A draws out for private purposes, $475. The concern agrees to pay a personal debt of B's of $800. A. adds to his investment $1,000. The net loss during the year amounts to $1,200, each partner sharing equally.

Required, The standing of each partner at the close of the year?

RESULTS OF PRECEDING EXERCISES.

CASH—Total Debit	$13,425	
" Credit	7,765	
On hand	5,660	
MERCHANDISE—Total Debit	20,900	
" Credit	20,350	25
Net loss	549	75
BILLS RECEIVABLE—Total Debit	3,920	
" Credit	3,070	
On hand	850	
BILLS PAYABLE—Total Credit	2,300	
" Debit	925	
Outstanding	1,375	
EXPENSE—Total Debit	717	
" Credit	0	
Net loss	717	
ROBERT JONES—Total Debit	8,000	
" Credit	8,000	
A. BROWN—Total Debit	1,500	
" Credit	700	
He owes me	800	
JAMES SMITH—Total Debit	750	
" Credit	750	
THOMAS GRAVES—Total Credit	800	
" Debit	0	
I owe him	800	

```
Stock—Total Credit.................................................$17,000
   "   Debit......................................................  1,125
                                                                    ------
       Net worth..................................................  15,875

"A."—Total Credit...............................................   7,000
   "   Debit......................................................  1,075
                                                                    ------
       Present worth..............................................  5,925

"B."—Total Credit...............................................   8,500
   "   Debit......................................................  1,400
                                                                    ------
       Present worth..............................................  7,100
```

QUESTIONS FOR REVIEW.

CHAPTER I.

What is Book-keeping? How many distinct methods of keeping accounts are there? What is the distinction between Single and Double Entry? Why is the Double Entry system to be preferred? What great feature of Double Entry particularly recommends it to business men? What do the terms " Debtor " and " Creditor " signify? What does an entry on the Dr. side of an account signify? What does an entry on the Cr. side of an account signify? What are the main books used in Double Entry? Describe the Day Book. For what is the Journal used? What is Posting? What is the Ledger? and what is its principal use? What are the advantages of keeping personal accounts in the Ledger? What is an account, as used in the Ledger? What is the object in keeping a Cash Account in the Ledger? When are entries made on the Dr. and when on the Cr. side of this account? How is the Cash Account closed? How are Merchandise and other similar accounts closed? Define Bills Receivable. Of what may Bills Receivable consist? What is the object in keeping this account? How is it kept? Define Bills Payable. Of what may Bills Payable consist? What is the object in keeping this account? How is it conducted and closed in the Ledger? For what purpose are accounts of Expense, Insurance, Charges, Interest and Discount kept? And how are they closed? Describe the object and manner of keeping Personal Accounts. What does the Dr. side of a personal Account show? What the Cr. side? Define "Stock" as a Ledger title. How is the Stock Account conducted and closed?

CHAPTER II.

DOUBLE ENTRY.

We introduce the learner, at once, to Double Entry Book-keeping, omitting any special instructions in Single Entry until the student has become familiar with the principles of the former system; for the reasons, first, that we do not desire to distract the mind from the more important considerations bearing upon the science of accounts; and, secondly, because a student who has mastered Double Entry requires nothing more than a perusal of Single Entry to understand it.

In Double Entry Book-keeping accounts are kept not only with individuals, but also with different kinds of property, and with the different branches of gains and losses in business.

Business transactions consist in exchanging various forms of value. Among these are Merchandise, Real Estate, Cash, Personal Debts, Written Obligations, Service, etc. In many kinds of business it is necessary that the amounts of these different forms of value in possession, as they exist at any one time, may be readily and easily ascertained; also how much is due to others, and how much has been paid out or received for any particular purpose. This information is required in order to know the exact condition of affairs, and to have a correct basis upon which to plan any future enterprise. To obtain the information fully, an account must be kept not only with the persons with whom business is transacted, but also with every form of value exchanged and with every source of receipt and expenditure.

The distinguishing feature in Double Entry consists in carrying out a mathematical principle of equilibrium, under the titles of *debtor* and *creditor*.

The variations introduced in the manner of working the following sets are merely peculiarities. The particular method or form in which books are kept is not essential, as long as they conform to the principle of equal debit and credit.

The forms in use in business houses vary according to the nature and extent of the business. In a small retail store a record showing the amounts which are due from persons who have purchased on credit is by many considered sufficient. In some cases an authentic record that can be used as evidence is all that is wanted; in others the workings of each series of operations, the results of each series of income or loss, and the comparative value of different undertakings must be fully set forth as a basis for future plans, and to determine what is requisite for the safe and successful conduct of affairs. A system of checks against omissions, mistakes and frauds is also in many establishments indispensable in order to guard against errors and serious losses. Without an accurate set of books proceedings must be upon vague and possibly erroneous conclusions, the results of which may be insolvency and bankruptcy.

The qualifications necessary to keep books properly will, therefore, depend very much upon the kind of business for which the books are required. In any business a knowledge of certain principles is indispensable; and a comprehensive acquaintance with the science of accounts will give many facilities and advantages not possessed by those who have no knowledge except what they have gained from a contracted routine of petty details.

The principal books used are the Day Book, Journal and Ledger. The Auxiliary Books vary according to the nature of the business, and are the Cash Book, Bill Book, Invoice Book, Sales Book, Letter Book, Receipt Book, Account Sales Book, etc.

The form and number of the auxiliary books used depend in all cases upon the nature of the business transactions; but as a knowledge of the auxiliaries is easily obtained it is not thought best to encumber the mind of the student with them at first, and they are accordingly omitted until a subsequent part of the work.

DIRECTIONS FOR JOURNALIZING.

Journalizing is ascertaining the proper *Drs.* and *Crs.* of business transactions recorded in the Day Book, and writing them in the Journal. This requires thought and study. Whenever a transaction occurs the book-keeper should reflect for a moment, and see what part of the property is affected by that transaction, and then the accounts that represent that property are the accounts to be made *Dr.* and *Cr. Every Dr. must have a corresponding Cr. of equal amount, and every Cr. must have a corresponding Dr. of equal amount.*

If the transaction takes from the one part of your property and adds to another, the account from which it is taken is made *Cr.* and the one to which it is added is made *Dr.* Whenever you buy property, the account representing that property is made *Dr.* to what you give in payment for it; or, if you buy it on trust, it is *Dr.* to the person that trusted you; and when you sell that property it is made *Cr.* by what you receive in payment for it; or, if it is sold on credit it is *Cr.* by the person trusted.

For example, if you buy merchandise of A. Brown on account, $500, Merchandise would be *Dr.* to A. Brown $500, and A. Brown *Cr.* by Merchandise, $500. If you pay him cash for it, Cash would be *Cr.*; if your note, Bills Payable would be *Cr.* Or if you sell merchandise on account to J. Meudell, he would be made *Dr.* to Merchandise, and Merchandise *Cr.* by J. Meudell. If he paid you cash, Cash would be *Dr.*, or gave you his note, Bills Receivable would be *Dr.* If you gave your note to A. Brown on account, he would be made *Dr.* to Bills Payable, and Bills Payable *Cr.* by A. Brown. When you redeem that note with cash, Bills Payable would be *Dr.* to Cash, and Cash *Cr.* by Bills Payable. If J. Meudell gives you his note on account, Bills Receivable would be made *Dr.* to J. Meudell, and J. Meudell *Cr.* by Bills Receivable. When he redeems that note with cash, Cash would be *Dr.* to Bills Receivable, and Bills Receivable *Cr.* by Cash.

Journalizing is considered the most scientific part of book-keeping, but will not be found difficult if you understand the following:

RULE FOR JOURNALIZING. — "*Debit what costs value, or the thing received.*" "*Credit what produces value, or the thing parted with.*"

The above rule is the *Key* to the principle of Double Entry Book-keeping, and a good understanding of it at the commencement will save time and many vexatious moments as you become further advanced.

Those persons are *Debtors* who owe us.

Those persons are *Creditors* whom we owe.

EXERCISES IN JOURNALIZING.

Transactions.	Journalized		
1—Bought of S. G. Beatty, on account, mdse., amounting to $4,500.	1—Mdse. Dr. To S. G. Beatty,	$4,500	$4,500
2—Sold W. B. Robinson, on acct. mdse., $750	2—W. B. Robinson, Dr. To Mdse.,	750	750
3—Paid S. G. Beatty, cash on account, $400.	3—S. G. Beatty, Dr. To Cash,	400	400
4—Received from W. B. Robinson, cash on account, $500.	4—Cash Dr. To W. B. Robinson,	500	500
5—Sold Geo. Sherry, on his note at one month, mdse., $200.	5—Bills Receivable, Dr. To Mdse.,	200	200
6—Bought of S. G. Beatty, on my note, mdse., $800.	6—Mdse. Dr. To Bills Payable,	800	800
7—George Sherry has paid his note in cash, $200.	7—Cash, Dr. To Bills Receivable,	200	200
8—Paid my note to S. G. Beatty in cash, $800.	8—Bills Payable, Dr. To Cash,	800	800
9—Received from W. B. Robinson cash to balance his acct., $250.	9—Cash, Dr. To W. B. Robinson,	250	250
10—Bought of F. Rous, mdse., $2,000. Gave in payment my note for $1,000, and cash for the balance, $1,000.	10—Mdse., Dr. To Bills Payable, To Cash,	2,000	1,000 1,000
11—Sold R. Gordon, mdse., $800. Received in payment his note for $500, and cash for the balance, $300.	11—Bills Receivable, Dr. Cash, Dr., To Mdse.	500 300	800

RECORD OF TRANSACTIONS.

A BUSINESS TRANSACTION consists nominally in an *exchange of values;* and each complete record of a transaction is based upon the theory that something is *received* and something *given.* This theory, however, is not always literally, though it may be constructively true.

One unvarying condition of a transaction is that its *complete* record requires at least *two* entries—one to the *Debit* of some account, and one to the *Credit* of some other account. Frequently, however, the record may involve more than two accounts; but under any circumstances, the *sum* of the debit and credit entries must be equal.

Preserving the *equality* of debits and credits, the records of a transaction may require any of the following four forms :

1. ONE DEBIT AND ONE CREDIT.
2. ONE DEBIT AND TWO OR MORE CREDITS.
3. TWO OR MORE DEBITS AND ONE CREDIT.
4. TWO OR MORE DEBITS AND TWO OR MORE CREDITS.

The main object of a business record is to show at any time *the condition of the business;* in other words, *what the concern is worth.* Inasmuch, moreover, as the real or net worth of a concern is *the difference between its property and debts,* it follows that any adequate system of business record must secure the ready means of ascertaining these necessary items.

The following Set is worked out in full, in order to show the pupil the proper form of carrying the transactions through the different books, and should be thoroughly understood in every particular before proceeding further.

The transactions are first taken from the "Record," which is supposed to be a memorandum of the merchant's business transactions in the date and order of their occurrence, and arranged properly in the Day Book, after which they are journalized and posted.

A faithful adherence to the foregoing instructions and applications will enable the pupil to record, readily and correctly, the following exercise, which should be first written on skeleton paper prepared for that purpose, or on blank paper ruled up by the student himself.

ACCOUNTS TO BE OPENED IN LEDGER
WITH NUMBER OF LINES REQUIRED FOR EACH.

For the benefit of the student, and in behalf of economy in the use of Ledger paper, we give below the number of lines required for each account in the nine following Sets :

This apportionment, it will be borne in mind, provides for the Ledger Headings, and also for the necessary space to close up the accounts in due form.

SET I.—Stock 6, Cash 14, Flour 9, Wheat 14, Bills Payable 10, Bills Receivable 8, James Rimmer 9, W. Lingham 6, Robert Thompson 7, H. Corby 7, James Miller 5, Expense 6, Loss and Gain 9, Balance 12.

SET II.—Stock 9, Cash 18, Merchandise 20, W. L. Hamilton 10, Sanderson & Co. 9, A. H. Skinner 9, B. M. Carman 10, R. S. Thompson 8, Expense 12, Loss and Gain 10, Balance 13.

SET III.—Stock 9, Cash 17, Merchandise 16, Bills Payable 10, Bills Receivable 11, Muir & Co. 9, Geo. Sherry 9, S. G. Beatty 9, H. Warren 8, Thomas Moore 10, Expense 12, Loss and Gain 10, Balance 12.

SET IV.—Stock 9, Cash 15, Merchandise 15, Bills Receivable 11, Bills Payable 11, G. S. Tickel 8, Jakes & Hayes 9, G. W. Maybee 8, H. Corby 8, Expense 11, Interest 8, Loss and Gain 11, Balance 10.

SET V.—Stock 8, Cash 25, Bills Receivable 10, Bills Payable 9, Merchandise 23, J. W. Campion 9, L. W. Yeomans 9, Ames, Holden & Co. 10, F. M. Clarke 8, W. T. Tilley 8, Shipment to Tilley 8, Interest & Discount 10, Expense 12, Ont. Trans. Co. Shares 5, Loss & Gain 10, Balance 13.

SETS VI and VII (under same headings)—Student 13, James Fenwick 10; Cash, 27; Merchandise, 18; Bills Receivable, 13; Bills Payable, 13; Furniture, 9; Expense, 11; Rent, 12; Insurance, 12; Montreal Bank, 26; Jones & Co.'s Consig't. No. 1, 10; W. B. Robinson, 10; Jones & Co.'s Consig't No. 2, 10; Charges, 14; Commission, 14; Jones & Co., 14; W. West's Consig't. No. 1, 9; Jones & Co.'s Consig't. No. 3, 9; H. Holden, 8; W. West's Consig't. No. 2, 9; Jones & Co.'s Consig't. No. 4, 9; Interest and Discount, 10; W. West, 9; Solomon Johns, 8; Good Will, 8; Loss and Gain, 18; Balance, 11.

SET VIII (Single Entry) and Set IX, under same headings—J. S. Miller, 9; F. Lane, 9; J. R. Marvin, 8; W. McKay, 12; Robert Carey, 13; James Goodwin, 13; H. Simmons, 13; Additional accounts after opening Set IX: Cash, 9; Merchandise, 13; Bills Receivable, 12; Bills Payable, 9; Real Estate, 8; Expense, 9; Interest and Discount, 8; Shipment to B. Way, 9; Loss and Gain, 9; Balance, 11.

Set 1.

PRODUCE BUSINESS.

In making the entries in the Day Book leave a line between each transaction, putting the date *over* it; and in making an entry of several items take a line for each item.

It is expected that the student will not merely copy the exercises in connection with this Set, but that he will work them out for himself according to the forms given.

RECORD OF TRANSACTIONS.

Quebec, January 1, 1889.

Commenced business, investing as follows, Cash	$4,000 50
500 bbls. Extra Flour, at $6.00	3,000 00
800 bush. Fall Wheat, at $1.25	1,000 00
Jan. 2—Bought of W. Lingham, for Cash, 50 bbls. Superfine Flour, at $6.00	300 00
" " Sold James Rimmer, on acc't., 100 bush. Fall Wheat, at $1.50	150 00
" " Bought of H. Corby, on my Note, 200 bush. Spring Wheat, at $1.00	200 00
" 3—Sold Robert Thompson, on acc't, 400 bush. Fall Wheat, at $1.50	600 00
" " Bought of W. Lingham, on my Note, 100 bbls. Superfine Flour, at $6.50	650 00
" " Bought of James Wilson, for Cash, 200 bush. Fall Wheat, at $1.50	300 00
" 4—Sold John Smith, for his Note, 100 bush. Fall Wheat, at $1.75	175 00
" " Received of James Rimmer, on acc't., Cash	100 00
" 5—Bought for Cash, 400 bush. Fall Wheat, at $1.40	560 00
" " Sold James Johnson, for Note, 100 bush. Spring Wheat, at $1.20	120 00
" 6—Bought of H. Corby, on account, 500 bbls. Extra Flour, at $6.00	3,000 00
" " Sold James Miller, on account, 200 bbls. Extra Flour, at $6.50	1,300 00
" " Sold for Cash, 100 bush. Spring Wheat, at $1.25	125 00
" 8—Sold James Rimmer, on acc't., 200 bush. Fall Wheat, at $1.40	280 00
" " Received of James Miller, his Note in full of acc't	1,300 00
" 9—Paid cash for Sundry items of expense	25 50
" " Sold Robert Thompson, on acc't, 250 bush. Fall Wheat, at $1.50	375 00
" 10—Bought of W. Lingham, on acc't., 450 bush. Spring Wheat, at $1.00	450 00
" " Paid H. Corby, on acc't	1,000 00
" 11—Sold Robert Brown, 380 bush. Spring Wheat, at $1.00	
" " Received in payment his Note for $150, Cash for bal. $230.	380 00
" 12—Bought of W. Lingham, on my Note, 50 bbls. Extra Flour, at $6.30	315 00
" " Paid Cash for my Note of the 3rd inst., favor of W. Lingham	650 00
" 13—Sold J. Rimmer, on acc't., 200 bbls. Extra Flour, at $7.00	1,400 00
" 15—Paid Cash in full for my Note, favor H. Corby	200 00
" " Received of R. Thompson, Cash in full of acc't	975 00
" " Received Cash in full for J. Smith's Note of the 4th inst	175 00
" 16—Gave H. Corby my Note on acc't	1,000 00
" 17—Bought of W. Lingham, on acc't., 550 bush. Spring Wheat, at $1.00	550 00
" " Sold J. Rimmer, on acc't., 150 bbls. Superfine Flour, at $8.00	1,200 00
" " Received Cash, in full for J. Johnston's Note of the 5th instant	120 00
" 18—Paid Sundry expenses in Cash	140 00
" " Goods unsold as per Inventory, Flour $3,915. Wheat $1,120.	

CAUTION.—In transcribing a set to your Day Book leave the column blank for the insertion of your own folios. ☞ The Ledger headings for the first nine sets will be found on pages 26 and 27.

SPECIMEN DAY BOOK.

TO THE STUDENT.

After becoming familiar with the preceding instructions and tracing through the examples on journalizing given on page 25, you may write up the Day Book according to the following form; then lay aside the printed book, and on a sheet of waste paper journalize the entries of the Day Book; after which compare with the printed journal to see if you have journalized correctly; then post to the Ledger as directed in explanations on posting independent of the printed book, and make out your Trial Balance and statements:

Quebec, January 1, 1889.

Journal Folio						
30	*——— this day commences the Produce Business, renting store from F. Johnston, and investing as follows:— Cash, 500 bbls. Extra Flour, 800 bush. Fall Wheat,	$6 00 1 25	$4000 3000 1000	50 00 00	$8000	50
	2					
30	Bought of W. Lingham for Cash, 50 bbls. Super. Flour, "	6 00			300	00
30	Sold James Rimmer on account, 100 bush. Fall Wheat, "	1 50			150	00
30	Bought of H. Corby on my Note, 200 bush. Spring Wheat, 3	1 00			200	00
30	Sold Robert Thompson on account, 400 bush. Fall Wheat, "	1 50			600	00
30	Bought of W. Lingham on my Note, 100 bbls. Super. Flour, "	6 50			650	00
30	Bought of James Wilson for Cash, 200 bush. Fall Wheat, 4	1 50			300	00
30	Sold John Smith for his Note, 100 bush. Fall Wheat, "	1 75			175	00
30	Received of James Rimmer on account, Cash, 5				100	00
30	Bought for Cash, 400 bush. Fall Wheat, "	1 40			560	00
30	Sold James Johnson for his Note, 100 bush. Spring Wheat, 6	1 20			120	00
30	Bought of H. Corby on account, 500 bbls. Extra Flour, "	6 00			3000	00
30	Sold James Miller on account, 200 bbls. Extra Flour.	6 50			1300	00
	Amt. carried forward,				15455	50

* Student to use his own name.

NOTE.—The figures in the narrow column to the left refer to the pages of the Journal upon which the transactions have been journalized, and should be placed in the Day Book, opposite the transaction, immediately after the Journal entry is made. This is called folioing, and serves the purpose of reference from one book to another, as well as indicating that the entry has been transferred.

If goods have been charged in Day Book, and the customer pay for them before the entry has been posted, just mark PAID in the margin in a bold hand, and put the money in the till, to be counted with that day's Cash Sales.

Quebec, January 6th, 1889.

	Amount brought forward,			$15455	50
30	Sold for Cash, 100 bush. Spring Wheat,	1 25		125	00
	8				
30	Sold James Rimmer on account, 200 bush. Fall Wheat	1 40		280	00
30	Received of James Miller his note. in full of account			1300	00
	9				
30	Paid Cash for Sundry Expenses;			25	50
31	Sold Robert Thompson on account, 250 bush. Fall Wheat	1 50		375	00
	10				
31	Bought of W. Lingham on account, 450 bush. Spring Wheat	1 00		450	00
31	Paid H. Corby Cash on account,			1000	00
	11				
31	Sold Robert Brown, 380 bush. Spring Wheat, Received in payment his Note, Cash for the Balance,	1 00	150 230	380	00
	12				
31	Bought of W. Lingham on my Note, 50 bbls. Extra Flour,	6 30		315	00
31	Paid Cash for my Note of the 3rd inst.			650	00
	13				
31	Sold J. Rimmer on account, 200 bbls. Extra Flour, 7 00			1400	00
	15				
31	Paid Cash in full for my Note, favor H. Corby,			200	00
31	Received of R. Thompson, Cash in full of account,			975	00
31	Received Cash in full for John Smith's Note of the 4th instant,			175	00
	16				
31	Gave H. Corby my Note on account,			1000	00
	17				
31	Bought of W. Lingham on account, 550 bush. Spring Wheat,	1 00		550	00
31	Sold James Rimmer on account, 150 bbls. Super. Flour,	8 00		1200	00
31	Received Cash in full for J. Johnston's note of the 5th inst.,			120	00
	18				
31	Paid Cash for Sundry Expenses,			140	00
	*Inventory of Goods unsold: Flour, Wheat,		3915 1120	26116	00
	Total,		$5035		

* The value of unsold property is not necessarily measured by its cost nor its selling price, although in ordinary cases the cost standard is adopted in taking " account of stock." The proper standard of value is the cost of goods in the purchasing market, or what it would cost to replenish them.
At the end of each set the value of goods left unsold is given. In business an inventory of stock is written into the " Stock Book," the amounts and quantities are extended, then added, and the total value of the goods on hand is shown.

SPECIMEN JOURNAL.

Some business men require their Journal to embody brief explanations of their transactions; but we do not introduce this plan now, because, in his incipient steps, everything that takes the learner's attention off the LEDGER TITLES has a tendency to perplex and embarrass him. Familiarity with the following form will prepare the student for using any other without difficulty:

Quebec, January 1st, 1889.

L.F.			D.B.F.				
34	Cash Dr.			$4,000	50		
34	Flour "		28	3,000	00		
34	Wheat "			1,000	00		
34		To Stock,				$8,000	50
		——2——					
34	Flour Dr.		28	300	00		
34		To Cash,				300	00
		"					
35	James Rimmer Dr.		28	150	00		
34		To Wheat,				150	00
		"					
34	Wheat Dr.		28	200	00		
34		To Bills Payable,				200	00
		——3——					
35	Robert Thompson Dr.		28	600	00		
34		To Wheat,				600	00
		"					
34	Flour Dr.		28	650	00		
34		To Bills Payable,				650	00
		"					
34	Wheat Dr.		28	300	00		
34		To Cash,				300	00
		——4——					
35	Bills Receivable Dr.		28	175	00		
34		To Wheat,				175	00
		"					
34	Cash Dr.		28	100	00		
35		To James Rimmer,				100	00
		——5——					
34	Wheat Dr.		28	560	00		
34		To Cash,				560	00
		"					
35	Bills Receivable Dr.		28	120	00		
34		To Wheat,				120	00
		——6——					
34	Flour Dr.		28	3,000	00		
35		To H. Corby,				3,000	00
		"					
35	James Miller Dr.		28	1,300	00		
34		To Flour,				1,300	00
		"					
34	Cash Dr.		29	125	00		
34		To Wheat,				125	00
		——8——					
35	James Rimmer Dr.		29	280	00		
34		To Wheat,				280	00
		"					
35	Bills Receivable Dr.		29	1,300	00		
35		To James Miller,				1,300	00
		——9——					
35	Expense Dr.		29	25	50		
34		To Cash,				25	50
		Amts. carried forward,		17,186	00	17,186	00

NOTE.—The figures in the narrow columns are the pages of the Day-Book and Ledger; those to the left are Ledger folios, and those to the right Day Book folios. By the latter we are able to refer readily to the book of original entry, and by the former to the Ledger account.

Quebec, *January 9th*, 1889.

35	Amts. brought forward,		29	$17,186	00	$17,186	00
34	Robert Thompson Dr.			375	00		
	To Wheat,					375	00
	——— 10 ———						
34	Wheat Dr.		29	450	00		
35	To W. Lingham,					450	00
	"						
35	H. Corby Dr.		29	1,000	00		
34	To Cash,					1,000	00
	——— 11 ———						
35	Bills Rec. Dr.		29	150	00		
34	Cash "			230	00		
34	To Wheat,					380	00
	——— 12 ———						
34	Flour Dr.		29	315	00		
35	To Bills Payable,					315	00
	"						
34	Bills Payable Dr.		29	650	00		
34	To Cash,					650	00
	——— 13 ———						
35	J. Rimmer Dr.		29	1,400	00		
34	To Flour,					1,400	00
	——— 15 ———						
34	Bills Payable Dr.		29	200	00		
34	To Cash,					200	00
	"						
34	Cash Dr.		29	975	00		
35	To R. Thompson,					975	00
	"						
34	Cash Dr.		29	175	00		
35	To Bills Receivable,					175	00
	——— 16 ———						
35	H. Corby Dr.		29	1,000	00		
34	To Bills Payable,					1,000	00
	——— 17 ———						
34	Wheat Dr.		29	550	00		
35	To W. Lingham,					550	00
	"						
35	J. Rimmer Dr.		29	1,200	00		
34	To Flour,					1,200	00
	"						
34	Cash Dr.		29	120	00		
35	To Bills Receivable,					120	00
	——— 18 ———						
35	Expense Dr.		29	140	00		
34	To Cash,					140	00
				$26,116	00	$26,116	00

SPECIMEN OF DAY BOOK AND JOURNAL *on same, or opposite pages of one Book, having Day Book and Journal entries directly opposite each other.*

DAY BOOK.			JOURNAL.			
——— 1st ———			——— 1st ———			
30 B'ht. of W. Lingham for cash			34 Flour Dr.		300 00	
50 bbls. Flour $6 00	300 00		34 To Cash, 28			300 00
——— 2nd ———			——— 2nd ———			
30 Sold J. Rimmer on acct.			35 J. Rimmer, Dr.		150 00	
100 bush. Wheat $1.50	150 00		34 To Wheat 28			150 00
"			"			
30 B'ht. of H. Corby on my Note			34 Wheat Dr.		200 00	
200 bush. Spring Wheat $1.00	200 00		34 To Bills Pay. 28			200 00

LEDGER.

You have now finished the most difficult part of your task, the problem being solved, for each Debit you have found a corresponding Credit. This, in the main, is the science of Double Entry Book-keeping, the remaining part being considered as a mechanical operation. The Journal items having been prepared, you will now carry them to the Ledger or *post* them.

Posting.—Each different account found in the Journal must have a place in the Ledger, and the carrying to that account from the Journal all for which it is Debited or Credited is called *posting.*

The Ledger is usually opened by placing Stock,* or the partners' names, at the beginning, in a clear text hand, followed by the most prominent accounts, such as Cash, Merchandise, Bills Payable, Bills Receivable, etc., as shown in Model Ledger. Insert the abbreviations Dr. and Cr. at the top of the page only. In expressing the entry upon the Ledger it will be seen that a debit is always "To" that account which receives credit for the sum, and the Cr. account expresses the same entry "By" the account that was made Dr. for the same sum.

Now under each account you place all the entries that belong to it, found in the Journal, transferring the entries from the Journal to the Ledger in the order in which they occur.

You first turn to Cash Account, and on the Dr. side place the words "To Stock." This signifies that Cash or the Cash Account owes Stock for the amount of investment. In the first ruled column, called the folio column, you place the page of the Journal and in the next columns the amount. You next turn to the Cr. side of the † Stock Account and place the words "By Cash," signifying that Stock is credited by Cash, and carry the Journal page, or folio, to first column and the amount to next columns, and thus proceed carrying all the Journal entries to their respective places in the Ledger. Then you will find in the Ledger, as in the Journal, for each debit there is a corresponding credit.

The learner will acquire the process of posting more readily by seeing it done on printed Ledger than by any other means.

INDEX TO THE LEDGER.

This is a small book, or space ruled in the account book, in which are arranged, in alphabetical order, the names of all accounts in the Ledger, together with the pages on which such accounts are entered.

The object of keeping it is to enable us to refer readily to the accounts in the Ledger. Whenever we open an account in the Ledger we enter the name of the account and the number of the page in the index. If an account should be transferred to another page, a red line should be ruled through the figures of the old page, and the number of the new page placed in the Index.

In real business the Index generally has a page allotted to each letter. The following illustrations will be sufficient to explain how it is kept:

---

* The Stock Acct. is almost universally used by Accountants instead of the proprietor's name; but it is rather an ill-chosen title, as young Book-keepers are apt to confound it with the Merchandise Acct. The term CAPITAL or some other title that would better express the nature of the Acct. would be more appropriate. We will not, however, conflict with established usages by changing the title of this account.

† There being three accounts representing Stock's investment it is usual to credit, in that case, Stock By Sundries—See Ledger.

INDEX.

A	Page	K	Page
B		**L**	
Bills Receivable,	35	Lingham, W.,	35
Bills Payable,	34	Loss and Gain,	
Balance,			
C		**M**	
Cash,	34		
Corby, H.,	35		
D		**N**	
E		**O**	
Expense,	35		
F		**P**	
Flour,	34		
G		**Q**	
H		**R**	
		Rimmer, James,	35
I		**S T**	
		Stock,	34
J		**U V W**	
		Wheat,	34

CAUTION.—Always index an account when opening it in the Ledger. Without this precaution it may be forgotten, and a second account opened with the same individual; and, unimportant as this may appear, it often leads to very troublesome mistakes.

When it is necessary, owing to the leaf being filled, to transfer an account to another page of the Ledger, don't balance the account, but add each side and carry the totals to the new page. Write on the last line, on each side of the old page " Carried to Folio—," and on the first line of each side of the new page, " Brought from Folio—," and put the new page in the Index. Also date the transfer in the new page.

SPECIMEN LEDGER.

DR. (Existing Debts at Starting. Amounts withdrawn and net loss, if any.) STOCK. (Investments and net Gain, if any.) CR.

					1889				
					Jan.	1	By Sundries,	30	$8,000 50

(Received.) CASH. (Paid out.)

1889									
Jan.	1	To Stock,	30	$4,000 50	Jan.	2	By Flour,	30	300 00
"	4	" J. Rimmer,	30	100 00	"	3	" Wheat,	30	300 00
"	6	" Wheat,	30	125 00	"	5	" "	30	560 00
"	11	" "	31	230 00	"	9	" Expense,	30	25 50
"	15	" R. Thompson	31	975 00	"	10	" H. Corby,	31	1,000 00
"	15	" Bills Rec.,	31	175 00	"	12	" Bills Pay.,	31	650 00
"	17	" "	31	120 00	"	15	" "	31	200 00
					"	18	" Expense,	31	140 00

(Cost.) *FLOUR. (Proceeds.)

Jan.	1	To Stock,	30	3,000 00	Jan.	6	By J. Miller,	30	1,300 00
"	2	" Cash,	30	300 00	"	13	" J. Rimmer,	31	1,400 00
"	3	" Bills Pay.,	30	650 00	"	17	" "	31	1,200 00
"	6	" H. Corby,	30	3,000 00					
"	12	" Bills Pay.,	31	315 00					

(Cost.) *WHEAT. (Proceeds.)

Jan.	1	To Stock,	30	1,000 00	Jan.	2	By J. Rimmer,	30	150 00
"	2	" Bills Pay.,	30	200 00	"	3	" R. Thompson	30	600 00
"	3	" Cash,	30	300 00	"	4	" Bills Rec.,	30	175 00
"	5	" "	30	560 00	"	5	" "	30	120 00
"	10	" W. Lingham,	31	450 00	"	6	" Cash,	30	125 00
"	17	" "	31	550 00	"	8	" J. Rimmer,	30	280 00
					"	9	" R. Thompson	31	375 00
					"	11	" Sundries,	31	380 00

(My Notes redeemed.) BILLS PAYABLE. (My Notes issued.)

Jan.	12	To Cash,	31	650 00	Jan.	2	By Wheat,	30	200 00
"	15	" "	31	200 00	"	3	" Flour,	30	650 00
					"	12	" "	31	315 00
					"	16	" H. Corby,	31	1,000 00

To the Student: Observe the analyses of the accounts and study them thoroughly.

* The analysis of Flour and Wheat is the same as Merchandise.

35

DR.	(Others' Notes received.)			BILLS RECEIVABLE.		(Others' Notes disposed of or collected.)			CR.
1889 Jan.	4	To Wheat,	30	$175	00	1889 Jan.	15	31	$175	00
"	5	" "	30	120	00	"	17	31	120	00
"	8	" J. Miller,	30	1,300	00					
"	11	" Wheat,	31	150	00					

(My Acct. against him.)   **JAMES RIMMER.**   (His Acct. against me.)

Jan.	2	To Wheat,	30	150	00	Jan.	4	By Cash,	30	100	00
"	8	" "	30	280	00						
"	13	" Flour,	31	1400	00						
"	17	" "	31	1200	00						

W. LINGHAM.   (His Acct. against me.)

						Jan.	10	By Wheat,	31	450	00
						"	17	" "	31	550	00

(My Acct. against him.)   **ROBERT THOMPSON.**   (His Acct. against me.)

Jan.	3	To Wheat,	30	600	00	Jan.	15	By Cash,	31	975	00
"	9	" "	31	375	00						

(My Acct. against him.)   **H. CORBY.**   (His Acct. against me.)

Jan.	10	To Cash,	31	1000	00	Jan.	6	By Flour,	30	3000	00
"	16	" Bills Pay.,	31	1000	00						

(My Acct. against him.)   **JAMES MILLER.**   (His Acct. against me.)

Jan.	6	To Flour,	30	1300	00	Jan.	8	By Bills Rec.,*	30	1300	00

(Outlay for Expense.)   **EXPENSE.**

Jan.	9	To Cash,	30	25	50						
"	18	" "	31	140	00						

*The plan is frequently adopted of ruling a special column on the Cr. side of personal accounts to show the due date of customer's notes. It may also, of course, be done on the Dr. side to show the due dates of your own notes.

TEST OF THE LEDGER.

The first thing to be done, after the transactions of a set have been posted, is to test the correctness of your work, by comparing the amounts of the two sides of the Ledger, and seeing that the sum of the Dr. side of all Ledger accounts equals the sum of the Cr. side.

This is accomplished by making out a

TRIAL BALANCE.

A Trial Balance is taken to ascertain if the Debits and Credits on the Ledger are equal, or balance.

As soon as you finish posting all the transactions to the Ledger, according to the principle of equal debits and credits, you take off a Trial Balance. This is done by first footing the items of the different accounts, placing the amounts in light pencil marks, which should be erased after the completion of the work. The totals of the accounts are carried to the Trial Balance, as per model form, leaving out such accounts as close themselves. By adding to the footings of the Trial Balance given, the footings of accounts that close themselves, you will find that they exactly correspond with those of the Journal, which would not be the case if any of the Journal entries were not posted; and as the footings of the Journal columns also tally with those of the Day Book, it is almost conclusive that all the original entries have found their way to the Ledger. There will remain but two chances of errors in the accounts, viz., from improper Journal entries, or from posting to the wrong accounts in the Ledger.

It will be observed from the foregoing remarks that the Trial Balance is not always a strict proof of the correctness of the work, though it is so nearly a test, that, under ordinary circumstances, it may be considered satisfactory.

A Trial Balance may be taken with the difference columns only (see the municipal set), or with the amount columns only. The former is very frequently used in business. In a real business, a Trial Balance may be taken monthly (see form of monthly Trial Balance), and should be taken as often as once in three months, even though the books are closed but once a year. Never attempt to close a set of books that are out of balance. The error, or errors, will be found somewhere by careful, patient checking. When a bookkeeper first takes charge of a set of books that have previously been kept by another, he should take off a Trial Balance to prove if the Ledger is in balance. If not in balance he should find the errors before making any entries in it.

TRIAL BALANCE—Set I.

Dr. Bal.		Dr. Footings.		L.F.	ACCOUNTS.	Cr. Footings.		Cr. Bal.	
				34	Stock	$8000	50	$8000	50
$2550	00	$5725	50	34	Cash	3175	50		
3365	00	7265	00	34	Flour	3900	00		
855	00	3060	00	34	Wheat....................................	2205	00		
		850	00	34	Bills Payable...........................	2165	00	1315	00
1450	00	1745	00	35	Bills Receivable........................	295	00		
2930	00	3030	00	35	James Rimmer...........................	100	00		
				35	W. Lingham	1000	00	1000	00
		2000	00	35	H. Corby	3000	00	1000	00
165	50	165	50	35	Expense				
11315	50	23841	00			23841	00	11315	50

NOTE.—The Ledger from which the foregoing Trial Balance was taken does not contain all the results of the business. Hence, in getting at the data from which to ascertain the net worth, or the net gain or loss, it will be necessary to go beyond the Ledger, and estimate the value of the unsold merchandise or other similar property.

In each of the statements which follow, an Inventory of unsold property is supposed to have been taken, the results being given.

CLASSIFIED STATEMENTS.

The foregoing "Statement" or "Trial Balance" is supposed to show the *footings* and *balances* of the Ledger accounts growing out of the transactions indicated in the "Exercise" just preceding; and, as far as the open Ledger is concerned, affords as completely as possible the exact condition of the business *at the time* the Statement purports to have been rendered. The form of this Statement, however, is not sufficiently compact, nor the specific *results* of the business so distinctly given as to present at a glance the *general* result which constitutes the objective point of all business record. To accomplish this, it becomes necessary to re-arrange or *classify* the separate results as shown on the Ledger.

The Trial Balance being a simple abstract of the Ledger accounts, and these accounts showing only the *cost* and *proceeds from sales* of property having a variable value, it follows that the *real* value of such property remaining on hand can be ascertained only by actual enumeration and valuation, a process known in business as "taking account of stock," or "taking an inventory." The value of property which does not vary, viz., Cash, Notes, and Personal indebtedness, is readily ascertained from the accounts themselves.

In classifying accounts, or specific results, two grand objects are kept in view, which, are, 1st, The *net gain* or *loss* during a specified time; and, 2nd, The *net* worth or insolvency of the business. The processes of arriving at these results are distinctly indicated above. The *classified* statements which follow only present them to the eye in a consecutive and logical form.

Note.—It is necessary that the student should understand well the classes into which accounts are divided; to attain this, study carefully the explanations, on page 39, and also the subjects on page 40.

I.—STATEMENT OF LOSSES AND GAINS.
(FOR THE PURPOSE OF ASCERTAINING THE NET GAIN OR LOSS.)

	LOSSES.		GAINS.	
Flour, unsold per Inventory $3915				
" Cr. or proceeds from sales.............. 3900				
" Total proceeds.......................... 7815				
" Dr. or cost............................. 7265				
" Difference or gain			550	
Wheat, unsold per Inventory................ 1120				
" Cr. or proceeds from sales............... 2205				
" Total proceeds......................... 3325				
" Dr. or cost 3060				
" Difference or gain			265	
Expense, Dr. or outlay, a loss	165	50		
* *Difference between Gains and Losses or Net Gain*...	*649*	*50*		
	$815	00	$815	00

The material for this and the following Statement is found in the Trial Balance on page 36, except the value of unsold property, which is taken from the inventory given at the end of the Day Book, page 29. The process of working it is so simple that it does not require an explanation.

* Italics indicate red ink.

STATEMENT OF RESOURCES AND LIABILITIES

(Analysis of Accounts that show Resources and Liabilities for the purpose of ascertaining the Net Worth or Net Insolvency of the Business.)

1.—From Inventories.		RESOURCES.		LIABILITIES.	
Flour unsold, as per Inventory		3915	00		
Wheat " " "		1120	00		
2.—From Ledger Accounts.					
Cash Dr. Amount received $5725 50					
" Cr. " paid out 3175 50					
Difference, amount on hand		2550	00		
Bills Payable Cr. My notes issued 2165 00					
" " Dr. " redeemed 850 00					
" " " Difference, my outstanding notes.....				1315	00
Bills Receivable Dr. Other people's notes received.. 1745 00					
" " Cr. Other people's notes disposed of.. 295 00					
Difference, other's notes on hand............		1450	00		
James Rimmer Dr. My acct. against him 3030 00					
" " Cr. His " " me 100 00					
Difference, he owes me—................		2930	00		
W. Lingham Cr. His Acct. against me—I owe him...				1000	00
H. Corby Cr. His Acct. against me............... 3000 00					
" Dr. My " " him............... 2000 00					
Difference I owe him				1000	00
*Stocks Net Investment *8000 50					
" " Gain per Statement................. 649 50					
" " Worth................................				*8650	00
Proof............		11965	00	11965	00

Questions for Review—Chapter II.

Of what does a business transaction consist? Upon what theory is it based? Is this theory always literally true? How many entries does the complete record of a transaction require? Mention the four forms the records of a business transaction may require? What is the main object of a business record? In what books are business transactions first recorded? What is the main feature of Book-keeping by Double Entry? How is the Ledger usually opened? What does the term "Stock" stand for? What other term would better express the nature of the Acc't.? Mention some of the most prominent accounts found in the Ledger. What is an Index to the Ledger? What is the principal object in keeping it? When an account is transferred to another page what should be observed? What is the first thing to be done after the transactions of a set have been posted? How is this accomplished? Why is a Trial Balance taken? Is the Trial Balance always a proof of the correctness of the work? How often should a Trial Balance be taken? How can the real value of property on hand be ascertained? What is this process called in business? In classifying accounts what two grand objects are kept in view? Analyze each of the Accounts on pages 34 and 35.

---

* Red Ink.

CHAPTER III.

CLASSIFICATION OF ACCOUNTS.

The science of Double Entry Book-keeping is by far more subtle and philosophical, in its theories and applications, than would appear from any of the fallible or infallible rules which authors claim as encompassing it. The mere fact of the *balance* or equilibrium of debits and credits, which is the inevitable condition of each complete record of a transaction —and so, of course, of the sum of any number of transactions—is interesting and important only as it points to other and more vital truths. The Science of Equations, which so aptly applies in each distinct entry, has a broader application to the entire subject of WEALTH, which lies at the very foundation, not only of business record, but of business itself.

It has been clearly shewn, in the preceding exercises, that the *results* of transactions may be readily grouped or classified so as to exhibit distinct facts, each important in showing the condition of the business; as, for instance, the amount of cash on hand, as shown in the Cash account; other people's notes on hand, as shown in the Bills Receivable account; our outstanding notes, as shown in the Bills Payable account; the *gain* or loss from dealing in goods, as shown in the Merchandise account, etc., etc.

We have also given in the preceding statements a form for gathering up these separate facts, and, by a proper combination and comparison of them, exhibiting the grand results which lie at the end of all faithful records, viz., the exact *present* condition of the business or its net worth, and the *current* condition of the business or its net *gain* or *loss* between any two given periods.

The accounts comprising the complete transactions of any business are susceptible of an arrangement or classification, which will show at a glance, not only the existing condition of the business, but its exact measure of prosperity or adversity during any stated period.

A thorough comprehension of the nature and purpose of each account will at once suggest its position in the statement or classification.

CLASSIFICATION.

Accounts are divided into two classes: *Real* and *Representative*.

Real accounts are those that show in the difference between their sides a *resource* or *liability*. They are Cash, Bills Receivable, Bills Payable, Bank, Personal Accounts, etc.

Representative Accounts are those that exhibit, in the difference between their sides, either a *gain* or a *loss*, and are usually subdivided into Speculative and Incidental.

Speculative Accounts are those kept with any species of property that has a fluctuating value; as Merchandise, Real Estate, Live Stock, Moveable Property, etc.

Incidental Accounts are those to which particular names are given in order to treat them separately; such as Expense, Rent, Salary, Interest, etc.

Every gain made in business is practically an addition to the Capital, and every loss a decrease; but it would not be practicable to credit or debit the account representing Capital as the separate gains or losses occur. They are shown through the representative accounts during the year, and at the end of it are closed into Loss and Gain account. If, when this is done, the credit side of Loss and Gain account is the larger, an addition to the Capital has resulted, and the Stock or Capital account will be credited with the sum made; if the debtor side is the larger, a decrease of capital has resulted, and the Stock or Capital account will be debited with the amount lost.

A good understanding of the above division of accounts will enable the student to discern at a glance under what head an account should be arranged in a balance sheet, and how it should be closed in the Ledger.

RESOURCES AND LIABILITIES.

The following preliminary propositions will aid you in making out statements:

A RESOURCE, or ASSET, in business language, is any species of property belonging to you, to which a financial value may be attached.

All Resources having a *fixed* value may be continually shown in the Ledger accounts representing them. These are Cash, Notes, Bank and Personal accounts.*

All Resources having a *fluctuating* or variable value must be *estimated* by a cash standard, whenever it becomes necessary to know their value. Of such resources are Merchandise of all kinds, Real Estate, Fixtures, etc.*

A LIABILITY is any debt owing by you.

LIABILITIES being debts owing, they cannot vary much in form. They are represented on the Ledger either by Personal accounts or Bills Payable account; the distinction being only as between what we owe, without having given a written obligation and what we owe on written obligations.

The difference between the Resources and Liabilities of a business is, when the Resources exceed the Liabilities, its *net worth*, and when the Liabilities exceed the Resources, its *net insolvency*.

One marked peculiarity of Resources and Liabilities, as shown in the Ledger, should not escape the learner's attention, viz.: Resources are invariably shown by excess of the *debit*, and Liabilities by an excess of the *credit* side of Real Accounts.

LOSSES AND GAINS.—A loss in business occurs when *less* value is received than given in exchange; and when property *depreciates* in value.

A Gain occurs when *more* value is received than given in exchange; and when property *increases* in value.

NET WORTH AND NET INSOLVENCY.

The NET WORTH of a concern is found by subtracting the sum of its *liabilities* from the sum of its *resources*.

The NET INSOLVENCY of a concern is found by subtracting the sum of its *resources* from the sum of its *liabilities*.

AGAIN.—The net worth of a concern is found by adding the *net gain* to, or subtracting the *net loss* from, the original capital or investment, and the *net* Insolvency by subtracting the original capital from the *net loss*.

Inasmuch as net worth or absolute wealth is measured by the excess of Resources over Liabilities, the increase in wealth must be the result either of increase of resources or decrease of liabilities; and decrease in wealth the result of decrease of resources or increase of liabilities.

NET GAIN AND NET LOSS.

The NET GAIN during any period is found by subtracting the net worth at the *commencement* from the net worth at the *close* of such period.†

The NET LOSS during any period is found by subtracting the net worth at the *close* from the net worth at the *commencement* of such period.†

AGAIN.—The NET GAIN during any period is found by subtracting the sum of the *individual losses* from the sum of the *individual gains*.

The NET LOSS during any period is found by subtracting the sum of the *individual gains* from the sum of the *individual losses*.

---

* Assume what is practically true, that Cash, which is the measure of all values, must be competent to measure itself. Hence, we call its value fixed. Personal indebtedness, whether in the shape of notes or personal accounts, being only cash deferred, is, of course, subject to the same restrictions.

† If during the term any new capital has been added or any capital has been withdrawn it must be taken into account.

EXERCISES.

The student will test his familiarity with the foregoing lessons by rendering analyses or statements of Losses and Gains, and of Resources and Liabilities from the following exercises, before proceeding to close the Ledger.

TRIAL BALANCE—SINGLE PROPRIETOR.

Dr. Bal.		Dr. Footings.		L.F.		Cr. Footings.		Cr. Bal.	
		$150		1	Stock	$7500		$7350	
1044	27	4170	17	2	Mdse. (unsold $2,000)...............	3125	90		
1532	17	5750	29	3	Cash...................................	4218	12		
500		500		4	Robert Baker.........................				
6685		7000		5	Real Estate (unsold $6,900)........	315			
1000		1500		6	Bills Receivable......................	500			
		400		7	Bills Payable..........................	1200		800	
79	25	154	25	8	Geo. Ritchie & Co....................	75			
1061		1200		9	Warner Bros..........................	139			
375		375		10	Expense...............................				
		1400		11	N. Jones...............................	2100		700	
				12	Hunt & Co	170		170	
45		120		13	Interest and Discount..	75			
				14	W. P. Graham.........................	3601	69	3601	69
300		300		15	Loss and Gain				
12621	69	23019	71		_____Equilibrium_____	23019	71	12621	69

Net capital at commencing, $7,350. Net Gain, $450.73.
Net capital at closing, $7,800.73.

TRIAL BALANCE.—PARTNERSHIP BUSINESS.

L.F.		Dr.		Cr.	
1	S. G. Beatty (*Partner*)*...................................	$3000		$16863	13
2	W. B. Robinson (*Partner*)*...............................			12000	
3	Cash...	9732	10	4719	22
4	Merchandise (*Value unsold*, $5,159.50)..............	7350		3719	50
5	Railroad Stock (*Value unsold*, $12,000).............	12000			
6	Bills Receivable..	7000		5000	
7	Bills Payable...	3180		6180	
8	Real Estate (*Value unsold*, $8,000).................	7500		150	
9	Robertson & Henry.....................................	1150		920	
10	G. C. Holton & Co......................................			1500	
11	Expense...	125			
12	Interest...	28		13	25
13	W. W. Jones..	1795		795	
14	John Cook..	1290		840	
15	Conger Bros..			1450	
		54150	10	54150	10

S. G. Beatty's net capital at commencing, $13,863.13.
W. B. Robinson's net capital at commencing, $12,000.
Total net gain, $2,039.25; each partner's share of gain $1,019.62½.
S. G. Beatty's net worth at closing, $14,882.75.
W. B. Robinson's net worth at closing, $13,019.63.

---

* Partners' accounts are treated precisely the same as the Stock Acct.; the net amount owing to the partners being the net worth or net investment of the concern. In this instance divide the gain equally.

BALANCING ACCOUNTS.

As all gains in business must appear either in an increase of resources or a decrease of liabilities, and as all losses must appear either in a decrease of resources or an increase of liabilities, it will be plain that the two classes of accounts, Real and Representative, must always run parallel.

Balancing accounts is placing a sufficient sum on the smaller side of an account to make it equal to the greater, and is done by adding the two sides of the account and subtracting the smaller from the greater, and entering the difference on the side that is less.

Real accounts close, " To," or " By Balance."

Before closing a *speculative* account, whatever property belonging to it remains unsold, must be entered on the credit side thus: " *By Balance Inventory* " as an off-set against its cost, which has already been placed on the debit side, after which the account closes into " Loss and Gain."

Incidental accounts close, " To," or " By Loss and Gain."

As *resources* are shown by an excess of the debit side of *Real* accounts, and *liabilities* by an excess of the credit side ; and as *losses* are shown by an excess of the debit side of the *Representative* accounts; and *gains* by an excess of the credit side of *Representative* accounts, it will be necessary to open two accounts for these general results ; one to contain the resources and liabilities, and the other the gains and losses.

You will, therefore, open these accounts under the titles of " *Loss and Gain* " and " *Balance*," * the former to contain the results of the *Representative*, and the latter of the *Real* accounts.

You will do well to observe particularly and follow out in practice the following

ORDER OF CLOSING ACCOUNTS.

1st.—Take off a trial balance and statements.

2nd.—Open an account with " Loss and Gain " (if not already opened), and another with " Balance," the former to contain the *Losses* and *Gains*, and the latter the *Resources* and *Liabilities*.

3rd.—Ascertain by taking stock the cost value of any property remaining unsold ; and enter this value on the credit side of its account, making the entry in *red ink*, " By Balance Inventory," and transferring the amount directly to the debit side of " Balance Account," making the entry in *Black ink*, " To Merchandise," or the name of the account from which the transfer is made. The Ledger accounts will each show, now, one of the four following results, viz.: a Resource, a Liability, a Gain or Loss, and are in a condition for closing.

4th.—Omitting Stock (or the Partners' accounts), commence with the next account in the Ledger. First ascertain whether it shows a resource or a liability, a loss or a gain, and make the closing entry accordingly. If the difference shows a resource or a liability enter upon the smaller side, in *red ink*, " To," or " By Balance," as the case may be, and transfer the amount in *black ink* to the opposite side of the " Balance account." If the difference represents a gain or loss, enter on the smaller side, in *red ink*, " To," or " By Loss and Gain," and transfer the amount in the same manner to Loss and Gain account. Close all the accounts (except Stock or Partners), and transfer the balances as directed. The Loss and Gain Account will now show, on the debit side, all the losses, and on the credit side all the gains, the difference being the net loss or net gain. The " Balance Account " will show on the debit side all the resources, and on the credit side all the Liabilities, the difference being the real interest or present investment of the proprietor or proprietors.

---

* When the business is to be continued, instead of closing the Real Accounts into Balance Account you bring down the balances, as is done in Set VI. To balance an account (which is usually done in red ink to distinguish it from ordinary entries) is to exhibit its condition ; if it shows an asset or resource it is closed temporarily, by balance, and ruled and footed to mark a period, and a condition at that period, for the same reason, if it shows a liability it is closed to balance, but it is immediately reopened by bringing down the balance on the opposite side.

5TH.—Close Loss and Gain account into Stock, or, if it be a partnership business, into the partners' accounts, dividing the gain or loss, according to agreement. The Stock or Partners' accounts will now show the original investment increased by the gain, or decreased by the loss; the difference being the *present* net investment. Inasmuch as the Balance account shows the same thing, they must of course agree.

6TH.—Close Stock (or Partners' accounts) into Balance account which must equalize that account, it showing now, on one side, the total Resources, and on the other side the total liabilities, and presenting in the most condensed form the exact present condition of the business.

CLOSING THE LEDGER.

In the preceding form it was thought best to leave the Ledger in its open or current condition, the results of the business being shown in separate statements. When the object is to know simply the condition of the business, this method is sufficient; but when it becomes necessary to mark the progress of the business in some enduring manner upon the Ledger, the accounts must be "closed," and the balance exhibited.

The object of closing the Ledger is to put an end to its current condition by disposing of the REPRESENTATIVE accounts; for inasmuch as the proprietor is to be credited with his net investment, whenever that net investment is increased by gains, his account should get the benefit of it. As it would be impracticable to carry the separate gains and losses to the proprietors' accounts when they accrue, they are permitted to remain in the accounts producing them. In real business, books are usually closed once a year, and in some establishments every six months, thus marking an era in the business.

We shall now take the student carefully through the process of "closing the Ledger."

Having gone through the process of Journalizing, and posting the transactions in Set I., and taken off a trial balance to satisfy ourselves that the work has been properly performed, we now proceed, according to the following instructions, to close the Ledger Accounts.

We open *"Loss and Gain"* and *"Balance"* accounts as directed. We then ascertain from the Inventory at the end of the Day Book, page 29, the value of goods unsold. The unsold Flour in this case is worth $3,915, and the unsold Wheat $1,120, which amounts we enter on the credit side of these accounts in red ink, "*By Balance Inventory*," and transfer the same immediately to the contrary or Dr. side of Balance account, making the entry in black, "To Flour $3,915," "To Wheat $1,120." The accounts are now in a condition to close; and we will take them in their order.

The first account (after Stock) is cash. This account represents a resource consisting of cash in hand, $2,550.

We *close* the account by entering the difference, *in red ink*, "By Balance," on the credit side, and footing up the sides, drawing double *red* lines underneath.

The red ink entry, or *balance*, is transferred immediately to the *debit* side of Balance account.

The next account, Flour, shows a *gain*, the Cr. or proceeds from sales, together with the value of that unsold, being greater than the Dr. or cost, and the difference is entered *in red ink*, on the debit side of the account, "To Loss and Gain, $550," and transferred to the *credit* side of Loss and Gain account. The next account, Wheat, is closed in the same way. The next, Bills Payable, shows a *Liability*, consisting of our unredeemed Notes, and is closed "To Balance $1,315."

This *balance* is transferred to the *credit* side of Balance account. Bills Receivable account is closed in the same manner as Cash, the balance being transferred as a resource to Balance account. The next account, James Rimmer, is closed in the same way. The next, W. Lingham, shows a *Liability*, and is transferred to the *credit* of Balance. Robert Thompson's account already balances, and we close it by simply footing and ruling it. H. Corby's account shows a *Liability*, and the balance is transferred to the *credit* side of Balance. The next account, James Miller, already balances, and as there is but one entry on each side, we close it by simply ruling the double red lines. Expense account shows a *loss*, and is closed "By Loss & Gain," $165.50, and transferred to the *debit* side of Loss and Gain.

We have now the result of all the accounts exhibited under the heads of Loss and Gain, and Balance, and if the balances have been properly transferred, these accounts, together with the (unclosed) Stock account, must be in equilibrium. To test this, we next take a Trial Balance of these three accounts, which we call the

SECOND TRIAL BALANCE.

		Dr.		Cr.	
Stock.............	....			$8000	50
Loss and Gain	....	$165	50	815	00
Balance	....	11965	00	3315	00
		12130	50	12130	50

After proving by this test that the balances have been properly transferred, we proceed to accomplish the grand object of closing the Ledger, by carrying the difference between the two sides of the Loss and Gain account, or, in this case, net gain of $649.50 to the Stock account.

The Stock account now contains the capital invested, increased by the gain, which must equal the *present worth*, as shown by the balance account. We now close Stock account into Balance, which must produce an equilibrium of the Balance account, and complete, in that account, the record of Resources and Liabilities.

The Balance account is used for its convenience in collecting, under one title, all the Resources and Liabilities. The same effect may be produced by bringing down the balances under the REAL accounts. The latter method is adopted in business, particularly where the record is continued in the same Ledger.

The student should remember that in no one thing does the proficiency of a practical accountant more plainly manifest itself than in the matter of neatness in arrangement and execution.

He should observe particularly the form adopted in ruling, and be careful to enter all Balances, Inventories and ruling with *red ink*, and all Transfers with *black ink*.

NOTE.—The form adopted in closing the Ledger on the following pages is submitted as a model to guide you hereafter.

SPECIMEN LEDGER—CLOSED.

See Explanation, pages 43, 44.

DR.   STOCK.   CR.

1889							1889					
Jan.	20	To Balance,	47	8650	00		Jan.	1	By Sundries,*	30	8000	50
							"	20	" Loss and Gain,	47	649	50
				8650	00						8650	00

CASH.

Jan.	1	To Stock,	30	4000	50		Jan.	2	By Flour,	30	300	00
"	4	" J. Rimmer,	30	100	00		"	3	" Wheat,	30	300	00
"	6	" Wheat,	30	125	00		"	5	" "	30	560	00
"	11	" "	31	230	00		"	9	" Expense,	30	25	50
"	15	" R. Thompson,	31	975	00		"	10	" H. Corby,	31	1000	00
"	"	" Bills Rec.,	31	175	00		"	12	" Bills Payable,	31	650	00
"	17	" "	31	120	00		"	15	" "	31	200	00
							"	18	" Expense,	31	140	00
							"	20	" Balance,	47	2550	00
				5725	50						5725	50

FLOUR.

Jan.	1	To Stock,	30	3000	00		Jan.	6	By J. Miller,	30	1300	00
"	2	" Cash,	30	300	00		"	13	" J. Rimmer,	30	1400	00
"	3	" Bills Payable,	30	650	00		"	17	" "	31	1200	00
"	6	" H. Corby,	30	3000	00		"	20	" Bal. Inventory	47	3915	00
"	12	" Bills Payable,	31	315	00							
"	20	" Loss and Gain,	47	550	00							
				7815	00						7815	00

WHEAT.

Jan.	1	To Stock,	30	1000	00		Jan.	2	By J. Rimmer,	30	150	00
"	2	" Bills Payable,	30	200	00		"	3	" R. Thompson,	30	600	00
"	3	" Cash,	30	300	00		"	4	" Bills Receivable	30	175	00
"	5	" "	30	560	00		"	5	" "	30	120	00
"	10	" W. Lingham,	31	450	00		"	6	" Cash,	30	125	00
"	17	" "	31	550	00		"	8	" J. Rimmer,	30	280	00
"	20	" Loss and Gain,	47	265	00		"	9	" R. Thompson.	31	375	00
							"	11	" Sundries,	31	380	00
							"	20	" Bal. Inventory	47	1120	00
				3325	00						3325	00

* Sundries, meaning several accounts, stands for the three accounts, Cash, Flour and Wheat.

E

BILLS PAYABLE.

Dr. | | | | | | **Cr.**

1889						1889					
Jan.	12	To Cash,	31	650	00	Jan.	2	By Wheat,	30	$200	00
"	15	" "	31	200	00	"	3	" Flour,	30	650	00
"	20	" Balance,	47	1 15	00	"	12	" "	31	315	00
						"	16	" H. Corby,	31	1000	00
				2165	00					2165	00

BILLS RECEIVABLE.

Jan.	4	To Wheat,	30	175	00	Jan.	15	By Cash,	31	175	00
"	5	" "	30	120	00	"	17	" "	31	120	00
"	8	" J. Miller,	30	1300	00	"	20	" Balance,	47	1450	00
"	11	" Wheat,	31	150	00						
				1745	00					1745	00

JAMES RIMMER.

Jan.	2	To Wheat,	30	150	00	Jan.	4	By Cash,	30	100	00
"	8	" "	30	280	00	"	20	" Balance,	47	2930	00
"	13	" Flour,	30	1400	00						
"	17	" "	31	1200	00						
				3030	00					3030	00

W. LINGHAM.

Jan.	20	To Balance,	47	1000	00	Jan.	10	By Wheat,	31	450	00
						"	17	" "	31	550	00
				1000	00					1000	00

ROBT. THOMPSON.

Jan.	3	To Wheat,	30	600	00	Jan.	15	By Cash,	31	975	00
"	9	" "	31	375	00						
				975	00					975	00

H. CORBY.

Jan.	10	To Cash,	31	1000	00	Jan.	6	By Flour,	30	3000	00
"	16	" Bills Payable,	31	1000	00						
"	20	" Balance,	47	1000	00						
				3000	00					3000	00

47

Dr.						JAMES MILLER.					Cr.
1889 Jan.	6	To Flour,	30	1300	00	1889 Jan.	8	By Bills Receiv.,	30	1300	00

EXPENSE.

Jan.	9	To Cash,	30	25	50	Jan.	20	By Loss and Gain,	47	165	50
"	18	" "	31	140	00						
				165	50					165	50

(Losses.)   **LOSS AND GAIN.**   (Gains.)

Jan.	20	To Expense,	47	165	50	Jan.	20	By Flour,	45	550	00
20	"	" Stock,	45	649	50	"	"	" Wheat,	45	265	00
				815	00					815	00

(Resources.)   **✱ BALANCE.**   (Liabilities.)

Jan.	20	To Flour,	45	3915	00	Jan.	20	By Bills Payable	46	1315	00
"	"	" Wheat,	45	1120	00	"	"	" W. Lingham,	46	1000	00
"	"	" Cash,	45	2550	00	"	"	" H. Corby,	46	1000	00
"	"	" Bills Rec.,	46	1450	00	"	"	" Stock,	45	8650	00
"	"	" Jas. Rimmer,	46	2930	00						00
				11965	00					11965	00

DETECTION AND CORRECTION OF ERRORS.

The Trial Balance is the best short test of correctness in posting yet discovered; but this is defective, inasmuch as errors may exist while the Trial Balance is apparently entirely correct:—such as posting to the wrong account, although on the right side; omitting to post a debit and a credit of equal amount, &c. But if the Trial Balance is not in equilibrium there is certainly an error, which must be sought and corrected.

DETECTION.

FIRST.—See whether the pencil footings on the Ledger, made preparatory to taking the Trial Balance, are correct, by adding both up and down, and whether the footings and balances of the different accounts have been transferred into the Trial Balance correctly.

SECOND.—If there is still an undiscovered error, examine each posting separately, checking the entries in both Journal and Ledger as you proceed, thus, √, until you have been over the whole; and then look through again, to see if any amount remains unchecked, and, if so, investigate the cause of the omission.

In this manner, you can scarcely fail to discover the mistake, provided the Journal is correct; but great care should be taken to see that the Journal is in equilibrium before posting, as any discrepancy there will give you much trouble in the Ledger.

✱ It will be observed that all those accounts that have been closed "By Balance" or "Balance Inventory" appear on the Dr. side of Balance Account, while those that close "To Balance" appear on the Credit side You will also see that Stock makes up the deficiency between the two sides, it being the concern's net capital, and also agrees with the balance of Stock account after the net loss or gain has been transferred to it. See foot note, page 42.

CORRECTION.

IN THE DAY BOOK (or any other book of original entry), erasures are not admissible, since this book is taken as evidence in Courts of Justice, and any thing obliterated or erased looks suspicious, and would probably render invalid the entry with which it is connected, and in some cases might even throw the whole book out of Court, as evidence unfit to receive. Errors in it should, therefore, be corrected by making other entries explaining them; or the erroneous entry, if it has not been journalized, may be marked "void," and remain without further alteration, a new and correct entry being made of the transaction.

IN THE JOURNAL, erasures are sometimes admissible, although it is generally advisable to treat errors as directed for the Day Book.

IN THE LEDGER, if any entry be posted to the wrong account, or to the wrong side of the account, make ciphers of the figures, and leave the remainder so as not to deface the Ledger; then post the entry to its proper place. If a wrong amount be posted, alter it to the right. And if a duplicate posting be made, make ciphers of the figures in the erroneous one. If two accounts be opened with the same person, close the one into the other. "To" or "By," name of account, page ——, foot and rule off the closed account, as a settled account; stating the particulars of each transfer to the open account. A further explanation of this will be found hereafter. See Index for "Cross Entries."

QUESTIONS FOR REVIEW—CHAPTER III.

Into what classes are Accounts divided? What is a Real Account? Name some Real Accounts? What is a Representative Account? How are Representative Accounts sub-divided? Define Speculative and Incidental Accounts. Give examples of each. What is a Resource? Define the term Liability. What is the measure of all value in business? By what Accounts are Liabilities represented on the Ledger? What will the difference between the Resources and Liabilities of a business show? How are Resources and Liabilities invariably shown in the Ledger? When do Losses and Gains occur in business? How may the net worth or net insolvency of a concern be found? How may the net gain or loss during any period be found? For what purpose is a Trial Balance taken? How should you proceed to take off a Trial Balance? In what way may the footings of the Trial Balance be made to correspond with the footings of the Day Book and the Journal? Is the Trial Balance always a strict proof of the correctness of the work? In what way may an error occur and the Trial Balance stand in equilibrium? What is necessary after taking a Trial Balance, before we can get at the data from which to ascertain the net worth, or net gain or loss? In Classifying Accounts, what two grand objects are kept in view? Define the term balancing an account. How do Real Accounts close? How do Speculative and Incidental Accounts close? What is the object of closing the Ledger? What two Accounts are opened to receive the results of the other Accounts? For what purpose is the Balance Account used? Which of the Statements shows the same as the Balance Account? When should red ink be used? How would you proceed to detect an error in the work, if the Trial Balance did not come right? How should corrections be made in books of original entry? If an entry be passed to the wrong Account in the Ledger, how should the correction be made? How should the correction be made when two Accounts have been opened for the same person?

CHAPTER IV.

BUSINESS SERIES.

The foregoing exercises and explanations are sufficient, if thoroughly understood, to familiarize you with the theory of Double Entry Book-keeping. It now remains with you to fasten these principles indelibly on your mind by the regular process of Book-keeping, which at the same time will serve to give you practice in business record, which is essential to real progress.

The sets which follow, while serving as a synthetical unfolding of the science, are intended, each in its turn, to present some specialty of business, and some radical feature which distinctly characterizes its purpose. In presenting the transactions, care has been taken to avoid, as far as possible, any special *form* of entry; but at the same time to present the *facts* as clearly and unmistakably as possible.

They are intended to cover a wide field of practice, and to present sufficient variety of transactions and knowledge of theory to give the student an excellent understanding of the science. Each set is complete within itself, and special in its purpose and teaching. Its characteristics are briefly announced at the start, and as its results only, with more or less detail, are given at its close, the student is obliged to accomplish the work of the set in order to arrive at the proper result.

This mode of arrangement is calculated to throw the learner upon his own resources, and rescue him from the too common error of copying down the work without understanding it. This feature will no doubt commend itself to all faithful students.

While performing the following work, remember that the three great qualities essential to success in Accountantship are: ACCURACY, NEATNESS, and DISPATCH.

SET II.

RETAIL DRY GOODS BUSINESS.

CHARACTERISTICS.—*Buying and selling for Cash and on Personal Account. Business Adverse.*

NOTE.—Instead of keeping a distinct account with each article of traffic, as in Set I, we classify all under the title of "Merchandise." This is the usual business method, and should always be adopted, except were it is essential to know the gains and losses on each particular kind of property or branch of business.

Halifax, February 1, 1889.—Invested in business, Cash $5,000.

2—Bought of W. L. Hamilton, on acct., merchandise amounting by invoice to $4170.75.
"—Bought of Sanderson & Co., on acct., an invoice of merchandise amounting to $1250.
3—Paid for repairing and cleaning store, $187.50; for advertising business, $15.50. Total, $203.
4—Sold A. H. Skinner, on acct., 5 yds. Black Broadcloth at $4; 2 yds. Farmer's Satin at 50c.; 1 yd. Silecia, 30c.; 1 yd. Canvas, 20c.; 1 yd. Hair Cloth, 60c.; 3 sheets Wadding at 5c.; 1 doz. Buttons, 25c.; 4 skeins Silk at 5c.; 1 Vest Pattern, $4.25; 5 yds. Red Flannel at 40c. Total, $28.95. *Cash sales this day,* $115.40.
5—Sold B. M. Carman, on acct., 1 pair Kid Gloves, $1.25; 12 yds. Merino at 60c.; 5 Linen Handkerchiefs at 25c.; 10 yds. Calico at 15c. Total, $11.20.
"—Sold R. S. Thompson, on acct., 15 yds. Muslin de Laine at 30c.; 5 yds. Alpaca at 50c.; 10 yds. Cambric at 10c.; 40 yds. Sheeting at 15c. Total, $14. *Cash sales this day,* $130.45.

NOTE.—Remember when recording the Day Book entries to separate each transaction, whether they occur on the same date or not, with a line, and use a separate line for each item sold or bought.

6—Paid Sanderson & Co., on acct., cash, $850.
" Bought of W. L. Hamilton, on acct., invoice of merchandise, $1500.
" Sold A. H. Skinner, on acct. (wife), 10 yds Linen Edging at 15c.; 15 yds. Muslin at 30c.; Trimmings, $1.20; 3 yds. Fine Linen at 50c. Total, $8.70.
". Paid W. L. Hamilton, on acct., cash, $2000. *Cash sales this day*, $192.65.
8—Bought for cash, invoice of merchandise, $450.
" Paid sundry items of expense $24.50.
" Sold B. M. Carman, on acct. (daughter), 18 yds. Black Silk at $1.10; Trimmings, $5.50; 1 pair Kid Gloves, $1.25; 5 spools Thread at 5c.; 6 yds. Edging at 20c. Total, $28. *Cash sales this day*, $211.30.
9—Received from A. H. Skinner, cash on acct., $25.00.
" Paid clerk's salary, $10.50; for wood, $18.50. Total, $29.
" Sold B. M. Carman, on acct., 15 yds. Shirting at 20c.; 4 yds. Black Cassimere at $1.75; 4 yds. Green Baize at 50c. Total, $12. *Cash sales this day*, $225.30.
10—Received from B. M. Carman, cash on acct., $15.
" Paid W. L. Hamilton, on acct., $350.
" Paid sundry items of Expense, $15.40.
" Bought of W. L. Hamilton, on acct., invoice of merchandise, $475.50.
" Paid Sanderson & Co., in full of acct., cash $400.

Inventory of Goods remaining unsold: Merchandise, $6950.
RESULTS (*not to be entered in Day Book.*)
Net capital at commencing, $5000; *Net loss,* $190.20; *Net worth at closing,* $4809.80.

SET III.
DRY GOODS AND GROCERY BUSINESS.

CHARACTERISTICS.—*Buying and selling for cash, on personal account and on notes.—Business prosperous.*

Belleville, March 1, 1889.—Invested in business—Cash $6500; Merchandise 3000.
2—Bought of Geo. Wallbridge, on my note, 56 hhds. Molasses, 3500 gals., at 40c., $1400.
3—Bought of Muir & Co., Montreal, on three months' credit, 4 cases, 5200 yds. Muslin, at 20c. $1040.
4—Sold George J. Sherry, on acct., 34 hhds. Molasses, 2100 gals., at 35c., $735.
5—Sold S. G. Beatty, on acct., 1 case Muslin, 1300 yds., at 25c., $325; 12 pieces of Tweed, 420 yds., at $1.25, $525. Total, $850.
6—Bought of Walker & Son, Toronto, for cash, 3 cases Prints, 3210 yds., at 10c., $321; and 4 cases do., 3500 yds., at 15c., $525. Total, $846.
8—Sold C. P. Holton, for cash, 11 hhds. Molasses, 700 gals., at 45c., $315.
9—Sold H. Warren, on acct., 6 pieces Tweed, 210 yds., at $1.25, $262.50.
10—Bought of S. G. Beatty, on acct., 18 half chests " Y. H." Tea, 370 lbs., at $1.00, $370.
11—Sold W. B. Robinson, for cash, 11 hhds. Molasses, 700 gals., at 40c., $280.
12—Paid cash for 1 Quarter's Rent of Store, $200; Gas Bill, $15. Total, $215.
13—Received from S. G. Beatty, his note for $480, in full of account.
15—Paid cash in full for my note of the 2nd inst., $1400.
16—Sold R. P. Dunning, on his note, 10 half chests " Y. H." Tea, 200 lbs., at $1.25, $250.
17—Gave Muir & Co., my note at three months, in part settlement of account, $500.
18—Bought of Walker & Son, Toronto, on my note, 4 cases Prints, 4300 yds., at 10c., $430.
19—Paid cash for Clerk's Salary, $175.
20—Received from S. G. Beatty, cash in full for his note of 13th inst., $480.
22—Paid for sundry items of expense, $180.
23—Sold G. J. Sherry, on acct., 4 pieces Tweed, 160 yds., at $1.50, $240; 1 case Muslin, 1200 yds., at 25c., $300. Total, $540.
24—Sold Thomas Moore, on acct., 11 hhds. Molasses, 700 gals., at 40c., $280.
25—Received from G. J. Sherry, cash on account, $100, and his note for $125.

26—Redeemed my note of the 18 inst., favor of Walker & Son, $430, for which I gave cash $305, and G. J. Sherry's note for balance $125.
27—Received from Thomas Moore, cash on account, $150.
28—Paid cash for Wood, $24; Cleaning Store, $4.50.
" Received from Thomas Moore, cash in full of account, $130.
" Paid cash for Clerk's Salary, $75.

Inventory of goods remaining unsold: Merchandise, $5,500.
Net Capital at commencing $9,500; Net gain, $1,253; Net worth at closing, $10,753.

REMARKS ON NOTES AND BILLS.

A new feature in connection with the work of the next set is the computing of interest on notes and bills. As beginners often experience difficulty in determining the day upon which notes and acceptances fall due, we shall endeavor, in the following directions, to make the matter plain.

In all computations in reference to notes or bills, in the following sets, three days grace is included. When the term of a note is expressed in days, the day after drawing or accepting is the first day counted, in the time to run. Thus, a bill drawn or accepted on January 1st, at 15 days, will fall due January 19th,—including three days' grace. A bill drawn or accepted on the 29th September, at 60 days, has to run

In September	1 day
In October	31 days
In November	30 days
In December	1 day
	63 days, due Dec. 1.

Again, a bill drawn or accepted 30th September, at 90 days, has to run

In October	31 days
In November	30 days
In December	31 days
In January	1 day
	93 days, due Jan. 1.

It will be observed in the last example, that no time is allowed for September, although the date is on the last day of that month, as, according to the rule, the day following the date is the first day counted in the time to run.

When the term of a note or bill is expressed in months, CALENDAR MONTHS are always understood, and it comes due in the last month of its term, upon the day corresponding with its date, to which are added the days of grace.

The time of payment is not extended, in business, on account of any deficiency in the length of the months, of which the term of the note is made up. For instance, a note drawn on the 31st August, at three months, and another drawn on the 30th August, also at three months, will both fall due on the same day, viz., 3rd December.

Bills of different dates running the same time will sometimes fall due the same day, and thus occasion unexpected inconvenience. Sometimes by obtaining one day's advance in the date, two, three and four days are gained in the time of payment. For example, a note or bill drawn or accepted on the 28th February, at six months, is due August 31st, but if dated on the 1st March, only one day later, it would not be due until the 4th September, thus extending the term of payment four days for one day's difference in the date.

In the following instances, one day's advance in the date will give the date of payment three or four days later. Notes drawn or Bills accepted February 28th.*

At 1 month, are due March 31, but if dated March 1 are not due till April 4.
" 2 months, " May 1, " " " May 4.
" 3 " " May 31, " " " June 4.
" 4 " " July 1, " " " July 4.
" 5 " " July 31, " " " Aug. 4.
" 6 " " Aug. 31, " " " Sept. 4.
" 7 " " Oct. 1, " " " Oct. 4.
" 8 " " Oct. 31, " " " Nov. 4.
" 9 " " Dec. 1, " " " Dec. 4.
" 10 " " Dec. 31, " " " Jan. 4.
" 11 " " Jan. 31, " " " Feb. 4.

One day's advance in the date will in the following cases give two additional days in the time of payment.

Notes drawn or Bills accepted April 30th.

At 1 month, are due June 2, but if dated 1st May are due June 4.
" 3 months, " Aug. 2, " " " Aug. 4.
" 4 " " Sept. 2, " " " Sept. 4.
" 6 " " Nov. 2, " " " Nov. 4.
" 8 " " Jan. 2, " ' " Jan. 4.
" 9 " " Feb. 2, " " " Feb. 4.
" 11 " " April 2, " " " April 4.

The above illustrations are sufficient to impress upon those having anything to do with bills, the fact that an error of one day in recording the maturity of a note or acceptance may cause the holder to lose his remedy against the endorser; and perhaps cause him to lose the amount of the note altogether. When the last day of grace falls upon Sunday or a bank holiday, the note is payable on the following day. We have next to point out the other feature alluded to, viz. : those instances in which several notes or acceptances, dated or accepted on different days, and having the same time to run, in months, will fall due on the same day.

If you give four notes dated—

August 28, at 6 months,
August 29, at 6 months,
August 30, at 6 months,
August 31, at 6 months,

these notes, although of different dates, and all of the same running time, will become due on the same day.

Again, if you give two notes dated—

March 30, at 3 months,
March 31, at 3 months,

they will both fall due on the same day.

---

* Our calculations are all made for ordinary years. Leap year makes a day's difference.

MEMORANDA.

The following memoranda will enable the learner to determine in the preceding cases when to date bills in order to advance the day of payment, and to tell the precise day upon which they become due :

1—*Notes drawn or bills accepted on the last day of February, with a running time in months, will advance the day of payment three or four days by dating forward one day.*

2.—*Notes drawn or bills accepted on the last day of a thirty-day month, with a running time in months, expiring in a thirty-one day month, will advance the date of payment two days by dating forward one day.*

3.—*Notes drawn or bills accepted on the last three days of thirty-day months, and the last four days of thirty-one day months, with a running time in months, expiring in February, will become due on the same day.*

4.—*Notes drawn or bills accepted on the last two days of thirty-one day months, with a running time in months, expiring in a thirty-day month, will fall due on the same day.*

SET IV.
FURNITURE BUSINESS.

CHARACTERISTICS.—*Buying for Cash, on Personal Account and on Notes.—Interest taken into consideration.—Commencing with a Net Capital, sustaining a loss greater than Capital, and closing Insolvent.*

BOOKS USED—DAY BOOK, JOURNAL, LEDGER AND BILL BOOK.
See form of Bill Book at the end of Set.

OTTAWA, MARCH 1, 1889.

Leased a store of T. B. Dean, at $600 per annum, and commenced the Furniture business, investing as follows :

Cash, $1800. Stock of Furniture on hand, $1500. Note against A. Overell for $750, dated Jan. 17th, 1889, at 2 months. Total investment, $4050.

Bought of G. S. Tickell, Belleville, on one Month's credit, 15 Carved Rosewood Centre Tables at $50, 6 doz. do Arm Chairs at $60. Total, $1110.

2—Sold W. R. Barber, on his note at 15 days, 10 Carved Rosewood Chairs at $8, 1 do. Centre Table, $75, 1 Gothic Hall Stand, $25. Total, $180.

3—Bought of Jakes & Hayes, Toronto, on acct., 10 sets Enamelled Furniture at $75, 6 do. Black Walnut at $150, 10 Extension Dining Tables at $25. Total, $1900.

4—Sold W. H. Sherman, for Cash, 1 set Enamelled Furniture, $100, 1 Extension Dining Table, $40, 8 Carved Chairs at $8. Total, $204.

5—Sold W. W. Jones, on his note at one month, with interest at 6 per cent., 1 set Enamelled Furniture, $100, one Extension Table, $40, 1 Dressing Bureau, $35, 1 Rosewood Tete-a-Tete, $50, 1 Gothic Hall Stand, $28, 1 Card Table, $5, 1 French Bedstead, $22, 1 Cottage Bedstead, $15. Total, $295.

*6—Settled with Jakes & Hayes, by giving them my note at 1 month, with interest at 9 per cent., in full of acct., $1900.

9—Bought of J. B. Ashley, on my note at 10 days, 15 Black Walnut Book Cases at $60, 2 doz. do. Arm Chairs at $60, 20 Curled Hair Mattrasses at $20, 20 Double-Leaf Secretaries at $35, 25 Music Racks at $5. Total $2245.

10—Sold G. W. Maybee, on acct., 1 Carved Rosewood Centre Table, $60, 2 doz. Arm Chairs at $50, 1 set Enamelled Furniture, $80, 1 Black Walnut Sofa Bedstead, $50, 2 Extension Tables at $30, 2 Gothic Chairs, B. W. stuffed at $15, 1 Easy Rocker, $12. Total, $392.

11—Bought of Jakes and Hayes, on 3 months' credit, an assortment of Furniture amounting, per invoice, to $3,500.

" —Paid Cash for Insurance, $125.

---

* This note is to bear interest, but you make the Journal entry as though it were not. At the maturity of the note you will deal with interest.

The Dr. side of Interest acc't shows what interest costs you, and the Cr. side what interest produces for you. It closes either to or by loss and gain.

15—Sold S. G. Beatty, for cash, 2 Black Walnut Bureaus at $30, 1 Rosewood Parlor Set, $400, 1 enamelled Bedroom Suite, $200, 1 Single Bedstead, $8, 1 Quartette Table, $9, 1 Lady's Arm Chair, $12, 1 Black Walnut Library Book Case, $75. Total, $764.

16—Sold W. McKeown, for cash, 1 Carved Rosewood Secretary, $120, 3 Patent Spring Beds at $60, 1 Walnut Centre Table, $50, 2 Rosewood Bureaus at $40, 2 Arm Chairs at $10, 2 " Sleepy Hollow " Chairs at $25, 1 Black Walnut Parlor Suite, $300, 1 Side What-not, $9. Total, $809.

17—Paid cash for three months' Rent, $150, Advertising, $25.

" —Bought of Jakes & Hayes, on acct., Furniture amounting, per invoice, to $2150.

" —Bought of H. W. Huffman, on my note at 3 months, Furniture amounting to $550.

18—Received from G. W. Maybee, cash on acct., $150.

" —Sold W. Johnson, on his note at three months, 1 Hall Stand, $5, 6 Parlor Chairs at $3.50, 1 R. W. Tete-a-Tete, $30, 1 Black Walnut Sofa, $30, 1 Large Dining Table, $14, 1 Piano Stool, $8, 1 Music Rack, $5. Total, $113.

19—Sold Warner Bros., for cash, 2 Bedroom Suites at $50.60, 2 Rosewood Parlor Suites at $200. Total, 501.20.

20—Received from G. W. Maybee, cash in full of acct., $242.

" —Received from A. Overell, cash in full for his note of Jan. 17, $750.

22—*J. B. Ashley renewed for one month my note for $2245, due this day. Charges on renewal $13.78.

24—Sold H. Corby, on acct., 20 doz. Kitchen Chairs at $8, 10 doz. Rush Bottom Chairs at $18. Total, $340.

28—Bought of Smith and Co., Kingston, on note at three months, assortment of Furniture, amounting, as per invoice, to $1500.

April 1st—Paid G. S. Tickell cash on acct., $500.

8—Received from W. W. Jones cash in full for his note of 5th ult., and interest thereon to date at 6 per cent. Face of note, $295. Interest, $1.62.

12—Paid Salaries, $180. Sundry expenses, $25.

16—Paid my note 6th ult., favor of Jakes & Hayes, with interest to date. Face of note, $1900. Interest, $19.

Inventory of merchandise unsold, $5336.34.

Net capital at commencement, $4050. *Net loss*, $6056.62. *Net insolvency at closing*, $2006.62.

REMARKS ON THE BILL BOOK.

The Bill Book should never be omitted in any business dealings with notes, either payable or receivable. It is so simple that the student will see, by inspection, its utility. All necessary explanations are made by the headings of the different columns.

The precaution of closing the Bill Book and showing the amount of bills unpaid is necessary in a business where any considerable number of Bills are given or received, in order to maintain harmony between this book and the Bills Payable and Bills Receivable accounts in the Ledger.

It will be seen that the Bills entered in the following forms are taken from the transactions of Set IV., and hence the notes on hand and notes outstanding, as shown by Bills footed up, will be found to agree with the balance shewn in the proper Ledger accounts.

NOTE.—The student is expected to work out the interest on all notes bearing interest.

The above calculations have been made by the short business method in common use for computing interest for days; but, since it considers the year as containing only 360 days, instead of 365, the result is too large by $\frac{5}{365}$, $\frac{1}{73}$ of itself. Hence, when perfect accuracy is desired, the interest for the days when obtained by the rule must be diminished by $\frac{1}{73}$ part of itself.

In business calculations it is not customary to enter fractions of a cent on the account books; consequently, in all computations throughout these sets where a fraction of a cent less than one-half occurs, we take no notice of it; but where a fraction of half a cent or more occurs, we call it one cent.

* Under the head of " Entries for Renewals of Notes," refer to Index, you will learn how to make this entry in the Journal.

FORM OF BILL BOOK.

BILLS RECEIVABLE.

No.	When Received.	Drawer or Acceptor.	In whose Favor.	For what Received.	Where Payable.	Date. Year	Date. Month.	Time to Run.	When Due. Year	Jan.	Feb.	Mar.	April	May	June	July	Aug.	Sept.	Oct.	Nov.	Dec.	Am't.	When and how disposed of.
1	March 1	A. Overell.	My own	Invest't.	My office.	1889	Jan. 17	2 m.	1889			20										750	Mar. 20 Rec'd. in cash.
2	" 2	W. R. Barber	"	Mdse.	"	1889	Mar. 2	15 d.	1889			20										180	
3	" 5	W. W. Jones,	"	"	Mont. Bk.	1889	Mar. 5	1 m.	1889				8									295	Apr. 8 Rec'd. in cash.
4	" 18	W. Johnson.	"	"	"	1889	Mar. 18	3 m.	1889						21							113	
																						293*	

BILLS PAYABLE.

No.	When Issued.	Drawer or Acceptor.	In whose Favor.	For what Given.	Where Payable.	Date. Year	Date. Month.	Time to Run.	When Due. Year	Jan.	Feb.	Mar.	April	May	June	July	Aug.	Sept.	Oct.	Nov.	Dec.	Am't.	When and how retired.
1	March 6	Myself.	Jakes & Hayes.	Mdse.	My office.	1889	Mar. 6	1 m.	1889				9									1900	Apr. 16 Paid in cash.
2	" 9	"	J. B. Ashley.	"	"	1889	Mar. 9	10 d.	1889			22										2245	Mar. 22 Ren'd by B. P. No. 4
3	" 17	"	H. Huffman.	"	Mont. Bk.	1889	Mar. 17	3 m.	1889						20							550	
D 4	" 22	"	J. B. Ashley.	Ren'l. No. 2.	"	1889	Mar. 22	1 m.	1889				25									2258 78	
5	" 28	"	Smith & Co.	Mdse.	"	1889	Mar. 28	3 m.	1889							1						1500	
																						4308 78 *	

NOTE.—In many large houses the Bill Book is kept as the only book of original entry for bills receivable and payable, and from it they are posted directly to the Ledger without journalizing. When this is done, a folio column, to show the Ledger Folios of the accounts debited and credited, is necessary, and the columns "For what Received" and "For what Given" should be wide enough to admit of explanations when necessary.
When notes are paid, or disposed of, rule a red line across the figures to show that they are cancelled.
*Amount of our notes unpaid, agreeing with Credit Balance of Bills Payable account in Ledger.

*Amount of unpaid notes, agreeing with Debit Balance of Bills Receivable account in Ledger.

BUSINESS FORMS.

A thorough acquaintance with the forms of business papers is indispensable to every one who would master the science of accounts. Not only should their nature and use be fully understood, but the ability to make them out readily and correctly should be acquired. For this reason we ask the student to make out formal bills and invoices of merchandise bought and sold, write proper receipts for moneys paid or received, draw up forms to represent bills receivable and bills payable, forms of the drafts and orders referred to in the transactions of the different sets, and copy them until he can write them out without referring to the book.

BILLS AND INVOICES.

A BILL OF GOODS is a description of the quantity and price of goods sold, with the date of the transaction and the names of the purchaser and seller.

AN INVOICE is a full account of merchandise, in which the marks, numbers, contents, and value of each package, together with all charges, are described.

When anything is purchased for another, or is to be charged in account, it is well to take a bill of it. The bill will be a reminder to make the proper entry in the books concerning it, and will also serve as a voucher for items, prices, etc. Even when cash is paid, the bill is frequently needed for reference.

Invoices are usually pasted in a book, or neatly folded and marked on the back with the name of the person from whom bought, the date and the amount, and then put up in monthly packages for safe keeping.

BILL NOT RECEIPTED.

Toronto, Nov. 1st, 1889.

MR. JOHN S. EWING,
    Toronto.

BOUGHT OF GEO. RITCHIE & CO.

Terms Cash.

4 yds. Black Broadcloth,	at	$4.25	$17	00
10 " Factory Cotton,	"	0.10	1	00
15 " Muslin,	"	0.25	3	75
20 " Red Flannel,	"	0.40	8	00
4 doz. Linen Hdkfs.,	"	2.00	8	00
5 lbs. Green Tea (Y. H.)	"	1.00	5	00
			42	75

BILL RECEIPTED.

MR. W. A. ROBLIN, *Belleville, Nov. 1st,* 1889.
Trenton, To CONGER BROS., *Dr.*

To 10 yds. Cambric,				$0.15	$ 1	50
" 20 " Gingham,				0.30	6	00
" 5 " Broadcloth,				4.00	20	00
" 2 doz. Spools Thread,				0.50	1	00
Received payment,					28	50

CONGER BROS.

Should the above bill be receipted by a clerk, his own name should be signed under that of the firm, with the word " per " placed before it.

ITEMS OF AN ACCOUNT.

MR. J. A. MOORE, *Halifax, Jan. 2nd,* 1889.
 To ROBERTSON & HENRY, *Dr.*

1889						
Feb.	1	To 4 yds. Broadcloth,		$5 00	$20	00
"	9	" 3 " Can. Tweed,		1 50	4	50
March	4	" 1 " Vest (Broadcloth),			5	50
		CR.			30	00
April	1	By Cash,		$20.00		
May	6	" Order on Beatty & Wallbridge,		5.00		
					25	00
		Balance due,			5	00

MONTHLY STATEMENT.

Montreal, Jan. 2nd, 1889.
MESSRS. SMITH & JONES, *Winnipeg,*
 To SINCLAIR, JACK & Co., *Dr.*

1889					
Nov.	1	To Mdse. as per Invoice at 3 months,		$100	20
"	8	" " " " at 4 "		500	00
"	28	" " " " at 30 days,		400	00
		CR.		1000	20
"	9	By Goods returned,		57	00
				$943	20

Gentlemen,—We shall draw upon you on Wednesday next at 90 days for amount of account. Please honor draft on presentation and oblige, Yours truly,
 SINCLAIR, JACK & CO.

INVOICE IN WHICH BOTH TRADE AND CASH DISCOUNTS ARE ALLOWED.

Belleville, Jan. 5th, 1889.
MESSRS. W. J. GAGE & Co., *Toronto,*
(Terms—3 *mos.* or 3 *p. c. dis. for cash.*) BOUGHT OF ROBINSON & JOHNSON.

50 copies " The Canadian Accountant " at $2	100 00		
Trade discount 30 per cent.	30 00		
		70	00
20 copies " Johnson's Joint Stock Book-keeping," " $1	20 00		
Trade discount 25 per cent.	5 00		
		15	00
		85	00
Cash discount, 3 per cent.		2	55
		$82	45

INVOICES.

*Sales, 24,
Folio, 325. } **DOMESTIC INVOICE.**

Montreal, Oct. 28th, 1889.

MESSRS. BEATTY & WALLBRIDGE,
                  Belleville, Ont.
Forwarded—G. T. R.

(Terms—*Note at 4 mos.
or 3 p. c. dis. for cash.*)

BOUGHT OF SINCLAIR, JACK & CO.
Importers and Wholesale Dealers in Groceries.

1	5	Hlf. chests Tea (Y. H.,) " S. J. & Co., 14."					
5		78, 14, 73, 14, 74, 14, 369, 75, 15, 69, 13, 70,	299	72	$215	28	
6	4	" Gunpowder, " Chinaman," 53					
9		83, 15, 82, 15, 331, 85, 15, 81, 15, 60,	271	80	216	80	
10	4	Bags Coffee, Java, " A.B.,"					
13		128, 4, 105, 4, 494, 131, 4, 130, 4, 16,	478	24	114	72	
14	2	" Laguayra, " C. T."					
15		228, 113, 4, 115, 4, 8,	220	18	39	60	
	5	Boxes (10c) Laundry Soap, 60 ea.	300	07	21	00	
	4	Doz. B. L. Brushes 2 2			11	00	
		2.50 3.00					
		Cartage,				25	
		E. J.			618	65	

FOREIGN INVOICE.

Glasgow, 5th August, 1889.

Invoice of *one* Package, marked and numbered as per margin, shipped per *Hibernian SS.* from *Glasgow* for and on account of

MESSRS. FOSTER & REID,
    Belleville, Canada.

BOUGHT OF ARTHUR & CO.

London Warehouse, Old 'Change,   F. & R.
Bradford Warehouse, Grange St.   B.   No. 238.

					£ s. d.	£ s. d.
1	4	Pcs. Check Wincey, 56½, 2 57½.	228	6	5 14 0	
		57,				
2	4	" " 56½, 57, 58, 59.	230½	7¾	7 8 10½	
3	1	Shepherd,	50½	8	1 13 8	
4	2	" 51½, 54.	105½	9½	4 3 6	
30	6	All-Wool Tartan,				
		39, 3 2	237½	13½	13 7 2	
35	6	Clan Serge, 39¼ 40,				
		31, 2 2 51.	246	16¾	17 3 4½	
		40, 42,	42¼	16¾	2 19 0	
	1	Super " Box			0 15 6	
						53 5 1

NOTE.—The figures on the left are the invoice number by which any particular line of goo ls would be dentified. The figures underneath the items are gross weights and tares, or measurements.
* Sales Book 24, folio 325

INVOICE OF SHIPMENT ON SOLE ACCOUNT.

Invoice of Merchandise shipped per Steamer " Neptune," 1st November, 1889, and consigned to E. T. Hambly, Port Hope, to be sold on commission.

500 bbls. Extra Superfine Flour, ...at $8	$4000		
100 " Baker's Spring " 7.50	750		
200 " Goderich Salt.... .... 1.50	300		
Paid Insurance	40		$5090
E. & O. E. Hamilton, Nov. 1, 1889.			
S. S. EDSALL,			
Consignor.			

NOTE.—The Student will use the above form of invoice for a single shipment, and the following for a joint shipment. Goods consigned for sale on commission must not be invoiced as though they were sold. Besides the difference in form you should know that if the man to whom you have consigned goods should fail, and you had taken the precaution to put upon the invoice "Consigned to" instead of "Bought of" you can step in and claim your goods. If invoiced in the ordinary way, although it was understood that the goods were only consigned, you would have to take rank with the Creditors.

INVOICE OF SHIPMENT ON JOINT ACCOUNT.

Invoice of Merchandise shipped per Steamer Passport, and consigned to John Cook, Belleville, to be sold on joint account of Shipper and Consignee.

500 bbls. Goderich Salt, ...at $1.50	$ 750			
400 " Extra Family Flour, ... 7.50	3000		$3750	
———Charges.———				
Insurance on $3750, at 1½ per cent.	56	25		
Drayage $25, Labor $10, Cooperage $4, Wharfage $13.	52		108	25
Hamilton, June 1, 1889.				
W. B. ROBINSON, *Consignor.*			$3858	25

CREDIT NOTE.

A Credit Note is an acknowledgment of an error in an invoice, or of goods returned, and is in form similar to an invoice. Instead of the words " *bought of,*" the words " *credited by* " are used, and it is usually printed in red ink, that it may readily be distinguished from an invoice.

FORM.

C. W. THOMPSON, ESQ.,   *Montreal, Jan. 29th, 1889.*
    Belleville.

CREDITED BY SINCLAIR, JACK & CO.

½ chest, 56 lbs. Y. H. Tea, ...	42c		$23	52
Short Invoice of 5th January.				

BILL FOR SERVICES.

Belleville, Oct. 26th, 1889.

THE HASTINGS SMELTING WORKS CO.

To J. W. JOHNSON,   DR.

For services as Auditor, ...	$50	00

ACCOUNT SALES.

An Account Sales is an exhibit of the sales of goods disposed of on commission, with the charges incurred thereon.

When goods received on commission are sold, the agent makes out, for the inspection of the consignor, a detailed account of the sales of said goods, together with such charges as have been made on account of the same. In making out an Account of Sales, the mode of procedure is, to turn to the proper account in the Ledger, and from thence refer to the necessary details as found in the books of original entry.

A variety of forms is in use: those given are most commonly adopted in business.

SHIPMENT ON SOLE ACCOUNT.

Account Sales of 100 *kegs Butter, on account and risk of* ASHLEY & Co., *Belleville, Ont.*

1889					
Oct.	23	Sold for cash			
		100 kegs—6800 lbs. net .... at 20c.,			$1360 00
		Charges.			
"	20	Freight in cash, ...	$92 00		
"	23	Commission, 5 per cent. on sales, ...	68 00		160 00
		Ashley & Co.'s proceeds			$1200 00
		Remitted by sight draft.			
		E. & O. E. H. M. ALEXANDER,			
		Consignee.			
		Belleville, Oct. 25th, 1889.			

JOINT ACCOUNT.

Account Sales of Merchandise received per Steamer Passport, June 3rd, 1889, *from* W B. ROBINSON, *Hamilton, to be sold on joint account of Shipper and myself each* ½.

1889					
Sept.	3	Sold James Smith for endorsed note at 4 mos., with interest at 9 per cent.			
		300 bbls. Goderich Salt, ... at $2·00	$ 600		
		200 " Extra Family Flour, ... at 8.50	1700		
Oct.	1	Sold Winters, Smith & Co., for cash,			
		200 bbls. Goderich Salt, ... at 1.75	350		
		200 " Extra Family Flour, ... at 8.25	1650		$4300
		Charges.			
June	3	Freight and drayage, ...	95	50	
		Wharfage, cooperage and labor, ...	25		
		Commission and Guarantee at 2 per cent., ...	86		
		Interest on charges paid, ...	3	50	210
		Total net proceeds			4090
		Your ½ net proceeds, ...	2045		
		Our ½ " "	2045		
		E. & O. E., J. J. SOLMES.			
		Kingston, Ont., Oct. 5th, 1889.	$4090		$4090

RECEIPTS.

A receipt is an acknowledgment in writing of having received a certain sum of money, or other valuable consideration.

When a payment has been made, a receipt should be taken as proof of the payment. It may not in all cases be necessary, but when important interests are involved nothing should be left to uncertainty, if it can so easily be avoided. A receipt often saves misunderstanding and loss of friends, as well as loss of money. Receipts should be carefully preserved, as many instances have occurred in which claims have been presented after they were paid.

When not written in a book specially prepared for the purpose, they should be kept in a place of security, so that they may be readily produced, if needed.

RECEIPT FOR PAYMENT ON ACCOUNT.

Toronto, Jan. 1st, 1889.

Received from W. H. Yourex, Fifty dollars on account.

$50   E. SCARLETT.

RECEIPT IN FULL OF ACCOUNT.

Belleville, Jan. 1st, 1889.

Received from W. R. Ross, Seventy-five dollars, in full of account to date.

$75   CHAS ADEN.

RECEIPT IN FULL OF ALL DEMANDS.

Napanee, Jan. 1st, 1889.

Received from Henry Bros., One hundred and fifty dollars, in full of all demands.

$150   J. A. FRASER.

RECEIPT FOR A PARTICULAR BILL.

Kingston Dec. 1st, 1889.

Received from Beatty & Wallbridge, Five hundred dollars, in payment for a bill of groceries of this date.

$500   J. CARRUTHERS.

RECEIPT FOR BORROWED MONEY (OR BORROWED MONEY DUE BILL).

Picton, Jan. 1st, 1889.

Borrowed and received from J. S. Miller, Four hundred and fifty dollars, which I promise to pay on demand, with interest.

$450   B. BORROW.

RECEIPT FOR SERVICES.

Hamilton, Dec. 1st, 1889.

Received from Geo. Wallbridge, Forty-seven dollars, in full for services to date.

$47   O. PAYMAN.

RECEIPT FOR A NOTE.

London, Dec. 1st, 1889.

Received from J. B. Ashley, his note of this date, at four months, for Five hundred dollars in full of account rendered to 1st inst.

$500   GEO. RITCHIE & CO.

NOTE.—See the method of filing papers at page 73.

RECEIPT FOR RENT.

Montreal, Dec. 1st, 1889.

Received from C. P. West & Co., One hundred and twenty dollars, in full for one quarter's rent of Store, No. 95 McGill street; due 20th ult.

$120   E. HARRISON.

RECEIPT FOR INTEREST DUE ON MORTGAGE.

Toronto, Dec. 5th, 1889.

Received from Robert Smith, Twenty-nine dollars and fifty cents, in full for six months' interest due this day, on his mortgage to me, bearing date Dec. 6th, 1878, for five hundred and ninety dollars, and which amount is also endorsed on the mortgage.

$29.50   S. G. BEATTY.

RECEIPT FOR PAYMENT BY THE HAND ON A THIRD PARTY.

Halifax, Jan. 1st, 1889.

Received from John Jones, by the hand of R. Howe, Fifty dollars, in full of his account.

$50   WM. R. DEAN.

ENDORSEMENT OF A PARTIAL PAYMENT OF A NOTE.

Bowmanville, Jan. 1st, 1889.

Received on account of the within note, Forty-five dollars.

$45   J. S. MILLER.

AGENT'S RECEIPT.

Brantford, Sept. 1st, 1889.

Received from M. L. Perkins, Two hundred dollars, to apply on his account with C. P. Stanwood.

$200   A. L. HOWARD, Agent.

NOTE.—Payments made by cheque, payable to the order of the individual, do not require receipts, as he must endorse the cheque before obtaining the money. See cheque No, 5. Refer to Index, under the head of Bank Cheque Book.

DRAFTS.

A draft is an unconditional written order, addressed by A. B. to C. D., directing him to pay E. F. a certain sum of money. A. B. is said to draw on C. D., in favor of E. F. A. B. is called the Drawer, C. D. the Drawee, and E. F. the Payee. A. B. may direct the money to be paid to himself, in which case he is Payee as well as Drawer.

To make it an obligation on the part of C. D. he must *accept* it, which is commonly done by writing the word " accepted " and his name across the face of it.

A Draft is of no value until the Drawee accepts it. Bank drafts are an exception, as they are payable on demand, and are issued on the credit of the Bank.

Drafts may be made payable at a certain time after date, a certain time after sight, *at* sight, or payable on demand. It is usual, and advisable, TO PRESENT FOR ACCEPTANCE all Drafts we receive, except those payable on demand. With regard to those payable at a certain time after sight, and even those payable *at sight*, where days of grace are allowed, presentment for acceptance is ABSOLUTELY NECESSARY in order to fix the date of payment: for which purpose the DATE OF ACCEPTANCE must also be written.

When accepting a Draft that is to be paid a certain time after date, write across its face the word *accepted* and *your name* only, as the maturity of the Draft is to be reckoned from the date of itself; but when accepting a Draft ordered to be paid a certain time after sight, place the *date of acceptance* also, as it is from this date the maturity of the Draft will be reckoned. If the Drawer has left the place of payment optional with you, insert it with the acceptance.

Three days' grace are allowed on all Drafts, except those payable on demand.

It is the usual custom to send Drafts through a Bank for acceptance or collection, as it insures prompt returns. The rate of commission or exchange generally charged by the Banks for collections is $\frac{1}{4}$ of one per cent. If you desire to draw upon a man so as to realize a certain amount, you must make the Draft for that amount *and the exchange*. When a Draft has to go through several Banks for collection, as, for example, if you draw upon a man in the United States, or a distant Province of the Dominion, and you don't know at the time of drawing what the exchange will be, add the words "*with exchange*" after the amount in the body of the Draft.

FORM OF SIGHT DRAFT.

$75.00   *Cobourg, Jan. 1st*, 1889.

At sight, for value received, pay * Henry Campion, or order, Seventy-five dollars, and charge to account of

‡ To A. R. HAMMER,
       Whitby, Ont.   †S. T. VANCE.

FORM OF DEMAND DRAFT.

$150.50.   *Belleville, Oct. 26th*, 1889.

On demand, for value received, pay to the order of myself the sum of One hundred and fifty dollars and fifty cents, and charge to account of

To A. R. McKIM,
      Montreal.   W. B. ROBINSON.

TIME DRAFT.

Accepted, payable at the Merchants' Bank, Oshawa. Isaac East.

$200.00   *Toronto, Nov. 1st*, 1889.

Thirty days after date pay to the order of W. R. Lingham, Two hundred dollars, value received, and charge to account of

To ISAAC EAST,
      Oshawa, Ont.   S. T. VANCE.

TIME RECKONED AFTER SIGHT.

Accepted January 5th, 1889. payable at my office in Oshawa. Isaac East.

$257.00   *Hamilton, Jan. 3rd*, 1889.

Thirty days after sight pay to the order of W. R. Lingham, Two hundred and fifty-seven dollars, value received, and charge to account of

To ISAAC EAST,
      Oshawa, Ont.   S. T. VANCE.

NOTE—*The words of the acceptance, the student will understand, are to be written across the face of the draft about the centre.*

A Bank Draft is bought from a bank for the purpose of making a remittance. Refer to Index

* Payee.   † Drawer.   ‡ Drawee.

ORDERS.

An Order is a written request to deliver or pay goods or money on account of the person signing the request. The signature is a voucher that the signer gave the order, and that he is responsible for the payment of what is ordered. When an order is received and acceded to, an entry should be made charging the signer; and, if the order is for the benefit of a third party, it is well to mention in the entry the name of the person to whom the goods or money is delivered. The order should be kept until settlement is made, as it is a confirmation of the charge.

ORDER FOR GOODS.

Messrs. Page, West & Co.   *Montreal, Jan. 1st,* 1889.
    Gentlemen :—Please deliver to H. S. Cathcart, or bearer, Fifty-seven dollars, in goods from your store, and charge to the account of
    $57.00   B. C. SANDERS.

ORDER FOR MONEY.

Mr. W. J. Gage,   *Toronto, Jan. 2nd,* 1889.
    Please pay to A. H. Jones, or order, One hundred and ten dollars, and charge the same to my account.
    $110.00   PETER COOPER.

DUE BILLS.

A Due Bill is a written acknowledgment of a debt. When it is intended that a due bill should be paid at a definite time in the future, the date of payment should be specified.

DUE BILL FOR MONEY.

Hamilton, Jan. 9th, 1889.
Due Samuel Clare, for value received, One hundred dollars.
    $100.00   GEO. H. CAMP.

The following is a common form of Due Bill, and is called an I. O. U.
Belleville, Jan. 1st, 1889.
        I. O. U. Fifty dollars.
    $50.00   JAS. SANDERSON.

DUE BILL FOR GOODS.

Kingston, Jan. 30th, 1889.
Due Sanford Farmer, Twenty dollars, in goods from our store.
    $20.00   ROSS & BAIN.

PROMISSORY NOTES.

A Promissory Note is a written promise to pay unconditionally, and at all events, a specified sum of money.

When a note is given or received, it should be entered in the person's account with whom the transaction occurs, in the same manner as cash would be entered. The note settles so much of the account, and may change hands many times before it becomes due, and it must be paid to the holder. Should suit be brought because not paid, it would be brought upon the note instead of upon the account.

FORMS OF NOTES.

NEGOTIABLE WITHOUT INDORSEMENT.

$100.   *London, Oct. 28th,* 1889.

Three months after date, I promise to pay †S. G. Beatty, or bearer, One Hundred Dollars, value received.
                                                                *THOMAS WILLIAMS.

NEGOTIABLE BY INDORSEMENT.

$100.   *Hamilton, Oct.* 28*th,* 1889.

Three months after date, I promise to pay S. Clare, or order, One Hundred Dollars, value received.
                                                     THOMAS WILLIAMS.

NON-NEGOTIABLE.

$100.   *Toronto, Oct.* 28*th,* 1889.

Three months after date, I promise to pay George Dean, One Hundred Dollars, value received.
                                                     THOMAS WILLIAMS.

PAYABLE ON DEMAND.

$100.   *Kingston, Oct.* 28*th,* 1889.

On demand, I promise to pay Messrs. Jones & Brown, or bearer, One Hundred Dollars, value received.
                                                    THOMAS WILLIAMS.

PAYABLE AT BANK.

$100.   *Brantford, Nov.* 25*th,* 1889.

Three months after date, I promise to pay John Smith, or order, at the Bank of Commerce, here, One Hundred Dollars, value received.
                                                    PETER J. WILSON.

PAYABLE AT BANK, WITH INTEREST.

$340.42.   *Belleville, Oct.* 28*th,* 1889.

Three months after date, we promise to pay Messrs. East & West, or order, at the Merchants' Bank of Canada, here, Three Hundred and Forty $\frac{42}{100}$ Dollars, with interest at seven per cent. per annum, value received.
                                                   SMITH, JONES & CO.

NOTE.—It is always desirable to *fix a place* for the payment of a note, which is usually the bank at which the maker keeps his account. Hence when making a note, state where you intend to provide funds for its payment, as in the last example. To secure interest at 7 per cent. after maturity, should the note not be paid when due, add the words, *as well after as before maturity until paid,* after the word annum.

* Drawer. † Payee.

JOINT NOTE

$300. *Montreal, Jan. 1st,* 1889.

Three months after date, we jointly promise to pay R. Brown, or order, Three Hundred Dollars, value received.

E. T. HAMBLY,
J. G. SHERRY.

JOINT AND SEVERAL NOTE.

$210. *Port Hope, Oct. 28th,* 1889.

Ninety days after date, we jointly and severally promise to pay Geo. Wallbridge, or order, Two Hundred and Ten Dollars, value received.

JOHN BROWN,
WILLIAM BROWN.

NOTE MADE BY A MAN WHO CANNOT WRITE.

$100. *Belleville, Nov. 5th,* 1889.

Three months after date, I promise to pay to the order of Nelson Lingham, One Hundred Dollars, for value received.

SYLAS THOMPSON, } *Witnesses.*
E. REID,

his
ROBERT + McNAUGHTON.
mark.

NOTE.—Read this over to the maker carefully, that you may be able to prove that he knew what he signed.

AN ACCOMMODATION NOTE

Is one made payable to the order of an endorser, for the purpose of raising money for the maker at a bank or from a private lender. After it is endorsed the holder would have recourse against both parties. If not paid at maturity, notice of non-payment must be send to the endorser, or recourse against him will be lost. See protests page 238.

QUESTIONS FOR REVIEW.—CHAPTER IV.

What three qualities of an Accountant are essential to success? What are the characteristics of Set II? Do you keep a distinct account with each article of traffic as in Set I? Under what general title do you classify them? What are the characteristics of Set III? How many days are allowed for the payment of a bill, after the time mentioned on its face expires? What are they called? When the term of a bill is expressed in days, when do you begin to count the time to run? Give examples. When the term of a bill is expressed in months, how do you determine when it falls due? Give examples of bills drawn on different dates and running the same time, falling due on the same day. Explain how the term of payment may be extended three or four days, by advancing the date of bills one day. When the last day of grace of a bill falls on Sunday or a bank holiday, when is it payable? Give examples of bills dated on different days and having the same time to run, in months, falling due on the same day. Give rules to determine when to date bills in order to advance the day of payment, and to tell the precise day when they become due. What are the characteristics of Set IV? What books are used in this Set? In business calculations do you enter fractions of a cent upon the account books? How do you proceed? Describe the Bill Book. What is a Bill of Goods? An Invoice? An Account of Sales? A Receipt? Give different forms of Receipts. Are Receipts necessary in business transactions? What is a Draft? How many persons are interested in a Draft? How is a Draft at sight considered by the drawee and payee? Give rules for making the Drawer's, Drawee's, and Payee's entries in case of a *Sight Draft.* In case of a *Time Draft.* How in a Draft accepted? How may Drafts be made payable? What is an Order? How is the signature to an Order considered? Give examples of different kinds of Orders. What is a Due Bill? Give examples of a Due Bill for Money. For Goods. What is a Promissory Note? Give different forms of Notes. What is a Credit Note? What is an Accommodation Note?

CHAPTER V.
DRAFTS—SHIPMENTS AND CONSIGNMENTS.

The learner should carefully study and fix in his mind the following explanations on Drafts and Shipments, before commencing the work of Set V.

A Draft is an order in the form of a request, usually payable at sight, or a specified time thereafter. A Draft at sight is considered the same as Cash by the payee and drawee.

There are three persons concerned (though often the same person acts both as drawer and payee), the drawer or maker; the payee, or the one in whose favor it is drawn ; the drawee, or the one who is obliged to pay it, or, in other words, the one who accepts it. Banker's Drafts are generally used to make remittances. When drawn upon any Bank in the Dominion they are payable on demand.

RULES FOR JOURNALIZING DRAFTS. *

CREDIT the person or bank you draw on, because that person or bank pays an amount on your account.

DEBIT the person who draws on you, because you pay a certain amount on his account.

SIGHT DRAFT.—Drawer's entry, " Payee Dr. to Drawee."
" " Payee's entry, " Cash Dr. to Drawer."
" " Drawee's entry, "Drawer Dr. to Cash."
TIME DRAFT.—Drawer's entry, " Payee Dr. to Drawee."
" " Payee's entry, " Bills Receivable Dr. to Drawer."
" " Drawee's entry, " Drawer Dr. to Bills Payable."

SHIPMENTS AND CONSIGNMENTS.

Merchants having goods, which they cannot dispose of to advantage at home, often send them to some person doing business in another place, by this means frequently finding a better market.

These transactions give rise to the above accounts.

Consignor is a name given to the shipper of goods or other property.

Consignee is the person to whom the goods are shipped.

Shipment, as a ledger title, is a fictitious name given to merchandise, or other property, shipped to be sold on account and risk of the Consignor. It is made Dr. when the goods are shipped for their full value and for all costs; it is credited by its net proceeds, when the account of sales is received, by making the person to whom the goods were shipped, or whatever he has remitted you in payment for it, Dr. to the shipment. After posting to the ledger it is closed "To" or " By *Loss* and *Gain* " if an Account of Sales has been received; if not, it is closed " By Balance Inventory," for what it was invoiced at and charged with when the shipment was made.

---

* The learner's mind should be thoroughly impressed with the meaning of these rules, otherwise it will take him a long time to divest himself of the idea that every draft or bill he draws upon his correspondent must appear in one or other of the Bill accounts.

"Consignment," as a ledger title, is a name by which you keep an account of goods or other property received by you to sell on account and risk of the consignor.

It is debited for all charges paid by you when received, and for all costs accruing on the same while in your possession, and credited for all its incomes and sales. It is closed by making it Dr. to your commission and to the consignor for his net proceeds, or to whatever you may remit him.

In either case the account balances when posted in the ledger.

The term "shipment," when used as a ledger title, should have the consignee's name or place of residence attached, and each one should be numbered, in order that you may distinguish between different shipments to the same person or place.

"Consignment," when used as a ledger title, should have the consignor's name prefixed, and each one should be numbered.

Thus,—If you ship goods to Joseph McKay, of Montreal, to be sold on your account and risk, your ledger title should be "Shipment to McKay No. 1," or "Shipment to Montreal No. 1," and his ledger title should be "Student's Consignment No. 1," or, as some merchants term it, "Student's Sales No. 1."

EXERCISES IN JOURNALIZING SHIPMENTS AND CONSIGNMENTS.

Transactions. *Journal Entries.*

(1) Adams shipped to Benson, to be sold on his own account, 100. bbls. Flour, valued at $550.

(1) Shipment to Benson, Dr. $550.00
    To Mdse.   550.00

(2) Benson on receipt of Flour pays $15, for freight, by check.

(2) Adams Con., Dr.   15.00
    To Bank   15.00

(3) Benson sells the goods at 12½ per cent. advance, and receives in settlement note at 1 month for one half and check for balance.

(3) Bills Receivable, Dr.   309.38
    Cash Dr.   309.37
    To Adams' Con.   618.75

(4) Benson renders an Account Sales, his unposted charges being as follows: Insurance $3, Storage $5.50, Cooperage $2.30, Commission 5 per cent., and remits net proceeds by draft on Bank of Montreal for which he pays cash.

(4) Adams' Con., Dr.   603.75
    To Charges   10.80
    " Commission   30.94
    " Cash   562.01

(5) Adams receives Account Sales with draft on Bank of Montreal, $562.01.

(5) Cash Dr.   562.01
    To Shipment to Benson   562.01

Remarks on 1st transaction.—If Adams had paid say $16 freight, insurance, or other charges on the shipment his Journal entry would have been:

Shipment to BENSON, Dr. $566.00
  To MDSE. $550.00
  " CASH [or Bank] 16.00

Remarks on 2nd transaction.—If Benson on receipt of Consignment had paid no charges he would simply have made a memorandum, but no journal entry, as there would have been no account affected. He takes no responsibility more than the safe care of the goods until he begins to make sales from them.

Remarks on 3rd transaction.—The individual purchasing or the account representing the thing received for, the whole or any portion of a Consignment is made Dr. to the Consignment.

Remarks on 4th transaction.—The method of making out Account Sales is shown in an example at page 60.

In making the Account Sales entry, first find what the total sales amount to, then the total charges, and by deducting the total charges from the total sales you obtain the amount which you are to remit the shipper, or credit him with.

The "Charges account" is a representative account opened to show income from such sources as the charge made for insuring the Consignment against fire while in your possession (your general policy covering the contents of your warehouse), the charge made for storing it, and the charge made for the time spent by your men in coopering the barrels.

The "Commission" account is of the same nature, opened to show income from commission charged for selling goods.

Remarks on 5th transaction.—If the Account Sales had been received without a remittance of any kind, Adams' entry would have been:

BENSON, Dr. $562.01
  To Shipment to BENSON $562.01

NOTE.—To understand the result of the above entries open a ledger account on a piece of paper with "Shipment to Benson," and post the entries affecting it, and you will find the gain upon the venture $12.01; then open an account with "Adam's Consignment," and post the entries affecting it, and you will find that the account closes itself.

SET V.
BOOT AND SHOE BUSINESS.

THE CASH BOOK SHOULD BE USED IN PERFORMING THE WORK OF THIS SET. SEE FORM AT THE END OF SET.

CHARACTERISTICS.—*Buying and Selling for Cash on Notes and on Personal account; Shipping to be sold on account of the Shipper; Commencing with a Net Capital, effecting a net gain, and closing with increased Capital.*

KINGSTON, April 1st, 1889.

*――――this day commences business with the following RESOURCES AND LIABILITIES. RESOURCES,—Cash as per C. B. $3,850; Thomas Holden's Note, dated Dec. 9th, 1888, at 4 months, $500; an Accepted Draft drawn by A. M. Foster on John Templeton, dated Feb. 1, at 60 days' sight, and accepted Feb. 4, $400; A. L. Bogart's Note for $250, dated Jan. 14, at 3 months, with interest at 8 per cent. Interest accrued on above note $4.33; J. W. Campion owes on account $450; L. W. Yeomans owes on account $375.—Total RESOURCES, $5,829.33. LIABILITIES,—Am owing on note, favor of F. Lockett, $325, dated Dec. 9, 1888, at four months; Ames, Holden & Co., Montreal, on account, $175; F. M. Clark, on account, $220. Total liabilities, $720.

2—Bought of Haines & Lockett, on my notes, for equal amounts, at 1, 2 and 3 months, Merchandise as per invoice $5,100.

" Bought of Ames, Holden & Co., on account, Merchandise, as per Invoice, $3,500.

" Paid Cash for a set of Books for store $12.50. For Freight, $8.25. Total, $20.75. *Cash sales this day,* $54.50.

4—Sold L. W. Yeomans, on account, 1 pr. Calf Stitched Boots, $6.50; 1 pr. Misses' Goat Laced Boots, $2.40; 1 pr. kid Slippers, $1.25. Total, $10.15. *Cash sales this day,* $70.80.

6—Paid F. M. Clarke, Cash on account, $150. Paid for Advertising, $15.75. Accepted Ames, Holden & Co.'s Draft at 10 days' sight, favor Thomas Smith, for $400. Received from J. W. Campion, Cash on account, $250. *Cash sales this day,* $85.40.

8—Received Cash for J. Templeton's draft of Feb. 4th, $400. *Cash sales this day,* $95.

9—Sold J. W. Campion, Belleville, on account:—

5 cases,	60 pairs	Men's Stout Boots	....	....	....	at	$2.20	$132.00
6 "	72 "	Men's Lasting Gaiters	....	....	....	"	1.75	126.00
8 "	96 "	Youths' Stout Boots	....	....	....	"	1.80	172.80
4 "	240 "	" " Brogans	....	....	....	"	60	144.00
4 "	240 "	Women's Split Boots	....	....	....	"	1.10	264.00
2 "	120 "	" Congress Gaiters	....	....	....	"	1.25	150.00
2 "	120 "	Pebbled Buff Bals	....	....	....	"	1.25	150.00

Cash sales this day, $115.40. Total $1138.80

10—Bought for cash 10 shares of the Capital Stock of the Ontario Transportation Co. at the par value $50, $500.

11—Shipped per Steamer Passport, and consigned to W. T. Tilley, Port Hope, Ont., to be sold on my account and risk: 10 sides No. 1 Sole Leather, "Hemlock Spanish," 240 lbs. at 25c.; 1 roll No. 1 Buffalo Sole, 300 lbs. at 22c.; 2 rolls Pebbled Cow, 280 feet at 15c. Total, $168. Paid Insurance on same in cash, $10.50.

---
* Your own name.

12—* Renewed Thomas Holden's note for $500, due this day, for 2 months; charges on renewal, $6.01. *Cash sales this day*, $114.70.
13—Sold L. W. Yeomans, on account, 1 pair Misses' Calf Stitched Boots at $2.75; 1 pair do. Lasting Gaiter Boots, $1.75. Total, $4.50.
" Redeemed my note of December 9, favor of F. Lockett, by giving him Draft at 30 days on J. W. Campion, $325. *Cash sales*, $124.
14—Sold John Mansard, Brockville,

10 cases	120 prs.	Men's Calf Stitched Boots		....	....	....'	at $5.00	$600.00
5 "	60 ".	" " Sewed	"	....	....	....	" 4.00	240.00
6 "	360 "	Women's Calf Lace	"	....	....	....	" 1.25	450.00
1 "	60 "	" Goat Buskins		....	....	....	" 1.20	72.00
1 "	60 "	" " Lace Boots		....	....	....	" 1.25	75.00
2 "	120 "	" Colored Gaiters		....	....	....	" 1.10	132.00
2 "	120 "	" Prunella Bals.		....	....	....	" 1.25	150.00

Received in payment, his notes, one at 30 days for $475   Total, ... $1719.00
" 60 "   544
" 90 "   700

16—† Received Dividend at the rate of 10 per cent. on stock held in the Ontario Transportation Co., $50. *Cash sales this day*, $125.75.
17—Received from A. L. Bogart, cash in full for his note of Jan. 14th, and interest thereon to date. Face of note, $250. Interest for 3 months and 3 days, at 8 per cent., $5.17. *Cash sales*, $118.25.
18—Paid Ames, Holden & Co., Cash on account, $500. Paid the following items of Expense: Painting Shop, $35. Repairing Windows, $140. Clearing Store, $4.50. Total, $179.50. *Cash sales this day*, $125.50.
20—Paid Ames, Holden & Co.'s Draft of the 6th inst., favor T. Smith, $400. *Cash sales*, $136.20.
22—Bought of Jno. McKeown, for cash, Merchandise, as per invoice, $1,200.
" Received from L. W. Yeomans, Sight Draft on John Smith, for $835.15.
" Bought of Thomas Brown for John Mansard's note of April 14th, Merchandise, $700. *Cash sales*, $175.50.
23—Received from W. T. Tilley, Port Hope, an account of sales of the Leather shipped him the 11th inst. The net proceeds, which have been entered to my credit, amount to $211.50. Paid F. M. Clark Cash, in full of account, $70.
24—Paid Ames, Holden & Co., Cash on acct., $200. Paid sundry expenses, $15.50.
30—Paid Rent, $100. Clerk's salary, $140. Gave Ames, Holden & Co. Draft at 30 days on W. T. Tilley for $211.50.

Merchandise unsold as per Inventory, $9173.25.   *Shares in Ont. Trans. Co.*, $500.
Net capital at commencing, $5109.33.   *Net gain*, $2673.05.   *Net worth at closing*, $7782.38.

When making out the Loss and Gain Statement of this set, show the dividend ($50.00) on O. T. Co. Shares under the head of Gains, and in the Resource and Liability Statement show the value of the shares ($500) under the head of Resources. Close this account to Loss and Gain for the $50, and By Balance for the $500.

TO THE STUDENT.

From the above Day Book you are required to make out the following business papers, using for the same such names and amounts as would be required in a *bona fide* business.

Draw the three notes received on the 14th, Draft paid on the 20th, and the Draft received on the 22nd.

All necessary forms of Notes, Drafts, etc., may be found in the foregoing Chapter.

See mode of filing business papers, page 73.

Note.—When notes, drafts, or other obligations fall due on Sunday, payment is not required by law until the next day.
   * Under the head of "Entries for Renewals of Notes," you will learn how to make this Journal entry.
   † See Note at foot of second page from this for an explanation of Dividend.

THE CASH BOOK.

This book is kept for the purpose of recording all Cash received and paid. There are various ways of keeping the Cash Book (see forms for Sets IX and XI), but the following form is perhaps as simple as any for beginners, and is sometimes used by persons whose Cash transactions are not very numerous, and who are not scientific accountants.

It contains two columns for dollars and cents.*

Whenever money is received from any source whatever, it must be entered in this book "To" (describing for what), and the amount be extended into the *left* hand dollar and cent column, which is called the *debit* column ; and whenever money is paid out for any purpose whatever, it must be entered in this book "By" (telling what for), and the amount extended into the *right* hand dollar and cent column, called the credit column. If the account is kept correctly, the difference between these two columns will show at all times the *balance* of Cash in hand, and will agree with the actual amount of money found in possession by counting. Any discrepancy must arise from error, which must be sought out and rectified before the account is balanced. The credit column can never be the larger, since it is impossible to pay out more money than you receive.

The Cash Book should be balanced at the end of each week (or daily when much business is done), by entering the balance of Cash in hand, in the credit column, in *red* ink to distinguish it from sums paid away. After footing the columns and drawing the lines, bring the balance down, in black ink, entering it in the debit column. The lines should be ruled exactly as in the form. They serve to keep the new account distinctly separated from the old ; a matter of greater importance than young bookkeepers generally imagine. It adds greatly to the appearance of your book to begin the words "To" and "By" all upon a perpendicular line. Leave a space between the name of the account and the explanation, and begin the latter on a uniform line. Note example.

The Cash account may be tested at any time, without balancing the Cash Book, by finding the difference between the debit and credit columns, on a scrap of paper, and comparing the difference with the Cash in hand. This should be done daily when the Cash-Book is balanced only once a week, as in the following form.

The small figures in the form of Cash Book given on page 72 to the right of explanations are the footings of the Dr. and Cr. sides. These figures should only be entered with pencil at the time of balancing the book, and erased as soon as the difference or Cash in hand is obtained.

---

*The student will observe that in speaking of the money columns we designate the space for dollars and the space for cents, united, as but one column.

CASH BOOK—SET V.   Dr.   Cr.

Date	Account	Description	Dr.		Cr.	
1889						
Ap'l 1	To Stock,	Amount invested,	3850			
" 2	By Expense,	Acc. Books, $12.50, Freight, $8.25			20	75
" "	To Merchandise,	Sales this day, 3975.30	54	50		
" 4	" Merchandise,	Sales this day, 20.75	70	80		
		*Balance in hand,			*3954	55
			3975	30	3975	30
" 6		Balance brought down,	3954	55		
" "	By F. M. Clarke,	Paid on Account,			150	
" "	" Expense,	Paid for Advertising,			15	75
" "	To J. W. Campion,	Received on Account,	250			
" "	" Merchandise,	Cash Sales,	85	40		
" 8	" Bills Receivable,	Rec. for Templeton's Draft, B.B.	400			
" "	" Merchandise,	Sales this day,	95			
" 9	" Merchandise,	Received for this day's sales,	115	40		
" 10	By O. T. Co. Shares,	Bought 10 Shares at par,			500	
" 11	" Ship't to Tilley,	Paid Insurance,			10	50
" "	To Merchandise.	Received for day's sales, 5015.05	114	70		
		676.25				
		*Balance in hand.			*4338	80
			5015	05	5015	05
" 13		Balance brought down,	4338	80		
" "	To Merchandise,	Received for sales this day,	124			
" 16	" Merchandise,	Sales this day,	125	75		
" "	" O. T. Co. Shares,	†Ann'l divi'd at the rate of 10 p.c.	50			
" 17	" Bills Receivable,	Received for Bogart's note, B.B.	250			
" "	" Interest,	Received on above note,	5	17		
" "	" Merchandise,	Received for day's sales,	118	25		
" 18	By Ames, Holden & Co.,	Paid on Account,			500	
" "	" Expense,	Painting, repairing and cleaning			179	50
" "	To Merchandise,	Sales this day, 5137.47	125	50		
		679.50				
		*Balance in hand,			*4457	97
			5137	47	5137	47
" 20		Balance brought down,	4457	97		
" "	By Bills Payable,	Ames, Holden & Co.'s draft of 6th			400	00
" "	To Merchandise,	Cash Sales,	136	20		
" 22	By Merchandise,	Bought of John McKeown,			1200	00
" "	To L. W. Yeomans,	Sight Draft on J. Smith,	835	15		
" "	" Merchandise.	Sales this day,	175	50		
" 23	By F. M. Clarke,	In full of Account,			70	00
" 24	" Ames, Holden & Co.,	On account,			200	00
" "	" Expense,	Sundry Items,			15	50
" 30	" "	Rent, $100; Clerk's salary, $140			240	00
		5604.82				
		2125.50				
		*Balance in hand,			*3479	32
			5604	82	5604	82

* Red Ink.
† This dividend might be credited at once to Loss and Gain, but it is better to show it through another acct. first. We here credit it to the acct. representing the investment, but you must be careful when closing your books to write it from this acct. into Loss and Gain before balancing the Shares acct., otherwise you would show in this acct. a decreased resource. Another way of dealing with dividend is to open a "Dividend acct." and credit it with the amount, and when closing the books write it into Loss and Gain.

FILING BUSINESS PAPERS.

The following forms represent Business Papers properly folded and filed. As the folding and filing of other papers, not represented here, should be after the same general form, we deem it unnecessary to give them. Fold all papers the same width, ¼ of a page of foolscap.

*Represent wrappers for different classes of business papers.

- A. L. Sample, Receipt, 20th May, 1889, $140. — *Receipts for May, 1889.*
- R. P. Jennings, Bill of Mdse., 4th May, 1889, $40.35. — *Bills of Mdse. for May, 1889.*
- S. G. Beatty, Acc't. of Sales, 18th Jan., 1889, $250.20. — *Acct. Sales for January, 1889.*
- Thos. Smith, Invoice, 14th Jan., 1889, $124.50. — *Invoices for January, 1889.*
- Trial Balance, Set I. Taken, Belleville 31st Jan., 1889, A. R. Brown, Acco'nt. — *Trial Balances, 1889.*

SET VI.
PRODUCE AND COMMISSION BUSINESS—Single Proprietor.

BOOKS USED.—*Day Book, Journal, Ledger, Bill Book, and Cash Book.*

CHARACTERISTICS.—*This, and the succeeding Set, are intended to illustrate the principles and practice of a simple commission, in connection with a general merchandise business; as also to some extent the giving and receiving of notes, drawing and accepting drafts, with allowance of interest and discount; keeping a bank account in the Ledger, drawing and receiving cheques, etc., etc. This Set illustrates the business of a single Proprietor, closing with a net loss, and arranging to admit a partner, for the continuance of the business, in Set VII.*

St. John, N. B., January 1st, 1889. Student invests in Cash $5000.

* Paid Cash for Office Furniture $350, and for Books and Stationery $50. Total $400.

2—Deposited in the Montreal Bank $4000.

3—Bought of W. Lingham, on my Acceptance at 10 days, 50 bbls. Extra Flour at $13.50, $675; 100 do Superfine Flour at $8.25, $825. Total $1500.

4—† Paid for three months' Rent in advance, per Cheque, $375; Received from Jones & Co., Hamilton, to be sold on their account and risk, 100 bbls. Extra Flour; paid Freight and Drayage on same per Cheque, $213.50.

5—Sold for Cash, from Jones & Co.'s Consignment No. 1, 50 bbls. Flour at $11.40, $570. Sold W. B. Robinson, on account, 75 bbls. Superfine Flour at $9, $675.

6—‡ Took out open Policy of Insurance on Warehouse and contents for $30,000 at ⅜ per cent., paid Premium, per Cheque, $225. Sold for Cash, 25 bbls. Extra Flour at $14, $350; 25 do Superfine Flour at $9, $225. Total, $575. Deposited in Bank $1000.

8—Received from Jones & Co., Hamilton, their second Consignment, consisting of 100 bbls. New Mess Pork; paid Freight and Drayage on same per Cheque, $247.50. Sold J. Cummings on his Note, at 30 days, from Jones & Co.'s Consignment No. 1, 50 bbls. Flour at $11.50, $575.

9—Rendered Jones & Co. Account of Sales of Flour, represented in " Consignment No. 1." My charges on same are as follows :—Storage, Insurance, Cooperage, etc., $21.43 ; ‖ Commission 2½ per cent. on Sales $28.62 ; Jones & Co.'s net proceeds $881.45 *Total debit to Jones & Co's Consignment No. 1, $931.50.*

10—Sold from Jones & Co.'s Consignment No. 2, 75 bbls. Pork at $20, $1500. Received in payment Sight Draft on James Wilson & Co., for $800; § Cash $700. Deposited in Bank $2000.

11—Accepted Jones & Co.'s Draft at 10 days' sight, favor of W. H. Davy, for $500.

12—Received from W. West, Toronto, to be sold on his account and risk, 1000 bush. Wheat; paid Freight and Drayage on same, per Cheque, $175.

13—Sold from W. West's Consignment No. 1, for Cash, 500 bush. Wheat at $3.25, $1625.

14—Received from Jones & Co., Hamilton, their third Consignment, consisting of 500 bush. Rye, 300 bush. Oats ; paid Freight and Drayage on same, per Cheque, $180.

15—Sold from Jones & Co.'s Consignment No. 2 to H. Holden, on account, 25 bbls. Pork at $21; $525.

16—Closed Jones & Co.'s Consignment No. 2, and rendered Account Sales of same. My charges for Storage, Cooperage, etc., $19.78 ; Commission 2½ per cent. on Sales, $50.62 ; Jones & Co.'s Net Proceeds, $1707.10. *Total debit to Jones & Co.'s Consignment No. 2, $1777.50.*

17—Received from W. West, Toronto, his second Consignment, consisting of 2000 bush. Canadian Club Wheat ; paid Freight and Drayage, per Cheque, $325.

---
* Open an Office Furniture account for this, and charge Books and Stationery to expense. † Open a Rent account for this. ‡ Open an Insurance account for this.

‖ A general " Charges" account is sufficient to represent the returns from all charges except your Commission, which requires a separate account.

§ The only distinction between a Sight Draft and a Cheque is that the former is drawn on an individual and the latter on a bank. Both being payable on presentment are considered the same as Cash. As this draft will be placed in the bank for Collection we shall reckon it as Cash at once.

18—Sold W. B. Robinson, on account, from Jones & Co.'s Consignment, No. 3, 500 bush. Rye at $1.40, $700. Bought of John Downing, on my note at 30 days, 400 bush. Timothy Seed at $3, $1200.

20—Received from Jones & Co., Hamilton, their fourth Consignment, consisting of 200 bbls. Extra Flour; paid Freight and Drayage on same, per Cheque, $425. Deposited in Bank $1000.

21—Paid my acceptance, favor of W. Lingham, due the 16th, per Cheque; Face of Acceptance $1500; Interest on same, 5 days, $1.25; *and protest charges $1.04. Amount paid $1502.-

29. And also discounted my Note favor of John Downing for $1200, due February 20th. Discount off, 30 days, $7. *Net amount paid, per Cheque, $1193.

23—Received of W. B. Robinson, cash in full of acct——†

24—Paid my acceptance favor W. H. Davy, due this day, per Cheque, $500. Deposited in Bank $1875.

INVENTORY OF RESOURCES NOT SHOWN ON THE LEDGER.‡

Merchandise: 25 bbls. Extra Flour at $13.50, $337.50; 400 bush. Timothy Seed at $2.75, $1100. Total $1437.50. ‖*Rent*, two months paid in advance, $250; *Insurance*, 11 months' unexpired policy, $206.25; *Furniture* valued at $350.

Net loss, $81.09.

NOTE.—What should be done at the time of closing the books, when the property represented by such accounts as Furniture has depreciated, will be learned under the head of Plant Account. See Index.

TO THE STUDENT.

Having journalized and posted this Set, take a Trial Balance and Statements, and prove your work to be correct. You will then close the accounts, open a Loss and Gain account, and transfer the net loss to the proprietor's account. Then bring down in black ink, all *Inventory Balances*. " To Balance," and Balance of *Real Accounts*, such as Cash, Bills Receivable, Personal Accounts, etc., either " To" or " By Balance," as the standing of the accounts may show, making no transfers to a Balance Acct.

If an account is closed " *To Balance*" bring down the balance on the credit side of the same " By Balance," and if an account is closed " *By Balance*," bring down the balance on the debit side " To Balance," dating the balance brought down. When all the balances are thus brought down, the *Resources* and *Liabilities* will be correctly located in the Ledger ready for the commencement and continuation of Set VII. See the foot note at page 42.

Before posting Set VII., take a Trial Balance of those accounts the balances of which have been brought down in the Ledger, to ascertain if the transfers have been properly made; or compare the balances brought down with the resources and liabilities in the statement, with which they should agree.

---

* As Interest and Discount are the same in nature and effect, both representing the use of money, and both indicating the amount paid or received for its use, we do not deem it necessary to keep two separate accounts. See " Discounting Notes and Entries " for full explanation. The protest charges is the amount of expense incurred by the holder of the acceptance in having it protested for non-payment by a Notary Public, and which he (the holder) collects from the acceptor. See " Protests " for full explanation.

† Leave this amount blank until you have posted thus far, then refer to the Ledger for amount.

‡ Among the open Ledger accounts are W. West's Consg't. No. 1, Jones & Co.'s Consg't. No. 3, West's Consg't. No. 2, and Jones & Co.'s Consg't. No. 4; the former two of which show an excess of the credit side, and the latter two an excess of the debit side. As the business for which these accounts were opened is not concluded, they are treated in this statement precisely like personal accounts, waiving our immature claims for charges and commission.

‖ The value of unexpired rent and insurance, based upon advances made, should unquestionably be reckoned among our resources. We therefore place the amount of these on the credit side of their respective accounts and treat them as we do inventories of goods unsold, and only close to Loss and Gain the expired portions. A moment's reflection will show you that in this way we charge the past year with only its own proper charge under these heads.

STATEMENT—Set VI.

Instead of making out the Trial Balance and Statements of Losses and Gains, and of Resources and Liabilities separately, you may now write them in one.

COMBINED STATEMENT.

Losses.	Gains.	Dr. Footing	L. F.	Ledger Accounts.	Cr. Footing	Resources	Liabilities
			38	Stock,	5000		
		10645	38	Cash,	10275	370	
12 50		2700	38	Merchandise,	1250	1437 50	
		575	39	Bills Receivable,		575	
		500	39	Jones & Co.,	2588 55		
		525	39	H. Holden,		525	2088 55
		9875	40	Montreal Bank,	5361 29	4513 71	
		350	40	Furniture,		350	
125		375	40	Rent,		250	
50		50	41	Expense,			
18 75		225	41	Insurance.		206 25	
	41 21		41	Charges.	41 21		
	79 24		42	Commission,	79 24		
		175	42	West's Consg't No. 1,	1625		1450
		180	42	Jones & Co.'s Consg't No. 3,	700		520
		325	43	West's Consg't No. 2.		325	
		425	43	Jones & Co.'s Cons'gt No. 4,		425	
	4 71	2	29	43	Interest and Discount,	7	
				*STOCK'S net Inv'st $5000			
	*81 09			" " " Loss 81 09			
				" " " Worth.			*4918 92
206 25	206 25	26927 29			26927 29	8977 46	8977 46

SET VII.
PRODUCE AND COMMISSION BUSINESS—*Continued.*
TWO PARTNERS.

CHARACTERISTICS.—*This is a continuation of the business represented in Set VI., under a new proprietorship; the business to be conducted precisely as in previous Set. The new partner, James Fenwick, invests cash equal to the net investment of the former proprietor, which is shown in his account after carrying to it the loss of the previous business.*

ST. JOHN, February 1st, 1889. The proprietor admits as a partner in the business, James Fenwick, who is to make a cash investment equal to the present net worth, the business to be conducted under the firm name of †———— & Co., each partner to give his time to the business, and the losses and gains to be divided equally. James Fenwick invests Cash, $————Deposited in Bank $40 00.

3—Sold George Wallbridge, on his Acceptance at 10 days, from W. West's Consignment No. 1, 500 bushels Wheat, at $3.40, $1700. Closed W. West's Consignment No. 1, and rendered him an Account of Sales of the same. Our charges for Storage, Insurance, etc., $22.91; Commission, $83.12; W. West's Net Proceeds, $3043.97. *Total debit to W. West's Consignment No. 1, $3150.*

* Red Ink. † Student's Name.

NOTE.—When forming a partnership, a written agreement, called "Articles (or Indenture) of Co-partnership," should be made out and signed in the presence of a witness (see form in a subsequent part of the book) embodying all matters of importance. This precaution may save expensive law suits, and endless trouble. A firm name and style is adopted at the outset and adhered to throughout; that is, you cannot sign "Jones & Brown" to-day, and to-morrow " Jones & Co."

4—Bought of S. White & Co., 8 hhds. Muscovado Sugar, 13,850 lbs., at 10½c., $1454.25. Paid them our Sight Draft, on H. Holden, for amount of his acct. $—— *Cheque for balance, $——
5—Paid Jones & Co.'s demand draft on us, per Cheque, $1500.
7—Sold James Jennings, on his Note at 30 days, 4 hhds. Muscovado Sugar, 6930 lbs., at 11c., $762.30.
8—Sold for Cash, 25 bbls. Extra Flour at $15, $375. Paid Cash for Postage Stamps and Stationery $10.
10—Received Cash in full for J. Cumming's Note of Jan. 8th, due this day, $—— Deposited in Bank, Cash $900.
12—Sold for Cash, 400 bushels Timothy Seed at $3.50, $1400.
15—Sold for Cash, from Jones & Co.'s Consignment No. 3, 300 bush. Oats at 65c., $195. Closed Jones & Co.'s Consignment No. 3, and rendered an account of the same. Our charges for Storage, Insurance, etc., amount to $13.87; Commission, $22.37; Jones & Co.'s Net proceeds, $678.76. *Total Debit to Jones & Co.'s Consignment No. 3, $715.*
16—Paid W. West's Sight Draft on us, favor Montreal Bank, per Cheque, $2500.
18—Sold Solomon Johns, on acct., from W. West's Consignment No. 2, 1500 bush. Canadian Club Wheat at $2.35, $3525; also, from Jones & Co.'s Consignment No. 4, 200 bbls Flour at $11.35, $2270. Total, $5795.
19—Closed Jones & Co.'s Consignment No. 4, and rendered an Account Sales of the same. Our charges for Storage, Cooperage, etc., $24.59; our Commission, $56.75; Jones & Co.'s Net Proceeds, $1763.66. *Total Debit to Jones & Co.'s Consignment No. 4, $1845.*
20—Sold for Cash, from W. West's Consignment No. 2, 500 bush. Canadian Club Wheat at $2.40, $1200.
21—Closed W. West's Consignment No. 2, and rendered Account Sales of the same. Our charges for Storage, Insurance, etc., $23.17; Commission at 2½ per cent., $118.12; W. West's Net Proceeds, $4258.71. *Total Debit to West's Consignment, $4400.*
24—Received Cash in full for George Wallbridge's Acceptance of the 3rd inst. Face of Acceptance, $1700; Interest on same, 8 days, $2.64; amount received, $1702.64.
25—Received Cash, less discount, for James Jennings' Note of the 7th inst., due March 10th. Face of note, $762.30; Discount, $2.22; Net amount received, $760.08. Deposited in Bank, $4500.
27—Received of Solomon Johns, Cheque in full of his acct. $—— †Deposited in Bank, $6000.
28—We have this day arranged with Smith & Moore, for the sale to them of our entire business, including Furniture, Lease, Good Will, etc. Possession to be given March 1st. Received their Note at 3 months, for the following considerations and amount:—Four years and ten months' lease of Store, together with one month's prepaid rent, $2000. Ten months' unexpired Policy of $30,000, on Store and contents, $187.50; Furniture, $300; ‡ Good Will, $2000; Total, $4487.50.
28—Accepted W. West's Draft at ten days, for balance of his acct., $—— *Sold for Cash, 4 hhds. Muscovado Sugar, 6920 lbs., at 12c., $830.40. Paid Jones & Co's Sight Draft, per Cheque, for balance of their acct., $—— *
Deposited in Bank, $2712.03.
Total net gain, $4512.52.

The following business papers are required to be made out, by the Student, from SETS VI and VII.
FROM SET VI.—Receipt for rent, paid Jan. 4th. Note received from J. Cummings Jan. 8th. Account of Sales rendered Jones & Co., Jan. 9th.
FROM SET VII.—Geo. Walbridge's acceptance of February 3rd. Sight Draft received from W. West, Feb. 16th. Account of Sales rendered W. West, Feb. 21st.

---
* Refer to Ledger for amount of these accounts.
† See balance of Solomon Johns' account in Ledger.
‡ The Good Will means the bonus paid for the privilege of securing an established business, one that is well known and possesses liberal patronage.

G

SINGLE ENTRY.

Exemplified in a partnership business, concluding with an illustration of the partnership settlement. Presenting, also, a practical illustration of the process of changing a set of books from Single to Double Entry.

Considerable space has been devoted to the following Set, in order that the Student may become thoroughly conversant with Single as well as Double Entry. The authors are not among those who condemn Single Entry as wholly inadequate to the demands of business and unworthy of consideration. To a person who understands and appreciates the advantages of Double Entry no further illustration than this Set affords will be necessary to show its superiority over the other system. But as there is a large class of dealers, who, for various reasons, are not inclined to keep their accounts by Double Entry, it will be serviceable and acceptable to every accountant to understand both systems.

The principles of Single Entry are so easy of comprehension as scarcely to need explanation. Accounts are usually kept only with the persons with whom you have dealings, and although a Cash Account, Merchandise account, and other Property accounts may be kept in the Ledger, yet just so far as you introduce any other accounts, except those with persons who owe you, or whom you owe, so far do you encroach upon the peculiar province of Double Entry. The principal books of Entry are a Day Book and Ledger.

Besides these we introduce the Cash Book and Bill Book, as they are very important books, and should never be dispensed with in a business where there are any considerable dealings in Cash or Notes.

These auxiliary books are kept in the same manner as in Double Entry.

All Transactions which require a debit or credit to any person with whom you have dealings are entered in the Day Book, and as this is the only book from which you post, every entry which you wish to bring into any account in the Ledger must be entered here.

In entering *purchases* it is allowable to say, " Amount as per Bill," or " Amount as per Invoice," and omit the details of items, since you have the invoice filed away, or pasted in a book so that you can refer to it at any time; but in entering *sales* on acct. the *items* should always be mentioned in the entry, whether your books are kept by Single or Double Entry, as this is your legal evidence of the transaction ; and in order to be taken as evidence, each article must be distinctly named. SEE FORM OF SINGLE ENTRY DAY BOOK, at the end of this Set, page 81.

SET VIII.
DRY GOODS BUSINESS.
TWO PARTNERS.

The work of this Set is to be done by Single Entry, according to form on page 81.

LONDON, March 1st, 1889. J. S. MILLER and F. LANE this day commence the Dry Goods business, at No. 114 St. James street; agreeing to share gains and losses according to capital invested.

J. S. MILLER invests:—
Cash, $1500; Merchandise, $800; Note for $600, favor J. S. M., signed by Thomas Gibbard, dated January 31st, at 30 days; an Accepted Draft for $400, drawn by J. Jones on D. Roblin, dated January 20th, at 90 days. Balance due from J. R. Marvin, $125. *Total investment*, $3425.

F. LANE invests:—
Cash, $1500; Merchandise, $1200; Real Estate, $700; Note against S. Fowler for $200, dated January 25th, at 60 days; Note against H. Jackson for $800, dated November 23rd, 1888, at 6 months, with interest at 7 per cent. Interest accrued on above Note to date, 3 months and 6 days, $14.94. *Total Investment*, $4414.94.

2—Bought of W. McKay, on acct., Invoice of Merchandise, amounting to $1800. Sold Robert Carey, on acct., 50 yds. Blk. Broadcloth at $2.25; 12 Fancy Neckties at $1 each; 15 doz. prs. Lisle Thread Stockings at $3.25 per doz.

3—Sold James Goodwin, on account, 50 yds. Flannel at 60c.; 25 yds. Broadcloth at $3.75; 66 yds. Cassimere at $1.25. Received his Draft at 10 days' sight on A. Benson for $55, the balance to remain on acct.

4—Bought of H. Simmons, on acct., Mdse. invoiced at $200; gave our Note, at 60 days, for $100; the balance to remain on acct.

5—Sold W. Harding, for Cash, 2 pcs. Irish Linen, 66 yards each, at 85c.; 35 yards Broadcloth at $2.50.

6—Sold W. Williams, for Note at 30 days, 2 pcs. Blue Broadcloth, 45 yards each, at $1.75; 90 yds. French Merino at 60c. Received from Robert Carey his draft at sight on W. Johnson for $50.

8—Sold James Goodwin, on account, 90 yards Scotch Tweed at $1.25; 45 do. Red Flannel at 55c. Bought of W. Harding, for our Note at 20 days, 5 pieces English Prints, 40 yards each, at 25c. Sold Richard Manning, for his Draft at 10 days, 10 yards Broadcloth at $2.25; 15 yards Mixed Tweed at $1.50.

9—Received from James Goodwin his Sight Draft on John James for $85. Bought of Richard Watson, for Cash, Merchandise invoiced at $200.

11—Sold Henry Simmons, 24 yards Brown Beaver at $3.25; received Cash, $40; balance on account. Bought of William McKay, Merchandise invoiced at $500; gave in payment Cash $350; balance to remain on acct.

12—Sold Robert Carey, on acct., 55 yards Blue Broadcloth at $1.75. Received from James Goodwin Cash, $50; Cheque on Montreal Bank, $30.

13—Paid William McKay Cash, $1200. Sold John Johnson, for his Sight Draft on J. Wilson, 15 pairs Pants at $3.75. Sold Robert Carey, on acct., 30 Vests at $2.25; 12 Ready-Made Coats at $5.50.

15—Sold H. Simmons, on acct., 9 Fine Overcoats at $16. Sold John Cummings, for his Note at 20 days, 12 Complete Uniforms at $15.

16—Bought of A. Vermilyea, for our Note at 30 days, Mdse. invoiced at $175. Received Cash for James Goodwin's Draft of the 3rd inst. Discounted our Note of the 4th inst., favor of H. Simmons, at 6 per cent., for unexpired time.

17—Received from Robert Carey, on acct., 50 Summer Coats at $2.50. Bought of W. McKay, on 3 months' credit, Mdse. invoiced at $275.

18—Received Cash in full for T. Gibbard's Note of Jan. 31st, with interest at 6 per cent., for time overdue 13 days. Received Cash from H. Simmons, $40.

20—Sold W. Manning, for Cheque on Merchants' Bank, 10 Military Coats at $11; 10 pairs Pants at $6. Sold Robert Carey, on acct., 5 doz. Byron Collars at $2 per doz.; 4 doz. Cravats at $3 per doz. Received from James Goodwin Cheque on Montreal Bank for $155.

21—Sold H. Simmons, on acct., 40 yards Blue Broadcloth at $1.80 ; 10 yds. Black Beaver at $3.75. Received Cash for R. Manning's Draft of the 8th inst. Sold W. West for his Draft at 10 days, on R. Bass, 50 yards French Cassimere at $3. Bought of W. McKay, on acct., Mdse. as per bill, amounting to $95.
23—Sold Robt. Carey, on acct., 10 Summer Coats at $2.50 ; 40 yards Red Flannel at 55c.
24—Gave W. McKay our Draft at 10 days' sight, on James Goodwin, for $100. Sold H. Simmons, on acct., 10 yards Broadcloth at $2.25 ; 6 doz. French Yoke Shirts at $18 per doz. Bought for Cash, Mdse., as per bill, amounting to $300. Sold James Goodwin, on acct., 10 doz. Undershirts at $7 per doz. ; 8 doz. pairs Knit Drawers at $8 per doz.
25—Paid W. McKay's Sight Draft on us, favor W. Barnes, for $500. Received from Robt. Carey Sight Draft on James Goodwin for $125.
26—Sold H. Simmons, on acct., 1 piece French Cassimere, 50 yds., at $1.25.
29—Sold James Goodwin, 15 complete Uniforms at $14 ; received in payment Sight Draft on Montreal Bank, $50; balance to remain on account. Had H. Jackson's Note of Nov. 23rd, 1888, discounted at Merchants' Bank. Face of Note, $800 ; Interest, less discount at 7 per cent., for unexpired time, 2 months, $18.81. Cash Received $818.81.* Gave W. McKay our Sight Draft on H. Simmons, $75. Bought for Cash Mdse., as per bill, amounting to $400. Received Cash in full for S. Fowler's Note of January 25th. Paid Cash for Gas Bill, $20 ; Wood, $15 ; Rent, $50.
30—Received Cash for D. Roblin's Draft of January 20th, less discount for unexpired time at 7 per cent. Paid Shop hands Cash in full for services to date, $120.
Inventory.—*Merchandise unsold* $3800 ; *Real Estate,* $700.
Total Net Gain, $425.60 ; J. S. MILLER's *share of Gain,* $185.93 ; F. LANE's *share,* $239.67.

REMARKS ON THE DISTRIBUTION OF GAINS AND LOSSES IN PARTNERSHIPS.

Although the gains and losses are in the above and subsequent sets divided *according to capital invested*, which is a common practice, and which appears at first sight an equitable arrangement, yet it may prove very unfair to the partner having the smaller capital. In a Joint Stock Company, where the shareholders give no time to the conduct of the business, the principle is right, as there is simply an investment of *money* on their part ; but in a partnership there is the investment of *time* and *skill* as well. The following example will illustrate our meaning : Suppose A and B go into partnership ; A is wealthy and invests $6000, but B, not possessing much capital, can only invest $2000, and they agree that gains and losses shall be shared according to capital invested, both giving equal time and skill to the business. They make a profit of $3000 ; according to the agreement A will receive $2250 and B only $750. Such a distribution is manifestly wrong and unjust, as it recognizes only *money* as a factor in securing the gain, whereas *time* and *skill* should also be reckoned.

The correct principle upon which to arrange a partnership where there is an unequal amount of money invested by the partners, but an equal investment of time and skill, is to allow each partner interest, say at 8 per cent., upon his investment, or allow the partner having the larger investment interest upon the sum he has invested in excess of the other, which amounts to the same thing, and then divide gains and losses equally. Were this done in the above example, A would receive only $320 in excess of B, instead of $1500, the $320 being a fair return for the use of his money, the equal distribution with the other partner of the gains after this sum for interest is deducted, being for his time and skill.

Inequality in skill or time would be adjusted by the one partner paying the other a sum to be agreed upon. At the end of the year an entry, debiting the one and crediting the other, will be made, and then gains and losses will be shared equally.

---

* It is the custom of Banks, when a Note bearing interest is discounted, to compute the interest for the full time on the face of the Note, and add it to the principal, then discount the amount. In this case, Jackson's Note bears interest at 7 per cent. for 6 months and 3 days, and will amount, when paid, to $828.47. The discount on this amount for the 2 months the Note has to run before it becomes due, at 7 per cent., is $9.66, and this deducted from $828.47 leaves $818.81, the net proceeds received from the Bank.

EXAMPLE OF SINGLE ENTRY—Set VIII.

London, March 1st, 1889.

L. F				
	J. S. Miller and F. Lane this day commence the Dry Goods business, investing and agreeing to share the gains and losses, according to articles of co-partnership.			
	_____Miller's investment._____			
57	J. S. Miller, Cr. For the following investment:			
	Cash as per Cash Book, ...	1500		
	Mdse. as per Inventory, ...	800		
	Note and Acceptance as per Bill Book, ...	1000		
	Balance due from J. R. Marvin, ...	125		3425
	_____Lane's investment._____			
58	F. Lane, Cr. For investment as follows:			
	Cash as per Cash Book, ...	1500		
	Mdse. as per Inventory, ...	1200		
	Real Estate, Lot Mountain St., ...	700		
	Notes as per Bill Book, ...	1000		
	Interest on H. Jackson's note, ...	14	94	4414	94
	"			
120	* J. R. Marvin, Dr. To Balance favor J. S. Miller, ...			125
	_____ 2 _____			
41	W. McKay, Cr. By Mdse., as per Invoice No. 1, ...			1800
	"			
29	Robert Carey, Dr.			
	To 50 yds. Black Broadcloth at $2 25	112	50	
	" 12 Fancy Neckties " 1 00	12	00	
	" 15 dozen prs Lisle Thread Stockings at.... 3 25	48	75	173	25
	_____ 3 _____			
39	James Goodwin, Dr.			
	To 50 yds. Flannel at $0 60	30		
	" 25 " Broadcloth at 3 75	93	75	
	" 66 " Cassimere at 1 25	82	50	206	25
	_____Cr._____ By Draft at 10 days, on A. Benson, ...			55
	_____ 4 _____			
45	H. Simmons, Cr. By Merchandise, as per Invoice No. 2			200
	_____Dr._____ To our Note at 60 days for			100
	_____ 6 _____			
29	Robert Carey, Cr. By Draft at sight on W. Johnson, ...			50

Note.—The sales of the 5th and 6th are merely entered in the Cash Book and Bill Book. As the goods were paid for in full at the time of purchase, no personal account is affected, and, consequently, no entry is required in the Day Book.

* This debt of Marvin's forms part of Miller's investment, but as this is Single Entry Bookkeeping you cannot debit it to Marvin from the entry in which Miller is credited with it, consequently, you make a separate entry in order to debit Marvin.

CHANGING SINGLE TO DOUBLE ENTRY.

Having finished the posting of this Set, according to the principles of Single Entry, you will now proceed to change the books to Double Entry. You have learned from the Sets already worked out that Double Entry comprises a *perfect* and continual record of Resources and Liabilities; and by examining the Ledger of the last Set as it now stands, you will find that Single Entry comprises an *imperfect* record of Resources and Liabilities, or a record of only a portion of them, viz., personal accounts. Whenever this deficiency is supplied, the requisites of Double Entry are met. Therefore,

TO CONVERT SINGLE ENTRY BOOKS TO DOUBLE ENTRY FOLLOW THIS RULE.

Carry the net gain or loss of the business to Stock, or the Proprietors' accounts, then open such additional accounts in the Ledger (with their respective amounts) as are necessary to exhibit the entire Resources and Liabilities of the concern.

It will be necessary, in order to effect the desired change, to ascertain the net worth, then the gain or loss. This is done by making out a statement of Resources and Liabilities; then, if no new capital has been invested, or none withdrawn, by taking the net capital at starting from the net worth at closing, you may ascertain the gain; or, in a losing business by taking the net worth at closing from the net capital at starting, you may ascertain the loss. Then find the proportion of gain or loss of each partner.

The Resources and Liabilities are found in Single Entry, by ascertaining from the Cash Book the amount of cash on hand; from the Bill Book the resource of Bills Receivable and the liability of Bills Payable; from the inventory the value of unsold merchandise; and from the Ledger the standing of personal accounts.

Having made out the statement of Resources and Liabilities, found the worth, and the gain or loss, and carried the proportion belonging to each partner to his account, then open Cash, Merchandise, Bills Receivable, Bills Payable and Real Estate accounts in the Ledger, entering the several amounts in each from the Statement. Prove that your Ledger is in equilibrium, then proceed with the transactions of the next Set by Double Entry, using the same Ledger, without disturbing any of the accounts already opened.

The Resource and Liability statement, if correctly made out, must be in balance when you include the proprietors' worth, consequently when you get your Ledger accounts to agree with it your Ledger must be in balance also.

TO CLOSE A SINGLE ENTRY LEDGER.

As we convert the Single Entry Ledger to Double Entry at the close of this Set, it is well that we should explain how a Single Entry Ledger, that is intended to be continued in that method, should be closed. Take stock, and make out a statement of Resources and Liabilities, the difference between which, is your capital. Find the gain by subtracting the worth when you last closed the books from the present worth, allowing in your calculation for any new capital added or any withdrawn. Credit the proprietor's account with the gain, then balance his account, and bring down the balance on the credit side, which is his worth at the beginning of the new business year; then balance each personal account and bring the balances down. It will be well, in order to have it permanently on record, and easy of reference in future years, to copy the Statement of Resources and Liabilities, as well as the work of finding the gain, into the Day Book.

SET IX.
DRY GOODS BUSINESS.
TO THE STUDENT.

The books to be used in working this Set by Double Entry are, Day Book and Journal combined, Cash Book, Bill Book and Ledger.

The eight previous Sets have all been conducted upon the *old Italian method.* Another style of keeping accounts will now be introduced, which is far more in use at the present time, and by which much useless writing may be avoided. It will at first require more thought on your part than the previous Sets have done, but you are now supposed to have mastered the elementary principles of Book-keeping, and to be prepared for a higher step on the road to a thorough knowledge of accounts. The plan of doing this Set is to entirely dispense with the *Day Book* in history form, and use instead a *Day Book in Journal form,* denominated the *Journal Day Book,* in which the entries are recorded in such a manner, as not only to present a complete history of the business transactions, but also to furnish debits and credits under the proper Ledger titles, ready for posting, thus rendering it useless to keep a Journal. The general rule for Journalizing now becomes a general rule for determining the proper debits and credits in making original entries. In writing up your Journal Day Book remember that *no Cash transactions appear in it.*

The Cash Book used in connection with Sets V. to VIII. inclusive, was only for the purpose of preserving the Cash account from error, and giving you an idea of how it should be kept; but as used in this Set it has a still more important office. *It is the exclusive and only book of original entry for Cash transactions, and these transactions are posted directly from it to the Ledger.* See form and explanation of Journal Day Book and Cash Book (or Cash Journal) at the end of the Set.

DRY GOODS BUSINESS.—SET IX.

NOTE.—*Before beginning the 9th set you must have changed the Single Entry ledger of the 8th set to Double Entry, as fully explained on page 82; and to the converted ledger you will post the entries of the 9th set.*

London, Ont., April 1st, 1889.—J. S. MILLER and F. LANE have this day changed their books from Single to Double Entry. Bought of J. R. Marvin, on acct., Goods as per invoice, $700. Bought of Jones & Co., on our note at 3 months, with interest at 9 per cent., Mdse., as per invoice, $2500.

2—Sold Robert Carey, on acct., 2 pieces Scotch Tweed, 35 yds. each, at $1.50; 4 pieces Cassimere, 30 yards each, at $2.

4—Bought for Cash 10 pieces Factory Cotton, 60 yards each, at 10c. Sold C. A. Langford, for his note as 2 months, with interest at 10 per cent., 2 cases Prints, 1500 yards, at 15c.; 3 cases Irish Linen, 1280 yards, at 25c.; 1 case Scotch Tweed, 450 yards, at $1.50; 1 case Broadcloth, 175 yards, at $4, *Cash Sales this day,* $134.75.

6—Shipped per Steamer Alexandra, and consigned to B. Way, Picton, to be sold on our account, 8 pcs. Broadcloth, 20 yards each, at $4. Paid freight on same, $6.50. *Cash Sales,* $136.20.

8—Sold Real Estate for $1250; received in payment Draft at 15 days on Thomas Davis for $850, cash for the balance, $400.

9—Gave W. McKay Draft at 30 days on James Goodwin for $287.50. *Cash Sales,* $195.

10—Received from Robert Carey, Cash on account $100. Sold A. Diamond, for Cheque, 4 yards Black Broadcloth at $5; 3 yards Scotch Tweed at $2; 1 Vest Pattern, $5. *Cash Sales this day,* $230.15.

12—Bought of Henry & Co. 20 pcs. Red Flannel, 40 yards each, at 30c.; 10 pcs. Wincey, 30 yards each, at 25c. Gave in payment Sight Draft on H. Simmons for $269.50; Cash for balance. *Cash Sales,* $200.

14—F. Lane withdrew on private account, $150. Paid Gas Bill, $14.50. Taxes, $45.70, *Cash Sales,* $170.

16—Received from B. Way, Picton, acct. of Sales of Mdse. shipped him 6th inst. The net proceeds remitted per Cheque (payable here at par) amount to $760.75.
17—Sold S. Edsall, on his Note at 3 months, 4 pcs. Summer Tweed, 35 yds. each, at $1.50. *Cash Sales*, $180.
18—Had S. Edsall's Note discounted at Montreal Bank. Discount off at 7 per cent., $—— Cash received, $—— * Paid Cash for a bill of Mdse. bought at auction, $75.20.
20—Paid Clerk's Salary, $140. For sundry Expenses, $18.50.
21—Bought for Cash, from T. J. Claxton & Co., Mdse., as per invoice, $1200. Paid for Cartage, $1.50. Sundry Expenses, $9. *Cash Sales*, $245.50.
22—Bought of J. G. Mackenzie & Co., Mdse., as per invoice, $800. Gave in payment our Acceptance at 5 days, $550. Cash for balance, $250. *Cash Sales*, $725.
23—Bought of J. McKay, for Cash, Mdse., $150. J. S. Miller withdrew on acct., $200. *Cash Sales this day*, $475.50.
26—Paid Cash for our Draft of 22nd inst., favor of J. G. Mackenzie & Co., $——. *Cash Sales*, $695.40.
30—Bought for Cash, of T. Anderson, Mdse., $100. Paid for Insurance, $14.75. Cartage, $3.20. *Cash Sales*, $480.25.

INVENTORY OF RESOURCES AND LIABILITIES NOT SHOWN ON THE LEDGER†

RESOURCES.—*Merchandise remaining unsold*, $4300. *Interest receivable accrued to date on Langford's, Note*, $13.87.

LIABILITY—*Interest payable—Accumulated on our Note favor Jones & Co.*, $18.12. *Total net gain*, $2022.64. *Miller's share*, $871.59. *Lane's share*, $1151.05.

TO THE STUDENT.

We would here again impress upon the student the necessity of study. There is no better test of a person's knowledge of Book-keeping than that connected with what you have just being doing,—changing books from Single to Double Entry. Here the matter is made clear, and easily understood. See that you master thoroughly the *principles* involved, so that if you are called upon, in the course of your business career, to change books from Single to Double Entry, you may be able to do so intelligently, and to explain and give the reason for what you do.

Impress this point upon your mind ; that the facts you require to ascertain to open books by Double Entry, or change books from Single to Double Entry, are the Resources and Liabilities of the concern.

TO CHANGE DOUBLE ENTRY BOOKS TO SINGLE ENTRY.

Discontinue in the Ledger all accounts but those with individuals, but continue the use of the auxiliary books, such as the Cash Book, Bill Books, etc.

---

* This is exclusively a cash transaction, and entered on both the debit and credit side of the Cash Book. Enter the full amount of Note on the debit side, as if the firm actually received it, and then enter the amount paid for discount on the credit side. See the Cash Book of Set IX. If the proceeds had been left in Bank you would also make cash credit by Bank, same as for a deposit.

† There is a marked peculiarity in the Inventory, viz., the showing of a liability as a necessary part of the Inventory. Another peculiarity growing out of this presentment of facts is the debiting of Interest Account with the liability of Interest, as well as crediting it with the resource of Interest, before closing the account. This enforcement of a correct theory should be thoroughly understood and carried out in the remaining Sets.

JOURNAL DAY BOOK—Set IX.

You are requested to observe particularly the following form, that you may be able to express, in this manner, any conceivable transaction, combining all the essential points of the separate Day Book and Journal. Very few large business houses adopt the old method of first entering transactions in a historical Day Book, and Journalizing therefrom. Where more practical forms, for the purpose of condensation, are not in use, the Journal Day Book meets with great favor, as being both plain and practical.

In writing up this book, make your Journal entry first, from the record of transactions; then write the explanation immediately under it in a smaller hand, commencing about half way between the centre of the page and the folio column, as is illustrated in the following:

FORM OF JOURNAL DAY BOOK.

London, April 1st, 1889.

Mdse. Dr. To J. R. Marvin, Bought on acct. Goods as per invoice.		700		700	
—————— " ——————					
Mdse. Dr. To Bills Payable, Bought of Jones & Co. on our Note, as per B. B., with interest at 9 per cent., Mdse. as per invoice.		2500		2500	
—————— 2 ——————					
Robert Carey Dr. To Mdse., Sold him on acc't. as follows: 2 pcs. Scotch Tweed, 70 yds., at $1.50 $105.00 4 " Cassimere, 120 yds., at 2.00 240.00		345		345	
—————— 4 ——————					
Bills Receivable Dr. To Mdse., Sold C. A. Langford, for his Note at 2 months, with interest at 10 per cent.: 2 cases Prints, 1500 yds., at $0.15 $225.00 3 cases Irish Linen, 1280 yds., at 0.25 320.00 1 case Scotch Tweed, 450 yds., at 1.50 675.00 1 case Broadcloth, 175 yds., at 4.00 700.00		1920		1920	
—————— 6 ——————					
Shipment to Way No. 1 Dr. * To Mdse., Shipped to B. Way, Picton, per Steamer Alexandra, to be sold on our acct.: 8 pcs. Broadcloth, 160 yds., at $4. Paid freight on the same as per C. B.		640		640	
—————— 8 ——————					
Bills Receivable Dr. To Real Estate, Sold Lot on Mountain Street for $1250. Received Draft as per B. B. and Cash as per C. B. for Balance.		850		850	
—————— 9 ——————					
W. McKay Dr. To James Goodwin, Gave McKay a Draft at 30 days on J. Goodwin, for above amount.		287	50	287	50
		7242	50	7242	50

NOTE.—Transactions in nowise connected with Cash are to be entered only in the Journal Day Book, and exclusive Cash transactions, such as the purchase of Cotton on the 4th, only in the Cash Book.
* These transactions being of a mixed nature are entered in both Journal Day Book and Cash Book.

CASH BOOK.

Dr. ——————CASH.——————

1889. Apr.	L.F.				Mdse.		Sundries.	
1			Balance from last month, $3015.04					
4	√	To Merchandise,	Sales from Petty C. B............		134	75		
6	√	" "	" "		136	20		
8	24	" Real Estate,	Lot Mountain Street, D. B........				400	
9	√	" Merchandise,	Sales as per Petty C. B..........		195			
10	25	" Robert Carey,	On account.....................				100	
10	√	" Merchandise,	A. Diamond's Check.............		31			
10	√	" "	Sales Petty C. B................		230	15		
12	√	" "	" "		200			
14	√	" "	" "		170			
16	26	" Ship't to Way No.	1 Net Proceeds per Check........				760	75
17	√	" Merchandise,	Sales from P. C. B..............		180			
18	24	" Bills Receivable,	Edsall's Note discounted,........				210	
21	√	" Merchandise,	Sales from P. C. B.,............		245	50		
22	√	" "	" " "		725			
23	√	" "	" " "		475	50		
26	√	" "	" " "		695	40		
30	√	" "	" " "		480	25		
	20		Total to cr. of Merchandise...............		3898	75	*3898	75
	21		Total to debit of Cash....................				5369	50
			From last month..........................				3015	04
							8384	54

The Cash Book is the most important of all the auxiliary books, for the Cash account is found to be the most difficult to keep correctly of the whole list of accounts, because Cash is the basis of all trade, and is constantly passing out for purchases, expenses, etc., and coming in for debts and sales.

In business the Cash Book is generally balanced every night. We could not, in a work like this, introduce a sufficient number of entries to carry this out; we have therefore left it open until the end of the month.

As the above Cash Book is the book of original entry for all such transactions as are entered upon it, great care is necessary in making these entries.

They should be made in such a manner that any person may be able to determine what account was intended to be debited or credited for the money paid or received. For this purpose accountants adopt the following RULE :

When money is received, write the *name* of the account to be credited for it, next the folio or date column on the left side, and the words of explanation, on the same line a little to the right. When money is paid, write the *name* of the account to be debited for it, next the folio or date column on the right side, and the words of explanation on the same line a little to the right.

The Ledger titles should be kept in a perpendicular column, separated by a slight space from the words of explanation. And it adds greatly to the appearance of the book to begin the words of explanation all on a perpendicular line, made by a light pencil mark, and write them one half smaller than the Ledger titles.

NOTE.—The balance from the last month, it will be observed, has not been extended in the money columns because it is already entered in the Ledger ; if extended it would be added with the total receipts, and posted a second time. It is necessary to add the Cash in hand from last month with the receipts during this month in order to obtain the proper balance. When you require to continue the Cash Book, after it has been closed, bring down the balance on the Dr. side, without extending the amount in the money columns, and continue it the same as above.

* Red Ink.

87

Set IX.

—————CONTRA.—————— Cr.

1889. Apr.	L.F.				Mdse.		Sundries.	
4	√	By Merchandise,	Invoice of Cotton.............		60			
6	26	" Ship' to Way No. 1	Freight on same...............				6	50
12	√	" Merchandise,	Invoice from Henry & Co.......		45	50		
14	24	" F. Lane,	Withdrew on Account..........				150	
"	24	" Expense,	Gas Bill, $14.50, Taxes, $45.70..				60	20
18	26	" Discount,	On S. Edsall's Note...........				3	76
"	√	" Merchandise.	Bought at Auction.............		75	20		
20	24	" Expense,	Wages, $140, Books, $18.50.....		•		158	50
21	√	" Merchandise,	T. J. Claxton & Co's Invoice.....		1200			
"	24	" Expense,	Cartage, $1.50; Repairing, $9....				10	50
22	√	" Merchandise,	Inv. J. G. MacKenzie & Co., D.B.		250			
23	"	" "	Invoice J. McKay.............		150			
"	25	" J. S. Miller,	Withdrew on Account...........				200	
26	25	" Bills Payable,	Draft favor J. G. McKenzie & Co.				550	
30	√	" Merchandise,	T. Anderson's Invoice..........		100			
"	24	" Expense,	Insur., $14.75; Cartage, $3.20....				17	95
	21		Total to debit of Merchandise....		1880	70	*1880	70
	20		Total to cr. af Cash................... BALANCE*................,.........				3038 *5346	11 43
							8384	54

* Red Ink.

Post from the Cash Book and Journal Day Book in the same order, as regards the dates when the transactions were entered.

The above is a very convenient form of Cash Book to be kept in connection with a general merchandise business. The feature of *special columns* may be extended, if desirable, as is shown in a subsequent part of the work.

It will be seen that all Cash Entries, debit and credit, are taken directly to the Ledger from this book, together with all accounts producing or costing Cash. The amounts distinguished as "Per Petty Cash Book" are entered here from a book showing cash sales corresponding with the contents of the till.

The columns headed "Mdse." will be found very convenient for posting. Should the Cash transactions of a month extend over several pages, the footings of these columns are brought forward to the end of the month, and posted in total. The check marks in the column following dates are made to indicate that the amounts opposite, in the "Mdse." column, are *not to be posted*, and the figures are the pages of the accounts in the Ledger to which the amounts in the "Sundries" column opposite have been posted. The method of posting from the Cash Book is extremely simple.

The amounts in the "Sundries" column on the Dr. side are posted to the *credit* of their respective accounts—the page of the Ledger being indicated in the folio column; and the amounts in the "Sundries" column on the Cr. side, to the *debit* of their respective accounts. The footing of the "Mdse." column, on the Dr. side, is posted at the end of

* Red Ink.

NOTE—In making entries in your Cash Book, always observe the above style of arrangement, and NEVER ENTER THE TITLE CASH anywhere in this book, except the heading at the beginning of the page; for you enter nothing in it but Cash. It is unnecessary to use the words "received" and "paid" in explaining an entry as nothing is entered on the debit side of this account except Cash received, and nothing but Cash paid out on the credit side.

In balancing the Cash Book always rule that side first upon which appears the greater number of entries and have the footings of the two sides directly opposite one another.

Where long explanations have to be given in a Cash Book, it may be desirable to put the name of the acct. on one line and the explanation on the line or lines (if more than one explanatory line is required) below.

the month to the *credit* of Merchandise account, and the total footing of the "Mdse." column, on the Cr. side, to the *debit* of Merchandise account. The Cash received, or amount of the Dr. side of the Cash book, is then posted to the *debit* of Cash account, and the total footing of the Cr. side, or Cash disbursed, to the *credit* of Cash Account in the Ledger.

As the *debit* side of the Cash Book contains the *credits* of all accounts producing Cash and the *credit* side the *debits* of all accounts costing Cash, it will be seen that when the above posting is completed a double entry is effected.

PUTTING CHEQUES THROUGH THE CASH BOOK.

Whether Cheques shall be Journalized, or put through the Cash Book (when the latter is kept as in this and subsequent Sets), is simply a matter of convenience. Either way is right, and has precisely the same effect. Adopt which you deem best for the business you may be engaged in.

When putting a Cheque through the C. B., first make Cash Dr. to Bank for Cheque No. —, just as though you had received the amount; then make Cash Cr. by the individual or the account for which you pay the Cheque, giving the usual explanation. The municipal Set treats Cheques in this way, but we deem it well to give here an

EXAMPLE.

You give a Cheque on Bank of Montreal to retire your note for $520.00 and interest accumulated $12.00 ; the following would be the entries :

Dr. ———CASH.——— ———CONTRA.——— Cr.

Oct. 29	To Bank. For Cheque No. 132	$532 00	Oct. 29	By Bills Payable. Retired B.P. No. 81 by Cheque 132 "Interest. For int. on above	$520 00 12 00

QUESTIONS FOR REVIEW—CHAPTER V.

What is a Draft? How many persons are concerned in a Draft? How is a Draft accepted? For what purposes are Drafts usually used? Give the Rule for Journalizing Drafts? What do you understand by the term "Consignor?" What by "Consignee?" What is "Shipment?" as a Ledger title? When is "Shipment" made Dr? With what is it credited? When is it closed "To" or "By" *Loss* and *Gain*? When by *Balance Inventory*? What is "Consignment" as a Ledger title? With what is it debited? With what credited? How is it closed? When "Shipment" is used as a Ledger title what should it have attached? When "Consignment" is used as a Ledger title what should it have attached? What are the characteristics of Set V.? When Notes, Drafts and other obligations fall due on Sunday, when is payment required by law? What is the Cash Book used for? Whenever money is received how is it entered in the Cash Book? Whenever money is paid out, how entered? How can the balance in hand be found at any time? With what must this agree? Can the Cr. column of the Cash Account be the greater? How often should the Cash Book be balanced? How is this done? Give forms for filing Business Papers? With whom are accounts kept in Single Entry? What are the principal books of entry? What other books are introduced, and why? From what books do you post in Single Entry? What does Double Entry comprise? What does Single Entry comprise? How do you convert Single Entry to Double Entry? How can you ascertain the Net Gain or Loss? How are the Resources and Liabilities found in Single Entry? How do you close a Single Entry Ledger? What old method has been observed in the preceding eight sets? What books are now dispensed with? What book is used instead? Which is the most important of all the Auxiliary Books? In general business how often is the Cash Book balanced?

THE
CANADIAN ACCOUNTANT.

PART II.

CONTAINING THE MOST

PRACTICAL FORMS OF KEEPING ACCOUNTS

ADAPTED TO THE VARIOUS DEPARTMENTS OF BUSINESS,

INCLUDING

COMPLETE SETS OF BOOKS

IN

WHOLESALE AND RETAIL MERCHANDISING, MANUFACTURING, STEAMBOATING, MUNICIPAL BOOK-KEEPING, SETTLEMENT OF ESTATES, WAREHOUSING, FARM ACCOUNTS, BOOK-KEEPING FOR PUBLIC INSTITUTIONS AND CHURCHES, PRACTICAL COUNTING HOUSE WORK, CHAPTERS ON BANKING, JOINT STOCK COMPANIES, Etc., Etc.

TO THE STUDENT.

You have now been presented with nine Sets of Books, eight by Double Entry and one by Single, representing you as carrying on different kinds of business, some of which have been prosperously pursued and others attended with misfortune. The exercises already passed over are considered sufficient to illustrate the opening and closing of Books, both individual and partnership, under the various positions of gains and losses, capital and insolvency.

A good understanding of the preceding Sets will ground you thoroughly in the principles of the science of Book-keeping. We will next present you with some of the most approved methods and practical forms of keeping accounts, such as are now in use in counting houses in the various branches of business.

Writers on the subject have by no means kept abreast of the changes and improvements effected by practical Accountants in the form and use of the different books, and the improvements made, with the object to adapt them to any particular kind of business. The want of practicability in the treatises on Book-keeping already in use was one of the chief reasons that induced the writing and publication of this work.

BUSINESS STATEMENTS.

There are many forms of business statements now in use, each possessing some peculiar merit, and all having the same general purpose in view, viz., that of exhibiting the real and progressive condition of the business represented. The forms hitherto used in this work, Part I., are both simple and comprehensive, and would probably be preferred by one not versed in book-keeping, as they are easily understood; but as it is necessary that you should understand different modes of making out business statements, and as we know of no form that compasses so much within such limited space as that given on the following page, we request you to make out a similar BALANCE SHEET from each of the following Sets.

A trial balance taken with Dr. and Cr. footings, similar to the following, will be sufficient to exhibit the necessary results of the Ledger, from which to render a Balance Sheet.

L. F.	ACCOUNTS.						DR. FOOTING.		CR. FOOTING.	
12	Stock	....	....	....	....	....			8000	50
12	Cash	....	....	....	....	....	6850	50	2725	15
13	Flour	....	....	....	....	....	5080		2810	
14	Wheat	....	....	....	....	....	2420		1630	
14	N. W. Phillips	....	....	....	....	....	710		50	
15	Robert Brown	....	....	....	....	....	930		1000	
16	Bills Payable	....	....	....	....	....	1280		1380	
17	Bills Receivable	....	....	....	....	....	620		450	
18	Expense	....	....	....	....	....	155	15		
							18045	65	18045	65

The following form taken from this Trial Balance will illustrate the process of making out a BALANCE SHEET. Full instructions for cases where two or more partners are engaged in a business are give on page 92.

BALANCE SHEET.

TAKEN, *Belleville, January 30th,* 1889.

	L. F.	TRIAL BALANCE.		INVENTORY.	REPRESENTATIVE.		STOCK.		REAL.	
		Dr.	Cr.		LOSSES.	GAINS.	Dr.	Cr.	RESOURCES.	LIABILITIES.
Stock	24		8000 50					8000 50		
Cash	24	6850	2725 15						4125 35	
Flour	25	6080	2810	3360		1090			3360	
Wheat	25	2420	1630	1050		260			1050	
N. W. Phillips	25	710	50						660	
Robert Brown	25	930	1000							70
Bills Payable	26	1280	1380							100
Bills Receivable	26	620	450						170	
Expense	26	155			155 15					
		18045 65	18045 65	4410						
			† Stock's Net Gain.		†1194 85	1350 00		†1194 85		
					1350 00	1350 00	†9195 35	9195 35	9365 35	†9195 35
					† Stock's Net Capital.		9195 35	9195 35	9365 35	9365 35

NOTE.—Should there be a large number of personal accounts, it will be found difficult to include them all SEPARATELY in this form. In such cases it is customary to employ the two general titles, "Accounts Receivable" and "Accounts Payable," the one embracing all amounts owing to us on personal account, and the other all amounts owing by us. This curtailment will enable the facts of any common business to be shown in this form.

If there are two or more partners each one should have two columns, as Stock has above. The balances brought down in a Ledger when it is closed should correspond with the Resources and Liabilities columns in the Balance Sheet.

† Red Ink. * Proprietor's name.

BALANCE SHEET.

In commercial language a "Balance Sheet" signifies the systematic arrangement of facts, for the purpose of exhibiting at a view the condition of business. The forms in use vary according to the necessities of the occasion or the ingenuity of the accountant. The following explanation will be found serviceable in preparing this sheet for the entries. The method of enforcing the facts will be apparent to any diligent student.

1. Take a sheet of paper of proper size, and for a border rule double red lines around the margin.

2. Rule parallel head lines, leaving proper space for double captions, as in the example.

3. Ascertain the number of the Ledger accounts to be represented, which will embrace all the accounts in the Trial Balance that do not cancel. If the business is that of a single proprietor, usually called "Stock" business, rule in pencil as many lines as will contain all the accounts and *five* additional. If it be a partnership business with two or more partners, rule three additional lines for each partner; thus, for "Stock" business, *five* lines more than all the accounts; for two partners, *eight* lines more than all the accounts; for three partners, *eleven* lines more, and so on.

4. Lay off proper spaces for debit and credit money columns; first for the footings of Ledger Accounts, second for Gains and Losses, third for Stock, or, if partners, for each partner—and fourth for Resources and Liabilities; also a *single* money column for Inventories and for Ledger titles and their Ledger folios. The position of these columns will be seen in the example given.

5. After denoting the proper space for each heading, which can be best done with pencil, commence to rule in red ink at the right hand, and bring all the lines of the two captions, "Real Accounts" and "Stock" or one of the partners, down to the lower pencil line. For the other partners drop two lines. For Losses and Gains drop two lines in "Stock" business, and one additional for each partner.

6. Rule the foot lines as shown, and the schedule will be ready to receive the accounts.

SHIPMENT CO'S AND MERCHANDISE CO'S.

"Shipment Company" is a term used to represent your interest in merchandise or other property shipped by you, to be sold on joint account and risk of yourself and other parties; or it may represent your interest where you receive intelligence that other parties have shipped to a third party and that you are interested.

It is made Dr. for your interest and share of the costs in the speculation when the shipment is made, and at the same time the parties interested with you are debited for their share of the merchandise and charges; it is credited with all incomes, and, after being posted to the Ledger, closes "To" or "By" Loss and Gain.

Should you wish to close the Ledger before an account of sales has been received, credit Shipment Company "By Balance Inventory" for the amount it cost you.

The title "Merchandise Company" is a fictitious name given to goods or other property received by you to sell on joint account and risk. It is made Dr. to the consignor when received for only your interest, and is debited for charges incurred until it is disposed of. The consignor should be credited for your share of the goods, unless settled for at the time of receiving them, the same as though bought of him on account.

In selling goods that have been received to sell on joint account, Cr. Merchandise Company for all sales.

In closing a Merchandise Company, deduct total charges from total sales. This leaves net proceeds in favor of all parties, each one having shared his part of the charges incurred.

Now, having in your possession the proceeds, each interested party should be credited with his share of them. In closing a Merchandise Company, it is made Dr. to Commission, to all charges which have not been posted, to the shipper or shippers for their net proceeds, and to Loss and Gain for your gain; if a losing operation, Loss and Gain is made Dr. to Merchandise Company for your loss. Should the goods, at the time of closing, be but partially sold, then Merchandise Company should be Cr. in the Ledger " By Balance Inventory," only for your share of the Merchandise remaining on hand, the remainder belonging to the shipper or shippers.

Shipment Companies and Merchandise Companies represent the temporary co-partnerships existing between the consignor and consignee, having reference to the sale of particular consignments of Merchandise. These co-partnerships differ from general co-partnerships only in their duration, and the manner of their sales. The consignee acts as a commission merchant, and in that capacity receives and disposes of the property as he would of a simple consignment; the only difference being that he is interested in the gains and losses.

A second method of considering these transactions is to recognize the principle that the holder of the property is responsible for it. Thus, when you receive from Pitceathly & Kelso an invoice to be sold on joint account, you debit Merchandise Company with the invoice and expenses, and credit the consignors with the cost of the invoice, thus making yourself responsible for the property as though it were all your own. The consignor's entry (recognizing the same principle) will be to debit you for the entire cost of the Merchandise. Where there are more than two parties interested, if the accounts are taken by this method, the consignee should debit the Merchandise Company with its entire cost—and credit the consignor with their (the consignee's and consignor's) joint share, and any other party or parties with his or their share.

The consignor's entry in such a case would be to debit the consignee with their joint share, and each of the other parties with his or their share. The other parties would, if making an entry to correspond, debit the consignee and credit the consignor each for his own share.

The foregoing illustrations, it is hoped, will be sufficient to fasten the principles of these accounts upon the mind of the learner. The only difference in the two methods is a simple matter of time. By the first method, the consignee is considered, as responsible for the property *when he has disposed of it*, and by the second *when he received it*. The final result is the same in either case; though, so far as right and responsibility are concerned, the first method is the correct and philosophical one—The principle recognized being that the owner of the property is responsible.

We submit these separate methods because we consider that the more the learner permits himself to dwell upon these principles, and the better he comprehends them in all their bearings, the more thorough and available will be his knowledge.

The Companies in their current condition are neither real nor representative, For this reason it is deemed best to close them by a Journal entry, when the property they represent is disposed of.

The exercises on the following pages will show the application of the foregoing principles.

H

EXERCISES ON JOURNALIZING SHIPMENT COS. AND MERCHANDISE COS.

You should lay a sheet of paper over the following solutions, and not refer to them while you are writing out the Journal Entries.

Transactions.	Journalized.

1—Jones ships Brown, to be sold on joint acct. and risk, Mdse. valued at $1200. And pays insurance on same $40.

1—Shipment Co. " A " Dr. $ 620
  Brown   .   620
    To Mdse. $1200.00
    " Cash   40.00

2—Brown on receipt of the goods pays freight and other charges amounting to $70.50.

2—Mdse. Co. " A " Dr. $690.50
    To Jones $620.00
    " Cash   70.50

3—Brown sells the goods for $1450. Receives in payment a Cheque for $500, Cash $500, and a Note for the balance.

3—Cash   Dr. $1000
  Bills Receivable   "   450
    To Mdse. Co. " A " $1450

4—Brown renders an account of sales; his charges are as follows: Drayage, $4.50; Storage, $5.00; Cooperage, $6.50; Commission, 3 per cent.
The following forms explain the manner of closing the Mdse. Co.:
Total Sales, $1450
Charges already posted, $70.50
" not "   16.00
Commission,   43.50   130

Total net proceeds,   1320
Brown's one half,   660.00
Cost of " "   620.00

Brown's gain,   40.00

4—Mdse. Co. " A " Dr. $759.50
    To Charges $ 16.00
    " Com.   43.50
    " Jones   660.00
    To Loss and Gain   40.00

In closing a Mdse. Co. and making the acct. sales entry, first find what all the sales amount to, then total charges (not including cost), and by deducting the total charges from the total sales you obtain the whole net proceeds. The individual net proceeds are found by dividing the total net proceeds by the number of parties interested. Your gain or loss is found by taking the difference between your proceeds and the amount you credited the shipper with when you received the goods.

5—Jones' entry on receipt of above account of sales.

5—Brown Dr. $660,
    To Shipm't. Co. " A " $660.00

6—Brown's entry on remitting am't. to balance Jones' acct. per Cheque.

6—Jones Dr. $1280,
    To Bank $1280.00

7—Jones' entry on receipt of above remittance.

7—Cash Dr. $1280,
    To Brown $1280.00

8—Received from Smith, for sale on joint acct., goods valued at $840. Paid freight on same, $100; wharfage, storage, drayage, etc., $60.

8—Mdse. Co. Dr. $580,
    To Smith $420.00
    " Cash   160.00

9—Having sold the goods for $850, I render an acct. of sales. Charges already posted, $160. After charges for drayage, etc., $10. Commission and guarantee, 5 per cent.

9—Mdse. Co. Dr. $270,
  Loss & Gain Dr. $101.25,
    To Smith $318.75
    " Commission   42.50
    " Charges   10.00

10—Suppose the above goods were sold for $1200, and I remit the amount due Smith with the acct. of sales.

10—Smith Dr. $420,
  Mdse. Co. Dr. $620,
    To Cash $905.00
    " Commission   60.00
    " Charges   10.00
    " Loss & Gain   65.00

11—Suppose the above goods were all destroyed by fire after coming into my possession.

11—Loss & Gain Dr. $500,
  Smith   "   80,
    To Mdse. Co. $580.00

12—Suppose the goods per No. 8 were partially destroyed and the balance sold for $150.

12—Loss & Gain Dr. $425,
  Smith   "   5,
    To Mdse. Co. $430.00

13—Shipped West, to be sold on joint account of East, consignee and myself each ½; goods valued at $1200. Paid Insurance on same, $30.

13—Ship't Co. Dr. $410,
  West   "   410,
  East   "   410,
    To Mdse. $1200.00
    " Cash   30.00

14—West returns the whole of the above goods. Charges paid by him, $60.

14—Mdse. Dr. $1200,
    To West $420.00
    " East   400.00
    " Ship't. Co.   380.00

15—Suppose that, in example No. 4, Brown has only sold ⅓ the goods for $700, at the time of rendering an account of sales, and that the charges and commission are the same as in the former case.

16—Suppose S. G. Beatty sends you $2000 worth of Mdse. for sale on joint acct., and you add goods to make up the joint property to $3500, what will your entry be?

17—What will S. G. Beatty's entry be in the above case, when he receives advice and invoice of goods added?

18—Supposing the whole of the speculation per No. 16 produce only $3000, and your charge for commission is 4 per cent., how would the account close?

19—Samuel ships Student on joint account and risk Mdse. $1200, and pays freight, $20 per Sight Draft on Student. Samuel's entry?

20—Student's entry on receipt of the goods accepting Samuel's Draft on him and at the same time paying $10 per check for cartage.

21—Student having sold the goods for $1500 renders an Account of Sales, and remits $50 to Samuel per Note. Unposted charges, $12. Commission, 2½ per cent. on Sales. Student's entry?

22—Student remits amount yet due Samuel per Time Draft on B, $800, and the balance in Cash. Student's entry?

23—Samuel's entry on receipt of last remittance?

15—Charges posted $70.50
   "   Unposted   16.00
Commission...............21.00 Total Sales...$700.00
Total Charges.........107.50.................107.50
                        Total Net proceeds. 592.50

Brown's Proceeds.....296.25 ⅓ Net Proceeds 296.25
Jones'   "   ....296.25 ⅔ Unsold Goods 300.00

Brown's ⅓ Invoice,   620.00 $596.25
Pro. and Inventory.   596.25

Net Loss...............$ 23.75
Mdse. Co. Dr.......... 309.50
Loss and Gain Dr.....   23.75
                    To Charges, $ 15.00
                    Commission,   21.00
                    To Jones,   296.25

16—Mdse. Co. Dr. $1750,
                    To S. G. Beatty $ 250.00
                    " Merchandise   1500.00
17—Ship't Co. Dr. $750,
                    To Student $750.00
18—Mdse. Co. Dr. $1250,
   Loss and Gain, 310,
                    To Commission $ 120.00
                    " S. G. Beatty 1440.00
19—Ship't Co. Dr. $610,
   Student   "   590,
                    To Mdse. $1200.00
20—Mdse. Co. Dr. $620,
                    To Samuel $590.00
                    " Cash   20.00
                    " Bank   10.00
21—Mdse. Co. Dr. $880,
                    To Charges $12.00
                    " Commission   37.50
                    " Samuel   670.25
                    " B. Payable   50.00
                    " Loss & Gain 110.25
22—Samuel Dr. $1260.25,
                    To B. $800.00
                    " Cash   460.25
23—Bills Receivable Dr. $800,
    Cash   "   460,
                    To Student $1260.25

You shall now analyse a number of similar entries, and find the correct amounts to form the Journal entry, which, as explained heretofore, when correct, will always close the account on the Ledger.

It is very difficult to understand the closing entry of either a Mdse Co. or a Consignment, unless you have before you the position of the account upon the Ledger. If your Ledger is not posted when closing a Mdse. Co. and making the account Sales Entry, open the account upon a piece of paper, and show its total debits and credits as they exist, and will appear in the Ledger when posted.

SET X.

(Corresponding with Set VIII. Part I.)

INCLUDING PRACTICAL FORM OF DAY BOOK AND JOURNAL COMBINED AND ILLUS-
TRATING THE DISTINCTION BETWEEN SINGLE AND DOUBLE ENTRY.

The transactions comprising this Set are the same as those in Set VIII, and are selected for the purpose of showing the exact difference between SINGLE and DOUBLE ENTRY. A careful study and comparison of the two sets in their similar and dissimilar points will open to the mind of the student a clearer distinction between the two methods of accounts than could be effected by any other form of reasoning.

This distinction is most apparent in the Ledger, where it will be seen that the *additional* accounts required by Double Entry are useful, mainly to denote special gains and losses.

In performing the work of this Set you are required to introduce the

SIX-COLUMN JOURNAL.

The principal feature of this book, that of affording special columns for the accounts most used, may be carried to any desirable extent; and in some business houses as many as *eight* special debit and credit columns are used.

Its advantages may be briefly stated as follows:

1st.—A vast saving of time and space in posting.
2nd.—Embracing the principles of *four* books in *one*, viz.: Cash Book, Invoice Book, Sales Book and Journal.
3rd.—Showing monthly totals of the principal accounts in the Ledger, that the same may be compared year after year.
4th.—Affording an opportunity to post personal accounts immediately, the debits and credits appearing separately in the " Sundries " column.
5th.—Giving additional security of the correctness of the Ledger, there existing no probability of admitting debits and credits of the same account.

This book is called the SIX-COLUMN JOURNAL, because it is ruled with six columns; three debits on the left and three credits on the right. In making an entry the same form of expression is used as upon the Journal Day Book of last Set. In entering a sale extend the particulars first, like Carey's or Goodwin's entries on form.

The method of posting from this Journal is very simple. The separate items in the " Sundries " column are posted the same as from the common Journal, while the amounts of the " Cash " and " Mdse." columns are posted in totals at the close of each month. Every time these accounts are posted, it makes a period in the amounts brought forward on the Journal, and the new period commences with the heads of the columns empty.

Before commencing this Set, observe closely the form of Six-column Journal given, as an understanding of it, at the beginning, will greatly facilitate your progress.

DRY GOODS BUSINESS.—SET X.
TWO PARTNERS.

LONDON, March 1st, 1889.—J. S. MILLER and F. LANE this day commence the Dry Goods business at No. 114 St. James Street, agreeing to share gains and losses according to capital invested. J. S. MILLER invests:

Cash, $1500. Merchandise, $800; Note for $600, favor J. S. M., signed by Thomas Gibbard, dated January 31st, at 30 days; an accepted Draft for $400, drawn by J. Jones on D. Roblin, dated January 20th, at 90 days. Balance due from J. R. Marvin, $125. *Total investment* $3425. F. LANE invests:

Cash, $1500; Merchandise, $1200; Real Estate, $700; Note against S. Fowler for $200, dated January 25th, at 60 days. Note against H. Jackson for $800, dated Nov. 23rd, 1888, at 6 months, with interest at 7 per cent. Interest accrued on above to date, 3 months and 6 days, $14.94. *Total Investment*, $4414.94.

2—Bought of W. McKay, on acct., Invoice of Merchandise amounting to $1800. Sold Robert Carey on acct., 50 yds. Bl'k Broadcloth at $2.25; 12 Fancy Neckties at $1 each; 15 doz. prs. Lisle Thread Stockings at $3.25 per doz.

3—Sold James Goodwin, on acct., 50 yards Flannel at 60c.; 25 yards Broadcloth at $3.75; 66 yards Cassimere at $1.25. Received his Draft at 10 days' sight on A. Benson, for $55; the balance to remain on acct.

4—Bought of H. Simmons, on acct., Mdse. invoiced at $200; gave our Note at 60 days, $100; the balance to remain on acct.

5—Sold W. Harding, for Cash, 2 pcs. Irish Linen, 66 yards each, at 85c.; 35 yards Broadcloth at $2.50.

6—Sold W. Williams, for Note at 30 days, 2 pcs. Blue Broadcloth, 45 yards each, at $1.75; 90 yards French Merino at 60c. Received from Robert Carey his Draft at sight on W. Johnson for $50.

8—Sold James Goodwin, on acct., 90 yards Scotch Tweed at $1.25; 45 do. Red Flannel at 55c. Bought of W. Harding for our Note at 20 days, 5 pieces English Prints, 40 yds. each, at 25c. Sold Richard Manning, for his acceptance at 10 days, 10 yards Broadcloth at $2.25; 15 yards Mixed Tweed at $1.50.

9—Received from James Goodwin his Sight Draft on John James for $85. Bought of Richard Watson, for Cash, Merchandise invoiced at $200.

11—Sold Henry Simmons 24 yards Brown Beaver at $3.25; received Cash, $40; balance on acct. Bought of Wm. McKay Merchandise invoiced at $500; gave in payment Cash, $350; balance to remain on acct.

12—Sold Robert Carey, on acct., 55 yards Blue Broadcloth at $1.75. Received from James Goodwin, Cash, $50; Cheque on Montreal Bank, $30.

13—Paid Wm. McKay, Cash, $1200. Sold John Johnson, for his Sight Draft on J. Wilson, 15 pairs Pants at $3.75. Sold Rbt. Carey, on acct., 30 Vests at $2.25; 12 Ready-made Coats at $5.50.

15—Sold H. Simmons, on acct., 9 Fine Overcoats at $16. Sold John Cummings, for his Note at 20 days, 12 complete uniforms at $15.

16—Bought of A. Vermilyea, for our Note at 30 days, Mdse. invoiced at $175. Received Cash for James Goodwin's Draft of the 3rd inst. Discounted our Note of the 4th inst., favor of H. Simmons, at 6 per cent. for unexpired time.

17—Received from Robert Carey, Cash, $100. Bought of James Goodwin, on acct., 50 Summer Coats at $2.50. Bought of W. McKay, on 3 months' credit, Mdse. invoiced at $275.

18—Received Cash in full for T. Gibbard's Note of Jan. 31st, with interest at 6 per cent., for time overdue, 13 days. Received Cash from H. Simmons, $40.

20—Sold W. Manning, for Cheque on Merchants' Bank, 10 Military Coats at $11; 10 pairs Pants at $6. Sold Robert Carey, on acct., 5 dozen Byron Collars at $2 per dozen; 4 dozen Cravats at $3 per dozen. Received from James Goodwin, Cheque on Montreal Bank for $155.

21—Sold H. Simmons, on acct., 40 yards Blue Broadcloth at $1.80; 10 yards Black Beaver at $3.75. Received Cash for R. Manning's Draft of the 8th inst. Sold W. West for his Draft at 10 days on R. Bass, 50 yards French Cassimere at $3. Bought of W. McKay, on acct., Mdse., as per bill, amounting to $95.

NOTE.—The names of Ledger accounts for this set and the number of lines to be left for each will be found on page 99.

23—Sold Robert Carey, on acct., 10 Summer Coats at $2.50; 40 yards Red Flannel at 55c.
24—Gave W. McKay our Draft at 10 days' sight, on James Goodwin, for $100. Sold H. Simmons, on acct., 10 yards Broadcloth at $2.25; 6 dozen French Yoke Shirts, $18 per dozen. Bought for Cash Mdse., as per bill, amounting to $300. Sold James Goodwin, on acct., 10 dozen Undershirts at $7 per dozen; 8 dozen pairs Knit Drawers at $8 per dozen.
25—Accepted W. McKay's Sight Draft on us, favor W. Barnes, for $500. Received from Robert Carey Sight Draft on James Goodwin for $125.
26—Sold H. Simmons, on acct., 1 piece French Cassimere, 50 yards, at $1.25. Had H. Jackson's Note of Nov. 23rd, 1888, discounted at Merchants' Bank. Face of Note, $800; interest, less discount, at 7 per cent., for unexpired time, 2 months, $18.81. Cash received, $818.81.*
28—Sold James Goodwin 15 complete Uniforms at $14; received in payment Sight Draft on Montreal Bank, $50; balance to remain on acct.
29—Gave W. McKay our Sight Draft on H. Simmons for $75. Bought for Cash, Mdse., as per bill amounting to $400. Received Cash in full for S. Fowler's Note, January 25th. Paid Cash for Gas Bill, $20; Wood, $15; Rent, $50.
30—Received Cash for D. Roblin's Draft of January 20th, less discount for unexpired time at 7 per cent. Paid Shop Hands Cash in full for services to date, $120.
At this date you will post the books and take off a Combined Statement without balancing or closing any of the accounts. The inventories are the same as those of Set VIII.
APRIL 1st—Bought of J. R. Marvin, on acct., Goods as per invoice, $700. Bought of James & Co., on our Note at 3 months, with interest at 9 per cent., Mdse. as per invoice, $2500.
2—Sold Robert Carey, on acct., 2 pieces Scotch Tweed, 35 yds. each, at $1.50; 4 pieces Cassimere, 30 yards each, at $2.
4—Bought for Cash 10 pieces Factory Cotton, 60 yards each, at 10c. Sold C. A. Langford, for his Note at 2 months, with interest at 10 per cent., 2 cases Prints, 1500 yards, at 15c.; 3 cases Irish Linen, 1280 yards, at 25c; 1 case Scotch Tweed, 450 yards, at $1.50; 1 case Broadcloth, 175 yds., at $4. *Cash Sales this day,* $134.75.
6—Shipped per Steamer Alexandria, and consigned to B. Way, Picton, to be sold on our account, 8 pcs. Broadcloth, 20 yards each, at $4. Paid Freight on same, $6.50. *Cash Sales*, $136.20.
8—Sold Real Estate for $1250; received in payment Draft at 15 Days on Thomas Davis for $850; cash for balance, $400.
9—Gave W. McKay Draft at 30 days on James Goodwin for $287.50. *Cash Sales*, $195.
10—Received from Robert Carey, Cash on account, $100. Sold A. Diamond, for Cheque, 4 yards Black Broadcloth at $5; 3 yards Scotch Tweed at $2; 1 Vest Pattern, $5. *Cash Sales this day*, $230.15.
12—Bought of Henry & Co., 20 pieces Red Flannel, 40 yds. each, at 30c.; 10 pieces Wincey, 30 yds. each, at 25c.; gave in payment Sight Draft on H. Simmons for $269.50; cash for balance. *Cash Sales*, $200.
14—F. Lane withdrew on private account $150. Paid Gas Bill, $14.50; Taxes, $45.70. *Cash Sales*, $170.
16—Received from B. Way, Picton, Acct. of Sales of Mdse. shipped him 6th inst, the net proceeds remitted per Cheque amounting to $760.75.
17—Sold S. Edsall, on his Note at three months, 4 pieces Summer Tweed, 35 yards each, at $1.50. *Cash Sales*, $180.
18—Had S. Edsall's Note discounted at Montreal Bank. Discount off at 7 per cent. $——. Cash received $——. Paid Cash for a bill of Mdse. bought at auction, $75.20.
20—Paid Clerk's salary, $140. For Sundry Expenses, $18.50.
21—Bought for Cash, from T. J. Claxton & Co., Mdse., as per invoice, $1200. Paid for Cartage, $1.50; Sundry Expenses, $9. *Cash Sales*, $245.50.
22—Bought of J. G. MacKenzie & Co., Mdse., as per invoice, $800. Gave in payment our Acceptance at 5 days, $550; cash for balance, $250. *Cash Sales*, $725.

* It is the custom of Banks, when a Note bearing interest is discounted, to compute the interest for the full time on the face of the Note, and add it to the principal, then discount the amount. In this case, Jackson's Note bears interest at 7 per cent. for 6 months and 3 days, and will amount, when paid, to $828.47. The discount on this amount for the 2 months the Note has to run before it becomes due, at 7 per cent., is $9.66, and this deducted from $828.47 leaves $818.81, the net proceeds received from the Bank.

23—Bought of J. McKay, for Cash, Mdse., $150. J. S. Miller withdrew on account, $200. *Cash Sales this day*, $475.50.
26—Paid Cash for our Draft of 22nd inst., favor of J. G. McKenzie & Co., $———. *Cash Sales*, $695.40.
30—Bought for Cash, of T. Anderson, Mdse., $100. Paid for Insurance, $14.75. Cartage, $3.20. *Cash Sales*, $480.25.

Make out a Balance Sheet at the end of this Set after the form on page 91. Rule it for two partners.

RESOURCES AND LIABILITIES NOT SHOWN ON THE LEDGER.

RESOURCES.—*Merchandise remaining unsold*, $4300.—*Interest Receivable—Accrued to date on Langford's Note*, $13.87.
LIABILITY.—*Interest Payable—Accumulated on our Note favor Jones & Co.*, $18.12.
Total Net Gain $2448.24.

The following are the Ledger Headings for Set X, and the number of lines required for each account.

J. S. Miller, 8; *F. Lane*, 8; *Cash* 9; *Merchandise*, 10; *Bills Receivable*, 17; *Bills Payable*, 12; *J. R. Marvin*, 7; *Real Estate*, 8; *Interest*, 10; *W. McKay*, 10; *Robert Carey*, 12; *James Goodwin*, 10; *Shipment to B. Way*, 8; *H. Simmons*, 10; *Expense*, 12; *Loss and Gain*, 10; *Balance*, 12.

INVENTORY (OR STOCK) BOOK.

When taking an inventory of stock it should be done methodically, and with the utmost care as to quantities and values. There should be a separate stock book for each year. Ordinary Journal paper, to the extent required, bound into limp covers, is the form usually adopted.

The necessary preliminary preparation of accurate measuring, counting and ticketing having been done, each department or assortment of goods will be taken in turn. The salesmen familiar with the departments will, classifying as they go along, call out the kinds, quantities, and prices of goods to the man entering in the Stock Book, who will call back each entry as he proceeds. When the entering has been done (which will be continuously until completed in a few hours or a day), the calculations will be extended and the additions made, and both will be verified by checking over.

The kinds, quantities and values of the goods in each department having been shown separately (this arrangement being desirable for reference in the future), then the recapitulation of the goods in all the departments is given at the end, with the final total of the stock on hand.

As a rule an inventory of goods is taken at the cost price, and in order that this may be done intelligently, the cost price must be marked upon the gooods when they are received and the invoice is being checked off. See page 198 for the method. The exception to the rule would be in the case of goods that have depreciated, say by shopwear, being out of fashion, or, as with iron goods, their value in the market being lower. The business year that is closing should bear the loss from depreciation.

If all business men would take stock yearly as we have indicated, and write off bad debts annually, as shown at page 179, there would be fewer failures.

The best conducted retail dry goods houses keep their stock of goods free from bad accumulations, to a great extent, by giving their salesmen a small premium for selling goods that are sticking too long.

SUNDRY DEBTORS' ACCOUNT.

An account with the above heading is frequently opened where there is a large number of small personal accounts, under the mistaken notion that labor will be saved by it. We have yet to see such an account used alone, without an auxiliary ledger containing the separate accounts in connection with it, that did not make a great deal of confusion and much trouble. If you give an individual credit at all, open a separate account for him. I is not necessary that these accounts should be in the General Ledger, they may be kept in a small, easily handled ledger, which may be called the Petty Ledger. To learn the way to deal with numerous small personal accounts, read, "Book-keeping for Churches and Public Institutions." See Index.

FORM OF SIX COLUMN JOURNAL.

London, March 1st, 1889.

Mdse.	Cash.	Sundries.	L.F.		L.F.	Sundries.	Cash.	Mdse.
				Sundries Dr., **To J. S. Miller.**	77	3425		
				Amounts invested.				
	1500		√	Cash,				
800		1000	√	Mdse.				
		125	75	Bills Receivable. As per inventory.				
			75	J. R. Marvin. T. Gibbard's Note B.B... ..$600				
				D. Roblin's Draft 400				
				Balance of Account				
				Sundries Dr. **To F. Lane.**	77	4414		
				Amounts invested.. ..				
	1500	700	√	Cash.				
1200		1000	√	Mdse.				
			78	Real Estate. As per inventory.				
			75	Bills Receivable. Lot No. 8, Mountain Street.				
		14 94	79	Interest. S. Fowler's Note as per B.B. $200				
				H. Jackson's " " 800				
				Accrued on Jackson's Note				
1800			√	**Mdse. Dr.** **To W. McKay.**	80	1800		
				Bought on acct. as per invoice of March 2nd.				
		173 25	82	**Robert Carey Dr.** **To Mdse.**	√			173 25
				For 50 yds. Broadcloth at $2.25 .. ..$112.50				
				" 12 Fancy Neckties " 1.00 .. .. 12.00				
				" 15 doz. prs. L. Thread Hose at $3.25 .. .. 48.75				
		55 00	75	**Bills Receivable Dr.** **To Mdse.**	√			206 25
		151 25	80	J. Goodwin, "				
				For 50 yds. Flannel at 60c. $30.00				
				" 25 " Broadcloth, at $3.75 .. .. .. 93.75				
				" 66 " Cassimere " 1.25 .. .. .. 82.50				
			3	Received in part payment Draft on A. Benson as per B.B. No.—				
3800	3000	3219 44		Amounts forward.		9639 94		379 50

London, March 4th, 1889.

Mdse.		Cash.		Sundries.	L.F		L.F.	Sundries.		Cash.		Mdse.	
3800	00			3219	44	✓		9639	94			379	50
200								100					
								100					
						✓	81						
							75						
		199	70	211	50	✓						199	70
												211	50
		50		137	25	75	82	50				137	25
						81							
50				45		✓	75	50				45	
						75							
200		85				✓	83	85					
4250	00	3334	70	3613	19	63	63	10024	94	200	00	972	95
				*3334	70	69	69	*200					
				*4250				*972	95				
				11197	89			11197	89				

Mdse. Dr. ..... Amounts forward ..... To Sundries.
    To H. Simmons,
    " Bills Payable,
    Bought of H. S. Goods as per invoice, gave in part payment,
    B.P. No. —

5

Cash Dr. ..... To Mdse.
    Sold H. Harding for Cash.

6

Bills Receivable Dr. ..... To Mdse.
    Sold W. Williams for his Note as per B.B. No. —

Cash Dr. ..... To Robert Carey.
    Received his Draft at Sight on W. Johnson.

8

James Goodwin Dr. ..... To Mdse.
    For 90 yds. Scotch Tweed at $1.25 $112.50,
    " 45 " Red Flannel " 0.55 24.75.

Mdse. Dr. ..... To Bills Payable.
    Bought of W. Harding as per invoice for our Note, B.P. No. —

Bills Receivable Dr. ..... To Mdse.
    Sold R. Manning for his acceptance, B.R.No.—,bill of above am't.

9

Cash Dr. ..... To James Goodwin.
    Received his Draft at sight on J. James.

Mdse. Dr. ..... To Cash,
    Bought of R. Watson as per invoice
        Sundries
        *Cash
        *Mdse.

The above is considered sufficient to illustrate the form of entering transactions in this book. *Red Ink.

REMARKS ON SET XI.

This Set is intended to illustrate a very practical form of keeping accounts; also some of the most important changes that take place in a partnership business. For this purpose it is continued four months, each month representing, so far as the closing of the books and the agreements of the partners are concerned, a year's business. At the end of the first year (represented by January), the existing partners, "Student" and "S. G. Beatty," admit a new partner, who is to share in the gains and losses according to capital invested. It is a settled principle in accounts, that whenever any change in the business occurs, the existing Resources and Liabilities of the concern should be made apparent; and, consequently, the proprietors' accounts should represent their investment at the time of the change. It is evident that if the accounts are all left in their current condition at the time of admitting a partner, he will unjustly become a joint partner in the gains which accrued before he had anything to do with the business. Therefore, before admitting a new partner, it becomes necessary to credit the original partners with their respective gains during business.

With this view we close the books at the end of January, credit each partner with his net gain, and bring down the balances as instructed on page 75.

At the end of the second year (represented by February), another partner is admitted, and the business changed from that of a Retail Grocery to a Wholesale Grocery and Shipping Business.

During the third year one of the partners disposes of his interest in the business to an outside party, who is allowed to assume the position of the retiring partner.

Through a disastrous fire at the end of the fourth year, the store and goods are entirely consumed, nothing being saved but the books and valuable papers. The accountant is required to effect a settlement with the Insurance Company, collect all Resources and pay off all Liabilities, as the partnership is to be dissolved and the business discontinued.

BOOKS USED.

The books necessary for this Set are JOURNAL DAY BOOK, INVOICE BOOK, CASH BOOK, BILL BOOK and LEDGER, and as there will be a large number of accounts, you will keep an Index for the Ledger.

A decided improvement in the Journal Day Book of this Set relates to the keeping of a column exclusively for *credit* sales of Merchandise, whereby the Journal and Sales Book are combined, and an opportunity afforded to post all credit sales of Merchandise in total. The Invoice Book and Cash Book are used as books of original entry. The transactions of the Invoice Book are journalized from that book at the end of the month, and the transactions of the Cash Book are posted directly to the Ledger.

See forms of Journal Day Book, Invoice Book and Cash Book immediately after the transactions for January.

SET XI.

SPACE REQUIRED FOR LEDGER ACCOUNTS.

Partners ½ page each. Merchandise, Bills Receivable, Bills Payable, Interest, A. Overell, S. Edsall, A. Forin, Merchants' Bank, a whole page each. Cash, Wm. Drewry, R. D. Anglin, Jos. Allen, W. Ponton, John Laird, T. B. Dean, Expense, Salary, Rent, Rimmer, Gunn & Co., Charges, Commission, J. W. Dickie, P. V. Dorland, W. B. Robinson, one half-page each. Loss and Gain, two pages, and all other accounts one-third of a page each.

RETAIL GROCERY BUSINESS.

(TWO PARTNERS.)

Gains and Losses to be divided in proportion to Capital invested.

Hamilton, January 1st, 1889.

*———— and S. G. Beatty this day form a co-partnership for the purpose of conducting the Retail Grocery Business, renting from Wm. Lottridge, Store No. 62 Macnab street, at $600 per year.

STUDENT invests Cash, $3800; Merchandise per inventory, $2500; George Stinson's Note, at three months, from October 10th, 1888, with interest at 6 per cent. per annum, $500. Interest accumulated to date, $————. A. Hamilton owes on account, $250. John Smith owes on account, $100.

Liabilities—Note favor W. Brown, $500, at 6 months, from October 12th, 1888. T. Durham on account, $275.

S. G. BEATTY invests Cash, $5,500, Note against W. Flemming, $1,750 at 6 months, from October 1st, 1888.

2—Engaged A. Overell, Alex. Forin, S. Edsall and John Laird as clerks, at $300 each per year. Sold Wm. Drewry, on account, 3 lbs. Japan Tea at 70c., 10 lbs. Soft Yellow Sugar at 9c., 1 lb. Cloves, 60c. Sold R. D. Anglin, on account, 10 lbs. Java Coffee at 40c, 2 boxes Layer Raisins at $3.25, 2 lbs. Pepper at 30c. *Cash Sales*, $96.

3—Bought of Rimmer, Gunn & Co., Montreal, on 4 months' credit, 5 bags Java Coffee, 142, 135, 136, 117, 150 lbs.; tare, 15 lbs. each, at 33c. Paid freight on above, $4.25. Sold Jos. Allen, on account, 100 lbs. Dry Cod, $6, 12 lbs. crushed "A" Sugar at 10½c. Deposited in Merchants' Bank, $1500. *Cash Sales*, $110.

5—Bought of James Gunner & Co., Montreal, 10 bbls. Canso Herrings at $3.50, 5 bbls. Round do at $3, 4 barrels White Fish at $5. Paid Freight, $2.50. Paid E. Harrison for Set of Books for use of store, $10.50. Sold S. Edsall, on account, 5 gallons Standard Syrup at 50c., 10 lbs. Sugar at 10c. Sold O. Vandervoort, on account, 2 bbls. Golden Syrup, 36 gallons each, at 45c., 2 bbls. Crushed Sugar at $25, 4 boxes Valencia Raisins at $3.25. Sold W. Ponton, on account, 5 lbs. Ground Ginger at 30c., 1 lb. Pepper, 25c., 12 lbs. Prunes at 20c. Received from A. Hamilton, on account, his Note at one month for $100. *Cash Sales*, $145.

7—Bought of J. Carruthers & Co., Kingston, at 30 days, 20 bbls. No. 2 Sugar, 220 lbs. gross; tare, 15 lbs. each, at 9½c. Paid freight, $4.60. Sold R. D. Anglin, 1 bbl. Sugar, 220 lbs. gross; tare, 20 lbs. at 12c. Sold A. Overell, 2 lbs. Tea at 95c. Sold Wm. Drewry, 20 lbs. Dried Apples at 15c., 1 bbl. White Fish, $7. Sold Alex. Forin, 1 lb. Tea. 90c, 1 lb. Candies, 50c. *Cash Sales*, $186.

---

* Student's name.
NOTE.—Consider all sales effected on account, unless settlement be mentioned in the entry.

8—Bought of S. E. Shibley, on our Note at 60 days, with interest at 7 per cent. per annum, 100 bush. Apples at $1.25, 40 bush. Chili Potatoes at 50c., 50 bbls. Extra Flour at $6.10, 10 bbls. Mess Pork at $15.50. Accepted J. Carruthers & Co.'s draft at 30 days, from the 7th inst., for amount of invoice and ¼ per cent. exchange. Sold Joseph Allen, 2 bushels Apples at $1.50, 2 lbs. Rice at 25c., Paid for Repairing Store, $25. Remitted Rimmer, Gunn & Co., Cash for their invoice of the 3rd inst., less discount at 2½ per cent. Discount. $—; Cash remitted, $—. Received of A. Hamilton, on account, $20. Sold John Laird, on account, 25 lbs. Salmon at 12c., 10 lbs. Raisins at 25c. Sold T. B. Dean, on account. 14 lbs. Sugar at 12c., 5 lbs. Dried Apples at 20c. Deposited in Merchants' Bank, $1000. *Cash Sales*, $250.

9—Bought of Pitceathly & Kelso, Belleville, 20 bbls. Mackerel at $5, 6 bbls. Trout at $8. Paid Cash for Freight, $12.50. Received of O. Vandervoort, his Note at 90 days, bearing interest at 7 per cent., for goods sold him the 5th inst. Bought of Sinclair, Jack & Co., Montreal, 5 half chests " Uncolored Japan " Tea, 75, 76, 78, 77, 79 lbs. gross; tare 11 lbs. each, at 56c., 4 half-chests Young Hyson, 78, 86, 75, 73 lbs., tare 9 lbs. each, at 74c., 5 boxes Pr. of W. Tobacco, 120, 125, 130, 132, 136 lbs., tare 16 lbs. each, at 30c. Paid Freight in Cash, $13.60. Sold Joseph Allen, 1 chest Tea, 130 lbs., at 90c. Sold Wm. Drewry, 55 lbs. Pr. of W. Tobacco at 45c. Sold S. Edsall, 3 lbs. Gunpowder Tea at 90c.. 3 dozen Nutmegs at 15c., 1 bush. Onions at $1.75. *Cash Sales*, $238.

10—Had O. Vandervoort's Note discounted at Merchants' Bank at 8 per cent. per annum ; discount $—; Cash received, $—. Paid Cash for Sundry items of Expense $22.40. Sold John Laird, 12 lbs. Prunes at 20c., 5 lbs. Raisins at 25c. Sold T. B. Dean, 1 bush. Apples $1.50, 2 lbs. Raisins at 25c. Sold Alex. Forin, 2 lbs. Macaroni at 20c., 5 Jars Coffee at 80c. *Cash Sales*, $174.

11—Sent Pitceathly & Kelso our Note at 3 months, with interest at 8 per cent., for their invoice of the 9th inst. Paid Cash for Stationery and Stamps, $4.80. Sold W. Ponton, 15 gallons Syrup at 40c., 1 lb. Tobacco, 50c. Sold A. Overell, 4 lbs. Candy at 50c., 1 lb. SS. Almonds, 55c. Received of John Smith, in full of account, Cash, $50, and his Note, at 30 days, with interest, at 8 per cent. for balance, $—". *Cash Sales*, $276.

12—Bought of A. Urquhart & Co., Montreal, on 4 months, 14 casks Bordeaux Vinegar, 50 gals each, at 35c., 5 cases Eleme Figs, 430, 32 ; 426, 27 ; 298, 31 ; 460, 30 ; 389, 32 lbs. †, at 16c., 10 bags S. S. Almonds, 130,5 each, at 21c., 100 boxes Layer Raisins at $2.25, 5 bbls. Zante Currants, 256, 31 ; 293, 27 ; 269, 29; 256, 27 ; 298, 31 lbs. at 5¾ cents. Paid Freight in Cash $22.40. Sold T. B. Dean, 4 lbs. Tobacco at 50c., 2 dozen Nutmegs at 30c. Paid A. Overell Cash, $5, John Laird, $3.50, S. Edsall, $4.50, Alex. Forin, $3. *Cash Sales*, $236.

14—Received Cash in full for George Stinson's Note of October 10th, with interest. Sold Wm. Vickers, at 30 days, 10 boxes Layer Raisins at $2.50, 1 bbl. Zante Currants, 293, 27 at 6½c., 1 bag S. S. Almonds, 130,5 at 24c., 1 box Pr. of W. Tobacco, 120,15 at 35c. Sold W. Ponton, ¼ case Eleme Figs, 210 lbs., at 18c., 1 bbl. Zante Currants, 233 lbs., at 6½c. Sold A. Overell, 20 lbs. Prunes at 20c. *Cash Sales*, $249.

15—Received from W. Vickers, his Note at 30 days from the 14th inst., for amount of goods sold him. Bought for Cash, 10 reams of Wrapping Paper at 95c. Sold T. B. Dean, 4 lbs. Coffee at 30c. Received of W. Ponton, on account, Cash, $20, Wm. Drewry, $15, R. D. Anglin, $10. Paid S. Edsall, $9. Paid sundry expenses, $4.40. Had W. Flemming's Note of October 1st discounted at Merchants' Bank, at 7 per cent. per annum. *Cash Sales*, $275.

16—Bought of J. H. R. Molson & Bros., Montreal, on 3 months, 10 bbls. Crushed " A " Sugar, 246,19 ; 238,20 ; 246,21 ; 232,19 ; 268,17 ; 262.17 ; 238,18 ; 258,17 ; 293,22 ; 246,19 at 12½c.; 5 bbls. Golden Syrup, 43, 44, 45, 46, 49 gals. at 61c. Paid Freight on above, $5.60. Sold W. Ponton, 1 bbl. Syrup, 44 gals. at 70c. Sold S. Thompson, 15 gals. Vinegar at 40c. Discounted our Note favor W. Brown, at 7 per cent. for unexpired time. Paid T. Durham on account, $45. *Cash Sales*, $268.40.

17—Sold R. D. Anglin, 1 bbl. White Fish, $12, 2 lbs. Tobacco at 50c. *Cash Sales*, $196.

18—Deposited in Merchants' Bank, $850. Paid Cash for Tax Bill, $15, Gas, $25, Coal $20. Sold John Laird, 20 lbs. Sugar at 13c. Received from Jos. Allen, on acct., $50. *Cash Sales*, $245.

---

* As soon as an entry of this kind is posted, the account should be ruled up in the Ledger, in order that it may not be brought in the Trial Balance at the time of closing, or use letters to show balance as explained under the head " To show settlements in Ledger accts. without ruling."

† The large amounts are the number of lbs. gross, and the small amounts to the right, separated from them by commas, are the lbs. tare allowed.

19—Discounted Sinclair, Jack & Co.'s invoice of the 9th inst. at 3½ per cent., and remitted amount per Draft on Bank of Montreal, for which we paid Cash. Received from A. Hamilton Cash in full of account. *Cash Sales*, $210.40.
21—Sold Wm. Drewry, 40 lbs. Sugar-cured Ham at 15c., 20 lbs. Mess Pork at 12c. Deposited in Merchants' Bank, $400. *Cash Sales*, $260.
22—Paid John Laird, Cash, $4.50; S. Edsall, $2.40; Alex. Forin, $3.60; A. Overell, $2.00. *Cash Sales*, $174.60.
23—Received from Wm. Drewry, on acct., $10. Sold R. D. Anglin, 1 bbl. Sugar, 216 lbs., at 13½c. Sold Joseph Allen, 1 bbl. Mess Pork, $16. Sold T. B. Dean, 10 bush. Apples at $1.40. *Cash Sales*, $172.
24—Deposited in Merchants' Bank, $386. Accepted T. Durham's Draft on us at 30 days, favor J. W. Campion, for balance of his acct. Sold M. Lingham for Note 60 days, 1 cask Vinegar, 40 gals., at 40c., 10 bush. Apples at $1.45, 50 lbs. Sugar at 14c. *Cash Sales*, $268.
25—Paid for Repairing Store, $20 per Cheque. Lent G. J. Sherry, $120, for which he gave his Note at 30 days, with interest. Sold Wm. Drewry, 5 lbs. Japan Tea at 95c. *Cash Sales*, $164.
26—Student drew on private acct., $250. Deposited in Merchants' Bank, $430. Sold R. D. Anglin, 30 lbs. Sugar-cured Ham at 15c. *Cash Sales*, $167.
28—S. G. Beatty drew on private account $167, 1 lb. Tea, 75c., 3 bush. Apples at $1.25. *Cash Sales*, $146.
29—Bought of Ross & Davies, for Cash, 10 bbls. Herrings at $5.50. Sold W. Ponton, 25 lbs. Dried Cod at 12c. *Cash Sales*, $100.
30—Received of Joseph Allen, on acct., $75. Paid A. Overell, $4. *Cash Sales*, $176.
31—Paid Alex. Forin, $3; S. Edsall, $2. *Cash Sales*, $260.

Open a Salary Account, and pass the amount of clerks' salary, for month, to their credit. Make Rent Account Dr. to the landlord for one month's rent of store.

As you are now to admit a new partner, it is necessary to ascertain the condition of the business, which you may suppose has been running a year, balance the accounts, and bring down the balances, deal with Loss and Gain, and make out the Balance Sheet.

Allow a profit of 25 per cent. on sales, in order to ascertain the inventory of merchandise. *

Total Net Gain, $779.24.

JOURNAL DAY BOOK.

The form of Journal Day Book used in this Set is similar to that of Set IX., except that the outside column is used exclusively for credit sales of Merchandise. This form is very practical and extensively used in large retail houses. It combines the Journal and Sales Book in one, and affords an opportunity of posting the sales of Merchandise in monthly totals. The column containing credit sales is forwarded to the end of the month, and the Cash Sales, from the Cash Book, added to this amount, gives the total sales, as illustrated in the following form.

---

* In order to ascertain the value of unsold Merchandise, divide the credit side of Merchandise Account by $1.25, the amount realized for each dollar of the cost, and the quotient will be the cost price of all Merchandise sold. The cost of Merchandise sold subtracted from the cost of Merchandise bought, will leave the cost price of unsold Merchandise.

NOTE.—As an additional partner will be admitted into the business at the beginning of the ensuing month, it becomes necessary to post all transactions up to the present time, take off a Trial Balance and Balance Sheet, to ascertain the condition of the business, and close all accounts in the Ledger, but instead of transferring balances to Balance Account, bring them down under their respective accounts writing "To" or "By Balance" in black ink. Compare the balances brought down with the resource and liability columns of the balance sheet, with which they should agree. Never neglect this.

JOURNAL DAY BOOK—Set XI.

Hamilton, January 1st, 1889.

							Merchandise	
	———and S. G. Beatty have this day entered into co-partnership, to carry on the Retail Grocery business, as per Articles of Agreement, renting from William Lottridge, Store No. 62 MacNab St., at $600 per year.							
112	Sundries Dr. To Student .... For effects invested.			$7156	83			
C. B.	Cash Amount invested as per C.B.	$3800	00					
114	Merchandise " " Inventory	2500	00					
115	Bills Rec. G. Stinson's Note as per B.B....	500	00					
118	Interest accrued on above Note to date	6	83					
115	A. Hamilton owes on account..............	250	00					
115	John Smith " "	100	00					
	"							
112	Student Dr. To Sundries................... For liabilities assumed by firm.			775	00			
115	Bills Pay., Note favor W. Brown for..					500		
120	T. Durham, bal. of acct. assumed					275		
	"							
113	Sundries Dr. To S. G. Beatty.............. For effects invested.					7250		
C. B.	Cash As per C.B.....................	5500	00					
115	Bills Rec., W. Fleming's Note as per B.B....	1750	00					
	"							
	Engaged A.Overell, A. Forin, S. Edsall & John Laird as clerks, at $300 each per year.							
	2							
121	Wm. Drewry Dr. to Mdse. For 3 lbs. Japan Tea at 70c...............			3	60		2	10
	" 10 " Soft Yellow Sugar at 9c.........							90
	" 1 " Cloves							60
123	R. D. Anglin, Dr. to Mdse. For 10 lbs. Java Coffee at 40c.............			11	10		4	00
	" 2 bxs. Layer Raisins at $3.25..........						6	50
	" 2 lbs. Pepper at 30c..................							60
	3							
121	Joseph Allen, Dr. to Mdse. For 100 lbs. Dry Cod at 6c...............			7	26		6	00
	" 12 " Crushed " A " Sugar at 10¼c..						1	26
	5							
125	S. Edsall, Dr. to Mdse. For 5 gals. Standard Syrup at 50c.........			3	50		2	50
	" 10 lbs. Sugar at 10c						1	00
	"							
124	O. Vandervoort, Dr. to Mdse. For 2 bbls. Golden Syrup, 72 gals., at 45c..			95	40			
	" 2 " Crushed Sugar at $25..........						32	40
	" 4 boxes Val. Raisins at $3.25..........						50	00
	"						13	00
130	W. Ponton Dr. to Mdse. For 5 lbs. Ground Ginger at 30c..........			4	15		1	50
	" 1 lb. " Pepper................							25
	" 12 lbs. Prunes at 20c....						2	40
	Amounts forwarded	$15306	84	$15181	83		$125	01

NOTE.—With each entry in the Journal throughout the XI Set, there must be full explanations.

Hamilton, January 5th, 1889.

							Merchandise.	
	Brought forward	$15306	84	$15181	83	125	01
115	Bills Receivable Dr.	100	00				
	To A. Hamilton			100	00		
	Received his Note as per B.B.(No.—)on acct. 7						
123	R. D. Anglin Dr. To Mdse.	24	00				
	For 1 bbl. Sugar, 200 lbs. net, at 12c...... "					24	00
114	Merchandise Dr. To Sundries.	1801	19				
	Invoices from the Invoice Book. Folio 108						
140	To Rimmer, Gunn & Co., invoice of Jan. 3.			199	65		
142	" James Gunner & Co., " " 5.			70	00		
141	" J. Carruthers & Co. " " 7.			389	50		
116	" Bills Payable, " " 8.			605	00		
146	" Pitceathly & Kelso, " " 9.			148	00		
349	" Sinclair, Jack & Co., " " "			389	04		
						149	01
114	*Merchandise Cr. by Sundries.			*149	01		
	*Red Ink.	$17232	03	17232	03		

The foregoing form is considered sufficient to illustrate the mode of entering transactions in this Journal. It will be observed that Cash transactions are not entered here, but carried into the Cash Book. Purchases of Merchandise are entered first in the Invoice Book and Journalized at the end of the month.

INVOICE BOOK.

This is a book in which to copy all bills of goods purchased, in order to have a book record of the details of such transactions, in case the original invoice should be lost or destroyed. This is practised by some merchants; but it is as convenient, and saves a great amount of writing, to paste the original invoices into a book made of some description of paper of a larger size than the invoices. By means of an index to this book, it will be found more convenient to refer to the original invoices than by seeking them from files.

In some business houses, where the invoices received are long, they are filed and numbered, and only an abstract of them entered in this book, with the number for reference. In whatever form the Invoice Book is kept, every entry affecting the debit side of Merchandise account should originate here; when this is done, it becomes a direct and perfect check upon the Dr. side of Merchandise account in the Ledger. This book is journalized at the close of the month, under the heading "Merchandise Dr. to Sundries," or you may post directly from it into the Ledger. In that case rule dollar and cent columns on the right, fold each Invoice neatly up to the name of the seller, write the explanation underneath each, carry the amount into the column, unless bought for Cash, carry forward each column. The footing at the mouth is the amount to make Merchandise Dr. for. After debiting Mdse., credit each Invoice to the individuals or Bills Payable, as the case may be, and put the Ledger folio on each Invoice in red ink.

Merchandise purchased for Cash is entered in this book, but posted from the Cash Book.

When a Cash purchase is entered, mark "C. B." in the folio column opposite the name of the seller, in order that it may not be journalized with the other transactions, and thereby posted twice.

The two sets of columns for dollars and cents on the right are used for extensions and sums total of purchases on time; a third, or inside, column may be ruled for Cash purchases.

Invoices of goods to be sold on commission are not entered in this book; they should either be kept in a separate book, or a memorandum of them made in the Day Book, and the invoices filed away for reference. Merchants who import goods from other countries keep a Foreign Invoice Book, in which they enter all goods purchased in foreign countries, and a Domestic Invoice Book for copies of all invoices of Merchandise purchased from persons in their own country.

Want of space prevents us from giving more than a few of the first purchases in the form of Invoice Book below; but those given are considered sufficient to show how the entries should be made.

When an invoice in a foreign currency is received, you may deal with it in two ways. In the case of a Sterling Invoice, for example, you may count it at the present rate of exchange, debit Mdse. account, and credit the firm from which you purchased; and if, when you settle for it, exchange is higher than you estimated, charge Mdse. or Discount with the difference, or if it is lower, credit it. The other way is to post the Invoice, leaving the figures blank until you have ascertained the actual cost.

INVOICE BOOK—Set XI.

Hamilton, January 1st, 1889.

Marks.	Nos.	D. B.				
			Mdse. invested by Student as per Inventory Book,		2500	00
			———3———			
		√	Rimmer, Gunn & Co., Montreal.			
			5 bags Java Coffee,			
			lbs. tare.			
			142—15 over 413—45			
			135—15 117—15			
			136—15 150—15			
			——— ———			
			413—45 680—75=605 at 33c.		199	65
			4 months' credit, or 2½ per cent. off for Cash.			
			———5———			
		√	James Gunner & Co., Montreal.			
			10 bbls. Canso Herrings at $3.50	35		
			5 " Round Herrings at $3.00	15		
			4 " White fish at $5.00	20	70	00
			4 months' credit.			
			———7———			
		√	J. Carruthers & Co., Kingston.			
			20 bbls. No. 2 Sugar, 4400 lbs. gross,			
			300 " tare,			
			———			
			30 days' credit, 4100 " net, at 9½c.		389	50
			———8———			
		√	S. E. Shibley, Belleville.			
			100 bus. Winter Apples at $1.25	125		
			40 " Chili Potatoes " 0.50	20		
			50 bbls. Extra Flour " 6.10	305		
			10 " Mess Pork " 15.50	155	605	00
			Note at 60 days.			
			———9———			
		√	Pitceathly & Kelso, Belleville.			
			20 bbls. Mackerel at $5	100		
			6 " Trout " 8	48	148	00
			3 months' credit.			
			———"———			
		√	Sinclair, Jack & Co., Montreal.			
			5 half-chests Uncolored Japan Tea,			
			lbs. tare.			
			75—11 over 229—33			
			76—11 77—11			
			78—11 79—11			
			——— ———			
			229—33 385—55=330 lbs. at 56c.		184	80
			4 half-chests Young Hyson,			
			78—9 over 239—27			
			86—9 73—9			
			75—9			
			——— ———			
			239—27 312—36=276 lbs. at 74c.		204 24	389 04
			2 months' credit.			
			*Total purchases, Journal, page 107.			1801 19

* Red Ink

CASH BOOK.

(See form on next two pages.)

The only distinction between the following form of Cash Book and that of Set IX. is the adoption of a greater number of special columns.

This form of Cash Book will be found applicable to almost any kind of business. The columns which we use for Merchandise, Interest, Bills Receivable, Expense and Freight, may be used for any other titles. Every business has particular accounts from which its principal income is derived, and for which its chief expenditure is paid. These accounts must always create a great number of entries, and any mode of posting these entries in accumulated amounts must materially diminish the amount of writing in the Ledger. The number of special columns used, and the titles adopted, depend upon the nature of the business. The special columns on the Dr. side should be headed with accounts for which Cash is frequently received, and the special columns on the Cr. side with accounts for which Cash is frequently paid.

It will be found practical and very convenient to use a column on each side for the Bank account, and put all bank transactions through the Cash Book as shown below. The mode of entering transactions in this book and posting therefrom has already been explained on pages 86 and 87.

After drawing the lines and posting the special columns, they may be entered in the extension to the " Sundries " column, with red ink. Observe closely the style of ruling adopted for closing this book, in the following form, and adhere to it throughout your work, as neatness and uniformity in this matter add greatly to the appearance of books, and are of more importance in preserving accuracy and order than many persons imagine.

METHOD OF KEEPING THE BANK ACCOUNT IN THE CASH BOOK.

The Bank Account is frequently kept in the Cash Book, and not opened in the Ledger at all, and by this means a saving of time and labor is effected. You will require a special column on each side,—the one on the Dr. side for Cheques or Notes, and Drafts charged to you in the Bank; and the one on the Cr. side for Deposits, Proceeds of Discounts or Collections.

When entering Cheques, Notes or Drafts charged to you in the Bank, don't write anything in the space where the names of accounts are usually placed, as you have to make no posting to the Ledger; but in the explanation space write, for example, Cheque 89, or, Note No. 87, and carry the amount into its own column; you will then make the regular Cash entry for Cash paid out.

When entering Deposits, or Proceeds of Discounts, don't write anything in the space where the names of the accounts are usually placed, but in the explanation space write Deposit, or Proceeds of Note No. 129, and carry the amount into its own column. For a deposit you would of course make no other entry, as you are simply moving the money from your own office to the Bank for safe keeping, but for a discount or collection you would make the regular Cash entry that would be made if the Proceeds were handed over to you in Cash.

EXAMPLES.—Suppose the following: you issue Cheque 89, for $150, to John Sutherland in full of account; the Bank has charged a Note for $153.

You deposit $397; you discount a Note for $120, the Proceeds $118.20 are left in Bank.

Dr. *Cash.* *Cr.*

			Bank.						Bank.		
		Bal. from last mo. $890						Bal. in Bank from last month.	$200	00	
N'v	8				N'v	8		By J. Sutherland in full of ac.			$150 00
	"	Check 89	$150	00		"		Bills Pay. Retired No. 87.			153 00
	"	Note 87	153	00		"		Deposit	397	00	
	"	To B. Rec. Dis. No. 129		120		"		Proc. of Note 129.	118	20	
		Balance in Bank	412	20		"		By Discount On Note 129.			1 80
		Cash Bal. from last mo.		890				Balance on hand and in Bank.			705 20
			$715	20	$1010				$715	20	$1010 00

I

Dr.   *Cash.*   CASH BOOK—

1889.	F.				Mdse.	In'st.	Bills Rec.	Sundries.
Jan. 1	D. B.	To Student,	Amount invested,					$3800 00
" "	D. B.	" S. G. Beatty,	" "					5500 00
" 2	√	" Mdse	Sales from Petty C.B.,		$ 96 00			
" 3	"	" "	" " "		110 00			
" 5	√	" "	" " "		145 00			
" 7	√	" "	" " "		186 00			
" 8	√	" Discount	On R. G. & Co.'s invoice,			4 99		
" "	98	" A. Hamilton,	On account,					20 00
" "	√	" Mdse.,	Sales from Petty C.B.,		250 00			
" 9	√	" "	" " "		238 00			
" 10	√	" Bills Rec.,	Had O.V.'s Note discount'd				95 40	
" "	√	" Mdse.,	This day's sales, P.C.B.,		174 00			
" 11	99	" John Smith,	Part Payment of account,					50 00
" "	"	" Mdse.,	This day's sales, P.C.B.,		276 00			
" 12	√	" "	" " "		236 00			
" 14	√	" Bills Rec.,	G. S.'s Note of Oct. 11 (B. R., No.—)				500 00	
" "	√	" Interest,	On above Note to date,			7 83		
" "	"	" Mdse.,	This day's sales, P.C.B.,		249 00			
" 15	94	" W. Ponton,	On account,					20 00
" "	90	" W. Drewry,	"					15 00
" "	87	" R. D. Anglin,	"					10 00
" "	√	" Bills Rec.,	W. Fleming's Note disc'ted				1750 00	
" "	√	" Mdse.,	This day's sales, P.C.B.,		275 00			
" 16	√	" Discount,	On our Note, favor W. Brown at 7 per cent.			8 65		
" "	√	" Mdse.,	This day's sales, P.C.B.,		268 40			
" 17	√	" "	" " "		196 00			
" 18	88	" Jos. Allen,	On account,					50 00
" "	√	" Mdse.,	This day's sales, P.C.B.,		245 00			
	52		Mdse., Cr. By Cash,		2944 40			*2944 40
	58		Interest, " "			21 47		* 21 47
	54		Bills Rec., " "				2345 40	*2345 40
	15	.	Total to Dr., " "					$ 14776 27

When discounting a number of notes or acceptances at the same time, and making the entries in the Cash Book, the following is a good form:

                         $500. $780. $390.50 $560.20 $300 $2530.70
Jan. 3.   To Bills Receivable   Dis. Nos.   438,   440,   443,   450,   451,

Then make entries on the other side of the C.B. for the discount, and the proceeds left in the bank.

* Extensions to Sundries column, Red Ink.

SET XI.

Cash. *Cr.*

1889.	F.			Exp'se.	In'st.	Freight.	Sundries.
Jan. 3	✓	By Freight,	On R. G. & Co.'s Invoice,			4 25	
" "	65	" Mer. Bank,	Deposited,				1500
" 5	✓	" Freight,	On J. G. & Co.'s Invoice,			2 50	
" "	✓	" Expense,	Set of Books for Store,	10 50			
" 7	✓	" Freight,	On J. C. & Co.'s Invoice,			4 60	
" 8	✓	" Expense.	Repairing Window of Shop,	25 00			
" "	81	" R. G. & Co.,	In full for Invoice 3rd inst.				199 65
" "	65	" Mer. Bank,	Deposited,				1000
" 9	✓	" Freight,	On P. & K.'s Invoice,			12 50	
" "	✓	" "	On S. J. & Co.'s Invoice,			13 60	
" 10	✓	" Discount,	On V.'s Note at 8 per cent.		26		
" "	✓	" Expense,	Sundry Items per P.C.B.,	22 40			
" 11	✓	" "	Station'ry,$4; p.stamps,80c	4 80			
" 12	✓	" Freight,	On Urquhart & Co.'s Inv.			22 40	
" "	74	" A. Overell,	On account of Salary,				5
" "	73	" John Laird,	" "				2 50
" "	70	" S. Edsall,	" "				4 50
" "	75	" A. Forin,	" "				3
" 15	✓	" Expense,	Wrapping paper, 10 rms. at 95c.	9 50			
" "	70	" S. Edsall,	On account,				9 00
" "	✓	" Expense,	Sundry items, P.C.B.,	4 40			
" "	✓	" Discount,	On Fleming's Note at 7 p.c.		26 88		
" 16	✓	" Freight,	On J.H.R. Molson Bros'Inv			5 60	
" "	56	" Bills Pay.,	Retired B.P., No.—				500 00
" "	81	" T. Durham,	On account,				45 00
" 18	65	" Mer. Bank,	Deposited,				850 00
" "	✓	" Expense,	Taxes,$15 ; Gas,$25 ; Coal,$20	60 00			
	61		Expense Dr. To Cash,	136 60			* 136 60
	58		Interest " "		27 14		* 27 14
	60		Freight "			65 45	* 65 45
	51		Total to Cr. of "				4348 84
			* *Balance in hand,*				*10427 43
							$14776 27

When retiring a number of notes or acceptances at the same time, and making the entries in the Cash Book, the following is a good form :

                                          $500 $397.50 $430.20 $600 $200 $2127.70
Jan. 3 By Bills Payable   Retired Nos.   183,   190,   195,   184,   191.

* Extensions to Sundries, Red Ink.

SECOND MONTH'S BUSINESS—Set XI.

February 1st, 1889.

We have this day admitted J. W. Dickie as partner, who invests, according to Articles of Agreement, Cash, $7500.

Bought of Carr, Chase & Raymond, Boston, 100 half Chests E. B. Souchong Tea, 20 lbs. net each, at 75c., U. S. currency; gold, $1.10.* Paid Customs Duty, 10c. per lb. Freight, $12.50. Received of Wm. Drewry, on account, $30. *Cash Sales,* $87.

2—Joseph Allan pays his account in full to date by contra account against S. G. Beatty, $15.60; Cash for balance. Paid S. Edsall, Cash, $3.50. *Cash Sales,* $145.60.

4—Sold Wm. Drewry, on acct., 14 lbs. Sugar at 10c.; 1 box Soap, $2; 2 lbs. Green Tea at 75c. Sold R. D. Anglin, on account, 1 box Candles, 50 lbs. at 10½c.; 10 gals. Syrup at 65c. *Cash Sales,* $176.

5—Bought of Rimmer, Gunn & Co., of Montreal, on four months, 100 bbls. Sup. Family Flour at $5.25; 5 casks Soda Ash, 1540,36; 1532,29; 1564,37; 1429,18; 1612,43 lbs., at 3½c. Paid Freight, $56. Sold W. Ponton, 1 bbl. Family Flour, $6.50; 1 box Soap, $2.25. *Cash Sales,* $135.

6—Paid sundry Expenses, $7.50. Sold R. D. Anglin, on acct., 1 bush. Dried Apples, $4.25; 20 lbs. Prunes at 20c. Paid Alex. Forin, Cash, $3.50. Sold W. Raymore, on account, 50 lbs. Sugar-Cured Ham at 17c., 3 lbs. Green Tea at 90c., 10 gals. Vinegar at 26c. *Cash Sales,* $174.

7—S. G. Beatty draws on private account, Cash, $50; 3 lbs. Tea at 60c.; 20 lbs. Sugar at 9½c.; 2 bbls. Flour at $6.25. Received of R. D. Anglin, on account, $25. Lent W. R. Barber, $150. Paid our Note favor S. E. Shibley, less discount for unexpired time. Remitted A. Urquhart & Co., a Draft on Bank of Montreal for amount of their Invoice of January 12th, less 2½ per cent. discount; Paid Cash for Draft and ¼ per cent. Exchange. *Cash Sales,* $146.

8—Bought of Dobson & Sons, Port Hope, on 60 days, 200 dozen Corn Brooms at $3.25, 50 dozen at $2.95, and 20 dozen at $4; paid Freight, $24.50. Sold Joseph Allan, 10 dozen Brooms at $3.50; 2 chests Y. H. Tea, 67,6½; 74,7½ lbs. at 75c. Paid for coal, $26. Paid W. Lottridge, for 2 months' rent of store per Check. Deposited in Merchants' Bank, $490. *Cash Sales,* $156.

9—Shipped per G.T.R. and consigned to C. Hutchinson, Toronto, to be sold on our acct. and risk, 100 half Chests E. B. Souchong Tea, 20 lbs. net each, at 79c.; † paid Freight on the same per Check, $15. T. B. Dean pays his acct. in full to date by contra account for repairing store, $4, and Cash for the balance. Sold S. Thomson, on account, 30 Boxes Bloom Raisins at $3. *Cash Sales,* $179.60.

11—Bought of David Cheesman & Co., London, on Note at 3 months, 16 boxes Mould Candles, 58 lbs. each, at 11¼c.; 30 boxes Bloom Raisins at $3; 2 chests Y. H. Tea, 96,7½; 110,12¼ lbs. at 69c. Paid Freight, $12. Deposited in Merchants' Bank, $1250. Sold W. Drewry, on acct., 1 box Candles, 58 lbs. at 13½c. *Cash Sales,* $172.

12—Received of Thomas Moore & Co., Toronto, to be sold on their account and risk, 100 brls. Flour invoiced at $6.50. † Paid Freight on the same per Check, $15. Paid sundry items of Expense, $9.50. Received of W. Raymore, on account, $5. Paid John Laird, $4. *Cash Sales,* $79.

13—Received of John Smith, Cash in full for his Note and Interest, due this day. Received of R. D. Anglin, on acct., $12. Paid A. Overell, Cash, $3. Received of S. Thompson his Note at 2 mos. in full of acct. *Cash Sales,* $87.

14—Sold Conger Bros., for their Note at 3 mos., 50 bbls. Flour, from Moore & Co.'s Consignment at $8. S. G. Beatty draws on private account, Cash, $40. Received from C. Hutchinson an

---

* Divide the amount of the invoice by 110 to convert it to gold value, as you cannot keep books in two currencies. Charge duties to Merchandise account, as they are part of the cost.

† The Freight on purchases might also be charged to Merchandise, but it is usual to keep a Freight account which may be closed into Merchandise, or, as we do, into Loss and Gain.

Amounts paid for freight on Consignments or shipments are not charged to Freight account but to the particular consignment or shipment.

"Acccount Sales" of the Mdse. shipped him the 9th inst., with net proceeds, $1580.50, by Sight Draft on Bank of Toronto; there being no agency of which in this place, it costs ¼ per cent. for collection. *Cash sales*, $156.

15—Sold R. Morris & Co., on their Acceptance at 30 days, the balance of Thos. Moore & Co's Consignment at $8 per barrel. Paid sundry expenses per Check, $36. Having become dissatisfied with our clerk, Jno. Laird, we settle with him in full to date and discharge him. *Cash sales*, $196.

16—Received Cash in full for W. Vicker's Note due this day. Closed Thomas Moore & Co's Consignment of the 12th inst. and rendered them an "Account Sales." Charges posted, $15. Charges for Storage, Cooperage, &c., unposted, $12.60; Commission 3½ per cent· on sales ; Moore & Co.'s net proceeds remitted by Draft on Montreal Bank. *Cash sales*, $196.

18—Deposited in Merchants' Bank, $750. Bought of J. Carruthers & Co., Kingston, on our Acceptance at 90 days, one hhd. Sugar,,1146 lbs., tare 10 per cent., at 8¼c ; 100 boxes Soda Biscuit at $2.50; 50 boxes Wine do. at $2.75. Paid Freight,'$14. Received Cash for A. Hamilton's Note with Interest for time overdue. Sold W. Raymore, on acct., 60 lbs. Cheese at 12½c ; 1 box Raisins, $3.25. *Cash Sales*, $219.60.

19—Sold John Templeton, 40 doz. Brooms at $4, for which he paid by contra acct. against Student $96 ; Cash for balance. Received from R. Mason & Son, London, to be sold on their acct. and risk, 50 bbls. Sugar, invoiced at $20; paid freight, $36. Remitted James Gunner & Co., Bank Draft to balance acct. Exchange ¼ per cent., paid Cash. *Cash Sales*, $158.

20—Paid Sundry Expenses, $5.50. Assumed the Sugar received from R. Mason & Son the 19th inst. at $25 per bbl., and shipped the same to Frank Smith & Co., Toronto, to be sold on our acct. and risk. Paid for Insurance on it $15 per Check. *Cash Sales*, $268.

21—Sold R. German, on acct., 2 bbls. White Fish at $10 ; 1 bbl. Vinegar, 42 gals., at 47c. Closed R. Mason & Son's Consignment and rendered an "Account Sales." Our Charges for Storage, &c., 3c., per bbl.; Commission 3 per cent. on sales ; R. Mason & Son's net proceeds, $——, settled by note at 60 days. *Cash Sales*, $216.

22—Bought of David Cheeseman & Co, London, on note at three months, 1 case Smyrna Figs, 165 boxes, 346 lbs., tare 73 lbs., at 14½c.; 1 case Eleme Figs, 40 boxes, 126,37 lbs, at 12½c. Paid Freight, $16.50. *Cash Sales*, $149.

23—Received advice from Frank Smith & Co., that they have re-shipped our Consignment of the 20th inst. to Ross & Davies, Belleville, having charged us $15 for receiving and re-shipping. Sold S. Edsall,·16 lbs. Sugar at 12c. ; 1 box Mould Candles, 58 lbs., at 12½c. *Cash Sales*, $140.

25—S. G. Beatty has taken, on private acct., 20 gals. Syrup at 50c., 10 lbs. Raisins at 30c· Paid Cash $4, for repairing counter in store. Student has taken, on private acct., 10 lbs. Figs at 12c., 3 lbs. Rice at 10c., 2 lbs. Prunes at 17c. *Cash Sales*, $163.

26—*Remitted Carr, Chase & Raymond, Boston, a Draft on First National Bank, payable in United States Currency, in full for their Invoice of the 1st inst.; Paid Cash for Draft and ¼ per cent. Exchange ; Gold, $1.15. Paid Cash for our Note of January 24th. *Cash Sales*, $119.

27—Deposited in Bank, $875. Paid Alex. Forin, Cash, $5. *Cash Sales*, $210.

28—Received of Ross & Davies, Belleville, an "Account Sales" of our Shipment to them by Frank Smith & Co., with net proceeds, $1360, by Draft on Merchants Bank, which we leave on deposit. *Cash Sales*, $146.80.

Inventory to be found same as in first month.
Total net gain, $1049.52.

NOTE.—As you have completed arrangements for admitting another partner into the firm at the beginning of March, and changing from a Retail to a Wholesale business, it is necessary to make out a Balance Sheet, and carry the result of the Loss and Gain Account to the accounts of the partners.

Close the Books the same as at the end of January, and bring down the balances. Compare the balances brought down with the resources and liabilities columns of the balance sheet.

---

* When these goods were received on February 1st, gold was at prem. of 10 per cent., and you converted the invoice at that rate into gold by dividing the amount by 1.10 ; now, when you come to remit, gold has gone up to 115, and it will cost less to pay for the goods than you anticipated. Divide the amount of the invoice by 1.15, the result will be the amount to remit· Next find ¼ of one per cent. of the latter amount, which is the bank commission. The entries will be, Cash by Carr, Chase & Raymond for the amount originally placed to their credit, and Cash to Discount (or Merchandise) for the difference between that amount and the actual cost.

REMARKS ON THE THIRD MONTH'S BUSINESS.

A new and important feature in this month is the changing of the business, and the introduction of the Sales Book. The books used after the change of business are, the JOURNAL, CASH BOOK, INVOICE BOOK, SALES BOOK, BILL BOOK and LEDGER. A form of the Sales Book, and explanations thereon, will be found at the end of this month's business. The other books are kept the same as heretofore, but without the special Mdse. Col. in the Journal.

The method of using these books, as books of original entry, has many advantages over consecutive entries in the Day Book, and is adopted in the majority of large business houses, where it is essential to divide labor, and avoid unnecessary writing. For instance, one clerk may keep the Invoice Book, another the Sales Book, another the Cash Book, and each book be so kept that posting may be done directly to the Ledger, instead of passing the transactions through the Journal. The separate departments of a large business may thus receive such special record as will present the facts in their clearest light. Thus, if any particular information is desired respecting purchases, all the facts can be obtained at once from the Invoice Book; and in the same manner, the facts and conditions of sales can be obtained from the Sales Book, the receipts and disbursements of cash from the Cash Book, etc.

The only objection to posting from special books directly to the Ledger is the tendency to debit and credit the same account *twice*. In order to avoid confusion in this respect, and to make the Invoice and Sales Books as plain as possible, journalize in one entry at the end of each month the entries from them; but post the Cash transactions directly from the Cash Book to the Ledger.

THIRD MONTH'S BUSINESS.—SET XI.

March 1, 1889.

We have this day closed our Retail business, and formed a partnership with P. V. Dorland for the purpose of conducting the Wholesale Grocery and Shipping business, renting from A. Diamond, store No. 96 James street, at $800 per annum. Gains and losses to be divided in proportion to capital invested.

P. V. DORLAND invests Stock of Groceries as per Inventory, $19,500; Cash, $6,000; Store Fixtures, $620. The firm assumes for him a Note of $1000, favor of George Lewis, dated February 28th at 3 months.

Engaged Thomas Way as Accountant at $900 per year.

Received from W. Drewry, Cash in full of account. Bought of Rimmer, Gunn & Co., Montreal, on 4 months, 12 bags Rio Coffee, 136,12; 143,13½; 127,11½; 128,12; 142,14; 147,14½; 146,12; 139,11½; 138,12; 152,16½; 146,14½; 156,16½ lbs., at 32c.; 10 chests Gunpowder Tea, 150,16; 148,14; 126,12½; 147,13½; 142,16; 145,14½; 156,17½; 143,21; 134,14; 144,12½ lbs., at 60c.; 15 casks Bordeaux Vinegar, 46 gallons each, at 35c. Sold Smith & Cook, Brockville, on their Note at 60 days, 4 bags Rio Coffee, 136,12; 127,11½; 128,12; 129,11½ lbs., at 40c.; 5 barrels Extra Flour at $7.50; 2 barrels Mess Pork at $14 50.

2—Bought of J. H. R. Molson & Bros., Montreal, on 3 months, 100 barrels Superfine Flour at $6.50; 10 boxes "Western Leaf" Tobacco, 115,10; 125,12½; 119,13; 117,11½; 116,12; 115, 9½; 118,10; 120,12½; 116,14; 113,10¼ lbs., at 42c. Received of W. Ponton Cash in full of account. Sold J. Waltham & Co., Guelph, on account, 20 barrels Apples at $3; 10 barrels Flour at $8.*

3—Received of R. D. Anglin his Note at 3 months with interest at 7 per cent. in full of account to date. Bought of J. Morris & Co., on our acceptance at 90 days, 800 barrels White Fish at $4.50; 50 barrels Mackerel at $6; 1000 lbs. White Cod at $4.75 per cwt.

4—Shipped per G.T.R., and consigned to W. R. Ross & Co., Montreal, to be sold on joint acct. and risk, each equally interested, 400 barrels White Fish at $5 per bbl. Paid Cash for repairing Store Fixtures, $75; Sundry Expenses, $24.

---

* Sales on account are intended to run 30 days, unless otherwise specified.

115

5—Bought of John Cook, Belleville, on 3 months' credit, 200 barrels Trout at $5.75; 60 barrels White Fish at $4.50. Paid Freight, $30. S. G. Beatty, with the consent of his partners, this day disposes of his entire interest in the business to W. B. Robinson for a certain consideration. * Received from V. Hudson, Montreal, to be sold on joint account of shipper and ourselves, ½ each, 600 barrels Superior Extra Flour at $6.50. Paid charges on same per Check on Merchants' Bank, $49.50. Sold Massie & Peterson, on their Note at 2 mos., 300 barrels Superfine Flour from Mdse. Co. " A." at $7.80.

7—Sold S. Moore, James Street, for his Acceptance at 2 months, 50 brls. Trout at $6.50; 20 brls. White Fish at $5.50; 5 bags Rio Coffee, 136,12; 152,16; 147,14½; 138,12; 156,16½ lbs., at 40c. W. B. Robinson withdraws on account, Cash, $40.

8—Received Cash in full for G. J. Sherry's Note of January 25th, with interest to date. Sold J. Farmer, Macnab Street, for Sight Draft on F. Stinson, a bill of Mdse. amounting to $540.† Sold for Cash the balance of Flour belonging to Mdse. Co. " A." at $7.90 per bbl.

9—Deposited in Merchants' Bank, $1200. Received from J. Wilson, Goderich, to be sold on joint account of shipper, George Moore and ourselves, each ½, 1000 barrels Salt at $1.50. Paid Freight and sundry expenses on same per Check, $47.50. Sold R. Eastman, on account, 500 barrels Salt from Mdse. Co. " B," at $2.20 per barrel.

10—‡Closed Mdse. Co. " A." and rendered Consignor an Account Sales. Our Charges, 3c. per bbl.; Commission, 2½ per cent. on sales. Bought of J. M. Hawley, 1000 bush. Barley at $1.10. Gave in payment Draft at 30 days on R. Eastman for amount of his account. Paid Freight, $50. Sold N. Boulter, for his Note at three months, the balance of Salt belonging to Mdse. Co. " B," at $2.15 per bbl.

11—Shipped to P. G. Close & Co., Toronto, to be sold on joint account, 150 boxes Bloom Raisins at $3; 125 boxes Layer Raisins at $2.40; 75 boxes Valencia Raisins at $3.25. Paid Freight on same, $15.30. Received from W. R. Ross & Co., an Account sales of our Shipment to them on the 4th inst., our net proceeds, $1060, received per note at 4 months.

12—Closed Mdse. Co. " B," and rendered Consignor and George Moore, each, an Account Sales. Our charges, 3½c. per bbl.; commission, 2½c. per cent. on sales. Remitted net proceeds to each per Check on Merchants' Bank, marked payable at par.

14—Remitted J. Wilson our Note at 3 mos. for our interest in Mdse. Co. received the 9th. inst. Had Massie & Peterson's Note of the 5th inst. discounted at Merchants' Bank, at 7 per cent. per annum. Received of R. Town, Kingston, to be sold on joint account, each equally interested, 800 barrels of Apples at $3. Paid charges on same, $75.

15—Shipped John Cook, Belleville, to be sold on our account and risk, 115 barrels Trout at $6.25; 40 barrels White Fish at $5. Paid Freight on same, $18.75.

16—Had S. Moore's Acceptance of the 7th inst. discounted at Merchants' Bank at 7 per cent. per annum. Sold T. Farmer, for Sight Draft on E. T. Hamley, Mdse. amounting to $1200.

17—Sold H. R. Mountain, London, on 30 days' credit, 150 bbls. Extra Flour at $7.25; 200 bbls. Spring Flour at $7; 1000 bbls. Goderich Salt at $1.50; 1000 lbs. Dry Cod, at $5 per cwt.

18—Received of John Cook, Belleville, an Account Sales of our shipment to him on the 15th inst.; our proceeds, $525.50, which he has entered to our credit.

19—Paid sundry expenses, $26. Remitted Rimmer, Gunn & Co., Draft on Montreal Bank, in full for their Invoice of the 1st inst., less 2½ per cent. discount; paid Cash for Draft and ¼ per cent. Exchange.

21—Shipped J. Griffith & Co., Toronto, to be sold on joint acct. and risk of ourselves, consignees and A. Brown, each ⅓, 10 hhds. Sugar, 11,200 lbs. net, at 8½c. Paid Freight on same, $44.50.

22—Had R. D. Anglin's Note of the 3rd inst. discounted at Merchants' Bank, at 7 per cent. per annum. Sold A. B. Jones, Toronto, for Cash, 10 bbls. White Fish at $5.50; 12 bbls. Spring Flour at $7.80; 4 hhds. Soft Yellow Sugar, 1420 lbs. net each, at 8½c.

23—J. A. Mathewson & Co., Montreal, and ourselves, have entered into an agreement to buy and sell Merchandise on joint account, each firm's interest in such speculations to be equal.

They now advance us Cash, $2000, to be invested in Goderich Salt under this agreement.§

---

* Joint Shipments and Merchandise Cos. are fully explained at pages 92 to 95.

† In transactions of this kind, where the articles are not stated, you are required to supply them. See this entry in Sales Book.

‡ Study thoroughly the method of making the Account sales entry or closing entry of Mdse. Co. at page 94; also read the last paragraph on page 95.

§ This amount has been placed in our hands for investment, we therefore treat it as a simple loan, and credit J. A. Mathewson & Co. for it.

24—Sold I. C. Chilman, on his Note at 3 months, 120 bbls. Extra Super Flour at $6.15; 50 bbls. Super Extra at $6.45; 50 bbls. Spring Extra at $5.70. Sold W. H. Graham, for Cash, an invoice amounting to $730.

25—Received from John Cook his Draft at 30 days on P. Miles for $1000. Received from H. R. Mountain, Sight Draft on L. W. Yeomans for $100. Received from J. Waltham & Co., Cash in full of account.

26—Remitted J. H. R. Molson & Bros., Draft on Montreal Bank for their Invoice of the 2nd instant less 2½ per cent.; paid Cash for Draft, and ¼ per cent. Exchange. Paid sundry Expenses, $10.

27—Had N. Boulter's Note of the 10th inst. discounted at Merchants' Bank at 8 per cent. per annum, and proceeds left to credit. Received Cash in full for M. Lingham's Note of January 24th.

29—*Had our Accommodation Note, at 3 months, drawn to the order of J. W. Parker, endorsed by him, discounted at Merchants' Bank at 7 per cent. per annum, net proceeds of which amount to $1260.

30—Paid our Note of Feb. 11th, favor D. Cheeseman & Co., less discount at 8 per cent. for unexpired time.

31—Paid one quarter's rent of store per check, which charge to the landlord's account.

SUFFICIENT MDSE. UNSOLD TO ALLOW A PROFIT OF 30 PER CENT. ON SALES, INVENTORY STORE FIXTURES AT THE AMOUNT CHARGED.

Total Net Gain, $3257.06.

As this ends the transactions of the third month, and a partner is about to retire from the firm, you are required to make out a Trial Balance and Balance Sheet. As this Set is supposed to end another year, close all the accounts in the Ledger, and bring down the balances as heretofore. It will be necessary to take clerks' wages into consideration before rendering a statement, and credit the landlord with one month's rent now due. Compare the balances brought down with the resources and liabilities columns of the balance sheet.

FORM OF A MONTHLY TRIAL BALANCE BOOK.
(*Refer to page* 135.)

Fol.	Accounts.	Dr. January.		Cr.		Dr. February.		Cr.		Dr. March.		Cr.	
50	W. H. Marsh,	1428		6974	90	230				146			
51	S. W. Manner,	2130		8768		475				239			
52	Cash,	4760		1278		2460	46	1450		1268	40	1174	80
53	Merchandise,	9764		3548		1342	50	3296	48	2164	80	2436	90
54	Bills Receivable,	8240		6400		2460	25	1720	25			1240	
54	Bills Payable,	1240		1560		574		465		175			
55	George Brown,	1850		840				248		246	20		
55	S. R. Smith,	200		100		268						158	
56	L. B. Lent,	1200		1360		743	40	176				248	70
57	S. O. Hess,	1400		1760						175			
58	G. A. Arner,	1250		1050		349	36					230	60
58	Interest,	18		21	60	26		46	30	10		5	60
59	Expense,	180				38				47	60		
	January.	33660	50	33660	50								
60	R. W. Post,					10							
61	Commission,							156	30			20	40
62	Loss and Gain,							276	40	146	30		
63	F. Rimmer,							1142	24	946	28	234	60
	February.					8976	97	8976	97				
64	Peter Huff,									200		100	
65	James Stanley,									596	70		
66	Robert Gordon,											511	68
	March.									6361	28	6361	28

* You are required to find the face of this note.

SALES BOOK—Set XI.

This book contains all the regular sales, either for cash or on time; the *Cash Sales*, being added in the inner columns, are not included in the amount for which Merchandise is credited from the Sales Book. These sales, together with petty sales not entered in the Sales Book, are posted from the Cash Book. This book is journalized in a similar manner to the Invoice Book, under the heading "Sundries Dr. To Merchandise," or may be posted direct to the Ledger.

Hamilton, March 1st, 1889.

Marks Nos. S. & C.								
	D.B.							
		√	SMITH & COOK, *Brockville, Ont.*					
			4 bags Rio Coffee,					
			lbs. tare					
			136—12 over 263—23½					
			127—11½ 128—12					
			— — 129—11¼					
			263—23½					
			520—47=473 lbs. at 40c.....	....	189	20		
			5 bbls. Extra Flour, at $7.50....	....	37	50		
			2 " Mess Pork, " 14.50....	....	29	00		
			Note at 60 days.				255	70
			2					
		√	J. WALTHAM & Co., *Guelph.*					
			20 bbls. Apples, at $3	....	60	00		
			10 " Flour, " 8.00	....	80	00		
			30 days' credit.				140	00
			7					
		√	S. MOORE, *James Street.*					
			50 bbls. Trout, at $6.50	....	325	00		
			20 " White Fish, at $5.50....	....	110	00		
			5 bags Rio Coffee,					
			lbs. tare.					
			136—12 over 435—42½					
			152—16 138—12					
			147—14½ 156—16¼					
			435—42½ 729—71=658 lbs. at 40c.	....	263	20		
			Acceptance at 2 months.				698	20
			8					
	C.B.		J. FARMER, *McNab St.*					
			4 bbls. Strong Baker's Flour, at $6.50	....	26	00		
			10 " Spring, " " " 6.00	....	60	00		
			20 " Extra, " " " 7.00	....	140	00		
			30 " Superior Extra, " " 7.25	....	217	50		
			10 " Salmon Trout, " " 8.00	....	80	00		
			3 " White Fish, " " 5.00	....	15	00		
			2 lbs. Y. H. Tea, " 75		1	50		
			Sight Draft.				540	00
			22					
	C.B.		A. B. JONES, *Toronto.*					
			10 bbls. White Fish, at $5.50	....	55	00		
			12 " Spring Flour, at $7.80	....	93	60		
			4 hhds. Soft Yellow Sugar, 5680 lbs., at 8½c.		482	80		
			Cash.		631	40		
*69			* Total Sales on time, Journal page—†				1093	90

NOTE.—The above Sales Book is merely given as a form, and not supposed to contain the entries in their order.

* Red Ink.

† This total might be carried to the credit of Mdse. at once, and each sale debited direct without journalizing.

FOURTH MONTH'S BUSINESS—SET XI.

April 1, 1889.

J. W. Dickie has this day retired from the business, selling his entire interest to the remaining partners at a discount of 10 per cent. from his net worth. Paid him ½ Cash and balance in Notes at 6, 9 and 12 months for equal amounts.

Bought of Rimmer, Gunn & Co., on 30 days, 10 bags Java Coffee, 130, 131, 134, 138, 136, 129, 143, 148, 151, 148 lbs., tare 4 lbs. each, at 30c.; 20 bags Jamaica Coffee, 128, 143, 164, 151, 147, 128, 127, 118, 131, 137, 146, 129, 144, 118, 132, 147, 131, 150, 141, 134 lbs., tare 5 lbs. each, at 29c.; 16 bags Ceylon Coffee, 149, 143, 158, 147, 162, 138, 127, 119, 154, 176, 138, 131, 144, 127, 124, 152 lbs., tare 5 lbs. each, at 27c.; 100 bbls. Crushed A Sugar, 225 lbs. gross, 25 lbs. tare each, at 10½c.; 200 bbls. Dry Crushed Sugar, 218' lbs., gross, 21 lbs. tare each, at 11c.; 115 bbls. Yellow Sugar, 222 lbs. gross, 22 lbs. tare each, at 8c.; 10 hhds. Porto Rico Sugar, 1107, 1141, 1113, 1121, 1127, 1116, 1099, 1142, 1130, 1117 lbs., tare 107 lbs. each, at 7½c. Paid Freight on same, $104.25.

2—Sold S. E. Shibley, for Cash, 10 Casks, Bordeaux Vinegar, 50 gals. each, at 35c; -9 bbls. Golden Syrup, 43, 47, 46, 41, 45, 43, 49, 42, 40 gals., at 40c.; 7 bbls. Standard Syrup, 37, 39, 42, 46, 44, 38, 31 gals., at 39½c.; 5 bbls. Clayed Molasses, 34, 38, 36, 32, 39 gals., at 26c.; 500 lbs. Dry Cod Fish at $5 per cwt.; 50 barrels Baker's Flour at $6.

4—Paid Cash for Sundry Expenses, $16.50 ; S. Edsall, on acct., $15.

Sold W. Ponton, on his acceptance at 30 days, 12 boxes P. of Wales No. 1 Tobacco, 120, 118, 117, 119, 114, 116, 117, 121, 120, 122, 119, 118 lbs. gross, tare 20 lbs. each, at 31c. ; 9 half-chests Y. Hyson, " Chinaman" No. 142—75, 73, 71, 70, 69, 74, 67, 71, 69 lbs. gross, tare 15 lbs. each, at 90c.; 5 half-chests Tea " Congou," 68, 72, 74, 73, 71 lbs. gross, tare 15 lbs. each, at 60c. Sold R. Gordon, for Cash, a bill of $850.

5—Received from John Cook, Belleville, for sale on joint acct. and risk, each ½, 1200 lbs. Cheese at 11c. Paid charges on same $10.50. Had Conger Bros, Note, of Feb. 14th, discounted at Merchants Bank at 7 per cent. for unexpired time.—Discount—; Cash received.—Paid A. Overell, on acct., $14 ; A. Forin, $10 ; S. Edsall, $5.

6—Sold A. M. Foster, for Cash, from Mdse. Co. " C." 10 bbls. Apples at $4 ; from Mdse. Co. " D." 600 lbs. Cheese at 12½c. Paid sundry items of expenses, $15.50. Remitted Rimmer, Gunn & Co., a draft on the Bank of Montreal for the amount of their invoice of the 1st instant, less 3 per cent. Paid Cash for draft and ½ per cent. Exchange.

7—Had W. Ponton's acceptance of the 4th instant discounted at Merchants' Bank at 7 per cent. for unexpired time. Discount $—. Cash received $—. Sold W. Bristol, for Cash, from Mdse. Co. " D.," 400 lbs. Cheese, at 12½c. Paid Gas Bill, $11.90.

8—Received from P. G. Close & Co., Toronto, an Account of Sales of the Raisins shipped them on the 11th ult. Our net proceeds and payment for ½ invoice remitted by Draft on Bank of Montreal $1131.25.

9—Bought of Sinclair, Jack & Co., Montreal, on 30 days, 11 half-chests Colored Japan Tea, 69, 64, 71, 70, 65, 68, 72, 73, 77, 74, 71, lbs. gross, tare 15 lbs. each, at 60c.; 21 half-chests Gunpowder Tea, Nos. from 114 to 135—55, 68, 74, 71, 73, 72, 71, 69, 68, 67, 64, 69, 73, 72, 71, 70, 72, 73, 68, 66, 70 lbs. gross, tare 14 lbs. each, at 66c. Paid Freight on above, $19.50. Sold for Cash from Mdse. Co. " D.," 200 lbs. Cheese at 12½c.

11—Closed Mdse Co. "D.," and rendered John Cook an account of Sales. Our Charges for Drayage, $3 ; Commission, 3½ per cent. Sold A. Henry, for Cash, a bill of goods amounting to $1500.

12—Paid a drayman $5 for carting from store remainder of Apples belonging to Mdse. Co. " C.," they having all decayed on account of exposure. Sold H. Armstrong, for Cash, a bill of goods amounting to $2100. Deposited in Merchants' Bank $2000.

13—Had our stock of goods insured in Imperial Insurance Co. for $20,000, at 2 per cent. Paid Premium per Check. Rendered R. Town, Kingston, a statement of the Apples received on the 14th ult., for sale on joint account, and remitted the amount due him per Check. Sold W. R. Barber, for Cash, a bill of goods amounting to $2500.

14—Sold John Cook, Belleville, on his acceptance at 30 days, 14 bbls. Muscovado Molasses, 42, 43, 46, 49, 45, 47, 40, 42, 48, 43, 44, 40, 41, 49 gals., at 30c. Sold W. R. Muir, for Cash, an invoice of Tea amounting to $2150.

15—Bought of A. Urquhart & Co., on our acceptance at 60 days, 80 casks Bordeaux Vinegar, 50 gals. each, at 30c.; 50 do Amber Syrup, 44 gals. each, at 69c.; 100 casks Barbadoes Molasses, 45 gals. each, at 32c. Paid for sundry Expenses, $13.50.

16—Had John Cook's Acceptance of the 14 inst. discounted at Merchants' Bank, at 7 per cent. for unexpired time, and net proceeds left to credit. Sold Charles Smith, for Cash, a bill of $1500. Received from S. Thompson, Cash in full for his Note of February 13th. Sold F. Dixon, for Cash, an invoice of $2150.

18—Shipped per Steamer Passport, and consigned to W. Bannan & Co., Toronto, to be sold on joint account and risk, each ½, 400 bbls. "Extra Superfine" Flour at $6.50; 150 bbls. "Spring Extra" at $6; 250 bbls. "Strong Bakers" at $5.90. Paid Insurance on same, $30. Sold for Cash, a bill of $750.

19—Remitted Sinclair, Jack & Co., a Draft on Montreal Bank for the amount of their invoice of the 9th inst., less 3 per cent. discount. Paid Cash for Draft and ½ per cent. Exchange.
" Bought of Geo. Flower, on our note at 3 months, 50 bbls. Salmon at $6.75. Sold C. W. Raney, for Cash, an invoice amounting to $1850.

20—Called upon H. R. Mountain, London, to effect a settlement, found him unable to pay his indebtedness, and compromised for 75c. in the dollar. Accepted Note against George Ritchie for $1200, dated February 1, at 3 months, and Cash for the balance.

21—Had Geo. Ritchie's Note, received 20th inst., discounted at Merchants' Bank at 7 per cent. for unexpired time, and net proceeds left to our credit.

22—Discounted our Note of the 19th inst., favor of Geo. Flower, at 10 per cent. for unexpired time. Discount off, $——. Amount paid per check, $——.

24—Sold W. R. Barber, for Cash, an invoice amounting to $850. Deposited in Merchants' Bank, $1000.
" Bought of J. Wilson, Goderich, on our Acceptance at 30 days, 300 bbls. Salt at $1.75; 200 bbls. Mess Pork at $16.

25—W. Bannan & Co. have this day returned the whole of the Flour shipped them on the 18th inst. Charges paid by them as per statement, $30.
" Sold John Cook, Belleville, on acct. 7 cases Bordeaux Vinegar, 38, 36, 39, 42, 41, 43, 40 gals. at 33c.

27—Received from P. Miles, Cash in full for his Draft of the 25th ult. Sold Geo. Wallbridge, for Cash, an invoice of Teas amounting to $1120. I. C. Chilman & Co. have failed, and are able to pay but 60c. in the dollar. Accordingly, we have received from the Assignees 60 per cent. of the Note we held against them in Cash. Lost the balance.

28—Bought from John Templeton, for Cash, 2000 bbls. Goderich Salt at $1.75, and shipped the same to J. A. Mathewson & Co., Montreal, for sale on joint acct. Paid insurance on same, $79.50.

29—Through a disastrous fire last night, our stock of goods was entirely consumed. Nothing saved but the books and other papers kept in the safe. Mdse. on hand yesterday as per Stock Book, $36,200.

30—J. P. Thomas, agent for the Imperial Insurance Co., in which we were insured, has promptly adjusted the loss by giving us the Company's Check for amount of insurance.

At a meeting of the partners, it has been mutually agreed that the business shall be discontinued, the books balanced, a settlement effected, and the partnership dissolved.

After journalizing the entries from the Invoice Book and Sales Book, journalize to the credit of the clerks their salaries to date, and credit the landlord with one month's rent now due.

In order to effect the above settlement, discount all Bills, both payable and receivable, at 7 per cent.; on overdue paper receive and pay for interest at the legal rate, if no rate mentioned. Receive Acct. Sales of the two Shipment Cos., each one to show a profit of $50, take off a Trial Balance and statements showing the condition of the business. Deal with Loss and Gain, balance the Accounts, and bring down the balances. Next proceed to wind the business up.* Collect all accounts owing you, and pay off all liabilities, including the partners, through the Cash Book. When you have posted these Cash entries to the Ledger, the business will be wound up and the books closed.

Net Loss, $1488.40.

* Remember that the sum of the Resources always equals the sum of the Liabilities and the Capital; so if you turn all your resources into cash you will have a sum sufficient to pay off all liabilities and pay the partners their capital. If a business is insolvent the sum of the Liabilities equals the sum of the Resources and Insolvency.

SET XII.
ADMINISTRATOR'S FORM.

An Administrator is a person appointed by the judge of the Surrogate Court to settle the affairs of an intestate—or a person dying without a will. His duties are specially described by the statutes, and pertain, first to the liquidation of outstanding debts and collection of amounts due the estate. Next, to the proper distribution of net assets among the heirs, or their legal representatives. That the position is a responsible one may be inferred from the fact that he is liable to those for whom he acts, in the amount of property or assets which he has in trust, and is required by law to give bonds with responsible sureties for at least that sum. None should accept the responsibility without careful consideration.

So far as the accounts are concerned they do not differ much in principle from those of an agent or single proprietor, except that in intent and scope they refer to liquidation. It very often occurs, however, that in the discharge of his duties an Administrator may increase the value of the property held, or circumstances may depreciate it. The accounts should be kept so as to show such gains or losses and their causes. Rich as one may die, unless his property is all in good shape, and his will and affairs generally clearly arranged, there is no certainty that his wife and children will derive much benefit from all that is left behind. Property sold through the probate courts generally brings only from one-half to two-thirds the price it would command if the late owner were alive and disposing of it himself.

This is due to the fact that, if there had been any irregularity in the legal proceedings connected with the sale, the heirs are very apt to rake the matter up, and try to recover the property. In addition to this injury to the property of deceased persons, come legal and court fees, referees' charges, advertising, and many other loop-holes which drain the estate. It is particularly unfortunate for heirs and legatees if the property left to them is covered by a mortgage. The man who loves his wife and children should endeavor to keep his affairs in such a state that, if he were suddenly called away by death, his property would be in such a well-arranged condition as to yield something like its real value.

In this set you will keep neither cash book, nor cash account in the ledger, but deal in cash transactions entirely with the Bank. You will deposit all cash received in the Bank, and make it debtor to the account for which the money is received. You will make all payments by cheque, crediting the Bank, and debiting the account for which it is paid.

The opening journal entries are:

Sundries (Resources) Dr. to Smith's Estate,
and
Smith's Estate Dr. to Sundries (Liabilities).

The difference between what is debited and credited to the estate being its value when you assume the functions of Administrator.

ADMINISTRATOR'S FORM—SET XII.

Belleville, Oct. 1st, 1889.

*————this day having received letters of administration, enters upon the duties of Administrator for the Estate of John Smith, deceased, and is to pay off all just liabilities and necessary contingencies, and after converting surplus into Cash and deducting commission, divide the remainder among the nine heirs in such proportion as the law provides.

---
* Student to use his own name.

The following is a list of such RESOURCES and LIABILITIES as can, at this time, be ascertained :

RESOURCES.

W. Jones owes on acct., $60; Thomas Gibertson, $37.50; George H. Dean, $78; N. W. Phillips, $54; W. Sutherland, $50; L. H. Bottoms, $32; W. Graham, $45; John S. Miller, $75; A. L. Geen, $28; W. A. Ostrom, $52. NOTES—William Lacy's for $250, dated January 1st, 1888, at 6 per cent. interest; W. H. Stinson's for $100, dated August 14, 1888, at 7 per cent; A. Overell's for $28, dated September 1st, 1889, at 8 per cent. Interest due on above notes to date, $—. Farm, as per valuation, $4,000; Farming Implements (as per Schedule A), $400; Live Stock as per valuation (Schedule B), $500; Furniture as per valuation (Schedule C), $250; Deposit in Merchants' Bank, $302; Deposit receipt Montreal Bank, $1000, dated Jan. 1st, 1889, at 4 per cent. interest; Mortgage from Thos. Jones, $400, dated March 1st, 1887, bearing 8 per cent. interest, payable half yearly; interest due on same from Sept. 1st, 1889, $—. 10 shares of Moira Cheese Factory Stock, par value $20 per share. Total Resources, $8008.52.

LIABILITIES.

L. W. Yeomans & Co., on acct., $50; G. C. Holton & Co., $25; J. S. Meudell, $28; John Lewis, $18. NOTES—Favor Robertson & Henry, $50, dated July 1st, 1889; John Cook, $35, dated August 1st, 1889. Total liabilities, $206.

3—Paid Lewis Roenigh, undertaker's bill per Check, $50; Paid Probate and Lawyer's fees per Check, $25; Paid Mrs. J. Smith for house expenses per Check, $25.

5—Sold Live Stock by auction for $600, less 1 per cent. for auctioneer's fees, paid to A. Keys; Paid for Advertising Sale in the "Intelligencer" and "Ontario," $10; Deposited in Bank, $—

7—Collected the following accounts : Thomas Gibertson, $37.50; George H. Dean, $78.

8—Paid L.W. Yeomans & Co.,in full of acct., $50 ; J. S. Meudell, in full of acct., $28, per Check.

9—Paid G.C. Holton & Co., in full of account per Check.

10—The following amounts due by the Estate were not enumerated in the original list: W. Johnson, $15; J. H. Hambly, $12.

12—Received Cash in full for the following accounts: W. Jones, $60; N. W. Phillips, $54; L. H. Bottoms, $32. Deposited amount in Bank.

13—Mrs. John Smith assumes the furniture (as per Schedule C.) at valuation, $250.

14—Transferred the 10 shares Moira Cheese Factory Stock to William Adams at 5 per cent. premium, deposited amount received in Bank.

15—Sold the Farm to John Smith, jr., son of deceased, at valuation, also sold him the Farming Implements (Schedule A.) for $400; received Cash (deposited), $4000; balance on account. Paid Mrs. Smith for house expenses, $25 ; on private account, $20, per Check.

16—Received Cash for the following Notes and interest on same to date ; W. Lacy's, $250 ; W. H. Stinson's, $100. Deposited amount in Bank.

17—Assigned to Mrs. John Smith, Thomas Jones' Mortgage ; Interest accumulated on same to date $—. Received payment for the following accounts: W. Sutherland, $50; W. Graham, $45 ; A. L. Geen, $28. Deposited amount in Bank.

19—A. Overell paid his Note with Interest to date $——, received from J. S. Miller in full of account, $75. Deposited in Bank.

21—Paid John Lewis and William Johnson in full of acct. per Check.

22—Paid Note favor Robertson & Henry per Check.

24—Paid Thomas Smith on account, per Check, $50 ; paid Note favor John Cook per Check.

26—Compromised with W. A. Ostrom for the amount of his indebtedness, he having produced a Receipt of $20 on the account, from the late John Smith, I accept $32 in full settlement. Received Cash for Deposit Receipt from Montreal Bank, with Interest to date. Deposited amount in Merchants' Bank. Paid J. H. Hambly in full of account per Check, $12. Appropriated for my services as Administrator $150, per Check.

To THE STUDENT.—You will now journalize and post the work, take off Trial Balance and Statements (or Combined Statement), which will show the undivided interest of the heirs in their representative account Smith's Estate. Having completed the work of converting resources into cash, and paying off liabilities, you will now credit the heirs with their respective interest. The widow will have ⅓ the net proceeds of the estate, and each of the other heirs ⅙ of the remainder.

You may next make the necessary entry for closing the accounts, which will be to pay off all the heirs per check.

Loss, $175.77.

CONDENSED SYSTEM OF BOOK-KEEPING FOR RETAIL BUSINESS.

The *principles* of Double Entry Book-keeping being fully understood, the Accountant can choose the particular style he may think best adapted to the business in which he is engaged. The prime object should, of course, be efficiency, and if a short condensed plan will give this result it should be adopted.

The Six Column Journal method (see Set X) is adopted by many retail houses, and is admirably adapted for many lines of business, so is the plan of keeping a special column for credit sales of merchandise in the Journal, and posting them monthly in one sum to the Credit of Merchandise account. (See first month of Set XI.) There are also the various methods of posting from Auxiliary Books direct, which large manufacturing and other establishments pursue.

We desire here to point out a system for a Retail Business other than those referred to, which we know by experience is thoroughly efficient and easily understood ; its main features being, keeping a Day Book Index, and Journalizing monthly.

The Books to be used are :—

DAY BOOK AND INDEX,   BLOTTER CASH BOOK.

MONTHLY CASH BOOK,   JOURNAL,

LEDGER,   BILL BOOK,

INVOICE BOOK.

The DAY BOOK should contain the plain history of all transactions, except those affecting Cash, as they occur during the day. It does not matter so much about the form of words used if the transaction is stated clearly and fully. You will at the close of each day's business index the transactions. For instance, if John Adams, J. Brown and R. Cummings have bought goods on credit during the day, under the letters respectively A, B, C, you will place the names (if they are not already there by reason of former transactions) and Day Book folio. If James Macfarlane gives you his note in settlement of account, you will in the Index under the letters B. R. (Bills Receivable) place his name and Day Book folio. If you give your note in favor of John Macdonald & Co., and accept a draft of Galbraith, Christie & Co., you will under the head of the letters B. P. (Bills Payable) place these names and the Day Book folio.

EXAMPLE OF DAY BOOK INDEX.

ADAMS, JOHN	Folio 57, 63, 71	A.
BROWN, J.	Folio 61	B.
CUMMINGS, R.	Folio 60, 63, 70	C.
MACFARLANE, JAS.	Folio 64	B. R.
GALBRAITH, CHRISTIE & Co.	Folio 69	B. P.
MACDONALD, JOHN, & Co.	Folio 70	M.

When the Day Book entries are Journalized, the fact will be shown in the Index by running the pen through the figures, thus ~~10~~.

The above is sufficient to indicate the method of Day Book indexing; circumstances may require you to vary it more or less.

THE BLOTTER CASH BOOK will be the ordinary form without special columns, and should be balanced every night, and cash checked at least twice a week.

THE MONTHLY CASH BOOK will be written up from the other at the end of the month, and will have special columns on each side representing the accounts for which money is most frequently received and paid out. See Cash Book for Set XI.

In connection with the method we here recommend, some Accountants keep the Blotter Cash Book only, and *Journalize* its transactions as is done in the Municipal Set in this book. Either is right; adopt which you deem most convenient.

THE JOURNAL will be written up monthly, and here you have the explanation why you index the Day Book.

As there is an interim of a month from one Journalizing to another, it is necessary that there should be an easy way of finding any particular transaction that has taken place in the meantime. For instance, Brown comes in to settle his account on the 20th of July, you first take the entries posted in the Ledger up to the 1st of the month; having written these on the bill, you take the Day Book Index, and find whether any debits or credits (other than cash) are indexed to him for the current month; if there are it will direct you to the folios of the Day Book on which they are recorded.

When Journalizing, first deal with the transactions other than those of Merchandise· You might begin with Bills Payable, then Bills Receivable, and so on till all the transac⁻ tions recorded in the Day Book, except those of Merchandise, are Journalized, and then Journalize the credit purchases of merchandise, and finally the credit sales.

If you put Checks through the Cash Book you should not Journalize them; but if you do not, you may either enter the Checks from the stubs of the Check Book to the Day Book at the close of each day, or Journalize them from the stubs direct; in the example we pursue the latter course.

The Invoices may either be entered in the Day Book to the credit of the parties from whom you purchase, as the goods arrive, or they may be kept on the file till the end of the month and journalized direct; the latter is the plan pursued in the example. Put the folio of the Journal upon the invoices in large figures near the date, in red ink, and either paste them into the Invoice Book or file them away; in either case, in consecutive Journal Folio order.

EXAMPLE OF MONTHLY JOURNAL.

JOURNAL.

Belleville, January, 1889.

Ledger Folio.						
192	Sundries Dr. To Bills Payable.					
260	John Macdonald & Co.,	D.B. folio 59.		420	96	
249	Sampson, Kennedy & Gemmel,	" " 60.		209	50	
232	Thos. Wall & Sons,	" " 64.		320	90	
241	Thos. May & Co.,	" " 72.		470	00	
						1421 36
159	Bills Receivable Dr. To Sundries.					
421	A. Forin,	D.B. folio 58.		79	20	
438	R. W. H. Duncan,	" " 62.		159	60	
491	W. R. Lett,	" " 69.		340	00	
						578 80
150	Sundries Dr. To Bank.					
23	Merchandise,	For Check 180.		75	00	
141	Expense,	" " 181.		24	80	
192	Bills Payable,	" " 182.		490	00	
250	John Wilson & Co.,	" " 183.		159	20	
192	Bills Payable,	" " 184.		223	20	
						972 20
23	Merchandise Dr. To Sundries.					
263	T. J. Claxton & Co., as per Invoice of Dec. 1, 1888.			459	60	
263	Ditto	" " " 2, "		272	50	
263	Ditto	" " " 20, "		74	00	
270	Young, McNaughton & Co.,	" " 3, "		160	00	
281	Ogilvy & Co.,	" " 7, "		342	40	
						1308 50
23	Sundries Dr. To Merchandise.					
		$42.20 $10.90 $4.00 $9.60				
450	A. Robertson, D.B. folios 59, 61, 68, 72.			66	70	
583	J. Tennent, " 60.			27	40	
		$39.20 $5.60 $41.50.				
476	E. Gillen, " 61, 64, 70.			86	30	
		$10.90 $21.20.				
458	M. C. Wild, " " 64, 70.			32	10	
471	H. Smith, " " 63.			29	20	
						241 70

THE LEDGER statements and method of closing the accounts of this Set do not differ from those already given, and therefore require no explanation.

THE BILL BOOK will be kept as in the example given in connection with Set IV. We would here simply emphasize the necessity of entering bills in the Bill Book, as well as in the Day Book, as they are given and received. If this be done, and you look at your Bill Book daily, in order to be aware of and advise your customers of paper coming due, and have knowledge of, and provide for your own bills maturing, there will be no danger of paper being dishonored and protested without your knowledge.

For an INVOICE BOOK we recommend a book about 12 x 21 inches of strong brown paper, well bound, containing about 150 pages. Into this the invoices should be pasted as they are journalized. As all that is necessary to see when looking for an invoice in the book are the name and Journal folio, you should fold the invoice so as to occupy as little space as possible.

SET XIII.

MANUFACTURING BUSINESS.

Books used—DAY BOOK, CASH BOOK, BILL BOOK, TIME BOOK and LEDGER.

The Day Book and Time Book to be used in this Set are explained, and a form of each given immediately after the record of transactions. Use the form of Cash Book adopted on page 110.

Belleville, April 1st, 1889.

*——— and A. M. Spafford have this day rented the Dominion Foundry, together with all its Machinery, Fixtures, etc., as shown per Schedules "A," "B," "C," and "D," from A. R. Patterson, at $2000 per year, for the purpose of carrying on business, as defined in their Articles of Co-partnership of this date. Each partner is to be allowed interest at 8 per cent. on amount invested, and charged at the same rate on sums withdrawn. Gains and losses to be shared equally.

STUDENT INVESTS : Cash, $8,500 ; Note against James Brown for $2000, dated December 11th, 1888, at 4 months. A. M. Spafford invests Cash, $12,000 ; Note against Peter Williams for $1500, dated October 21st, 1888, at six months, with interest at 8 per cent. Interest accrued on same, $54. Accepted Draft on F. J. Dixon for $1000, dated March 24th, 1889, at 30 days. Paid for a set of Books, $21.40.

2—Bought of A. R. Patterson his entire stock of manufactured implements, iron, etc., amounting, as per inventory, to $15,500 ; 100 cords of Wood at $5. Gave in payment our 4 Notes at 3, 6, 9, and 12 months, for $4000 each. Engaged Irwin Foster, as Accountant, at $800 per year ; John Davis, as Foreman of the Finishing Shop, at $2.75 per day ; George Abrahams, as Foreman of the Moulding Shop, at $2.50 per day ; Alexander Winters, Blacksmith, at $2.25 per day ; Robert Jones, Wm. West, Henry Darnley, Stephen Post, Warner Potts, Isaac Raming, George Everett, Samuel Lynn, Thomas Petre, Arch. Ewing and David Liddell at $1.50 each per day ; A. M. Fraser, S. H. Hudson and P. M. Grass at $1.25 per day ; Wm. Stoneberg, as Engineer, at $1.75 per day, and Thos. Roberts, James Long and W. H. Spring at $1.20 per day. Services to commence on Monday.

4—Made arrangements with W. A. Foster & Co., to supply machinery for a new mill, which they are about to erect ; also with W. W. Jones & Co., and A. S. Page & Co., to supply and repair machinery, as specified in the Articles of Agreement. Sold M. R. Coleman, for Cash,1 Double Crook Hurlburt Plough, $15 ; 1 Scotch Canadian do, $12 ; 1 Ten-horse power and Rods for same $100 ; 1 Maple Leaf Cooking Stove and Trimmings, $32. Robert Abrams, who is acting as agent for the sale of our implements, has this day received 7 Scotch Canadian Ploughs at $10 ; 4 Mohawk Valley Clipper do at $9 ; 6 Double Crook Hurlburt do at $12.*

5—Bought of Frothingham & Workman, Montreal, on acct., Round Bar Iron, amounting as per invoice to $490. Paid Freight on above, $27.40.

Bought of W. & F. P. Currie & Co., Montreal, on acct., invoice of Pig Iron, amounting to $950. Paid Freight and Cartage on same, $35.70.

FOREMAN'S REPORT.—Lost time ½ day Winters ; ¼ day Raming ; ¼ day Post ; ¼ day Darnley ; and ½ day Davis. Work to be charged, 5 hrs. Winters, 2 hrs. West, 7 hrs. Everett ; drilling and dressing spiders for A. S. Page & Co., at $4 per day. †

6—Delivered per order of our agent, Robert Abrams, 2 Reynolds' Water Wheels at $68 ; 1 Sellick's do, $90 ; 2 Leffell's do at $125.

Sold Wm. Cook, for Note at 3 months, 1 Wood's Mowing Machine, $75 ; Reaping attachment for same, $25 ; 2 Steel Ploughs at $10. Paid sundry expenses, $4.20. Student withdrew on acct., $150.

---

* As Mr. Abrams has taken these implements away from the shop, charge him with them the same as though he actually bought them, and give him credit for anything he may return.

† The hands who are not reported by the foreman, under the lost time, are credited each evening in the Time Book, with a full day, and all others with the time they have worked. Extra work, repairing machinery, etc., is charged to the parties for whom it is done with the men's time, at from $3 to $5 per day, according to the machinery used and the men required to perform the work. Observe this entry in the form of Journal.

Foreman's Report.—Lost time, Isaac Raming, reported sick; Warner Potts, ¼ day, and S. Post, ½ day. Extra work for W. A. Foster & Co., 6 hrs. Davis, 2 hrs. Liddell, and 2 hrs. Ewing; fitting and finishing Binding Rollers, 8 hrs. West; cutting off 7 inch Hammered Shaft, 5 hrs. Lynn, and 4 hrs Darnley, cutting bolts at $4 per day.

7—Delivered to W. W. Jones & Co. 2 Steam Engines, 45 H.-P., at $800; 1 Shingle Mill, $100; 2 Feed Rollers with Gear and Shafts; 2 Binding Rollers and Shafts; 1 Spider for 5½ in. Shaft—weight, as per memorandum given them, 1680 lbs. at 8c.; 15 pcs. Maple Scantling, 600 feet at 3c. A. M. Spafford withdrew on acct. $100.

Had Wm. Cook's Note of the 6th inst. discounted at Montreal Bank, at 7 per cent., and net proceeds left to credit.

Foreman's Report.—Lost time, Robert Jones, ½ day; William West, ¼ day, and Isaac Raming 1 day. Extra work for W. W. Jones & Co., 5 hours Liddell and 7 hours Ewing; cutting off and dressing Hammered Shaft, 5 hours Petre and 3 hours Lynn; cutting off and fitting a 3-inch Shaft, 5 hours Everett and 2 hours Davis, on old Pulley, at $4 per day.

8—Bought of Frothingham & Workman, for Cash, 12 sheets Boiler Plate, 6 x 3 x ¼. 2116 lbs. at 5c. Received from Robert Abrams cash on account, $200. Paid for painting and papering office, $30.

Foreman's Report.—Lost time, G. Everett, ¼ day; Isaac Raming, absent; W. Potts, ¾ day Extra work for A. S. Page & Co., 6 hours Jones and 2 hours West, taking length of pipe; 1 day Darnley and 7 hours Post, on old Shaft.

9—Received from W. W. Jones & Co. their Note at 3 months for amount of machinery delivered to them 7th instant. Paid sundry expenses, $10. Remitted Frothingham & Workman Draft on the Montreal Bank for the amount of their invoice of 5th inst., less discount at 3 per cent.; paid cash for draft and ⅛ per cent. exchange. A. M. Spafford withdrew on account, $250.

Foreman's Report.—Lost time, A. Winters, ¾ day; R. Jones, ½ day; I. Raming, sick; W. West, ¼ day. Extra work for A. S. Page & Co., 2 hours Winters, 5 hours Jones, 5 hours West, 1 day Darnley, 1 day Ewing, on wooden Rollers, at $4 per day. Paid hands cash in full for services, as per Time Book.

11—Had W. W. Jones & Co.'s Note of the 9th inst. discounted at Montreal Bank, at 7 per cent. per annum, and net proceeds left to credit. Shipped to Shannonville, per order of Robert Abrams, 3 Side Hill Ploughs at $9; 10 Double Crook Hurlburt do at $12; 12 Mohawk Valley Clipper do at $9.

Foreman's Report.—Lost time, Robert Jones, ¼ day, W. West, ½ day. Extra work for W. A. Foster & Co., 2½ hours Potts, on Collars; 8 hours Raming, 3½ hours Everett, 4 hours Lynn, on Stave Machine, at $4 per day.

12—Delivered to W. A. Foster & Co., 1 Arch Door and Frame, 126 lbs. at 5c.; 5 Arch Bolts, 22 lbs. at 5c.; 5 pieces Cast Pipe, 480 lbs. at 7c.; 15 Marking Hammers at $1; 4 Roller Shafts (2½ inch), 376 lbs. at 7c.; 4 Cast Rollers, 1348 lbs. at 7c.; 1 Hammered Shaft, 1322 lbs. at 13½c.; 66 lbs. Washers at 7c. Sold W. R. Coleman, on account, 1 Cumming's Straw Cutter, $25; 1 Circular Saw Carriage with head blocks, $400.

Foreman's Report.—Lost time, Winters ¾ day. Extra work for A. S. Page & Co., ¼ day blacksmith and helper at $5; 4 hours Darnley and 8 hours Post, on old boiler at $4 per day.

13—Received from W. A. Foster & Co., their Note at 3 months for amount of machinery delivered 12th instant, and had the same discounted at Montreal Bank at 7 per cent., proceeds left to credit. Remitted W. & F. P. Currie & Co., Draft on Montreal Bank in full for their invoice of the 5th inst., less 2½ per cent. discount; paid for Draft and ⅛ per cent. Exchange per Check.

Foreman's Report.—Men all put in full time. Extra work for W. A. Foster & Co., 1 day Fraser, 8 hours Hudson, 7½ hours Grass, on Wooden Rollers at $3 per day.

14—Delivered by order of Robert Abrams, at Madoc, 14 Scotch Canadian Ploughs at $10; 10. Side Hill do at $8; 4 Maple Leaf Cooking Stoves at $30. Bought of Frothingham & Workman, on our acceptance at 10 days, invoice of iron amounting to $1200.

Foreman's Report.—Lost time, Winters, ½ day; Liddell, ¼ day; Ewing, ¼ day; and Petre, ½ day. Extra Work for W. W. Jones & Co., 5 hours blacksmith and helper, 7 hours Jones, and 4 hours West, on connecting boilers at $4 per day.

15—Received Cash in full for James Brown's Note of December 11th. Received from Robert Abrams, on account, J. Johnson's Note for $250, dated April 12th, at 3 months, with interest at 8 per cent. Sold W. R. Coleman, on account, 1 Iron Horse Power (for 2 horses) $30 ; 1 Band Wheel for same $5 ; 1 Steel Plough, $12.
Having become dissatisfied with our blacksmith, A. Winters, we have paid him in full and discharged him.
FOREMAN'S REPORT.—Lost time : Liddell, ½ day ; Ewing, ¼ day ; Long, ¼ day, and Spring; ½ day. Extra work for A. S. Page & Co., 1 day Roberts, 6 hours Long, 4 hours Spring, on Wooden Rollers, at $3 per day.

16—Received from A. S. Page & Co., their Note at 3 months for the following machinery delivered to-day : 4 Saw Arbors (2½ in.), with Pulleys and Collars, 354 lbs. at 8c.; 4 Bevel Wheels (2½ in.), Shafts and Pinions on same, 738 lbs. at 8c.; 4 Pillar Blocks for 5½ in. Shaft, and 4 do for 7 in. Shaft, 2738 lbs. at 8c.; 1 Hammered Shaft. 7 in., 1490 lbs at 12½c.
Had J. Johnson's Note of 12th instant discounted at Montreal Bank, at 7 per cent., and proceeds left to Cr., Bought of Frothingham & Workman, Montreal, on account, invoice of Bar Iron, amounting to $1500 ; Paid Freight on same, $53.20.
FOREMAN'S REPORT.—Lost time, Grass, ½ day, and Hudson ¼ day. Extra work for W. A. Foster & Co., 8 hours Jones, 2 hours West, 6 hours Darnley and 7 hours Post, on connecting rods, at $4 per day. Paid our hands in full as per Time Book.

18—Robert Abrams has returned 1 Reynolds' Water Wheel, $68, sent him 6th instant, and 5 Double Crook H. Ploughs at $12. Bought of W. & F. P. Currie & Co., Montreal, on account, invoice of Scotch Pig Iron amounting to $850. Paid Freight on same, $57.60. Engaged Peter Huff, blacksmith, at $2 per day, services to commence to-morrow.
FOREMAN'S REPORT.—Lost time, Lynn ¼ day. Extra work for A. S. Page & Co., 4 hours Post, 6 hours Everett, 2 hours West and 1 hour Davis, on connecting rods, $4 per day.

19—Received from W. W. Jones & Co., their Note at 3 months for the following machinery delivered to-day : 2 Steam Boilers, 14 x 5 feet, at $1,500 ; 2 Globe Check Valves (1½ in.) at $5 ; 4 Globe Check Valves at $3.30 ; 2 Butting Chains, 240 lbs., at 12c.; 2 Sawdust Grates, 174 lbs. at 8c. Received from Robert Abrams, Cash on account $100.
FOREMAN'S REPORT.—Lost time, Jones ¼ day. Extra work for A. S. Page & Co., 8 hours Liddell, 1 day Ewing, ½ day Petre, 5 hours Davis, on connecting rods, at $3.50 per day ; 4 hrs. Darnley, 8 hours Post and 5 hours blacksmith and helper, on pumps and connections, at $4 per day.

20—Had A. S. Page & Co.'s Note of the 16th inst. discounted at Montreal Bank at 7 per cent. Discount $—; Cash received $—; Shipped per order of R. Abrams, 4 Reynolds' Water Wheels at $75 ; 6 Sellick's do at $100 ; 1 Excelsior Horse Power, $80.
FOREMAN'S REPORT.—Lost time, D. Liddell and A. Ewing, 1 day ; T. Petre, ¼ day. Extra work for W. A. Foster & Co., 4 hours Davis, 7 hours Jones, 1 day West, and 1 day Darnley on connecting rods and keys for same, at $4 per day.

21—Had W. W. Jones & Co.'s Note of the 19th inst. discounted at Montreal Bank, at 7 per cent. Discount, $—; Cash received, $—. Remitted W. & F. P. Currie & Co., Montreal, Bank Draft for amount of their invoice of 18th instant, less 2½ per cent. discount ; paid Cash for Draft and ⅛ per cent. Exchange.
FOREMAN'S REPORT.—Lost time, D. Liddell and A. Ewing, absent all day. Extra work for W. A. Foster & Co., 1 day blacksmith and helper, $5 ; 7 hours Post, 4 hours Jones, 6 hours Petre on connecting rods, at $4 per day.

22—Paid D. Liddell and A. Ewing in full for services to date, and discharged them. Received from R. Abrams, on acct., W. T. Heaslip's note at 3 months for $500. Paid John Davis, Foreman, $10 on acct.* Sold Gilmore & Co., for Cash, 2 Steam Engines, " 14 x 16," with Heaters and Set Gear, $1800 ; 2 Steam Boilers, 14 x 5ft. at $1550 each, less 2 per cent. from the total amount.
FOREMAN'S REPORT.—Lost time, Robert Jones, reported sick. Extra work for W. W. Jones & Co., 4 hours Petre, 6 hours Grass, 1 day Hudson, 7 hours Fraser, dressing and fitting Wooden Rollers at $3.50.

---

* When hands receive anything on account during the week, deduct the amount from their wages on pay day, and just keep a memo. in the till to represent it till then.

23—Engaged Robert Way, S. Boyle and H. Cover, at $1.50 per day, services to commence on Monday, the 25th inst. Had H. T. Heaslip's Note of the 22nd inst. discounted at Montreal Bank at 7 per cent., and proceeds left to credit.

FOREMAN'S REPORT.—Lost time, Robert Jones, absent. Extra work for A. S. Page & Co., 8 hours Potts, 4 hours Everett, cutting Bolts; 1 day Lynn, 7 hours West, bushing old Pulleys at $4 per day. Paid hands in full for services.

25—Received from Peter Williams, Cash for his Note of Oct. 21st, and interest thereon. Remitted Frothingham & Workman, Montreal, a Bank Draft for the amount of their invoice of the 16th inst., less 2½ per cent. paid Cash for Draft, and ⅛ per cent. Exchange. Delivered per order of R. Abrams, 12 Scotch Canadian Ploughs at $10; 8 Double Crook Hurlburt do at $12; 4 Side Hill do at $8.50; 2 Reynold's Water Wheels at $75.

FOREMAN'S REPORT.—Lost time, Petre, ¼ day; Lynn, ½ day. Extra work for W. A Foster & Co., 4 hours blacksmith and helper, making keys for connecting rods, at $5 per day. Stoneburg, Davis, Post and Lynn worked overtime ¼ day.

26—We are necessitated to suspend operations in consequence of putting in a new boiler, the old one being considered unsafe. The hands required to assist in making the change are, Davis, Jones, West, Post, Potts, Lynn and Huff; the others are not required until we commence operations again.

29—We allow A. R. Patterson $600 for the old boiler, and credit him with that amount and charge him $1800 for the new one, the connections there for and labor in making the change; the difference will remain at his debit, but the debit will be reduced as rent accrues due and is placed to his credit. Received from R. Abrams, Cash on account, $200.

FOREMAN'S REPORT.—Lost time, Lynn, ½ day. Extra work for W. W. Jones & Co., 1 day Roberts, 7 hours Long, 8 hours Spring, 3 hours cogging wheels, at $3 per day. Stoneburg, Davis, Huff, Spring, Long and Post have each worked overtime ¼ day. Received from F. J. Dixon, Cash in full for his Acceptance of March 24th. Paid our Acceptance of the 14th instant favor of Frothingham & Workman, per Cheque.

30—R. Abrams has returned 4 Double Crook H. Ploughs at $12; 3 Scotch Canadian do at $10; 1 Side Hill do, $8.50. Sold Robert West for Cash, 2 Steam Engines (35 H. P.), at $750; 2 Steam Boilers (50 H. P.), at $1000.

FOREMAN'S REPORT.—Lost time, Huff ½ day. Extra work for A. S. Page & Co., 1 day Post, 5 hours Huff, fixing pumps at $4 per day. The following hands have each put in ¼ day extra time: Davis, Jones, Everett, Petre and West.

Pay the hands in full to date, make Rent Dr. to the landlord, take off a Trial Balance and Balance Sheet, and close the accounts.

Inventory, $8262.96.

Merchandise credit in Journal, $10,969.44.

Net Gain, $4438.02.

Cash on hand, $33,141.28.

Time sheet footings, No. 1, $181.67, No. 2, $187.97, No. 3, $181.61, No. 4, $143.61.

If Wages account is closed into Merchandise, the cost of raw material being already debited to that account, the Dr. side of Merchandise will show total cost.

REMARKS ON SET XIII.

The material from which the transactions of this Set are constructed was obtained from an extensive foundry and machine shop, and the routine has the merit of being practical. The forms of the books, and arrangement of the various records, are submitted as being very simple and in general use throughout the country.

The form of Day Book adopted is similar to that of Set XI., all *credit* sales of merchandise being extended into the outside column, and forwarded from page to page until the end of the month, when the total amount is posted to the credit of Mdse. account. When work is charged by the day it is extended and posted to the credit of merchandise the same as though it were the sale of a manufactured article. This plan is adopted in the majority of machine shops, because the labor of hands is continually engaged on implements or machinery of some kind, which, when sold, will go to the credit of Merchandise account, and it would be very troublesome to keep the cost of material and work separate from one another.

In manufactories where the hands are not paid weekly, and are allowed to draw on their wages accordingly, there is no way of keeping a running account with each of the hands with less trouble and greater accuracy than by adopting the plan of keeping a small Ledger exclusively for the accounts of the hands employed, called the " Hands' Ledger." The adoption of this plan saves the opening of so many accounts in the General Ledger, keeps the accounts of hands together, and separated from all other accounts, and avoids trouble and detention at the time of making out a Trial Balance or balancing the General Ledger. A column should also be kept on the credit side of the Cash Book for amounts paid hands, and when money is paid to one of the hands it should be placed in this column and immediately posted to the debit of his account in the Hands' Ledger. When a " Hands' " column is kept in the Cash Book, it is footed and forwarded to the end of the month, and then posted in total to the debit of Hands' acc't. In cases where the Hands' Ledger is adopted, it is necessary to keep a " Hands' Account " in the General Ledger, and credit it from the Time Book, at the end of each week or month, as the case may be, with the following entry: "Wages account Dr. to Hands acc't." This plan keeps the two Ledgers entirely distinct from each other, the one account in the General Ledger containing the result of all the accounts in the other Ledger, and showing at any time the amount owing to hands. When the hands are all paid off and the Hands' Ledger balanced, this account must balance also.

PLANT ACCOUNT.

It will be observed by the student that the proprietors of this business *rent* the Foundry already fitted for their purpose, but suppose they had *purchased* it, and the necessary machinery to carry on their operations, they would require an account in the Ledger to represent these, which is called PLANT ACCOUNT. To the debit of this account is placed the cost of the permanent plant of the concern,—by this we mean the machinery and tools by the use of which its goods are produced, and not anything that may be purchased to be sold or manufactured. When closing the Ledger there are two ways of dealing with the Plant acc't. Owing to wear and tear the plant of the concern is now not worth so much as it was when you purchased it, or when you last closed your books; hence you must " write off " a portion of the amount charged to the account to Loss and Gain, so as to leave the debit at the figure you estimate you could sell the plant for. You may write off say 5 per cent. by making this journal entry, and posting it:

Loss and Gain, Dr.
  To Plant Account.
For 5 per cent. written off for wear and tear ;

then close the account By Balance; or, you may take an inventory of each part and piece that makes up the plant of the concern, place the amount of the Inventory on the credit side of the account, and close it By Loss and Gain. Any property account, such as office furniture, would be dealt with in like manner.

130

Want of space prevents us from recording more than a few of the first transactions in the following

FORM OF DAY BOOK—Set XIII.

Belleville, April 1st, 1889.

Led Fol.						Merchandise	
	Sundries Dr. to Student			$10500	00		
	For following investment:						
	Cash as per C.B.	$8500	00				
	Bills Receivable, J. Brown's Note, B.B. ...	2000	00				
	"						
	Sundries Dr. to A. M. Spafford			14554	00		
	For investment as follows:						
	Cash as per C. B.	12000	00				
	Bills Rec., Note against Williams and Draft on						
	Dixon, as per B.B.	2500	00				
	Interest accrued on above Note	54	00				
	2						
	Merchandise Dr.			15500	00		
	Fuel Dr.			500	00		
	To Bills Payable...					16000	00
	Bought of A. R. Patterson, Implements, Iron, &c., as per invoice, and 100 Cords of Wood at $5, for which we gave 4 Notes at 3, 6, 9 and 12 months, for equal amounts, as per B.B.						
	4						
	Robert Abrams Dr. to Mdse.						
	For 7 Scotch Canadian Ploughs, at $10.00...	70	00				
	" 4 Mohawk Valley " 9.00...	36	00				
	" 6 Double Crook H. " 12.00...	72	00			178	00
	5						
	Merchandise Dr.			490	00		
	To Frothingham & Workman					490	00
	Bought of them on acct. as per invoice of this date.						
	"						
	Merchandise Dr.			950	00		
	To W. & F. P. Currie & Co					950	00
	Bought of them as per invoice of this date.						
	"						
	A. S. Page & Co.* Dr. to Mdse.						
	To 5 hrs. Winters	2	00				
	" 2 " West	0	80				
	" 7 " Everett	2	80			5	60
	Drilling and Dressing Spiders,						
	Mdse. Cr. by Sundries.					183	60

* A. S. Page & Co. are charged for this work at the rate of $4 per day [10 hours work, 40c. an hour], which is considerably more than we pay the same men, but it must be remembered that we furnish the machinery, tools and other necessaries, and are under heavy expense aside from men's wages.

TIME AND WAGES REGISTER OF THE DOMINION FOUNDRY.

For the Week ending Saturday, April 9th, 1889.

No	NAME.	M.	T.	W.	T.	F.	S.	Total	Rate per day.	Amount.		Rec. the am't set opposite our respective names.
1	John Davis,	1	½	1	1	1	1	5½	2	75	15	12	John Davis.
2	G. Abrahams,	1	1	1	1	1	1	6	2	50	15	00	G. Abrahams.
3	A. Winters,	1	½	1	1	1	¼	4¾	2	25	10	69	A. Winters.
4	Robert Jones,	1	1	1	½	1	½	5	1	50	7	50	R. Jones.
5	Wm. West,	1	1	1	¾	1	¾	5½	1	50	8	25	W. West.
6	H. Darnley,	1	½	1	1	1	1	5½	1	50	8	25	H. Darnley.
7	S. Post,	1	½	½	1	1	1	5	1	50	7	50	S. Post.
8	Warner Potts,	1	1	¾	1	¼	1	5	1	50	7	50	Warner Potts.
9	Isaac Raming,	1	¾	—	—	—	—	1¾	1	50	2	62	I. Raming.
10	George Everett,| 1	1	1	1	¾	1	5¾	1	50	8	62	Geo. Everett.
11	Samuel Lynn,	1	1	1	1	1	1	6	1	50	9	00	Samuel Lynn.
	Ent'd Cash Book Folio —										96	48	

When men are paid every week, the above form will enable the accountant to keep a correct record of each man's time. In cases where men work extra time, it may be entered in the same column immediately over the day's work, and all extended in the Total column at the end of the week, or it may be recorded in a column headed "Extra time." If the men are paid every two weeks, twelve day columns are necessary. In business the above $96.48 is brought forward into the head of the "Amount" column upon the next page, and so continued from page to page until the whole list of workmen is complete. On pay-day the whole list is extended as above. The men assembled, the Pay Clerk calls the names in their order upon the register, hands each the amount due him, and checks it upon the left of the money column, thus √, and each signs his name. The total amount is entered in the Cash Book and charged to Wages Acc't.

By having a large book, one space for names will serve for four weeks; the ruling for the third and fourth week to extend upon the opposite page.

In case the men are not paid in full, extra columns, headed "Paid" and "Due," should be kept, and wages standing over should be entered in the "Due" column, and added to their earnings on the next register.

The few names entered in the above form are sufficient to show how this book should be kept.

WEEKLY TIME AND WAGES REGISTER.

The following form is designed for paying men by the piece in weekly payments, and will answer to keep an account of work either done in the manufactory or by parties at their own shops. By adopting the following plan one page answers for two weeks, and if opposite pages are taken they will answer for four weeks, and thus save the necessity of writing the names so frequently.

TIME AND WAGES REGISTER OF THE DOMINION BOOT AND SHOE MANUFACTORY.

Name.	June 1, 1889.					June 8, 1889.		
	Quantity.			Rate.	Amount.	Quantity.	Rate.	Amount.
James Amos,	5 prs	Boots,	2	10				
John Bates,	4 "	"	1 75	7				
R. Corn,	5 "	"	1 75	8	75			
L. Date,	3 "	"	2	6				
H. Evans,	4 "	"	2	8				
L. Favor,	6 "	Shoes,	1 15	6	90			
R. Goven,	5 "	"	1 75	8	75			
S. Hand,	3 "	Boots,	2	6				
T. Irwin,	2 "	"	2	4				
P. Jones,	6 "	Slippers,	0 60	3	60			
J. Words,	5 "	Boots,	2 15	10	75			
Forward,*				79	75			

* The footing of each page may be forwarded until the whole list of workmen is paid off, and then carried to the Cash Book in total.

S. G. BEATTY & CO.'S
PAY ROLL FOR THE BAY OF QUINTE MILL.
For the month ending July 31st, 1889.

We, the undersigned, do hereby severally acknowledge the receipt from Messrs. S. G. Beatty & Co., of the sums opposite our respective names in full payment for work done in the above Mill, to the above date:

No.	Names.	Occupation.	Wages rate per month.	Days.	Am'nt.	Deduction Items.	Am'nt	Net Amn't	Signatures.
			$ c.		$ c.	$$$ c.	$ c.	$ c.	
1	John Armer	Millwright	78	25	75 50	10.3.5 50	18 50	57	John Armer
2	James Avert	Foreman	65	25	62	8.2.4 50	145 0	47 50	James Avert
3	J. W. Archer	Blacksmith	52	25	50	10.4	14	36	J. W. Archer
4	S. W. Bull	Filer	52	25	50	10.	10	40	S. W. Bull
5	F. H. Burk	Gang	39	24	36	10.	10	26	F. H. Burk
6	S. R. Bones	Gang	39	24	36 00	10.	10	26	S. R. Bones
7	T. Camp	Gang	39	23	34 50			34 50	Thos. Camp
8	H. L. Cross	Gang	39	25	37 50	4.3.5	12	25 50	H. L. Cross
9	P. T. Chime	Gang	39	25	37 50	6.2.2	10	27 50	P. T. Chime
10	L. H. Davis	Circular	39	25	37 50	5.8.7	20	17 50	L. H. Davis
11	T. R. Day	Setting	32 50	24	30	10.	10	20	T. R. Day
12	H. M. Dews	Circular	32 50	23	28 75	10.	10	18 75	H. M. Dews
13	R. T. Evens	Edger	32 50	25	31 25	10.	10	21 25	R. T. Evens
14	S. W. Forks	Tailing	32 50	25	31 25	10.	10	21 25	S. W. Forks
15	A. B. Fife	Sorting	32 50	20	25	15.	15	10	A. B. Fife
16	Chas. Gover	Sorting	32 50	25	31 25	4.1.5	10	21 25	Chas. Gover
17	D. L. Ham	Engineer	52 00	25	50	3.7	10	40	D. L. Ham
18	H. S. Horn	Fireman	32 50	25	31 25	10.	10	21 25	H. S. Horn
19	James Irvin	Piling	32 50	20	25	10.	10	15	Jas. Irvin
20	James Jakes	Piling	32 50	21	26 25			26 25	James Jakes
21	S. N. Long	Piling	32 50	24	30			30	S. N. Long
22	H. P. Marvin	Piling	32 50	24	30	10.	10	20	H. P. Marvin
23	W. B. Moon	On boom	26 00	25	25			25	W. B. Moon
24	C. North	On boom	26 00	25	25	4.2.4	10	15	C. x North his mark Witness R. Nesbitt
25	David Port	Teamster	32 50	20	25	5.	5	20	David Port
26	G. H. Rover	Yard	26 00	21	21	10.	10	11	G. H. Rover
27	John Sokes	Yard	26 00	23	23	10.	10	13	Jno. Sokes
28	J. Wright	Yard	26 00	23	23	10.	10	13	Jas. Wright
	Entd C. B. Fol.				968 50		269 00	699 50	

NOTE.—The above form of Pay Roll is very convenient, when hands are paid by the month, and extensively used by mill owners. The Foreman keeps a Time Book at the mill, and at the end of the month makes out a Time List which is sent in to the head office, and from which the above Pay Roll is made out. The Time List made out by the foreman is merely a list of the men's names, rate per month, and the number of days they have worked.

CHEESE FACTORY MILK BOOK—NAMES OF PATRONS.

No. of cheese made daily.	Month of May, 1889.	Nelson Boulter.	Jas. Coulson.	D. J. Osterhout.	N. Gaffield.	John Hasl.	Irwin Foster.	Geo. G. Kerr.	T. Durham.	C. McLaurin.	W Badgley.
10	1	178	436	382	562	439	653	359	647	726	841
		196	450	390	579	446	648	366	659	734	879
12	2	185	443	367	583	453	672	361	652	752	864
		197	456	396	576	450	681	367	648	761	847
11	3	172	452	384	564	462	674	362	636	738	753
		180	450	390	573	453	658	360	653	749	861
9	4	186	463	397	578	461	676	364	649	758	872
		191	461	392	581	455	682	372	681	746	886
13	5	193	470	379	546	439	647	367	656	731	873
		198	466	391	554	448	659	376	663	752	889
11	6	196	462	369	567	456	674	371	652	749	857
		202	471	376	578	459	681	368	641	763	868
66	7	2274	5480	4613	6841	5421	8009	4393	7837	8995	10290
		√	√	√	√	√	√	√	√	√	√
14	8	196	446	390	567	452	659	368	641	721	856
		204	452	387	573	438	668	357	658	732	862
12	9	189	439	389	564	426	687	349	669	719	847
		197	447	396	579	431	674	366	686	743	863
10	10	190	453	378	556	453	659	372	649	726	861
		210	461	389	571	426	666	348	672	735	852
13	11	198	449	392	582	445	672	369	693	751	867
		204	458	382	574	432	658	384	668	742	853
12	12	201	462	386	569	451	683	391	659	738	866
		206	456	391	586	426	647	376	667	751	854
11	13	197	438	392	562	438	654	369	672	731	847
		206	452	387	579	419	676	387	681	745	862
72	14	2298	5413	4662	6864	5237	8003	4436	8015	8834	10290
		√	√	√	√	√	√	√	√	√	√

The above is the form generally adopted by cheesemakers for keeping a daily and weekly record of the amount of milk received from patrons. We have seen no less than eight different forms in use, each having particular merits; the above recommends itself on account of its simplicity. The amounts between the doubled ruled lines represent the total number of pounds of milk received daily from the patron under whose name they appear. In the upper space amount received in the morning is entered, and in the lower that received in the evening. At the end of each week the amounts are added together, and the totals carried to their respective accounts in the regular book kept for that purpose, placing a check mark beneath each sum as in the above when transferred.

We have only given a few of the patrons' names, and continued the entries for two weeks, as the form is so simple that it can be readily understood. The other books of account in connection with the business of a cheese factory do not differ from ordinary books.

DETECTING ERRORS IN TRIAL BALANCES.

By care in posting, and by *always* adding both up and down when making additions, a bookkeeper will avoid errors. The most careful person, however, will occasionally find his ledger out of balance.

If every addition has been verified by adding both up and down, one may safely conclude that the error or errors cannot be in the additions, and this knowledge gives confidence that the mistakes will soon be found by checking the postings. By experience we have found the following method of adding the best:

594327 23√
830560 28√
734251 38√
953872 22√
642501 28√
724956 47√
302416

The result of the addition of each line is set down, so that if the adder is disturbed, or if he finds a mistake when checking down, say in the fifth row of figures, he only requires to add that one line again, instead of all the lines from the first. The √ mark shows the verification, *i. e.*, that each line has been added twice. The result of the addition in the example is 4782883. Faint blue lines ruled in the Ledger between the red lines of the dollar column will prevent units being placed under tens, tens under hundreds, and so on, and much trouble be thereby avoided. The same precaution in ruling should be taken with the trial balance.

In the majority of offices a trial balance of the Ledger is taken monthly, or at least every three months. To the novice in bookkeeping the work involved in taking a trial balance of a Ledger containing from five hundred to a thousand accounts, twelve times in the year, would be appalling. It would be a laborious task, even for the man of long experience and habitual accuracy, if there were no labor-saving methods. Trial Balance Books, ruled and arranged so that the names of the accounts have only to be written once in the year, and having twelve separate columns, one for each month, can be obtained from any first class stationer. Refer to page 116 for an example of a Monthly Trial Balance Book, which shows balances for three separate months. The opposite page would contain three months more, and if each alternate sheet in the book be left untouched as you proceed, and a piece cut down on the right the width of the space that the names of the accounts occupy, you have simply to continue the balances for the last six months on these. Books containing this simple device are patented in Canada and the United States.

Taking a trial balance each month in this way, if a ledger is found out of balance, a month's checking is a comparatively trifling labor. Think for a moment of the difference between it and the work involved in checking eleven or twelve months' posting.

Many suggestions are made in regard to locating mistakes or detecting errors; few of them amount to anything. Perfect accuracy in addition by the method we have mentioned leaves the bookkeeper, in the event of the ledger being out of balance, just one thing to do, namely, to check back the postings. This must be done systematically. Take each book in turn from which the postings to the Ledger were made, and check each entry, placing a √ mark against each separate entry in the book posted from and the one posted to. Do this with a hard black lead pencil, not in the column with the figures, but just on the red line between the figure column and the folio column. The marks made by a hard black pencil can be easily erased, if this is desirable. If they are allowed to remain, being out of the figure column, they will cause no confusion or slovenliness. You should soon discover the errors by this process. Should they not be found, cast your eyes carefully down the columns of each ledger account, and if you find an entry without a check mark, then you have discovered an entry that has been by mistake posted twice. Omitting the check marks this would not have been so easily found.

ON THE CORRECTION OF ERRORS.

In correcting errors in the regular books, it is not sufficient to make matters come out right by writing "To error" or "By error," as you are directed to do in the old school treatises. You must make the correction explain itself by a distinct reference to where the error exists, and at the place where the error is made note the date and place of correction. Thus, if you have journalized any entry wrongly, and have discovered it before posting, write on the margin of the entry, "VOID, CORRECTED PAGE —," and preface your new entry with "To rectify error page —." For obvious reasons there are very strong objections to erasing either figures or writing on any book of original entry; but if a post be made to a wrong account or to the wrong side of an account in the Ledger, if the account is not footed, there can be no great objection to erasing the figures in the money column and replacing them with ciphers, allowing the date and other words of the entry to remain. Let the amount then be correctly posted. No man of taste ever thinks of scoring out entries in his Ledger for the purpose of rectifying them, or for any other purpose.

CROSS ENTRIES.

Cross entries are made for the purpose of rectifying mistakes. Where there is a "snarl" or complication in an account, caused by several mistakes, it is usually necessary to make several cross entries to "straighten" it. We give below examples of simple cross entries.

If Wm. Green purchased goods on credit, and by mistake in Journalizing or posting you charged them to Jas. Brown, the cross entry in the Journal to rectify the error would be:

Wm. Green, Dr.

To Jas. Brown.

For Goods charged the latter in error, Sept. 29th.

Again, supposing that when Journalising the entries of the IV. Set you had made the following errors and posted them to the Ledger: on the 8th credited Bills Receivable with both the amount of Jones' note and interest, $296.62; on the 16th charged Bills Payable with both the amount of Jakes & Hayes' note and interest, $1919.00; to rectify them you would make the following cross entries: For that on the 8th,

Bills Receivable   Dr.   1.62

           To Interest,   1.62

For error in crediting B. R. with an item of interest, April 8th.

For that on the 16th,

Interest   Dr.   19.00

           To Bills Payable, 19.00

For error in charging B. P. $19.00 Interest on April 16th.

Remember that Bills Payable account is never charged with more in connection with any bills than it was credited with, and Bills Receivable account is never credited in connection with any bill with more than it was charged with. Interest for or against must be put through Interest Account.

BANKING.

Banks exist primarily for the purpose of loaning money, which they do principally upon the security of promissory notes and bills of exchange. They not only loan the capital belonging to the stockholders, but also the money deposited by the public. The loans made by the banks are called discounts. Wholesale trade is largely done on credit, the customers giving their notes or acceptances at three or four months for the goods they buy. This paper, after being endorsed, is discounted—that is, money is borrowed upon it at the banks, the amount paid for the loans being the interest (usually about 7 per cent. per annum) on the face of the paper from the date of discounting to the date of maturity, which always includes the three days of grace. The net proceeds are usually placed to the firm's credit, as a deposit would be, and is available thereafter. It will be observed that in discounting a note payment is made for the use of the money, not at the end of the period for which it was borrowed, but at the beginning, and in this will be seen the difference between bank discount and true discount.

Besides discounting commercial paper, the banks make collections, advance money on warehouse receipts covering grain and other agricultural produce, on lumber and other merchandise, and buy and sell foreign exchange, created by the exports and imports of the country. They are also empowered to issue paper currency, limited only by the amount of their paid-up capital.

The system of banking pursued in Canada is partly British and partly American, but sufficiently distinct from either to be Canadian. The British system has been followed so far as establishing institutions with large capital, having a head office in an important centre, with branches in various cities and towns. The Bank of Montreal, for instance, has a paid-up capital of twelve millions of dollars, and a rest, saved out of earnings, of six millions, and has over thirty agencies, in each of which deposits are received, discounts granted, and the same general banking business carried on as at the head office. There is a general Banking Act of the Dominion Parliament, dealing with the currency and other matters, but each bank in Canada possesses a separate charter.

In two of the points just mentioned American banks differ materially from the Canadian institutions. American banks confine their business to one locality, and possess a comparatively small capital. They do not require a separate charter, but are formed under a general incorporation Act, by the promoters complying with the forms prescribed.

The most radical difference between Canadian and American banking is in the matter of securing the currency. The notes of American banks are secured by the deposit of United States bonds with the Government at Washington. The holders of Canadian bank bills can only look to the banks that issued them for their redemption, but they are a first lien on their assets. We believe the American system is the best, and that it will, as inter-provincial trade increases, recommend itself to our law makers. While admitting that the present security for the redemption of the currency issued by the banks of Canada, which consists of the double liability of the shareholders, as well as the existing assets, has hitherto been found fairly satisfactory, we shall point out the disadvantages connected with the system in comparison with the American.

A currency that is the only medium of exchange should be national; it should be as acceptable in one province as another. Our system fails in this respect. Nowhere in the Province of Ontario, for example, can a holder dispose of the bills of a Nova Scotia bank except at a discount, and even then only to a bank. The public, knowing nothing of the bank that issued the notes, will not receive them, and bankers will often refuse to take them except for collection. This is a hindrance to Intercolonial trade, as well as an obstacle to national aspirations and the homogeneity of the Dominion. Under the system prevailing in the United States the people have a *national* currency, that is everywhere accepted throughout their own country from Maine to California, and is also taken without hesitation in Canada, although often issued by banks of doubtful standing. The holders know that the Government of the United States is responsible for its redemption, and therefore they care nothing for the solvency of the bank of issue, as it has deposited with the Government bonds to secure its notes.

The failure of a Canadian bank invariably entails loss upon those bill holders, who cannot afford to wait for the redemption of its currency until the assets have been realized upon. These unfortunate people—and they always form a large proportion of the holders—are obliged to sell to speculators often at heavy discounts. The bills of the late Consolidated Bank were sold in the Province of Ontario for half their face value immediately after the bank's suspension, although they were redeemed at par in less than eighteen months from that time. Under the American system there can be neither delay nor loss in realizing upon the bills of a defunct bank.

The officers of a bank branch are, the manager, accountant, teller (receiving and paying), ledger keeper, discount clerk and junior.

Private banks are quite common, but they are in no way connected with the chartered banks. Those who do business with them have no recourse beyond the individuals who conduct them.

For further information relating to Joint Stock Banks, see the chapter on Joint Stock Companies.

DEALINGS WITH BANKS.

An account may be opened with a bank by calling upon the Manager. Evidence as to integrity or reliability of character on the part of a stranger is required. If that is satisfactory, he will be requested to write his name in the signature-book in the style in which his checks will be signed. If the account is opened in the name of a firm, the signature of the firm is written by each member, and his own name opposite. This is for the purpose of comparison, should a check with a doubtful signature be presented. The necessary blanks and books for keeping a bank account are furnished by the bank. The Deposit Slips are filled up by the depositor, who, in addition to writing his name and the date, specifies the particular kind of funds deposited, according to the printed divisions of the Slip, and also writes the total amount deposited. The Slip should be handed in to the Teller along with the money deposited. These Slips enable the Teller not only to see at once if the money, as counted by him, agrees with the depositor's statement, but also to recall the transactions of the day if necessary, in case of an error.

BANK PASS BOOK.

The entries made in the Bank Pass Book by the Teller are the depositor's vouchers for all sums left with the bank, and therefore nothing should be written in this book by the depositor himself. When a note is left for collection, the Bank Pass Book is handed with the note to the Teller, and a memorandum is made by him, but the amount is not placed in the money column until the note is collected.

Notes that have been discounted and ordered to be placed to the credit of the depositor are entered in the Bank Pass Book, less the discount, to his credit, the same as a note that has been collected.

CHECK BOOK.

The Check Book contains blank Checks, with a margin or stub for a description of the Checks as they are filled. The account with the bank is sometimes kept in this book, on the back of the margins from which Checks have been taken, as shown in the form of Bank Account given in a subsequent part of the work, the difference between the total amount deposited and that withdrawn showing the balance in bank. At certain intervals, usually at the end of each month, the Bank Pass Book should be left at the bank that it may be balanced. The amount of the Checks that have been drawn are entered at these times; and when the Bank Pass Book is returned, it should agree with the bank account kept by the dealer, if all Checks issued have been paid. No account need necessarily be kept in the Ledger, the balance being counted as so much Cash in hand, as it is subject to order at any time, and such account can contain nothing which may not be shown in the Check Book.

There are two methods for keeping the account with the bank in the Check Book adopted by business houses: that on page 142, in which the sums are added as soon as deposited, and the amounts of the Checks are subtracted as they are drawn, which is best when the business is limited. According to the other system, the deposits are entered as they are made, but are only added when the account is balanced, which is done by adding the amounts of Checks drawn since the last balancing and taking the sum from the total deposited. This method is adopted in large houses, whose deposits and Checks are numerous.

SUGGESTIONS TO DEPOSITORS.—A Check drawn payable to a person, " or bearer," is transferable without indorsement, and unless there is good reason for withholding the money, the Check is payable to any one who may present it.

A Check drawn payable to a person, " or order," must be indorsed by the person (called the payee) in whose favor it is drawn, before the bank will pay it. Checks drawn in this form are safer for holding and for making remittances, as they cannot be used until indorsed by the proper person. When so indorsed, and held by the bank or drawer, they are evidences of payment, and are therefore often used as receipts.

The payment of a Check may be countermanded by the drawer of it any time before it is paid by the bank.

A Check given by the drawer is not absolute payment; and if there are no funds in the bank at the time it is given, with which to meet it, it can be returned, and the Cash demanded.

If a Check is held beyond a reasonable time, and the bank or drawer should fail before it is presented, the holder must bear the loss. It must be presented in a reasonable time after it was received, or the holder retains it at his own risk. Every holder is liable to every subsequent holder only for a reasonable time.

The inexperienced should pay particular attention to the following suggestions:

Make your deposit as early in the day as convenient.

Use the Deposit Slips furnished by the bank, and do not make deposits without your Bank Pass Book.

All Checks deposited (that are not certified) must be indorsed by the depositor, whether drawn payable to " bearer " or " order."

To prevent their being used by other parties, stamp or write on all Checks sent for deposit the words " For Deposit " over your indorsement.

SUGGESTIONS FOR DRAWING CHECKS.—Avoid as much as possible giving Checks to strangers, and make it an invariable rule to give Checks only out of your own Check

Book; and when not in use keep it under lock and key. When giving a Check, write the particulars (always) on the stub first. Number your Checks consecutively, and always date them. If you desire a Check to be a definite receipt, draw it to the person or order, and state under the written amount what it is in payment of; as the Check, when drawn thus, cannot be cashed without the person's indorsation, his signature will be an acknowledgment that he received the money, and of what it was received for. Blank Checks have usually the word "bearer" printed; run your pen through the word, and write "order" over it. Write your signature with your usual freedom, and always in the same style.

At least once a month, and as frequently as occasion may require, send your Bank Pass Book to the Ledger keeper, that it may be balanced; and, as soon as returned, check it with your own account. Deface the signatures of cancelled Checks, arrange them according to their numbers, and place them in safe keeping, where they can be easily referred to.

Care should be taken in filling a Check to do it in such a manner that alterations cannot easily be made. Payment by the bank of a forged Check, if the forgery can be proven, will be the loss of the bank; but if the Check is filled so negligently as to invite, or facilitate forgery, any loss that occurs will fall on the drawer.

The amount of a Check should always be written out in words, and should also be placed in figures in one corner of the Check (care being taken to begin on the extreme left, and fill any space unused on the right by ruling), as a precaution against alterations, and that the sum may be readily seen when counting. Should the mistake occur of writing the sum in figures different from that expressed in words, the latter is taken as the sum of the Check.

A Check that is intended to be paid in the future should be dated the day it is given, and should state in the body of the Check the day when it is to be paid. If dated in the future, circumstances may arise before the time of its date that will render it void.

A Check is certified or marked "good" by an officer of the bank, and the bank thereby becomes responsible for its payment, thus making it more reliable for third parties. Certified Checks are chiefly used to avoid the risk and inconvenience of counting and carrying large sums of money that are to be immediately paid to others.

When any blanks are needed to supply duplicate Checks, mention in the margin the purpose for which they are used, and take them from the back of the Check book.

Avoid drawing numerous small Checks. When you have several sums to pay draw one Check for the whole, and ask the Teller for such denominations as will enable you to distribute the amount among those for whom the money is intended.

Checks are a convenient method by which to remit money to a distance. In order that your Check may realize the amount you desire the party to receive, you must add the commission, which is generally ¼ per cent. Example, when remitting $100 you must make the Check for $100.25. For some customers banks will mark Checks for remittance payable "at par."

Certificates of Deposit are given by banks to those who deposit a special amount for temporary safe-keeping. They may be drawn to the order of the depositor, or to any other person whom he may designate.

Drafts and Bills of Exchange for making remittances can be obtained from the bank.

Notes and Bills for collection should be sent to the bank a few days before they become due, in order to give the bank-clerk ample time to make the proper record and send notices to the makers or acceptors. A Check that is drawn on a different bank from that in which the Note is left for collection, unless certified, will not be received in payment for a Note in Bank.

Notes taken to a bank to be discounted are presented to the Manager, who decides whether they shall be discounted or not. In general, those Notes that are not within three months of maturity are not discounted; and there must be at least one name on the Note besides the maker, either as drawer or indorser. As a rule, banks discount only for depositors, and there must be satisfactory security that the Notes discounted will be paid when due.

In order to get a Note discounted at a bank it must be properly indorsed, and the residence of the drawer and endorser should be written on the Note in pencil. It is well to offer Notes at an early day that other sources may be applied to in case the Notes are refused by the bank. The chances for discount will usually depend upon the average amount kept on deposit, the reliability and standing of the names on the Notes that are offered, and the state of the money market.

Do not attempt to overdraw your account, and do not offer for discount Notes that are not likely to be punctually paid at maturity; and should any that have been discounted be protested and returned to you, for your own credit pay them immediately.

In case a Draft or customer's Note is handed in to the bank for collection, and you entertain doubts of its being paid at maturity, and do not wish the extra cost of protest charges incurred, pin a slip of paper to it with the memorandum, "NOT TO BE PROTESTED. TAKE THIS OFF BEFORE PRESENTING." The bank will follow your instructions, and, should the Note or Draft not be paid, you can get it from the bank at any time without paying charges.

A Note indorsed requires to be presented at the proper time for payment, and, if dishonored, it should be protested, and the indorser promptly notified, in order that he may be held for the amount. Sometimes, however, an arrangement is made between the parties, and the indorser writes on the back of the Note, "Notice of non-payment received without Protest," or, "Protest waived," and signs his name, after which he is held the same as though the Note had been protested. See index for Protests.

The holder of a note is not bound to notify the maker of the date of maturity, and request him to make provision for payment; but it is customary for firms to send such a printed notice ten days or so before notes mature, so that careless customers, will not have the excuse, " Oh, I forgot about it."

The Banks, when necessary, for instance, when any doubt about the genuineness of a signature exists, now notify makers and endorsers of notes which they have discounted, that they hold such paper.

CLEARING HOUSE.

Each day there accumulates in the banks, the currency and the notes and drafts of other banks, and daily settlements must be made. In the absence of a Clearing House Association, these settlements would involve the labor and time of many clerks. Where a Clearing House exists, the business of each day's settlements is conducted as follows: A manager is appointed by each of the banks in turn (or he may be a permanent officer, appointed and paid by the associated banks), and every morning a clerk and a messenger from each bank attends at the Clearing House at 10 o'clock, to deliver to and receive from each other the checks, drafts and notes which are payable by each to the other, these being made up in packages. At the same time a statement will be handed from each bank to the manager, showing the amount due by or to each bank, to or from each other bank. About noon the representatives of the different banks will pay to or receive from the Clearing House (which may be one of the banks) the amount so appearing due.

The sum of the amounts owing to (say) the Clearing House will just equal the sum of the amounts owing by (say) the Clearing House, so that there is a perfect balancing of each day's business, hence the term "clearing."

DEPOSIT SLIP.

BANK ACCOUNT.
KEPT ON BACK OF STUB.

Merchants' Bank,
MONTREAL, *Jan.* 2nd, 1889.
Credit James Smith with $1800.
Deposited by Self.

15 x 1 =	$ 15	
2 =		
25 x 4 =	100	
55 x 5 =	275	
40 x 10 =	400	
20 x 20 =	400	
		$1190
Gold		
Silver	60	
Checks	550	
		$1800

ANOTHER FORM.

DEPOSITED AT THE

Merchants' Bank,
BELLEVILLE, *Jan.* 3rd, 1889.
By Chs. Anderson & Co.

Bank Notes	$1500
Specie	1000
Checks as follows:	
	500
	150
	250
	$3400

BANK DRAFT.

No. 412.

Ontario Commercial College Bank,
BELLEVILLE, *Nov.* 1st, 1889.
$500.00.

On demand, for value received, pay to the order of Messrs. *John Jones & Co., Montreal, Five Hundred Dollars,* which charge with or without advice to this Bank.

James Hughes, Man.
To the   *John Smith,* Acc't.
BANK OF MASSACHUSETTS,
Boston, Mass.

1889.			
Jan. 2	Deposited.	$1800	00
" 15	Check No. 1.	175	50
" 24	Note No. 1 Col.	1624	50
		2000	00
		3624	50
Feb. 12	Check No. 2.	515	50
		3109	00
" 16	Wilson's Note. No. 2 Collected.	800	00
		3909	00
March 1	Check No. 3.	202	50
		3706	50
April 1	Check No. 4.	46	25
		3660	25
" 10	Check No. 5.	125	00
		3535	25
" 19	Deposited.	1325	00
	Carried forward	$4860	25

STUB.			CHECK-BOOK.	CHECK.
No. 1. Jan. 15, 1889. Favor of Robert North, For Tweed.	$175	50	No. 1. Montreal, Jan. 15, 1889. To the Manager of the **Merchants' Bank,** Pay to ROBERT NORTH, or Bearer, One Hundred and Seventy-five $\frac{00}{100}$ Dollars, $175 $\frac{00}{100}$	James Smith & Co.
No. 2. Feb. 12, 1889. Favor of Conger Bros., For Sugar.	515	50	No. 2. Montreal, Feb. 12, 1889. To the Manager of the **Merchants' Bank,** Pay to CONGER BROS., or Bearer, Five Hundred and Fifteen $\frac{50}{100}$ Dollars, $515 $\frac{50}{100}$	James Smith & Co.
No. 3. March 4, 1889. Favor of George Brown, Insurance.	202	50	No. 3. Montreal, March 4, 1889. To the Manager of the **Merchants' Bank,** Pay to GEORGE BROWN, or Bearer, Two Hundred and Two $\frac{50}{100}$ Dollars, $202 $\frac{50}{100}$	James Smith & Co.
No. 4. April 1, 1889. Favor of Ourselves, For Till.	46	25	No. 4. Montreal, April 1, 1889. To the Manager of the **Merchants' Bank,** Pay to OURSELVES, or Bearer, Forty-six $\frac{25}{100}$ Dollars, $46.25.	James Smith & Co.
No. 5. April 10, 1889. Favor of R. A. Smith & Co., For rent to date.	125	00	No. 5. Montreal, April 10, 1889. To the Manager of the **Merchants' Bank,** Pay to R. A. SMITH & Co., or Order, One Hundred and Twenty-five Dollars. (In full for rent to date.) $125.00.	James Smith & Co.

NOTE.—No. 5 would serve as a receipt, as R. A. Smith & Co. would have to indorse it before receiving payment at the bank. When drawing cheques be careful to leave no space unfilled either before or after the amt. n which anything might be wr tten. It is usually better to make checks payable to order. When the word ea rer is printed, run your penthrough it and write order over it.

STEAMBOATING.

The Books of Steamboats, like those of any other business, are kept in various forms. But the principles of accounts apply to every kind of business, and when thoroughly mastered can be readily adapted to any form that the peculiarities of the business may require. Skilful men adopt such forms of books as are most convenient and best adapted to their peculiar kinds of business, and which may be kept in the easiest and simplest manner, but it is only in some minor details, which are easily understood after the principles of accounts have been fully mastered, that any novelty is possible.

We have examined a number of different forms in use on some of the principal vessels that navigate the lakes and rivers of our country, and recommend the form here presented on account of its simplicity and practicability.

The books used are the Hands Register, Fuel Book, Freight Book, Passage Book, Cash Book, Journal and Ledger. Sometimes a Hands Ledger is also used, in which an account is kept with each hand employed. Also Pocket Memorandum Books for taking down freight (when no bill of lading is furnished) as delivered to the boat, and a Deck Passage Book.

THE HANDS REGISTER

contains the name, occupation, the day upon which service commenced, rate of wages per month, &c., of each employee, and is similar in use to the Time Book in a Manufacturing business. It is used to record the amount of labor performed and paid for.

THE FUEL BOOK,

as its name implies, contains a statement of the amount of fuel purchased, from whom, and the date of purchase.

THE FREIGHT BOOK, OR MANIFEST,

contains a classified list of the goods received for transportation; being plainly arranged, it exhibits its features and use without further explanation.

THE PASSAGE BOOK

is intended to record the names and numbers of the passengers, the places of embarkation and destination, and the amount of fare paid.

THE CASH BOOK,

as in ordinary business, contains a record of all Cash received and paid out. It is made up from the items recorded in the foregoing books, and from it and the Journal the entries are posted to the Ledger, which is the same form as in general use.

TRANSACTIONS.

TRIP I.—FROM BELLEVILLE TO MONTREAL.

June 1st, 1889.—J. W. Johnson and Geo. H. Pope have this day formed a partnership and purchased the STEAMER CITY OF THE BAY for $35,000.

They invest equal amounts, and are to share gains and losses equally, as per articles of co-partnership of this date.

They have paid for the boat as follows: Cash, $20,000, for which each advances $10,000, and the balance in two Notes, one at 3 months for $10,000 and the other at 15 months for $5,000, both Notes bearing interest at 6 per cent.

J. W. Johnson has advanced for incidental expenses, Cash, $750.
Geo. H. Pope.   "   "   "   "   "   " 860.

The boat will ply between Belleville and Montreal, and the present crew will be retained. The following list embraces the Officers and Crew, and their salaries:

Geo. H. Pope, Captain, ...	$100 per month.	H. Maitland, Cook	$25 per month
J. W. Johnson, Purser, ...	75 " "	J. B. Simpson, Deck Hand,	20 " "
Wm. Ireland, First Mate, ...	50 " "	R. P. Strong, "	20 " "
John F. Steel, Second Mate,	40 " "	B. C. Murney, "	20 " "
G. P. Mansard, Wheelsman,	30 " "	George Pearson, "	20 " "
John Frost, "	30 " "	Susan Broady, Chambermaid,	10 " "
O. R. Whaley, First Engineer,	70 " "	Isaac Epicure, Cabin Boy,	12 " "
A. B. West, Second "	40 " "	Daniel Alert, Watchman,	12 " "
M. Peterson, Fireman, ...	30 " "	A. B. Stunners, Porter.	10 " "
John P. Ray, "	30 " "		

June 1st.—Paid Downey & Pope for 20 tons Coal, at $5.50, $110; R. Price, for Provisions, $100; John Grainger, for Meat, $20.50; A. Henry for Ice, $6.50; Henry Blair, 8 cords of Wood, at $6, $48.
Received the following goods:—
BILL OF LADING No. 1.—From Victoria Foundry, Belleville, to William Watson & Co., Cornwall, marked " W. W. & Co., C.," 50 Excelsior Coal Stoves at $2.
BILL OF LADING No. 2.—From George Wallbridge, Belleville, to Jones & Smith, Brockville, marked " J. & S., B.," 100 bbls. Pork at 50c., 40 casks Bacon at 60c., 10 boxes Sundries at 40c.
BILL OF LADING No. 3.—From Foster, Barber & Brignall, Belleville, to Joseph McKay & Co., Montreal, marked " J. McK., M.," 12 boxes, 3500 lbs., at 30c. per hundred.
Received the following passengers at the Port of Belleville: Wm. Jones for Picton, $1.* S. G. Beatty for Montreal, $4.50. F. Hart, wife and daughter, Brockville, $3.50. Miss S. Johnson, Cornwall, $3. Jas. Parker and wife, Cornwall, at $3.
RECEIVED AT PORT OF PICTON: BILL OF LADING No. 4.—From J. K. Frimmier, to Sampson Young & Co., Montreal, marked " S., Y. & Co., M., " 240 boxes Eggs at 25c., 55 firkins, Butter at 15c. Also the following passengers: J. Kerr for Montreal, $4. J. P. Forrester and wife, Montreal, at $4. Peter West, Cornwall, $2.50. S. G. Palmer, Gananoque, $1.50.
BILL OF LADING No. 5.—From J. Carruthers & Co., Kingston, to R. Smith, Montreal, marked " R. S., M.," 500 bbls. Flour at 40c., 20 tons Bran at $2.
BILL OF LADING No. 6.—From Parker & Sons, Kingston, to G. P. Easterbrook, Montreal, 15 kegs of Nails at 10c., marked " G. P. E., M."
PASSENGERS FROM KINGSTON.—Geo. W. Easton, for Cornwall, $2. A. Diamond, Montreal, $3- B. C. Daymond, wife, and two daughters, Montreal, at $3. R. P. Daley and wife, Brockville, at $1.50. Discharged J. P. Ray.
June 2nd.—Paid J. R. Moser, Gananoque, for 5 cords Wood, $20.
BILL OF LADING No. 7.—From B. A. Abbott, Gananoque, to James Tiller, Montreal, marked " J. T., M.," 40 Cast Iron Rollers, 1600 lbs., at 15c. per cwt.; 35 Cumming's Straw Cutters at 60c.
PASSENGERS FROM GANANOQUE.—John West and wife, Cornwall, at $1. Miss W. Manion, Miss Susan Brown and Miss Nellie Peterson, for Montreal, at $2.50 each.
BILL OF LADING No. 8.—From L. G. Smart & Co., Brockville, to W. & F. P. Currie & Co., Montreal, 275 boxes Sundries at 75c., 280 kegs Nails at 10c.
Delivered to agent at Brockville the goods consigned to Jones & Smith. The Freight being unpaid is charged to the agent, George Webber. Paid Geo. West, for 10 cords Wood, $50
PASSENGERS FROM BROCKVILLE.—S. Spangenberg and wife, Chas. Corby and Geo. Sutherland, for Montreal, $2 each. Jno. Wilson and wife, for Cornwall, $1.00. Collected Freight at Cornwall.
BILL OF LADING No. 9.—From J. Weller & Co., Cornwall, to J. G. Mackenzie & Co., Montreal, marked " J. G. M. & Co., M.," 50 Cases Tweed at 25c., 80 Cases do at 30c.
RECEIVED PASSENGERS FROM CORNWALL.—Jno. Macoun and wife, and J.P. Linger, wife and two daughters, for Montreal, $1.50 each. Paid A. H. Stephenson, for ten tons Coal, $60.
June 4th.—Delivered to the agent at Montreal the goods consigned to that port, and received Cash for Freight. Paid Canal Toll, $7.50. Discharged A. B. Stunners. Deck Passage, $41.50.

FUEL RECEIPTS, STEAMER "CITY OF THE BAY."
TRIP I.—FROM BELLEVILLE TO MONTREAL.

Date, 1889.		Where Bought.	Tons Coal.	Cords Wood.	Prices.		Amount.	Received Payment.
June	1	Belleville,	20		5	50	$110	*Downey & Pope.*
"	"	"		8	6		48	*Henry Blair.*
"	2	Gananoque,		5	4		20	*J. R. Moser.*
"	"	Brockville,		10	5		50	*George West.*
"	"	Cornwall,	10		6		60	*A. H. Stephenson.*
			30	23			$288	Entered C.B. page 149.

*The berths assigned passengers should be entered as in Passage Book. This being a mere matter of detail, we leave the student to enter the numbers himself.

HANDS REGISTER, STEAMER "CITY OF THE BAY."
TRIP I.—FROM BELLEVILLE TO MONTREAL, 1889.

Name.	Occupation.	Date of Employment.	Time.	Wages per month.	Amn't.	Paid.	Remarks.
Geo. H. Pope,	Captain,	June 1	3 ds.	100	10		
J. W. Johnson,	Purser,	" "	3 "	75	7 50		
Wm. Ireland,	1st Mate,	" "	3 "	50	5	5	
John F. Steel,	2nd "	" "	3 "	40	4	4	
O. R. Whaley,	1st Engineer,	" "	3 "	70	7	7	
A. B. West,	2nd "	" "	3 "	40	4	4	
G. P. Mansard,	Wheelsman,	" "	3 "	30	3	3	
John Frost,	"	" "	3 "	30	3	3	
S. M. Peterson,	Fireman,	" "	3 "	30	3	3	
J. P. Ray,	"	" "	2 "	30	2	2	Paid and Discharged.
H. Maitland,	Cook,	" "	3 "	25	2 50	2 50	
D. B. Simpson,	Deck Hand,	" "	3 "	20	2	2	
R. P. Strong,	"	" "	3 "	20	2	2	
B. C. Murney,	"	" "	3 "	20	2	2	
George Pearson,	"	" "	3 "	20	2	2	
Susan Broady,	Ch'ber Maid,	" "	3 "	10	1	1	
I. Epicure,	Cabin Boy,	" "	3 "	12	1 20	1 20	
D. Alert,	Watchman,	" "	3 "	12	1 20	1 20	
A. B. Stunners,	Porter,	" "	3 "	10	1	1	Discharged.

Total wages this trip, 63 40

Amount paid this trip, 45 90 Ent'd C.B., F. 149.

PASSAGE BOOK STEAMER "CITY OF THE BAY."
TRIP I.—FROM BELLEVILLE TO MONTREAL.
June 1st, 1889.

Names of Passengers.	Embarkation.	Destination.	No.	Berth.	Fare.	Amount,
Wm. Jones,	Belleville,	Picton,	1	4	1 00	$1 00
S. G. Beatty,	"	Montreal,	1	8	4 50	4 50
F. Hart and wife,	"	Brockville,	2	6	3 50	7 00
Miss Ida Hart,	"	"	1	2	3 50	3 50
Miss S. Johnson,	"	Cornwall,	1	10	3 00	3 00
James Parker and wife,	"	"	2	16	3 00	6 00
J. Kerr,	Picton,	Montreal,	1	20	4 00	4 00
J. P. Forrester and wife,	"	"	2	13	4 00	8 00
Peter West,	"	Cornwall,	1	6	2 50	2 50
S. G. Palmer,	"	Gananoque,	1	5	1 50	1 50
Geo. W. Easton,	Kingston,	Cornwall,	1	7	2 00	2 00
A. Diamond,	"	Montreal,	1	11	3 00	3 00
B. C. Daymond and wife.	"	"	2	17	3 00	6 00
Jane and Sarah Daymond,	"	"	2	18	3 00	6 00
R. P. Daly and wife,	"	Brockville,	2	19	1 50	3 00
John West and wife,	Gananoque,	Cornwall,	2	15	1 00	2 00
Miss W. Manion,	"	Montreal,	1	22	2 50	2 50
Miss Susan Brown,	"	"	1	21	2 50	2 50
Miss Nellie Peterson,	"	"	1	24	2 50	2 50
S. Spangenberg and wife,	Brockville,	"	2	26	2 00	4 00
Charles Corby,	"	"	1	29	2 00	2 00
Geo. Sutherland,	"	"	1	30	2 00	2 00
John Wilson and wife,	"	Cornwall,	2	34	50	1 00
John Macoun and wife,	Cornwall,	Montreal,	2	27	1 50	3 00
J. P. Linger and wife,	"	"	2		1 50	3 00
Miss Mary Linger,	"	"	1		1 50	1 50
Miss Susan Linger,	"	"	1		1 50	1 50

Cabin P'gers, 38
*Deck D.P.B. 22

41 50

Total Rec'ts entered C.B. page 148, $130 00

*D. P. B. stands for Deck Passage Book, a small memorandum book in which the names, places of embarkation and destination of the deck passengers are registered. The total receipts of this book are transferred to the Passage book before posting.

OBSERVATIONS ON BOOKS.

We have in the Hands Register extended the time each hand worked during the trip and the amount he earned in the proper columns. This would not be done in regular business until such time as the hands would be paid or credited with their wages. It will be observed that the hands are all paid except the owners of the vessel, the Captain and Purser, whose salaries are journalized and placed to the credit of their respective accounts.

The books should all be paged, and references between them should always be made by the page instead of by the trip.

The Fuel Book is so arranged as to give all necessary information respecting all fuel purchased. The amounts paid in Cash for fuel are here collected, and carried forward from page to page until the end of the trip, or such time as a statement is required, when it is entered in one sum in the Cash Book. The columns for inserting the number of tons of coal and cords of wood enable you to carry forward the quantity of each, and exhibit in the statement the amount of each purchased.

According to the style of Passage Book adopted with this set, the names, places or embarkation, and destination are registered as the passengers engage their passege and choose their berths. It thus serves the purpose of a passage list and a Cabin Register, but for large boats, where many passengers are getting on and off frequently, this book would not answer. The Cabin Register, where one is kept separately, is usually left on the table for the use of the passengers.

Sometimes through tickets are issued by boats, and passengers re-shipped on other steamers or railways. In such case PASSAGE account may be credited with the whole fare and debited with the cost of re-shipping. The same rule is also followed in re-shipping freight.

The Freight or Manifest Book is explained by the headings of the different columns. A Steamboat is not supposed to do a credit business, but there will be times when the agent to whom goods are delivered will not have change to pay the freight, and it becomes necessary to keep track of it. In a case of this kind make a note of it in the column for remarks, and if it is not paid before the Freight Book is posted, make a Journal entry charging the agent with it. See amount charged G. Webber in the following Freight Book. When goods are delivered to you by another Steamer or an Express Co., on which there are back charges which you are required to pay, see that the shipper inserts the amount on your bill of lading. This gives you the same authority to collect the charges that you have for collecting your own freight. In case you re-ship goods, take a Bill of Lading from the boat or company with which the goods are entrusted, in order to hold it or them responsible for their safe delivery. No entry is required for sums advanced for back charges on freight from other boats or companies, except it should remain unsettled at the time of making out your statement, when it should be entered in the Cash Book. See note, Freight Book, page 148.

FREIGHT BOOK

TRIP 1st STEAMER "CITY OF THE BAY," FROM

Shipper.	Where Shipped.	Consignee.	Destination.	Numbers and Marks.
Victoria Foundry,	Belleville,	Wm. Watson & Co.,	Cornwall,	1, " W. W. & Co., C.,"
Geo. Wallbridge,	do	Jones & Smith,	Brockville,	2, " J. & S., B.,"
Do do	do	do	do	do do
Do do	do	do	do	do do
Foster,Barber&Brg'll,	do	Jos. McKay & Co.,	Montreal,	3, " J. McK. & Co., M.
J. K. Frimmier,	Picton,	Sams'n, Young& Co.	do	4, " S., Y. & Co.," M.
Do do	do	·)YT6 do	do	do do
J. Carruthers & Co.,	Kingston,	R. Smith,	do	5, " R. S., M.,"
Do do do	do	do	do	do do
Parker & Sons,	---- do	G. P. Easterbrook,	do	6, " G. P. E., M.,"
B. A. Abbott,	Gananoque,	James Tiller,	do	7, " J. T., M.,"
Do do	do	do	do	do do
L. G. & Co.,	Brockville,	W.&F.P.Currie&Co.	do	8," W.&F.P.C.&Co.,M.,"
Do do	do	do	do	do do
J. Weller & Co.,	Cornwall,	J.G. McKenzie & Co.	do	9, " J. G. M. & Co., M.,"
Do do	do	do	do	do do

NOTE.—In case back charges are paid another Steamer or an Express Co., from which you receive Freight, the amount is entered in the column kept for that purpose, and a ticket placed in the Cash Box until the money is again collected. No other entry is required, as it is similar to a simple loan.

CASH BOOK, STEAMER
TRIP 1st.—FROM

Dr   CASH.

Date.	F.		Receipts.	Passage.		Freight.		Sundries.	
1889									
June 1		150	To G. H. POPE, Investment,					10800	
" "		150	" J. W. JOHNSON, Amount invested,					10750	
" 4	√		" PASSAGE, as per Passage Book,	130					
" "	√		" FREIGHT, as per Freight Book,			714	40		
		151	Passage Cr. by Cash	130				130	
		151	Freight " " "			714	40	714	40
		151	Total to debit of "					$22394	40

OR MANIFEST.

BELLEVILLE TO MONTREAL, JUNE 1ST, 1889.

Articles.	Rate.	Items.	Amounts.	Back Charges	Collected.	Remarks.
50 Excelsior Coal Stoves,	2 00		100		100	
100 bbls. Pork,	50	50				
40 casks Bacon,	60	24				
10 boxes Sundries,	40	4	78			Charged G.
12 boxes 3500 lbs., 35 cwt.,	30		10 50		10 50	Webber.
240 boxes Eggs,	25	60				
55 firkins Butter,	15	8 25	68 25		68 25	
500 bbls. Flour,	40	200				
20 tons Bran,	2 00	40	240		240	
15 kegs Nails, 15 cwt.,	10		1 50		1 50	
40 Cast Iron Rollers, 1600 lbs.,	15	2 40				
35 Cumming's Straw Cutter,	60	21 00	23 40		23 40	
275 boxes Sundries,	75	206 25				
280 kegs Nails,	10	28 00	234 25		234 25	
50 cases Tweed,	25	12 50				
80 " "	30	24 00	36 50		36 50	
			792 40		714 40	Ent'd C.B., p. 148
		Charged G. Webber,—			78	" Journal, Page 150
					792 40	

"CITY OF THE BAY."

BELLEVILLE TO MONTREAL, 1889.

CASH.   *Cr.*

Date.	F.		Disbursements.	Wages.	Fuel.	Stores.	Sundries.
1889							
June 1		150	By STEAMER, Paid on her acct.,				20000
"	"	√	" STORES ACCT. Supplies at Belleville			127	
"	4	151	" EXPENSE, Toll passing Canal,				7 50
"	"	√	" WAGES, As per Hands Register,	45 90			
"	"	√	" FUEL, As per Fuel Book,		288		
		152	Wages Dr. to Cash,	45 90			45 90
		151	Fuel " " "		288		288
		151	Stores " " "			127	127
		151	Total to Cr. of "				20468 40
			Balance.				1926
							22394 40

JOURNAL.

TRIP 1st.—FROM BELLEVILLE TO MONTREAL, JUNE 1st, 1889.

150	Steamer " City of the Bay," Dr.		15000			
151	To Bills Payable,				15000	
	Gave our notes in part payment of the vessel.					
	2					
151	G. Webber, Dr.		78			
151	To Freight,				78	
	Freight unpaid per Freight Book.					
	4					
152	Wages acct. Dr.		17	50		
150	To G. H. Pope,				10	
150	" J. W. Johnson,				7	50
	Proprietors' salaries unpaid.					
			15095	50	15095	50

LEDGER.

Dr.　　　　　　　　　　　　GEO. H. POPE.　　　　　　　　　　　　Cr.

1889					1889					
June	4	To Balance,	11028	25	June	1	By Cash, C.B.,	148	10800	
					"	4	" Wages,	150	10	
					"	4	" Loss and Gain,	152	218	25
			$11028	25					11028	25
							By Balance,		$11028	25

J. W. JOHNSON.

June	4	To Balance,	10975	75	June	1	By Cash, C. B.,		10750	00
					"	4	" Wages,		7	50
					"	4	" Loss and Gain,		218	25
			10975	75					10975	75
							By Balance,		$10975	75

STEAMER " CITY OF THE BAY."

June	1	To Cash, C.B.,	149	20000	June	4	By Balance,		35000
"	1	" Bills Pay.,	150	15000					
				35000					35000
		To Balance,		35000					

Dr.   BILLS PAYABLE.   Cr.

1889 June	4	To Balance,	$15000	1889 June	1	By Steamer,	150	$15000
						By Balance,		$15000

CASH.

June	4	To Sundries, C.B.,	148	22394	40	June	4	By Sundries, C.B.	149	20468	40
						"	"	By Balance,		1926	
				22394	40					22394	40
		To Balance,		$1926	00						

GEO. WEBBER.

June	2	To Freight,	150	78	June	4	By Balance,		78
		To Balance,		$78 00					

PASSAGE ACCOUNT.

June	4	To Loss & Gain,	152	130	June	4	By Cash,	148	130

FREIGHT ACCOUNT.

June	4	To Loss & Gain,	152	792	40	June	2	By Geo. Webber,	150	78	
						"	4	By Cash,	148	714	40
				792	40					792	40

STORES ACCOUNT.

June	1	To Cash,	149	127	June	4	By Expense,	151	127

FUEL ACCOUNT.

June	1	To Cash, C.B.,	149	288	June	4	By Expense,	151	288

EXPENSE.

June	3	To Cash, C.B.,	149	7	50	June	4	By Loss & Gain,	152	48	90
"	4	" Stores acct.,	151	127							
"	4	" Fuel "	151	288							
"	4	" Wages "	152	63	40						
				485	90					485	90

Dr. WAGES ACCOUNT. *Cr.*

1889 June	4 4	To Cash, C.B., " Sundries,	149 150	$45 17	90 50	1889 June	4	By Expense,	151	$63	40
				63	40					63	40

LOSS & GAIN.

June " "	4 " "	To Expense, " G. H. Pope, " J. W. Johnson,	151 150 150	485 218 218	90 25 25	June "	4 4	By Passage acct., " Freight "	151 151	130 792	40
				922	40					922	40

EXPLANATION.

It will be observed that there is no necessity for a Day Book, and that the Journal is only used to record such transactions as cannot be entered in the auxiliaries. Before posting the C. B. the money received for freights and passages is transferred from the Freight and Passage Books to the Dr. side of the C. B., and the amounts for fuel and wages from the Fuel Book, and Hands Register to the Cr. side.

In a regular business the hands would in all probability be paid monthly, and would no doubt occasionally require small sums of money, through the month, to defray their expenses. In such case a special column might be kept in the C. B., in which items paid to hands could be charged. We have not space in a work like this to continue the transactions for a whole month, and consequently close the books on reaching Montreal, in order to fully illustrate the Set. We will now give manuscript for the return trip to be worked out in the same style. The balances may be brought down as is done with the Real accounts, and the return trip posted in the same Ledger accounts.

MEMORANDUM, STEAMER "CITY OF THE BAY."

TRIP I.—FROM MONTREAL TO BELLEVILLE, JUNE 5TH, 1889.

Engaged P. Graham, as porter, at $12 per month, and J. Reynolds, as fireman, at $30, services to commence to-day.

Paid A. Emerson, for 10 tons Coal, at $6; 12 cords of Wood, at $5.50; A. F. Wood, for Provisions $25; E. G. Forbes, for Meat, $8.75. Paid for repairs, $4.

BILL OF LADING No. 10.—From Alex. Buntin & Co., Montreal, to E. Harrison, Belleville, marked " E. H., B.," 10 boxes Stationery, 2425 lbs., at 20c. per cwt.

BILL OF LADING No. 11.—From Frothingham & Workman, Montreal, to Lewis & Price, Belleville, marked " L. & P., B., 400 kegs, at 10c.; 40 boxes Hardware, 5750 lbs. at 10c. per cwt.

BILL OF LADING No. 12.—From James Sutherland, Montreal, to J. C. Overell, Belleville, marked "J. C. O., B.," 4 boxes Books, 1250 lbs., at 25c. per cwt.; 6 boxes Sundries, 840 lbs., at 30c. per cwt.

BILL OF LADING No. 13.—From J. McKay & Co., Montreal, to M. Empey, Belleville, marked "M. E., B.," 20 boxes Tweed, 4300 lbs., at 25c. per cwt.; 10 boxes Sundries, 2460 lbs., at 20c. per cwt.

BILL OF LADING No. 14.—From J. McKay & Co., Montreal, to W. H. Doxsee, Kingston, marked "W. H. D., K.," 10 boxes Cloth, 3420 lbs., at 20c. per cwt.; 100 boxes Tweed, 18,760 lbs., at 20c. per cwt.; 40 boxes Sundries, 1275 lbs., at 25c. per cwt.

PASSENGERS FROM MONTREAL—W. J. Carman and wife, Belleville, $9; E. Potts, J. Squires, Wm. Jeffs and R. Noon, for Belleville, $4.50 each; E. C. Wartman, R. Sanders, W. M. Parker, A. Brady, S. Davison and B. Carper, for Picton, at $4 each; Miss Mary Downey, W. C. Niles, G. Golson, S. Grinder and John Ivason, for Kingston, $3 each; John Turner, C. B. Rogers, Isaac Westman, A. Munro and Miss S. Allen, for Gananoque $2.50 each; A. Overell and wife, Brockville, $4; John Brown, Mary Brown and Jane Brown, for Cornwall, $1.50 each. Paid Canal Tolls for up trip, $9.60.

BILL OF LADING No. 15.—From Robert Shannon, Cornwall, to Chas. Vannorman, Belleville, marked " C. V., B.," 400 bundles of Paper at 10c.; 14 boxes Sundries, 1850 lbs. at 20c. per cwt.

JUNE 6.—BILL OF LADING No. 16.—From Pason & Post, Cornwall, to S. Stephenson, Gananoque, marked " S. S., G.," 80 bundles Waggon Spokes at 60c. each; 12 boxes Sundries, 3140 lbs., at 15c. per cwt.

BILL OF LADING No. 17.—From A. B. Walsh, Cornwall, to J. & H. Carson, Picton, marked "J. & H. C., P.;" 25 Iron Ploughs, at 75c.; 25 Harrows, at $1.

PASSENGERS FROM CORNWALL.—Isaac Blair, Belleville, $3; Patrick Murray, Kingston, $2; M. Hamilton and wife, Picton, $5; Jas. Rombeau, Deseronto, $2.75.

BILL OF LADING No. 18.—From John Simpson, Prescott, to Geo. Easton, Belleville, marked "G. E., B.," 300 boxes Tobacco, at 15c.; 20 boxes Sundries, 2160 lbs., at 18c. per cwt. Paid wharfage at Prescott, $2.40.

PASSENGERS FROM PRESCOTT.—George Bull and wife, A. McFee and wife, and R. Thompson and wife, for Belleville, $2.75 each; Adam Leslie, Deseronto, $2.25; R. Bottford, Picton, $2.

Paid S. Gorman, for 8 cords of Wood, $44.

JUNE 8.—BILL OF LADING No. 19.—From H. Bottoms, Brockville, to J. A. Agnew, Kingston, marked " J. A. A., K.," 10 boxes Tweed, 3200 lbs., 15c. per cwt.

BILL OF LADING No. 20.—From J. C. McGannon, Brockville, to L. H. Henderson, Belleville, marked " L. H. H., B.," 400 sacks Flour, at 10c.; 800 bushels Wheat, at 5c.

PASSENGERS FROM BROCKVILLE.—A. L. Morden, S. Young, E. B. Fraleck and M. Jellett, for Belleville, at $3 each; R. Moses and wife, Kingston, $3; Miss J. Sanderson and Miss R. Gordon, for Picton, at $2 each.

Paid W. Gaffield, for Provisions, $12.60.

BILL OF LADING No. 21.—From J. Johnson, Kingston, to " Intelligencer " Publishing Co., Belleville, marked " I. P. Co., B.," 500 bundles of Paper, 6800 lbs., at 12c. per cwt.

BILL OF LADING No. 22.—From R. Town & Co., Kingston, to W. Dickens, Belleville, marked "W. D., B.," 200 bbls. Apples at 15c.

PASSENGERS FROM KINGSTON.—J. H. Way and wife, Picton, $1; A. Thomas, W. Weaver, R.P. Dowe and Miss D. Lazier, for Deseronto, at $1.25 each; John Rowe, Belleville, $1.50.

BILL OF LADING No. 23.—From P. K. Norris, Picton, to R. Dick, Belleville, marked " R. D., B.," 12 boxes Sundries, 3225 lbs., at 15c. per cwt.

PASSENGERS FROM PICTON.—Henry Norris and wife, Belleville, $2; Susan Wills, Annie Banker, Mary Sweet, John Porter and Peter Smith, for Deseronto, at 25c. each.

BILL OF LADING No. 24.—From The Rathbun Company, Deseronto, to J. Forin, Belleville, marked "J. F., B.," 10,000 ft. Lumber, at 65c per M.

Bought for Cash of L. Moody, 15 cords Wood at $4.

9.—Arrived in Belleville, discharged cargo and paid hands in full for 3 days.
Deck Passage, $62.50.
Gain for return, $298.61.

MUNICIPAL ACCOUNTS.

Municipal book-keeping differs only in form and detail from ordinary mercantile methods of double entry. As Municipal Treasurers occupy positions of public trust, and as the credit of a municipality is an exceedingly sensitive thing, requiring honesty and competence in those who administer the affairs of a corporation, it is exceedingly desirous that municipal books should be kept in a manner at once clear, concise, and comprehensive, in order that the taxpayer or the debenture creditor may at any time inform himself "from the books" of the financial condition, and verify the statements of the auditors. If it is incumbent upon a merchant, who is a private individual, to keep his books after a method and in such a manner as will inspire confidence in his creditors, how much greater is the necessity that municipal corporations, which are continually borrowing, should have their affairs managed by a well-defined and thoroughly understood system. The absence of this produces confusion and mystifies the true state of affairs, induces fraud and peculation, and lowers the municipality's credit in the money market, so that it is difficult to dispose of its debentures, except at a heavy discount.

In the Set which follows you are supposed to be commencing a new set of books on the basis of the city's assets and liabilities, and bringing truly ascertained balances forward from the old books. In carrying on the monetary affairs of a municipal corporation, two prominent matters have to be considered, and on these all minor details depend: they are the yearly estimates of expenditures and the method of raising the revenue necessary to meet them. It usually devolves upon the Chairman of the Finance Committee, aided by the Treasurer, to consider these matters, and prepare them for submission to the council, which usually adopts their recommendations. We will suppose that the following is the

ESTIMATED EXPENDITURE.

Interest, Commission and Exchange,	$2,338.32
Market Buildings,	700.00
City Hall,	1,720.00
Market Square,	850.00
Market No. 2,	50.00
Insurance,	600.50
Police Department,	8,544.87
Public Schools—appropriation for 1876,	11,500.00
Fire Department,	3,710.00
Lighting Streets,	2,155.00
Salaries,	7,500.00
Streets,	13,320.91
Public Park,	356.00
Printing and Stationery,	900.00
Election Expenses,	438.00

MISCELLANEOUS PROPERTY:

New Hose	$600.00	
Water Sprinklers	45.00	
		645.00
Interest on debentures, issue of 1st April, 1866,	2,100.00	
Interest on debentures, issue of 1st August, 1870,	7,000.00	
		9,100.00
To pay County of Windsor on account of award		25,040.00
Carried forward,		$89,468.60

CONTINGENCIES:

Brought forward,		$89,468.60
Prop. of Jury Expenses, 1875,	$1,902.58	
Support of prisoners in gaol,	4,130.00	
Appropriation High School	498.75	
" Collegiate Institute,	375.00	
" General Hospital,	200.00	
" to compensate John Smith for loss of property by Fire,	275.00	
" to compensate J. Brown for injuries received as fireman,	252.50	
Post-Mortem examination and medical evidence,	250.00	
Law Expenses,	100.00	
Pauper Passages,	200.00	
Coffins and Interments,	50.00	
Bill Posting,	20.00	
Postage and Telegrams,	30.00	
Registration,	115.00	
Taking Census.	100.00	
Dog Medals,	41.05	
Incidentals,	775.75	
		9,315.63
*Estimated Expenditure		$98,784.23

You now proceed to find out what the revenue will likely be.

ESTIMATED REVENUE.

Surplus of Revenue over Expenditure, 1875,	$2,736.99
Rents,	6,206.70
Licenses,	11,296.10
Fines Police Court,	1,000.00
Clergy Reserve Fund,	600.00
Taxes, lands of non-residents,	200.00
Gravel, Road, section of	73.62
Instalments on Lots sold,	1,139.06
Frontage,	292.50
Dominion Government for Public Clock,	430.00
	$23,974.97

The difference between the above revenue and the estimated expenditure has to be raised by taxation. We will suppose that the assessors have completed their work and placed the assessable property of the city at $5,112,246.

A rate of 16 mills on the Dollar will amount to			$81,795.93
Less S. Schools		$1,600.00	
Remissions		3,000.00	
Uncollectable		500.00	
		5,100.00	76,695.93
Total Revenue			$100,670.90
Estimated Expenditure			98,784.23
Surplus			$1,886.67

*NOTE.—The Sinking Fund Levy is omitted this year, for the reason stated in explanatory notes at the end of Set.

The preceding revenue and assessment will cover the expenditure, and leave the above surplus. Occasionally it becomes necessary to raise money for special objects, such as improvement of various kinds, buildings, bridges, &c., the cost of which it is desirable to spread over a number of years. To do this, resort is usually had to the issue of Debentures, which are promises to pay of the nature of notes of private individuals or firms, differing only in form. These sell at a premium, par, or discount, according to the interest they draw, the length of time they have to run, or the credit of the municipality offering them. They are frequently made payable in 20 years, with interest half-yearly. Attached to each debenture are interest coupons which the holders at the proper time detach and present for payment. When a municipality issues Debentures, it usually provides for their payment by creating a " SINKING FUND, " deposit or investment, obtained from a special rate levied yearly for the purpose ; and this fund, when wisdom and prudence are characteristic of the management, is held intact for the purpose for which it was created. A good plan for creating this fund to retire debentures that are to run 20 years, and pay the interest upon them, is to levy the amount of the yearly interest and 5 per cent. of the total debenture issue each year of the 20 years, the latter to be deposited or invested, and at the end of the time the whole capital sum will have been accumulated and the interest duly met. The interest accruing from the Sinking Fund deposit or investment you regard, and use, as any other yearly income. For example, debentures to the amount of $30,000 are issued, payable in 20 years from date, with interest at 6 per cent. ; if you levy $1800, and 5 per cent. of $30,000, which is $1500 yearly for 20 years, pay the interest with the former, deposit or invest the latter, using the interest it produces as a yearly income of the corporation, you will at the date of the maturity of the debentures be in possession of the sum necessary to retire them, and will have duly met the interest periodically.

Sinking Funds are sometimes dealt with differently from the method indicated above. The Ontario Municipal Statute requires that such a sum shall be levied yearly as will, capitalized at 5 per cent., produce the amount borrowed when it becomes due. Example, suppose the City of Belleville desires to raise $90,000, payable in twenty years. To find the amount you must levy for Sinking Fund proceed by this rule. Find what $1.00 will produce levied yearly for 20 years, and interest on the fund at 5 per cent. This gives $33.06682639 ; then if $1.00 produces $33.06682639, how much will it take to produce $90,000, as much as times that sum is contained in $90,000, which is $2721.76 to be levied yearly.

The levying and collecting of this Sinking Fund are not all the important features connected with it. It is highly important that an account in your Ledger should show at its DEBIT the amount of this fund. It will not do to only collect the amount, debit cash and credit tax account. In that case, the money goes into the general funds, and would be used for general purposes. You must take from the collections at certain times the proportion properly belonging to this fund, and either deposit it in a bank or invest it in a good security. The Sinking Fund account in the Ledger will be debited with the sums invested for this account, showing an existing tangible asset. It is sometimes desirable to provide a Sinking Fund for each of the several issues of debentures when the whole debt is not consolidated.

The principal books of entry required in this Set are, Cash Book, Journal and Ledger, and the minor books, Debenture Register, somewhat after the form of a Bill Book ; a Warrant Book in which the authority of the Council for the payment of accounts is entered, each one of which is consecutively numbered ; a Receipt Book in which receipts are entered, each bearing a corresponding number with the authority for payment in the Warrant Book ; a Non-resident Tax Book giving the particulars respecting the lands of non-residents, the taxes on which the Treasurer usually collects, and any other minor books or forms which peculiar circumstances may demand.

The method of dealing with the Collector is an extremely important consideration in municipal matters, for, upon the prompt collection of taxes, and the no less prompt handing over by the Collector to the Treasurer of the money, depends the satisfactory running of the municipal machine in accordance with the estimates.

If the collector be allowed to retain the money in his possession, and at his convenience pay over to the Treasurer such sums as he may choose, it is quite apparent that an opportunity for other than honest dealing is afforded. It is desirable that EACH DAY the Collector should pay over to the Treasurer all sums of money collected by him, exhibiting at the same time in a book kept by him for the purpose, or from stubs of his receipt book, the names of the parties from whom it has been received, and the amounts, which should be checked by the Treasurer, and a receipt given, in the book, for each day's collections. This course will obviate the necessity of opening an account with the Collector in the Ledger, a plan which, although pursued in some places, is not adopted in our principal cities, for reasons given in the explanations at the close of the Set. At the close of each year the Collector should be required to make an interim return of taxes remaining uncollected at that time and for that year, the total amount of which, and the money paid over, would exactly tally with the tax rolls; then, after the lapse of considerable time, when it is not possible to collect any more of that year's taxes, he should make out a final return and be relieved of further responsibility. Having so much premised for your general information, you will now proceed to open the Set by journalizing the assets and liabilities. (*See form of Journal.*) After journalizing, you will open accounts in the Ledger under the names of those titles used in the Journal, and proceed to post the items; this being done, you are ready to proceed with the current work of the year. As you are aware, there must be an account under some name in all double entry book-keeping, to keep the Ledger in balance, or show capital. In this set use "City of Ontario" account for this purpose. You will observe that on the start this account shows $10,553.65 at its debit, which of course means that the city's liabilities exceed its assets by that amount.

(*See the fuller explanations at the end of the Set.*)

JOURNAL.

City of Ontario, January, 1876.

L.F.					
166	Sundries Dr. to City of Ontario account.*				
166	Cash Acct. For Balance on hand,	$ 250	00		
166	Molsons Bank. For Amt. on deposit,	395	85		
166	Real Estate. For value of City Buildings and Lots D., B. and C. in Victoria Ward,	57000	00		
166	Property Account. For miscellaneous property, as detailed in Schedule A., B. and C., on file in this office,	45000	00		
166	Sinking Fund No. 1. For amount on deposit to meet accruing debentures of the issue of 1st April, 1866,	15300	00		
166	Rents Receivable. For sundry amts. owing 1st January, 1876, as per statement on file in this office,	274	50		
167	Non-Resident Taxes. For amount outstanding and considered good as per non-resident Tax Book,	897	00		
167	Taxes, 1875. For outstanding Taxes as per Collector's Interim Return to 1st January, 1876,	25329	00		
167	Sinking Fund No. 2. For amt. on deposit to meet accruing debentures of the issue of 1st Aug., 1870,	30000	00		
				174,446	35
166 167	City of Ontario Acct. Dr. to Sundries.† Debenture Acct. For issue of 1st April, 1866, as per Register, " " 1st Aug., 1870, " "	30000 100000	00 00		
167	Bills Payable. For Note No. 5 under discount, due 1st July, 1876,	20000	00		
167	County of Windsor. For amt. owing it, as per Arbitrators award,	35000	00		
				185,000	00

*This entry represents the City's assets on the 1st Jan., 1876.
† This entry represents the City's liabilities on the 1st Jan., 1876.

JOURNAL—Continued.
City of Ontario, January, 1876.

L.F.					
166	*Cash Acct. Dr. to Sundries.				
167	Taxes, 1875. For January receipts as C.B.,	$14339	65		
166	Rents Receivable. For January receipts as C.B.,	627	50		
166	Molsons Bank. For Checks drawn in January as C.B.	504	50		
167	Licenses Account. For January receipts as C.B.,	555	00	$16,026	65
166	Sundries Dr. to Cash Account.				
168	Indigent Account. For payments in January as C B.,	103	74		
168	Interest Acct. For payments in January as C.B.,	350	00		
168	Streets Acct. For payments in January as C.B.,	2403	10		
168	Fire Dept. Acct. For payments in January as C.B.,	282	95		
168	Thos. McNaughton. For payments in January as C.B.,	45	00		
167	County of Windsor. For payment in January as C.B.,	3000	00		
168	Election Exp. Acct. For payment in January as C.B.,	409	00		
166	Molsons Bank. For deposits in January as C.B.,	8000	00		
168	E. Robinson. For payment in January as C.B.,	100	00		
169	Contingent Acct. For payments in January as C.B.,	25	00		
169	Fuel Account. For payments in January as C.B.,	195	50		
166	Property Acct. For payments in January as C.B.,	984	20	$15,898	49

*Cash is Journalised from the Cash Book at the end of each month in this Set. We have done this to illustrate the method of journalizing from Cash Book; but there is no necessity for journalizing Cash, as it might be posted directly from Cash Book into Ledger, as is done in Sets IX. and XI.

JOURNAL—Continued.

City of Ontario, January, 1876.

L. F.											
169	Sundries Dr. to Assessment Acct.										
	Ward.	Value of Real Property.	Value of Personal Property.	Total Assessment.	Statute Labor.	Dogs.	Total amt. of Taxes.				
169	Taxes, 1876.										
	For Dog Taxes,						$50.00				
	" Statute Labor Taxes,						78.00				
	" Resident Taxes, $5,072,246										
	at the rate of 16 mills on $						81,155.93	$81,283	93		
167	Non-Resident Taxes.										
	For Taxes on lands of non-residents,$40,000										
	At the rate of 16 mills on $						640	00			
	Total Assessment, $5,112,246										
	Total Taxes,									$81,923	93
	Corresponding with above abstract from Assessment Rolls duly certified by Auditors.										
169	Assessment Acct. Dr. to Sundries.										
169	Taxes, 1876.										
	For remissions and deductions made by Court of Revision as per City Clerk's Remission Book, folios 43 and 44, certified by auditors,						$2575.00				
	For proportion of Separate School Tax as noted on Assessment Roll,						1729.00				
							4304	00			
169	Public Schools Account.										
	For appropriation for 1876 as applied for by the Board of Education as per their Budget submitted to City Council,						11,750	00			
										$16,054	00
169	Bonus Acct. Dr.						10,000	00			
167	To Debenture Acct.									$10,000	00
	For 20 Debentures for the sum of $500 each, issued to the Ontario Rolling Mills Co. with the sanction of a majority of the Ratepayers obtained by vote on the 3rd day of January, 1876, and confirmed by the Council on the 5th day of the same month and year, payable in 10 years from 1st January, 1876, with interest at the rate of 6 per cent. per annum, and duly entered and numbered C. 1 to 20 in Debenture Register.										

JOURNAL—Continued.

City of Ontario, January, 1876.

L.F.					
166	CITY OF ONTARIO ACCT. DR.		$10000	00	
169	To Bonus Acct.				$10000	00
	For amount of Bonus granted to the Ontario Rolling Mills Co. transferred.				
	February, 1876.				
166	CASH DR. TO SUNDRIES.				
	For receipts in February as per C.B.				
166	Rents Receivable, ...	5500	00		
167	Licenses, ...	10700	00		
169	Police Court, ...	960	00		
170	Clergy Reserve, ...	600	00		
167	Non-Resident Taxes, ...	450	00		
170	Gravel Road, ...	73	62		
166	Real Estate, ...	1050	00		
170	Frontage, ...	250	00		
170	Dominion Government, ...	430	00		
169	Taxes, 1876, ...	57550	00		
167	Taxes, 1875, ...	10000	00		
				$87563	62

166	SUNDRIES DR. TO CASH.				
	For payments in February as per C.B.				
168	Interest, ...	$ 8750	00		
170	Market Buildings,....	720	00		
170	City Hall, ...	1700	00		
170	Market Square, ...	850	00		
171	Market No. 2, ...	48	00		
171	Insurance, ...	600	00		
171	Police Department, ...	8540	00		
169	Public School, ...	11750	00	
168	Fire Department, ...	3420	00		
171	Lighting Streets, ...	2129	00		
171	Salaries, ...	2480	00		
168	T. McNaughton, ...	955	00		
168	E. Robinson, ...	900	00		
168	Streets, ...	10900	00		
171	Public Park, ...	329	00		
171	Printing and Stationery, ...	928	50		
167	County of Windsor, ...	22000	00		
.69	Contingent, ...	9429	00		
166	Molsons Bank, ...	1000	00		
				$87428	50

JOURNAL—Continued.

City of Ontario, February, 1876.

L.F.					
171	SALARIES ACCT. DR. TO SUNDRIES.	$1000	00		
168	T. McNaughton, for Salary, 1876,	1000	00		
168	E. Robinson, " " "			$2000	00
	NOTE.—The foregoing journal entries having been posted you will now take off Trial Balance to prove correctness of work, after which close the working accounts into revenue as per following journal entries.				
171	SUNDRIES DR. TO REVENUE ACCT. For amounts transferred to close working accounts for 1876.				
166	Rents Receivable, ...	5853	00		
167	Licenses, ...	11255	00		
169	Assessment, ...	65869	93		
169	Police Court, ...	960	00		
170	Clergy Reserve, ...	600	00		
170	Gravel Road, ...	73	62		
170	Frontage, ...	250	00		
170	Dominion Government, ...	430	00	85291	55
171	REVENUE ACCT. DR. TO SUNDRIES. For amounts transferred to close working accounts for 1876.				
168	Indigent, ...	$ 103	74		
168	Interest, ...	9100	00		
168	Streets, ...	13303	10		
168	Fire Department, ...	3702	95		
168	Election Expense, ...	409	00		
169	Contingent, ...	9454	00		
169	Fuel, ...	195	50		
170	Market Buildings, ...	720	00		
170	City Hall, ...	1700	00		
170	Market Square, ...	850	00		
171	Market No. 2, ...	48	00		
171	Insurance, ...	600	00		
171	Police Department....	8540	00		
171	Lighting Streets, ...	2129	00		
171	Salaries, ...	4480	00		
171	Public Park, ...	329	00		
171	Printing and Stationery	928	50	56592	79
171	REVENUE ACCT. DR.	28698	76		
166	To CITY OF ONTARIO ACCT. For amount transferred to close acct.			$28698	76

JOURNAL AND CASH BOOK.

You do not use what is ordinarily called a Day Book in this set of accounts, and the reason is obvious. In mercantile business, or when any kind of trade is being carried on, of course a book of this nature is desirable, but in the Treasurer's department of a municipality there are few transactions occurring other than the receiving and disbursing of money, and hence the Cash Book should contain the original entries of these; the form of Journal which is here used affording you the opportunity, when the necessity arises, to make entries other than those affecting cash in a full and comprehensive manner. It may be desirable, and would be quite proper, to keep a memorandum book in which to write the particulars of rents or other matters until you are prepared to journalize.

Monthly journalizing of Cash and all other entries, as here pursued, is admirably suited to municipal book-keeping in this form. At a glance the Cash Book shows each entry for the month in detail, with explanations as full as desired; and in the Journal these are grouped under the names of the accounts affected, and in the aggregate transferred to the Ledger; while any other entries that it may be necessary to make for the month follow in the Journal, and are likewise transferred to the Ledger. We put checks drawn upon, and deposits made in the bank through the Cash Book, because it is desirable to show all details of cash transactions in one book. It would be quite proper, however, if preferred, to confine the record of checks to the Journal and Ledger. The numbering of checks, and the preservation of them and the stubs, are matters which should receive your attention. We have placed the Journal first in the Set, as its first page is taken up with the entries necessary to open the books. Were there no opening entries to make, of course the Cash Book would have been first in order. You will, however, act as though the Cash Book, Journal and Ledger were separately before you, and having studied the first page of the Journal, take the Cash Book as next in order. In it you are supposed to have the record of transactions clearly and distinctly made. If it be desirable to make longer explanations than any of the examples given, make them; use half a dozen or a dozen lines if necessary, for this is the book of original entry, and each one should be accompanied by full and clear information. Where reference can be made to some document, paper, or book giving explanation or authority, of course a simple reference to these is sufficient, as for example taken from Cash Book:—

"FUEL ACCOUNT," "J. B. Warren's account for coal as per warrant No. 2" refers to the Coal Merchant's account, and by number to the warrant of the council for its payment. The Cash entries for the month being made, you will ascertain the aggregate of amounts to be debited or credited respectively to each account, and proceed to journalize these (as done on page 159); taking care when journalizing the total debit and credit of each, not to include the balances. Having journalized Cash for the month, your next business is to make any other journal entries that may be required (as done on page 160), and when they are made, and the items of the Journal are posted to the Ledger, the month's work, so far as the books are concerned, is complete, and you are prepared, as required by many municipal bodies, to furnish an intelligent and intelligible statement of the month's transactions.

CASH

Dr.

1876					
Jan.	1		To balance on hand as per asset entry in Journal,	$ 250	00
	"	To Taxes, 1875,	Amount as per receipt No. 1 given Collector,	3200	00
	"	" Rents Rec.,	J. Armstrong Market fees 3 mos. in advance,	495	50
	7	" Taxes, 1875,	Amount as per receipt No. 2 given Collector,	575	00
	9	" Molsons Bank,	Check No. 1,	45	00
	12	" Licenses,	Tavern License, William Wilson, $75.00		
			" " John Purdy, 75.00		
			Saloon " Wm. Redmer, 100.00		
			" " Jas. Todd, 100.00		
			Auctioneer " T. Hamilton, 20.00		
			Cab, " John O'Hara, 5.00		
			" " M. Sullivan, 5.00		
				380	00
	15	" Taxes, 1875,	As per receipts No. 3 to 7 given to Collector,	5400	00
	17	" "	Amount as per receipt No. 8 given Collector,	1500	00
	21	" "	As per receipts Nos. 9 to 12 given Collector,	2500	00
	"	" Molsons Bank,	Check No. 2,	459	50
	22	" Taxes, 1875,	Amount as per receipt No. 13 given Collector,	432	50
	23	" "	" " " " 14 " "	195	25
	26	" Licenses,	Tavern License, J. Brodie, 75.00		
	"	" "	Billiard " A. Norris, 100.00		
				175	00
	27	" Taxes, 1875,	Amount as per receipt No. 15 given Collector,	394	60
	"	" Rents Receivable,	Lessee of Lot on Water Street in full for 1875,	132	00
	30	" Taxes, 1875,	Amount as per receipt No. 16 given Collector,	142	30
			Entries Journalized, folio 159.	$16276	65
			To balance brought down,	378	16
Feb.		To Rents Receivable,	For balance of collections for 1876,	5500	00
		" Licenses	" " " "	10700	00
		" Police Court,	" Fines for year 1876,	960	00
		" Clergy Reserves,	" Income from that source for 1876,	600	00
		" Non-resid't Taxes,	" Collections for 1876,	450	00
		" Gravel Road,	" Income from that source for 1876,	73	62
		" Real Estate,	" Lots sold in 1876,	1050	00
		" Frontage,	" Income from that source for 1876,	250	00
		" Dominion Gov'nt.,	" Allowance for lighting clock,	430	00
		" Taxes, 1876,	" Collections, 1876,	57550	00
		" Taxes, 1875,	" Balance of collections in 1876,	10000	00
			Entries journalized, folio 161.	$87941	78

(See explanation given at the end of Set for making Receipts so large in one month.)

BOOK.
Cr.

1876					
Jan.	1	By Indigent,	Amount paid as per Relief Committee order,	$ 23	90
	3	" Interest,	Coupons Debentures A, Nos. 1 to 20,	350	00
	7	" Streets,	Prop. of Pay List No. 1,	410	00
	7	" Fire Dept.,	" " "	193	00
	9	" Thos. McNaughton,	Check No. 1, account salary,	45	00
	10	" County of Windsor,	Payment on account of award,	3000	00
	12	" Election Expense,	As per Clerk's receipt,	409	00
	15	" Molsons Bank,	Amount deposited,	5000	00
	18	" Indigent,	Amount paid as per Relief Committee order,	79	84
	"	" E. Robinson,	Account Salary,	100	00
	21	" Streets.	Prop. of Pay List No. 2,	397	50
	"	" Fire Department,	" " "	89	96
	23	" Contingent,	Expenses of deputation to Toronto, as per Warrant No. 1,	25	00
	25	" Fuel,	J. B. Warren's account for coal, as per Warrant No. 2,	195	50
	25	" Streets,	Lumber, J. Morden & Co., as per Warrant No. 3,	1595	60
	28	" Property,	Hose, R. Volney & Co., as per Warrant No. 4,	984	20
	30	" Molsons Bank,	Amount deposited,	3000	00
			Balance,	378	16
			Entries Journalized, folio 159,	16276	65
Feb.		By Interest Acct.,	For Balance of payments in 1876,	8750	00
		" Market Buildings,	For payments in 1876,	720	00
		" City Hall,	" " "	1700	00
		" Market Square,	" " "	850	00
		" Market No. 2,	" " "	48	00
		" Insurance,	" " "	600	00
		" Police Dept.,	" " "	8540	00
		" Public Schools,	For appropriation for 1876, paid in full,	11750	00
		" Fire Dept.,	" balance of payments in 1876,	3420	00
		" Lighting Streets,	" payments in 1876,	2129	00
		" Salaries,	" " "	2480	00
		" T. McNaughton,	" bal. of salary for 1876,	955	00
		" E. Robinson,	" " "	900	00
		" Streets,	" payments in 1876,	10900	00
		" Public Park,	" payments in 1876,	329	00
		" Printing and Statn'y,	" " "	928	50
		" County of Windsor,	" " on account of award,	22000	00
		" Contingent,	" balance of payments in 1876,	9429	00
		" Molsons Bank,	Deposit,	1000	00
			Balance,	513	28
			Entries Journalized, folio 161,	$87941	78

(See explanation given at the end of Set for making disbursements so large in one month.)

LEDGER.
Dr. CITY OF ONTARIO. Cr.

1876						1876				
Jan.	To Sundries.	158	185000	00	Jan.	By Sundries,	158	$174446	35
"	" Bonus acct.	161	10000	00	Feb.	" Revenue acct.	162	28698	76
	Balance,		8145	11					
			$203145	11				203145	11
						By Balance,		$8145	11

CASH ACCOUNT.

Jan.	To City of Ont.ac.	158	250	00	Jan.	By Sundries,	159	15898	49
"	" Sundries,	159	16026	65	Feb.	" Sundries,	161	87428	50
Feb.	" Sundries,	161	87563	62		Balance,		513	28
			$103840	27				103840	27
	To Balance,		513	28					

MOLSONS BANK.

Jan.	To City of Ont.ac.	158	395	85	Jan.	By Cash acct.,	159	504	50
"	" Cash acct.,	159	8000	00		Balance,		8891	35
Feb.	" "	161	1000	00					
			$9395	85				9395	85
	To Balance,		8891	35					

REAL ESTATE.

Jan.	To City of Ont.ac.	158	57000	00	Feb.	By Cash acct.,	161	1050	00
						Balance,		55950	00
			$57000	00				57000	00
	To Balance,		55950	00					

PROPERTY.

Jan.	To City of Ont.ac.	158	45000	00		Balance,		45984	20
	" Cash acct.,	159	984	20					
			$45984	20				45984	20
	To Balance,		45984	20					

SINKING FUND No. 1.

Jan.	To City of Ont.ac.	158	15300	00					

RENTS RECEIVABLE.

Jan.	To City of Ont.ac.	158	274	50	Jan.	By Cash acct.,	159	627	50
Feb.	" Revenue acct.	171	5853	00	Feb.	" "	161	5500	00
			$6127	50				$6127	50

NON-RESIDENT TAXES.

Dr									Cr
1876 Jan.	To City of Ont.act	158	897	00	1876 Feb.	By Cash acct., Balance,	161	450	00
"	" Assessment ac	160	640	00				1087	00
			$1537	00				1537	00
	To Balance,		1087	00					

TAXES, 1875.

Jan.	To City of Ont.act	158	25329	00	Jan. Feb.	By Cash acct., " " Balance,	159 161	14339 10000 989	65 00 35
			25329	00				25329	00
	To Balance,		$989	35					

SINKING FUND No. 2.

Jan.	To City of Ont.act	158	30000	00					

DEBENTURES.

					Jan.	By City of Ont.act " " " " Bonus acct.	158 160 160	30000 100000 10000	

BILLS PAYABLE.

					Jan.	By City of Ont.act	158	20000	

COUNTY OF WINDSOR.

Jan. Feb.	To Cash acct., " " Balance.	159 161	3000 22000 10000	00 00 00	Jan.	By City of Ont.act	158	35000	00
			$35000	00				35000	00
						By Balance,		10000	00

LICENSES.

Feb.	To Revenue acct.	162	11255	00	Jan. Feb.	By Cash acct., " "	159 161	555 10700	00 00
			$11255	00				$11255	00

Dr.   INDIGENT.   Cr.

1876 Jan.	To Cash acct.	159	103	74	1876 Feb.	By Revenue acct.,	162	103	74

INTEREST.

Jan. Feb.	To Cash acct., " "	159 161	350 8750	00 00	Feb.	By Revenue acct.,	162	9100	00
			$9100	00				9100	00

STREETS.

Jan. Feb.	To Cash acct., " "	159 161	2403 10900	10 00	Feb.	By Revenue acct.,	162	13303	10
			13303	10				13303	10

FIRE DEPARTMENT.

Jan. Feb.	To Cash acct., " "	159 161	282 3420	95 00	Feb.	By Revenue acct.,	162	3702	95
			$3702	95				3702	95

THOS. McNAUGHTON (City Clerk).

Jan. Feb.	To Cash acct., " " "	159 161	45 955	00 00	Feb.	By Salaries acct.,	162	1000	00
			$1000	00				1000	00

ELECTION EXPENSE.

Jan.	To Cash acct.,	159	409	00	Feb.	By Revenue acct.,	162	409	00

E. ROBINSON (City Treasurer).

Jan.	To Cash acct., " " "	159 161	100 900	00 00	Feb.	By Salaries acct.,	162	1000	00
			$1000	00				$1000	00

Dr.   CONTINGENT.   Cr.

1876								
Jan.	To Cash acct.,	159	25	00	Feb.	By Revenue acct.,	162	$9454 00
Feb.	" " "	161	9429	00				
			$9454	00				$9454 00

FUEL.

Jan.	To Cash acct.,	159	195	50	Feb.	By Revenue acct.,	162	195	50

TAXES, 1876.

Jan.	To Assessment ac	160	81283	93	Jan.	By Assessment ac	160	4304	00
					Feb.	" Cash acct.,	161	57550	00
						Balance,		19429	93
			81283	93				$81283	93
	To Balance,		$19429	93					

ASSESSMENT.

Jan.	To Sundries,	160	16054	00	Jan.	By Sundries,	160	81923	93
Feb.	" Revenue acct.,	162	65869	93					
			$81923	93				$81923	93

PUBLIC SCHOOLS.

Feb.	To Cash acct.,	161	11750	00	Jan.	By Assessment act	160	11750	00

BONUS.

Jan.	To Debenture act	160	10000	00	Jan.	By City of Ont. act	161	10000	00

POLICE COURT.

Feb.	To Revenue acct.,	162	960	00	Feb.	By Cash acct.,	161	960	00

Dr. CLERGY RESERVE. *Cr.*

1876 Feb.	To Revenue acct.	162	600	00	1876 Feb.	By Cash acct.,	161	$600	00

GRAVEL ROAD.

Feb.	To Revenue acct.,	162	73	62	Feb.	By Cash acct.,	161	73	62

FRONTAGE.

Feb.	To Revenue acct.,	162	250	00	Feb.	By Cash acct.,	161	250	00

DOMINION GOVERNMENT.

Feb.	To Revenue acct.,	162	430	00	Feb.	By Cash acct.,	161	430	00

MARKET BUILDINGS.

Feb.	To Cash acct.,	161	720	00	Feb.	By Revenue acct.,	162	720	00

CITY HALL.

Feb.	To Cash acct.,	161	1700	00	Feb.	By Revenue acct.,	162	1700	00

MARKET SQUARE.

Feb.	To Cash acct.,	161	850	00	Feb.	By Revenue acct.,	162	850	00

Dr. MARKET No. 2. *Cr.*

| 1876 Feb. | To Cash acct., | 161 | $48 | 00 | 1876 Feb. | By Revenue acct. | 162 | $48 | 00 |

INSURANCE.

| Feb. | To Cash acct., | 161 | 600 | 00 | Feb. | By Revenue acct. | 162 | 600 | 00 |

POLICE DEPARTMENT.

| Feb. | To Cash acct., | 161 | 8540 | 00 | Feb. | By Revenue acct. | 162 | 8540 | 00 |

LIGHTING STREETS.

| Feb. | To Cash acct., | 161 | 2129 | 00 | Feb. | By Revenue acct. | 163 | 2129 | 00 |

SALARIES.

Feb.	To Cash acct.,	161	2480	00	Feb.	By Revenue acct.	162	4480	00
"	" Sundries,	162	2000	00					
			$4480	00				4480	00

PUBLIC PARK.

| Feb. | To Cash acct., | 161 | 329 | 00 | Feb. | By Revenue acct. | 162 | 329 | 00 |

PRINTING AND STATIONERY.

| Feb. | To Cash acct., | 161 | 928 | 50 | Feb. | By Revenue acct. | 162 | 928 | 50 |

REVENUE.

Feb.	To Sundries,	162	56592	79	Feb.	By Sundries,	162	85291	55
"	" City of Ont.ac.	162	28698	76					
			$85291	55				85291	55

*TRIAL BALANCE.

Fol.	Account.	Dr.		Cr.	
166	City of Ontario,	$20553	65		
166	Cash,	513	28		
166	Molsons Bank,	8891	35		
166	Real Estate,	55950	00		
166	Property,	45984	20		
166	Sinking Fund No. 1,	15300	00		
166	Rents Receivable,			$5853	00
167	Non-Resident Taxes,	1087	00		
167	Taxes, 1875,	989	35		
167	Sinking Fund No. 2,	30000	00		
167	Debenture account,			140000	00
167	Bills Payable,			20000	00
167	County of Windsor,			10000	00
167	Licenses account,			11255	00
168	Indigent account,	103	74		
168	Interest account,	9100	00		
168	Streets,	13303	10		
168	Fire Department,	3702	95		
168	Election Expenses,	409	00		
169	Contingent account,	9454	00		
169	Fuel account,	195	50		
169	Taxes, 1876,	19429	93		
169	Assessment account,			65869	93
169	Police Court,			900	00
170	Clergy Reserve,			600	00
170	Gravel Road,			73	62
170	Frontage,			250	00
170	Dominion Government,			430	00
170	Market Buildings,	720	00		
170	City Hall,	1700	00		
170	Market Square,	850	00		
171	Market No. 2,	48	00		
171	Insurance,	600	00		
171	Police Department,	8540	00		
171	Lighting Streets,	2129	00		
171	Salaries,	4480	00		
171	Public Park,	32	00		
171	Printing and Stationery,	928	50		
		$255291	55	$255291	55

* This Trial Balance exhibits the *balances* of the accounts, not the footings.

ASSETS AND LIABILITIES,

STATEMENT.

Ledger Folio	Assets.			Ledger Folio	Liabilities.		
166	Cash,	513	28	167	Debentures,	140000	00
166	Molsons Bank	8891	35	167	Bills Payable,	20000	00
166	Real Estate,	55950	00	167	County of Windsor,	10000	00
166	Property,	45984	20	166	City of Ontario being balance showing amount of assets over liabilities		
166	Sinking Fund No. 1,	15300	00				
167	Non-Res. Taxes,	1087	00				
167	Taxes, 1875,	989	35			8145	11
167	Sinking Fund, No. 2	30000	00				
169	Taxes, 1876,	19429	93				
		$178145	11			$178145	11

EXPLANATORY NOTES.

Owing to the limited space which any one set of books may occupy in a work of this kind, curtailment is of course a necessity, and hence we have been obliged to compress into two months what ordinarily would be spread over a year. In the first month, however, ordinary receipts and expenditures are recorded, but in the second, in order to be in a position to instruct you how to close the books at the end of a year, aggregate sums for the balance of the year are entered; for the months which these aggregate sums represent, our entries would be similar to, and made after the manner of the examples given in the first month.

The method of making the assessment entry is important, and should receive your careful attention. It is desirable, as you will presently see, that there should be, in the Ledger, a Tax account for each year; the proper time for opening it being when the Assessors have completed their work, and the Assessment Rolls are in the Collector's hands, and money is being paid on its account, the sums so received being of course passed to its credit. Afterwards, when the Court of Revision has made all remissions and deductions, and these, properly certified by the Auditors, have been ascertained from the City Clerk's remission book, and the Rolls have been handed to you by the Auditors with their certificate of correctness, you will be in possession of the data from which to accurately make the Assessment entry, in the manner shown on page 160. As Auditors for any past year are not appointed till the first meeting of the Council of the succeeding year, your assessment entry is necessarily delayed till December, hence the necessity of the year's tax account being opened before then. You will see that in making the assessment entry in the form prescribed, you show accurately each year's revenue within the year. All the taxes for the year will not have been collected at the time you make the entry, but the amount outstanding is shown by the balance (corresponding with the Collector's interim return mentioned before) at the Tax account's debit when you close the books for the year. The Tax account for any one year should be kept open just so long as there are unpaid taxes on the roll likely to be collected. When it becomes impossible to collect any more, probably after the lapse of a few years, it should be closed into City of Ontario account.

The blank form given in the assessment entry, page 160, is used to show, in abstract, the amounts of the various taxes on the Assessment Rolls, with the totals of which it ought of course to correspond.

N

If you will consider the assessment entry, the foregoing explanations, and what is said on page 157 regarding the method of dealing with the Collector, you will perceive the advantage afforded by separate yearly tax accounts in securing prompt returns, clearly defined and reliable records of each year complete within itself, and the prevention of a lax system, either on the part of the treasurer, collector or other official.

The reason why we have adopted the plan of dealing with the Collector here pursued, instead of opening an account for him in the Ledger, and debiting him with the amount of the Assessment Rolls placed in his hands for collection, and crediting him with sums collected for taxes, is that we have observed in more than one instance, where the latter system is in vogue, the absence of promptness in making returns, and what follows as the natural result of this, an unsatisfactory condition of affairs between the Collector and the city, and in the Treasurer's books, laxity, incompleteness, and a deceptive and unreliable state of the accounts. We are acquainted with the books of one municipality, in the Ledger of which there stands at the debit of the Collector a sum of over $100,000, brought down as a balance from the previous year; the Collector not having returned the Assessment Rolls for three years, and no attempt having been made during that time to effect a settlement with him. In the method we adopt, we recognize but one Treasurer, and treat the Collector simply as a channel through which the daily collections of taxes reach his hands.

The bonus granted to the Ontario Rolling Mills Co. is charged to Bonus account (see Journal 160) because it is desirable to turn to this account, at any time, to see by direct reference the particulars of bonuses; but it is by the next entry (see Journal 161) written off to the City of Ontario account, and not allowed to stand in the form of an asset, which, of course, being a gift, it is not.

It is scarcely necessary to say that at the maturity of any debenture issue, for which a Sinking Fund has been provided, in the manner recommended on page 156, the amount at the credit of Debenture account, representing the issue, would be written off by a debit, the corresponding credit of which would close its Sinking Fund account.

As the proportion of Separate School Taxes does not come into the Treasurer's hands, we credit the Tax account of any year with its amount, the total of the Assessment Roll having been charged. (See Journal 160.)

We have given two accounts with salaried officers of the corporation, and charged the amounts supposed to be paid to the other officials direct to Salary account. You will see by referring to these individual accounts that at the end of the year they are closed by Salary account. Of course in actual work more of the officials would have individual accounts.

Rents we have put through Rents account, but it is desirable when there are many tenants to have individual accounts with them.

The Sinking Fund levy, which we recommended to be made yearly, except under peculiar circumstances, we have omitted, with the understanding that this year is a very hard one, and that next year a double levy will be made. For the same reason we do not pay off the note under discount which matured on 1st. July, but continue to use the loan, paying there-for a rate of interest as agreed upon with the bank.

Revenue account is similar to a Loss and Gain account, and is used, as you will see on page 162, to close the accounts for the year that are neither assets nor liabilities, but representative, or working accounts. It does not show all the revenue and expenditures, for of course when an amount is received for property sold, as for instance the sale of lots, it is passed to the credit of Real Estate account, and likewise when a sum has been paid on the reduction of a liability which is already in your Ledger, that account is debited with it; for example, see County of Windsor account. To ascertain, therefore, the receipts and expenditures for the year you will go through the several Ledger accounts which show them. Should there be any outstanding debts at the end of a year, which you have been unable to pay, you will credit the parties to whom they are owing, and debit the accounts to which they should be charged. This should be done before closing the accounts that are transferred to Revenue account. In actual work the amount of interest accrued on the note overdue since the 1st of July would be debited to interest account and credited to the bank. The aim is to make the transactions of each year complete within the books before they are closed.

At the opening of the set, the City of Ontario account showed that the city's liabilities exceeded its assets by over $10,000; but at the close this is reversed, and the assets exceed the liabilities by over $8,000. If you study the matter you will see that this has been brought about by the reduction, by $25,000, of the liability to the County of Windsor; an addition to the bank deposit of over $8,400, a few other minor reductions of liabilities, and per contra the payment of a $10,000 bonus, and a few minor reductions in the assets. We may remark that the assets shown on the books of a municipal corporation are, to a large extent, nominal. Its ability to pay its liabilities is not reckoned by what the corporation of the city may own, but by the value of the city's whole assessable property. You will understand this after a few moments' thought. For instance, the cost of a bridge is shown on the books to be $10,000. That bridge is nominally worthless, so far as its saleable value is concerned, but it is a thing of value to the corporation, and is, therefore, regarded as an asset, and its cost stands at the debit of an account from year to year.

It might be desirable, however, to write off a certain percentage of this account yearly, as the bridge becomes worn and useless; certainly in ordinary business this principle should be carried out, Loss and Gain being made debtor yearly to the account for the estimated depreciation.

During the year you are supposed to have kept all papers, warrants, checks, and vouchers, in a neat and convenient form for reference; the warrants, checks, and vouchers being consecutively numbered, and on the appointment of the auditors you are prepared to submit your work for their examination, exhibiting with your Ledger the Trial Balance and Asset and Liability statement in the forms given on pages 172 and 173. Their duty, of course, will be to first check your work, and afterwards prepare in detail an abstract from your books, showing the year's receipts and expenditures, and also the items composing the several asset and liability accounts, and to make any suggestion or recommendation that may seem desirable.

PRIVATE LEDGER.

All judicious merchants are aware of the importance of avoiding needless exposure of their affairs. This in some establishments is unavoidable where the partner's accounts and the results of the business are all exhibited on the same Ledger. In order to avoid this inconvenience, a Ledger, with clasp and lock, may be kept for accounts that are to be kept private. The keeping of these accounts in a separate book entails no additional trouble, as they are dealt with as though they were in the General Ledger. Some merchants, who adopt the plan of keeping a Private Ledger, also make the opening entry of the business upon a PRIVATE JOURNAL. We have not deemed it necessary to give an illustration of this Ledger, as the mode of keeping it will be apparent to any person who understands the science of accounts. We may mention, however, that the accounts usually kept in it are Merchandise, Loss and Gain, and the proprietors.

BOOKS AS EVIDENCE IN COURT.

BOOKS of ORIGINAL ENTRIES are the only ones admitted as evidence in Courts of Justice.

For proving many transactions there is no written signature nor testimony of witnesses, and the entries in the books are the only vouchers for millions of dollars. The law has laid down certain rules in regard to them which should be universally known, as debts are frequently lost from some defect of entry which might have been saved had they been recorded in a proper manner.

A book of ORIGINAL ENTRIES is evidence of the SALE and DELIVERY of goods and of work done. The book, however, may be set aside on sufficient proof of incorrectness. It must be proved by the affidavit or oral evidence of the person who made the entries, or if such person be dead or cannot be reached, proof of death or absence, or of the handwriting, is sufficient.

To entitle a person's books to be received as evidence in Court, the following facts must be proved, viz. :

1st. By whom the entries were made.

2nd. That the books produced are his account books, and come from the proper custody.

3rd. That some of the articles charged have been delivered.

4th. That he keeps fair and honest accounts, and this he must show by those who have dealt and settled with him.

If the entries in a book were made by a clerk, and he be dead, on showing that fact, and proving his handwriting, and that he was a clerk of the party, such entries would be received as evidence.

ENTRIES FOR RENEWALS OF NOTES.

Suppose M. MacCormick & Co., of Belleville, have a note for $200, in favor of McLachlan Bros. & Co., of Montreal, coming due at the Merchants' Bank in Montreal four days hence, which they cannot meet, they request the house to retire it, and renew, say, for three months; the request is granted, and the first or second day after the maturity of the note they receive the following statement :

(The Usual Heading.)

1879
Jan. 25---To Cash to retire your note, $200.00
" Interest on renewal for three months and Bank Comm.   5.09

$205.09
Cr.
By Draft at three months, $205.09
McLachlan Bros. & Co.

Your journal entries for above will be:
Bills Payable,   *Dr.* $200.00
Interest,   5.09
    To McLachlan Bros. & Co., $205.09
For B. P. No. 58, retired by them, and renewed for three months. as per st'mt.
McLachlan Bros. & Co.   *Dr.* $205.09
    To Bills Payable. $205.09
For their Draft at 3 months from Jan. 25, in renewal of B. P., No. 58.

Or, if you don't desire to put the transaction through the personal account, the following Journal entry will have the same effect, and be much shorter :

Bills Payable,   Dr. $200.00
Interest,   "   5.09
    To Bills Payable,   ———$205.09

The entries of the firm that renewed the note would be, if the note were under discount and retired by Check:

M. MacCormick & Co.,   Dr. $205.09
  * To Bank,   " $200.00
  " Interest,   5.09
For their Note due this day (B. R., No. 120) retired by Check, No. 170, renewed for three months.

Bills Receivable,   Dr. $205.09
    To M. MacCormick & Co. $205.09
For Draft at three months in renewal of B. R., No. 120.

Or, if you don't desire to put the transaction through the personal account (after charging back the note to Bills Rec. and crediting Bank), the following Journal entry will have the same effect, and be much shorter :

Bills Receivable,   Dr. $205.09
    To Bills Receivable, $200.00
    " Interest,   5.09

PARTIAL RENEWALS.

Brown renews for you half the amount of a note for $500, due to-day. You pay $250 cash, and give a new note for half the amt. of the old one and interest on renewal, $3.50.

1. YOUR ENTRY.
Bills Payable Dr. $500.00
Interest,   3.50
    To Cash, $250.00
    " Bills Payable,   253.50

2. HIS ENTRY.
Bills Receivable Dr. $253.50
Cash   "   250.00
    To Bills Receivable.   500.00
    " Interest,   3.50

Brown renews for you half the amount of a note for $600 due to-day. You pay $303, being half the amount, plus the interest on renewal, and you give a new note for half the amount of the old one.

3. YOUR ENTRY.
Bills Payable Dr. $600.00
Interest,   "   3.00
    To Cash,   303.00
    " Bills Payable,   300.00

4. HIS ENTRY.
Bills Receivable Dr. $300.00
Cash   "   303.00
    To Bills Receivable,   600.00
    " Interest,   3.00

Where a Cash Book is kept of course the cash would have to be put through it. In that case the entries for No. 1 would be as follows :—

---

*If the note were not discounted, as in the example in Set V. McLachlan Bros. & Co's. first entry would be * M. MacCormick & Co. Dr. to Bills Receivable and Interest. Suppose that instead of the note being due in Montreal it were due in Belleville, M. MacCormick & Co. would request permission from McLachlan Bros & Co., say four days before it matured, to draw upon them, at sight, for the amount required ; and having obtained written permission, would present it with the Draft to one of the Banks (most probably the Bank at which it is payable), and obtain the amount of the Draft for which they would debit cash and credit McLachlin Bros. & Co.., (the fifty cents paid for collection would be credited to cash and charged to Interest), and when the statement is received they will credit McL. Bros. & Co. with the interest, &c., on renewal. At the maturity of the Note they would pay it, and of course credit Cash by Bills Payable.

Cash Cr.
By Bills Payable. For part payment on No. 92 $250.00
renewed as per Journal and Bill Book.

Journal.
Bills Payable *Dr.* $250.00
Interest   "   3.50
     To Bills Payable, $253.50
On the same principle work the other examples for yourself.

DISCOUNTING NOTES * AND ENTRIES.

There are two senses in which the expression *discounting a note* or bill may be taken. It may mean paying a note outstanding against you before it comes to maturity, and getting a discount off; or it may mean raising money on your own note, having an endorser (which is called an accommodation note), or on a note you hold against another.

TO DRAW AN ACCOMMODATION NOTE.

Make it payable to the order of the person who is going to endorse it, get him to endorse it, then the bank discounting it will hold you as the maker and the endorser responsible in case you should fail to meet it.

ENTRIES FOR DISCOUNTING NOTES.

AN ACCOMMODATION NOTE made by yourself, endorsed by John Jones, for $300, the discount being $3.20, and the proceeds left to your credit in Bank.

Bank   *Dr.* $296.80
Discount "   3.20
     To Bills Payable, $300.

Through the Cash Book, producing the same effect upon the Ledger, the entries would be:

Cash Dr.   *Cash Dr.*
To Bills Payable, No. 91, disct'd, $3.00   By Bank. Proceeds of Note, $296.80
                                          " Discount. Dis. on above,   3.20

If you received the cash into your hands, Cash account would take the place of Bank in the Journal Entry, and in the Cash Book entry only Discount would appear on the *Cr* side.

A CUSTOMER'S NOTE, one for $420, you hold against R. Brown, discount, $4.90, proceeds left to Cr.

Bank *Dr.* $415.10
Discount "   4.90
     To Bills Receivable, $420.00

Through the Cash Book, producing the same effect upon the Ledger.

Cash Dr.   *Cash Cr.*
To Bills Receivable, No. 87, disct'd $420.   By Bank. Proceeds of Note, $415.10
                                            " Disc't. Dis. on above,   4.90

---

* Discounting Bills, might be the term employed, as the entries for discounting Drafts or Acceptances and Notes are the same.

If you received the cash into your hands, Cash account would take the place of Bank in the Journal entry, and in the Cash Book entry only Discount would appear on the Cr. side.

PAYING A NOTE BEFORE MATURITY.

J. H. McMurtry holds a note against you for $275, due 2 months hence; you pay it to-day, and he allows you a discount of $4.

Bills Payable Dr. $275.00
  To Cash, $271.00
  " Discount,   4.00

Through the Cash Book, producing the same effect in the Ledger.

Cash Dr.	Cash Cr.
To Discount. For dis. on No. 78, $4.	By Bills Payable. Retired No. 78, $275.00.

THE METHOD OF WRITING OFF BAD DEBTS.

Few merchants or manufacturers can do business without making bad debts. Every man doing a credit business should at each periodical closing of the books (which should be at least once a year) go through his Ledger, and take a list of the accounts that he considers bad or very doubtful, in order that they may be written off. It may be asked, Why write them off at all? What harm can there be in allowing them to remain on the books? The answer is, if you continue them they stand as resources or assets of your business, which, being worthless, they are not.

In nearly every case of insolvency, the book debts yield on an average not more than 50 per cent.; and in not a few instances the insolvency itself is in a large measure produced by allowing worthless accounts to remain on the ledger, and regarding them, and representing them to creditors, as assets of the business.

Suppose you have upon your ledger the following accounts considered bad:—Jones, $57; Brown, $31.50; Green, $41.90; write them off by the following journal entries:—

Bad debts account,   Dr. $130.40
  To Jones, $57.00
  " Brown,   31.50
  " Green,   41.90

For amounts at their debit that we consider impossible to collect.

Loss and Gain Account,   Dr. $130.40
  To Bad Debts account, $130.40

For amounts written off transferred.

It will be observed that the accounts are first written into Bad Debts Account, and the latter is closed into Loss and Gain. If they were left in Bad Debts Account, or in a Suspense Account, they would still be in the form of assets. Of course they might be written into Loss and Gain, at once, but the object desired in dealing with them as we do here is to have an account, showing distinctly the sum written off yearly for bad debts, as well as the *names* of delinquents, each of which occupies a line by itself in the account. Recording them thus in the ledger you can turn to the account at any time, and have the whole list, extending, it may be, over many years, before you.

Should you collect any of the accounts subsequently, you would make Cash debtor to Bad Debts, and in the explanation give the individual's name and other particulars.

A worthless note would be dealt with as you deal with the open accounts above, adding to the words "Bills Receivable" in Bad Debts account, the name of the maker in parenthesis.

TO SHOW SETTLEMENTS IN LEDGER ACCOUNTS

WITHOUT RULING.

It is a great assistance to a bookkeeper to pursue a method of showing clearly the various settlements in the course of a year, and the settled items of a large, or even a small account in the ledger; but it is not desirable to *rule* an account oftener than the ledger is balanced. We therefore recommend the plan shown in the example below.

Dr. R. B. BEATTY. *Cr.*

1882						1882						
Jan.	2	To Mdse.	49	A	197	50	Feb.	1	By Bills Rec.,	70	A	436	70
	15	" "	64	A	239	20	April	1	" "	101	B	749	90
Feb.	17	" Cash,	120		100	00	May	10	" "	170	C	57	50
Mar.	7	" Mdse.,	84	B	597	20							
	21	" "	91	B	152	70							
April	3	" "	102	C	57	50							
May	10	" "	120		143	20							
	29	" "	125		49	15							

The letters of the alphabet are used consecutively, and should always be in lead pencil. A hard black that will not blur is the best. You will note that the debits in January are settled by note in February, and the settlement is indicated by the letter A opposite each debit and the credit. The March and April debits are also settled, and the letters B and C on each side show the respective settlements. Suppose that on the first of June, when making out statements, you come to this account, you see at a glance the unsettled items. We have found in long, complicated accounts that this system of showing settlements is exceedingly valuable. In practice we have also used it in the Bills Receivable and Bills Payable accounts, to show notes retired, each bill of course being posted singly.

WORKING ACCOUNT.

This account is practically the same as a Loss and Gain account, and would be used to close the representative accounts in a ledger, say, of a public institution. Take a church for instance. It is desirable to show income and expenditure under such Ledger titles as the following: Collections, Pew Rent, Missionary Fund, &c., for income; and Lighting, Sexton, Organ Expenses, &c., for expenditure. At the close of the year, instead of closing these accounts into Loss and Gain, as would be done where trade is being carried on, you would close them into WORKING ACCOUNT, and it would show either excess of income or expenditure, and be closed into the "CHURCH" account, which is the one that keeps the Ledger in balance, or represents the net worth or insolvency, as does the Stock account of an individual.

For a more extended explanation and illustration of Working Accounts, see "Johnson's Joint Stock Company Bookkeeping."

WAREHOUSING.

The following SET OF WAREHOUSE BOOKS illustrates the method of keeping a record of, and dealing with Grain or Goods stored in a PUBLIC WAREHOUSE.

STUB.

No. 127.
Belleville, September 29, 1889.
Received from SILAS ALLAN,
1350 bush. No. 2 Barley,
Entered
Warehouse Ledger,
Folio 1,
" 2,

WAREHOUSE RECEIPT.

No. 127.
Belleville, Sept. 29, 1889.
RECEIVED into store from SILAS ALLAN, in good order and condition, thirteen hundred and fifty bushels No. 2 Barley, subject to his order.
R. W. CAMERON,
Warehouseman.

The above is the form of receipt granted for grain, flour, or other commodity stored in a warehouse. It is called a WAREHOUSE RECEIPT, and serves a very useful purpose in business transactions. It is made subject to the order of the individual, and is thereby negotiable by endorsement. The thing it represents may be sold and transferred without the buyer personally seeing the stuff. The bargain being concluded, the holder simply endorses the Receipt and hands it to the purchaser, who now becomes the owner of what is stored.

Loans are made by Banks upon Warehouse Receipts, and in other ways it is a valuable and convenient business paper.

The blank forms should be printed and bound in books containing about 250, and should be consecutively numbered

STUB.

No. 250.
Belleville, Oct. 18, 1889.
DELIVERED 1350 bush. No. 2 Barley on Warehouse Receipt, No. 127.
STORED originally by SILAS ALLAN, Entered
Warehouse Ledger,
Folio 1,
" 2,

DELIVERY ORDER.

No. 250.
Belleville, Oct. 18, 1889.
WAREHOUSE RECEIPT No. 127, having been properly endorsed and delivered up, you are authorized to DELIVER to the bearer thirteen hundred and fifty bush. No. 2 Barley, stored originally by SILAS ALLAN.
R. W. CAMERON,
per J. R.

The above is a DELIVERY ORDER that would be written in the Warehouseman's office, and sent with the teamster to the Werehouse when delivery of the stuff is required, and when the Warehouse Receipt is given up after being properly endorsed.

The Blank forms should be printed and bound in books containing about 250, and should be consecutively numbered.

WAREHOUSE LEDGER.

The Ledger is kept with quantities only. It is to show the quantity of the various kinds of grain or other stuff stored and the owners of it. It is kept on the double entry principle, and is exceedingly simple and correct. *It is posted from the stubs of the Warehouse Receipt and Delivery Order books.*

EXAMPLES.

Suppose you have received into store, for which you have granted Warehouse Receipts as shown in 6 different stubs, as on the form preceding :

1350 bush.	No. 2 Barley from	Silas Allan,
2000	" No. 1 "	" R. NcNaughton,
500 bbls. Flour		" Jas. Norris
1375 bush. Peas		" A. M. Gunn,
780 "	"	" T. H. Smallman,
1875 "	"	" John Walker,

and have made the following deliveries for which orders were given, and which are shown in 7 different stubs in your Order Delivery Book, as per the form preceding :

1000 bush.	No. 2 Barley,	Silas Allan,
500 "	Peas,	John Walker,
500 bbls.	Flour,	Jas. Norris,
370 bush.	Peas,	John Walker,
150 "	No. 2 Barley,	Silas Allan,
257 "	Peas,	A. M. Gunn,
1000 "	No. 1 Barley,	R. McNaughton,

you would post to the respective accounts as follows: For stuff received, debit the account representing the stuff received, and credit the individual from whom received. For stuff delivered, debit the individual from whom originally received, and to whom Warehouse Receipt was granted, and credit the account representing the stuff delivered. You will keep this book posted each day, and thereby show *at all times* the commodities, and the respective quantities stored and the owners of them.

A trial balance of balances taken from time to time will prove its correctness or otherwise.

From this Ledger you will also be able to make out accounts for storage.

No. 2. BARLEY.

1889			W.R. No.	Bushels.	1889			D.O. No.	Bushels.
Sep.	29	To Silas Allan,	127	1350	Oct.	18	By Silas Allan,	250	1000
					"	29	" Silas Allan,	254	150

No. 1. BARLEY.

			W.R. No.	Bushels.				D.O. No.	Bushels.
Sep.	30	To R.McNaughton	128	2000	Nov.	5	By R.McNaughton	256	1000

FLOUR.

1889			W.R. No.	Bbls.	1889			D.O. No.	Bbls.
Sep.	30	To Jas. Norris,	129	500	Oct.	20	By Jas. Norris,	252	500

PEAS.

			W.R. No.	Bushels.				D.O. No.	Bushels.
Sep.	30	To A. M. Gunn,	130	1375	Oct.	19	By John Walker,	251	500
Oct.	1	"T.H.Smallman,	131	780	"	29	" John Walker,	253	370
"	3	" John Walker,	132	1875	Nov.	1	" A. M. Gunn,	255	257

SILAS ALLAN.

1889 Oct.	18 "	ToNo.2 Barley, " "	D.O. No. 250 254	Bushels. 1000 150		1889 Sept	29	ByNo.2Barley,	W.R. No. 127	Bushels. 1350

R. McNAUGHTON.

Nov	5	ToNo.1 Barley,	D.O. No. 256	Bushels. 1000		Sept	30	By No.1Barley,	W.R. No. 128	Bushels. 2000

JAS. NORRIS.

Oct.	20	To Flour,	D.O. No. 252	Bbls. 500		Sept	30	By Flour,	W.R. No. 129	Bbls. 500

A. M. GUNN.

Nov.	1	To Peas,	D.O. No. 255	Bushels, 257		Sept	30	By Peas,	W.R. No. 130	Bushels. 1375

T. H. SMALLMAN.

						Oct.	1	By Peas,	W.R. No. 131	Bushels. 780

JOHN WALKER.

Oct.	19 "	To Peas, " "	D.O. No. 251 253	Bushels. 500 370		Oct.	3	By Peas,	W.R. No. 132	Bushels. 1875

REMARKS ON THE LEDGER.

The DEBIT BALANCE of the Barley, Flour and Peas accounts will show the quantity of each in store, and the *Credit balance* of the individual accounts will show the owners. A trial balance should be taken from time to time to prove if the Ledger is being correctly posted, and an abstract statement, showing what is in store and the owners of it, may be taken at any time, in a few minutes.

OPENING LEDGERS UNDER VARIOUS CIRCUMSTANCES.

JOURNALIZING RESOURCES AND LIABILITIES FOR SINGLE PROPRIETOR.

When a single proprietor commences business, possessed of certain resources, the journal entry necessary to open the Ledger is

SUNDRIES (the accounts representing each resource) *Dr.*

To STOCK (or the proprietor's name).

If he has debts or liabilities, as well as resources, they must be shown in the Ledger also, consequently a journal entry would require to be made for them as follows :—

STOCK (or the proprietor's name) *Dr.*

To SUNDRIES (the accounts representing each liability).

When the foregoing entries have been posted to the Ledger, you will show on the *Dr.* side each resource under its own title, and on the *Cr.* side each liability, and in the stock account the net capital.

JOURNALIZING RESOURCES AND LIABILITIES FOR PARTNERS COMING TOGETHER FOR FIRST TIME.

When two or more partners come together for the first time, each bringing in resources and liabilities, you will make the resources which each brings in *Dr.* to himself, and make each *Dr.* to his own liabilities. For example:—

Cash	*Dr.*	$1500.00	
Bills Receivable	"	750.00	
Real Estate	"	1000.00	
To J. W. Neal			$3250.00
Effects invested			
J. W. Neal	*Dr.*	900.00	
To J. Runciman			150.00
" Bills Payable			750.00

His liabilities assumed by the partnership.

Cash	*Dr.*	$2000.00	
Merchandise	"	1000.00	
M. MacCormick	"	89.00	
To John L. Kerr			3089.00
Effects invested.			
John L. Kerr	*Dr.*	425.00	
To Bills Payable			250.00
" Andrew Shaw			175.00

His liabilities assumed by the partnership.

NOTE.—If no day book entry has been made full explanations should accompany each entry in the journal

The resources and liabilities of each now become the resources and liabilities of the partnership; the individual partner's accounts showing each one's capital or insolvency. A partnership cannot have an account with itself.

JOURNALIZING TO OPEN NEW ACCOUNTS FOR A PREVIOUSLY EXISTING PARTNERSHIP.

An accountant is frequently called upon to open a new set of accounts for a previously existing partnership. The data from which it is to be done will be a balance sheet or statement, showing the firm's resources and liabilities, and the amount of the capital or insolvency of each partner.

The student will observe that it would not be possible to journalize in this case, as is done when partners come together for the first time, because you cannot say that any particular resource or liability is that of any one partner. We suggest either of the following methods :

Sundries *Dr.* to Sundries:

(*Resources*).

Cash	$570.20
Merchandise	4220.00
Bills Receivable	1500.00
John Macoun	78.20
J. W. Loudon	57.50
R. A. Van Allan	125.90
	6551.80

(*Liabilities.*)

To Bills Payable	$1570.00
" J. H. Watlington	340.00
" F. Macaulay	170.00
" Joseph Elliott	58.50
	2138.50
" (Partner) Jas. Johnson, Capital	2100.00
" Partner) W. H. Fuller, "	2313.30

NOTE.—When posting, debit each Resource To Sundries, and credit each Liability By Sundries.

The Sum of the Assets equals the sum of the Liabilities and Capital, or the Liabilities to the public and the proprietor.

ANOTHER METHOD.

Sundries *Dr.* to Capital $6551.80

(*Resources.*)

Cash	$570.20
Merchandise	4220.00
Bills Receivable	1500.00
John Macoun	78.20
J. W. Loudon	57.50
R. A. Van Allan	125.90

Capital *Dr.* to Sundries 6551.80

(*Liabilities.*)

Bills Payable	$1570.00
J. H. Watlington	340.00
F. Macaulay	170.00
Joseph Elliott	58.50
	2138.50
(Partner) Jas. Johnson, Capital	2100.00
(Partner) W. H. Fuller, "	2313.30

NOTE.—If preferred, Capital might be made Dr. to the partners in a separate entry.

When either of the above entries has been posted to the Ledger you will show on the Dr. side each resource under its own title, on the Cr. side each liability, and on the Cr. side of each partner's account the amount of his capital. You will observe that the " Capital Account " is simply used as a medium through which the other accounts are opened.

PROPRIETOR'S OR PARTNER'S CAPITAL ACCOUNT, AND PARTNER'S CURRENT (OR PERSONAL) ACCOUNT.

It is often desirable to keep the Capital Account of a proprietor or partners distinct from the account showing their withdrawals for family and other personal expenses or against salary. In that case open, say, J. W. Johnson's Capital Account, and J. W. Johnson's Current (or Personal) Account. The former will show the capital, and the latter the withdrawals. At the end of the business year close the Current Account with this journal entry :

J. W. Johnson's Capital Account Dr.

To J. W. Johnson's Current Account.

For amount withdrawn during the year transferred.

If the proprietors are allowed a certain salary, then credit this account at the end of the year, by Salary or Expense, and if the individual has overdrawn his account he should pay back the overdraft in cash, which would be passed to its credit.

TRANSFERRING ACCOUNTS FROM AN OLD LEDGER TO A NEW ONE.

When transferring accounts from an old Ledger to a new one proceed as follows : Call the old Ledger, Ledger A., and in the accounts which show a debit balance write on the credit side, By Balance to Ledger B, Folio—, and in the accounts which show a credit balance write on the debtor side, To Balance to Ledger B, Folio—. Call the new Ledger, Ledger B ; write in a bold hand the names of the accounts as you transfer them; on the debtor side of those that closed in Ledger A, By Balance, write To Balance from Ledger A, Folio—, and on the credit side of those that closed in Ledger A, To Balance, write By Balance from Ledger A, Folio—. Immediately after transferring an account index it. The best time to make such a transfer is when the annual closing time comes round, you will then only require to transfer the Resources and Liabilities and Partners' accounts, and open new representative accounts as required. There is very little more labor in transferring balances to a new Ledger than bringing them down in the old one.

FARM ACCOUNTS.

Originally prepared by J. W. Johnson, at the suggestion of the Honorable the Provincial Treasurer of Ontario, for the Royal Commission appointed to take evidence on agricultural matters in the year 1880, and recommended by the Commissioners.

TO TEACHERS.

The keeping of accounts by Farmers is strongly recommended, and in this connection we would say to Teachers in rural sections desiring to add something of practical value to their curriculum, that they can teach any boy of ordinary ability to keep books on the farm after this method.

Commence with, say the first seven Sets in this book, then let them write up the Day Book transactions only of this Set, and work out the Journal, Ledger and statements for themselves.

FARM ACCOUNTS.

Township of Thurlow, April, 1880.

DAY BOOK.   JOURNAL.

John Robin this day commences to keep a set of books by double entry for the purpose of recording the business of his farm, and to determine yearly his gains and losses, and assets and liabilities.								
INVENTORY OF PROPERTY.								
Real Estate, 50 acres, as under:								
Field No. 1. 8 acres.								
Field No. 2, 8 "								
Field No. 3, 8 "								
Field No. 4, 4 "								
Field No. 5, 4 "								
Field No. 6, 8 "								
Field No. 7. 6 "								
Orchard, Garden and Buildings, 4 "								
50 acres valued, including buildings, at $75 per acre......	$3750	00	1	Real Estate Dr	$3750	00		
			1	Furniture "	520	00		
Household Furniture....	520	00	1	Plant "	890	00		
			1	Live Stock "	215	00		
Plant as under	890	00	2	Cash "	525	00		
2 Teams $400.00			2	Farm Produce Dr..........	320	00		
1 Reaper 100.00			3	Field No. 6 "	10	00		
1 Mower 75.00			1	To Capital,			$6230	00
2 Ploughs,at$15 30.00								
1 Harrow 15.00								
2 Sets Harness. at $25 ..... 50.00								
2 Whiffletrees, at 2.50 ...... 5.00								
1 Waggon 75.00								
1 Buggy 100.00								
1 Cultivator ... 10.00								
1 Horse Rake ... 24.00								
Sundry Implements 6.00								
890.00								
Live Stock, as under:	215	00						
5 Cows 150.00								
10 Sheep 50.00								
3 Hogs 15.00								
Cash	525	00						
Farm Produce, oats, hay &c., &c., on hand,	320	00						
Field No. 6,	10	00						
For value of timothy and clover seed in ground.								
	6230	00		Carried forward,	$6230	00	$6230	00

Township of Thurlow, April, 1880.

DAY BOOK. JOURNAL.

3rd.						3rd. Forward,	$6230	00	$6230	00
Paid Cash for Seed:					3	Fields Nos. 1 & 2 Dr.	24	00		
Fields Nos. 1 & 2, 32 bush.					3	Field No. 3 "	16	00		
Barley at 75c.,	$24	00			3	" " 4 "	4	00		
Field No. 3, 16 bush.					3	" " 5 "	5	00		
Wheat at $1,	16	00			2	To Cash,			49	00
Field No. 4, 8 bush. Oats at 50c.,	4	00								
Field No. 5, Indian Corn and Potatoes,	5	00								
11th.			$49	00		11th.				
Credit John Thompson,	9	00			3	Fields Nos. 1 & 2 Dr.	18	00		
Credit Wm. Wilson,	9	00			4	To John Thompson,			9	00
For 9 days' labor each on Fields Nos. 1 and 2.			18	00	4	" Wm. Wilson,			9	00
16th..						16th.				
Credit John Thompson,	4	50			3	Field No. 3 Dr.	9	00		
Credit Wm. Wilson,	4	50			4	To John Thompson,			4	50
For 4½ days' labor each on Field No. 3.			9	00	4	" Wm. Wilson,			4	50
19th.						19th.				
Credit John Thompson,	2	25			3	Field No. 4 Dr.	4	50		
Credit Wm. Wilson,	2	25			4	To John Thompson,			2	25
For 2¼ days' each on Field No. 4.			4	50	4	" Wm. Wilson,			2	25
23rd.						23rd,				
Credit John Thompson,	4	50			3	Field No. 5 Dr.	9	00		
Credit Wm. Wilson,	4	50			4	To John Thompson,			4	50
For 4½ days each on Field No. 5.			9	00	4	" Wm. Wilson,			4	50
28th.						28th.				
Paid Cash for Garden seed,					4	Garden & Orchard Dr.	6	00		
Ohio Corn for green feed Vetches, Millet, &c.,			6	00	2	To Cash,			6	00
"						"				
Paid Cash for labor on Orchard and Garden,			9	00	4	Garden & Orchard Dr.	9	00		
30th					2	To Cash,			9	00
Paid John Thompson on account.	10	00				30th.				
Paid Wm., Wilson on acct.	10	00			4	John Thompson Dr.	10	00		
			20	00	4	Wm. Wilson "	10	00		
The Milk from our 5 Cows is taken by the "Allan Cheese Factory," at the rate of &c. for a gallon of 10 lbs.					2	To Cash,			20	00
May 5th.						May 5th.				
Received from "Allan Cheese Factory" for milk in April, Cash,			15	70	2	Cash Dr.	15	70		
					5	To Cows,			15	70
29th.						29th.				
Paid John Thompson account in full,	10	25			4	John Thompson Dr.	10	25		
Paid Wm. Wilson account in full.	10	25			4	Wm. Wilson Dr.	10	25		
			20	50	2	To Cash,			20	50
						Carried forward,	$6390	70	$6390	70

Township of Thurlow, June, 1880.

DAY BOOK.   JOURNAL.

June 1st.						Amts. forward,	$6390	70	$6390	70
Paid Cash for Groceries,	$7	50				June 1st.				
" " " Dry Goods	17	00	$24	50	5	House Expenses Dr.	24	50		
30th.					2	To Cash,			24	50
Have clipped and sold for						30th.				
Cash,					2	Cash Dr.	43	00		
60 lbs. Wool at 30c.,	18	00			5	To Sheep,			43	00
Sold for Cash 10 lambs at						"				
$2.50,	25	00	43	00						
"					2	Farm Produce Dr.	200	00		
Have harvested from					3	To Field No. 6,			200	00
Field No.6, 20 tons Hay,						"				
assumed to be worth										
$10 per ton,			200	00						
"										
Paid for harvesting Hay,			7	00	3	Field No. 6 Dr.	7	00		
					2	To Cash,			7	00
July 31st.						July 31st.				
					2	Farm Produce Dr.	420	00		
Have harvested and					3	To Fields Nos. 1 & 2,			420	00
threshed from Fields										
Nos. 1 and 2, 560 bush.										
Barley (average 35 to										
acre) for which I have										
been offered and have										
accepted for October										
delivery, 75c. per bush.			420	00						
August 5th.						August 5th.				
Have harvested, threshed										
and sold 240 bush.										
Wheat for Cash from										
Field No. 3, at $1.20,	288	00			2	Cash Dr.	288	00		
Put into Barn for use					2	Farm Produce "	24	00		
from same Field, 20					3	To Field No. 3,			312	00
bush. Wheat, at $1.20,	24	00	312	00		"				
"										
Credit John Thompson, 4										
days, Fields 1 and 2,	4	00			3	Fields 1 and 2 Dr.	7	00		
Credit Wm. Wilson, 3					4	To John Thompson,			4	00
days, Fields 1 and 2,	3	00	7	00	4	" W. Wilson,			3	00
"						"				
Credit John Thompson										
3½ days, Field 3,	3	50			3	Field No. 3 Dr.	7	00		
Credit Wm. Wilson, 3½					4	To John Thompson,			3	50
days, Field 3,	3	50	7	00	4	" W. Wilson,			3	50
15th.						15th.				
Paid for threshing Barley,										
Fields Nos. 1 and 2, 560										
bush., at 5c.,	28	00			3	Fields Nos. 1 & 2 Dr.	28	00		
Paid for threshing Wheat,					3	" " 3 Dr.	15	60		
Field No. 3, 260 bush.,					2	To Cash,			43	60
at 6c.,	15	60	43	60		"				
" "										
Have harvested & thresh-					2	Farm Produce Dr.	80	00		
ed from Field No. 4, 160					3	To Field No. 4,			80	00
bush. Oats, assumed to										
be worth 50c. a bush,			80	00						
						Carried forward,	$7534	80	$7534	80

Township of Thurlow, August, 1880.

DAY BOOK.   JOURNAL.

Day Book entry						Journal entry				
30th.						30th. Forward,	$7534	80	$7534	80
Paid Cash for harvesting Oats, Field No. 4,	$ 5	00			3	Field No. 4 Dr.	9	80		
Paid Cash for threshing Oats, Field No. 4,	4	80	$ 9	80	2	To Cash,			9	80
"						"				
Received from " Allan Cheese Factory," Cash in settlement to date Sept. 15th.			62	60	2 5	Cash Dr. To Cows, Sept. 15th.	62	80	62	80
Have harvested from Field No. 5, 120 bush. Corn, assumed to be worth 70c.,	84	00			2	Farm Produce Dr.	144	00		
150 bush. Potatoes, assumed to be worth 40c.,	60	00	144	00	3	To Field No. 5,			144	00
"						"				
Paid John Thompson, Cash in full of acct.,	7	50			4	John Thompson Dr.	7	50		
Paid Wm. Wilson, Cash in full of acct.,	6	50	14	00	4 2	Wm. Wilson " To Cash,	6	50	14	00
"						"				
Paid for labor on Field No. 5,			19	00	4 2	Field No. 5 Dr. To Cash,	19	00	19	00
"						"				
Paid for Dry Goods as per bill of Foster and Reid,			47	50	5 2	House Expenses Dr. To Cash,	47	50	47	50
30th.						30th.				
Have harvested from 3 acres of Orchard, 468 bbls. Apples, which I sold for Cash to a Montreal buyer, at $1.25.			585	00	2 4	Cash Dr. To Garden and Orchard,	585	00	585	00
"						"				
Paid for picking and barrelling the above apples			50	00	4 2	Garden & Orch'd Dr. To Cash,	50	00	50	00
Oct. 29th.						Oct. 29th.				
Received Cash for Barley, as per agreement recorded July 31st.			420	00	2 2	Cash Dr. To Farm Produce,	420	00	420	00
Nov. 30th.						Nov. 30th.				
Received from " Allan Cheese Factory," Cash in full for season			47	10	2 5	Cash Dr. To Cows,	47	10	47	10
"						"				
Paid " Allan Cheese Factory," for Butter and Cheese got during the season for house use,			15	20	5 2	House Expenses Dr. To Cash,	15	20	15	20
Dec. 15th.						Dec. 15th.				
Sold 40 bush. Oats for Cash, at 48c.,			19	20	2 2	Cash Dr. To Farm Produce,	19	20	19	20
1881.						1881				
Jan. 20th.						Jan. 20th.				
Sold 20 bush. Potatoes for Cash, 50c.			10	00	2 2 4	Cash Dr. To Farm Produce, " Field No. 5,	10	00	8 2	00 00
						Carried forward,	$8978	40	$8978	40

Township of Thurlow, January, 1881.

DAY BOOK.　　　　　　　　　JOURNAL.

20th.						20th Forward,	$8978	40	$8978	40
Paid subscription to Church for one year.			$20	00	5 2	House Expenses Dr. To Cash,	20	00	20	00
March 31st.						March 31st.				
Paid Conger Brothers their account for Groceries to date,	$14	90			5 2	House Expenses Dr. To Cash,	18	90	18	90
Paid subscription to "Weekly Globe,"	2	00								
Paid subscription to "Farmers' Advocate,"	2	00	18	90						
"										
Paid Taxes for 1880,	27	00				31st.				
" J. B. Graham for 1 suit Clothes for self and 2 for the boys,	53	00			5	House Expenses Dr.	138	10		
Paid Geo. Walbridge for Groceries in full to date	42	50			2	To Cash,			138	10
Paid John McKeown for Boots and Shoes.	15	60	138	10						
. "										
Credit Farm Produce account with Horse Keep, Oats, Hay, etc., used,			210	00	5 2	Horse Keep Dr. To Farm Produce,	210	00	210	00
"						"				
Credit Cows with Milk used in House,			30	00	5 5	House Expenses Dr. To Cows,	30	00	30	00
"						"				
Charge Cows as under. For Pasture—Field No. 7,	25	00			5 6	Cows Dr. To Field No. 7,	95	00	25	00
For Garden Feed—Garden and Orchard,	10	00			4	" Garden & Orchard			10	00
For Hay, Straw, &c.,—Farm Produce,	60	00	95	00	2	" Farm Produce,			60	00
"						"				
Charge Sheep as under, For Pasture—Field No. 7,	5	00			5 6	Sheep Dr. To Field No. 7,	15	00	5	00
For Hay, &c.,—Farm Produce,	10	00	15	00	2	" Farm Produce,			10	00
"						"				
Give Farm Produce account Credit for Stuff used for House,			65	00	5 2	House Expenses Dr. To Farm Produce	65	00	65	00
"						"				
Write off from the value of Plant 10 per cent. for wear and tear.			89	00	6 1	Loss and Gain Dr. To Plant,	89	00	89	00
							$9659	40	$9659	40

Dr. CAPITAL. Cr.

1881 April	1	To Balance,	6	$7185	50	1880 April	1	By Sundries,	1	$6230	00
						"	1	" Loss and Gain,	6	955	50
				$7185	50					$7185	50

REAL ESTATE.

1880 April	1	To Capital,	1	3750	00	1881 April	1	By Balance,	6	3750	00

FURNITURE.

April	1	To Capital,	1	520	00	April	1	By Balance,	6	520	00

PLANT.

April	1	To Capital,	1	890	00	1881 March	31	By Loss and Gain,	5	89	00
						April	1	" Balance,	6	801	00
				$890	00					$890	00

LIVE STOCK.

April	1	To Capital,	1	215	00	1881 April	1	By Balance,	6	215	00

CASH.

1880						1880					
April	1	To Capital,	1	525	00	April	3	By Sundries,	2	49	00
May	5	" Cows,	2	15	70	"	28	" Garden & Orchard	2	6	00
June	30	" Sheep,	3	43	00	"	28	" do	2	9	00
Aug.	5	" Field No. 3,	3	288	00	"	30	" Sundries,	2	20	00
"	30	" Cows,	4	62	80	May	29	" Sundries,	2	20	50
Sept.	30	" Garden & Orchard	4	585	00	June	1	" House Expenses,	3	24	50
Oct.	29	" Farm Produce,	4	420	00	"	30	" Field No. 6,	3	7	00
Nov.	30	" Cows,	4	47	10	Aug.	15	" Sundries,	3	43	60
Dec.	15	" Farm Produce,	4	19	20	"	30	" Field No. 4,	4	9	80
1881						Sept.	15	" Sundries,	4	14	00
Jan.	20	" Sundries,	4	10	00	"	15	" Field No. 5,	4	19	00
						"	15	" House Expenses,	4	47	50
						"	30	" Garden & Orchard	4	50	00
						Nov.	30	" House Expenses,	4	15	20
						1881					
						Jan.	20	" do	5	20	00
						March	1	" do	5	19	90
						"	1	" do	5	138	10
						April	1	" Balance,	6	1503	70
				2015	80					$2015	80

Dr.   FARM PRODUCE.   Cr.

1880							1880				
April	1	To Capital,	1	$320	00	Oct.	29	By Cash,	4	$420	00
June	30	" Field No. 6,	3	200	00	Dec.	15	" Cash,	4	19	20
July	31	" Fields Nos.1 & 2	3	420	00	1881					
Aug.	5	" Field No. 3,	3	24	00	Jan.	20	" Cash,	4	8	00
"	15	" Field No. 4,	3	80	00	March	31	" Horse Keep,	5	210	00
Sept.	15	" Field No. 5,	4	144	00	"	31	" Cows,	5	60	00
						"	31	" Sheep,	5	10	00
						"	31	" House Expenses	5	65	00
						April	1	" Balance,	6	395	80
				$1188	00					$1188	00

FIELD No. 6.

(*Grass.*)

1880						1880					
April	1	To Capital,	1	10	00	June	30	By Farm Produce,	3	200	00
June	30	" Cash,	3	7	00						
1881											
April	1	" Loss and Gain,	6	183	00						
				$200	00					$200	00

FIELDS Nos. 1 & 2.

(*Barley.*)

April	3	To Cash,	2	24	00	July	30	By Farm Produce,	3	420	00
"	11	" Sundries,	2	18	00						
Aug.	5	" Sundries,	3	7	00						
"	15	" Cash,	3	28	00						
1881											
April	1	" Loss and Gain,	6	343	00						
				$420	00					$420	00

FIELD No. 3.

(*Wheat.*)

April	3	To Cash,	2	16	00	Aug.	5	By Sundries,	3	312	00
"	16	" Sundries,	2	9	00						
Aug.	5	" Sundries,	3	7	00						
"	15	" Cash,	3	15	60						
1881											
April	1	" Loss and Gain,	6	264	40						
				$312	00					312	00

FIELD No. 4.
(Oats.)

Dr. / *Cr.*

1880											
April	3	To Cash,	2	$4	00	Aug.	15	By Farm Produce,	3	$80	00
"	19	" Sundries,	2	4	50						
Aug.	30	" Cash,	4	9	80						
1881											
April	1	" Loss and Gain,	6	61	70						
				$80	00					$80	00

FIELD No. 5.
(Corn and Potatoes.)

April	3	To Cash,	2	5	00	Sept.	15	By Farm Produce,	4	144	00
"	23	" Sundries,	2	9	00	1881					
Sept.	15	" Cash,	4	19	00	Jan.	20	" Cash,	4	2	00
1881											
April	1	" Loss and Gain,	6	113	00						
				$146	00					$146	00

JOHN THOMPSON (Hired Man.)

1880						1880					
April	30	To Cash,	2	10	0	April	11	By Fields 1 and 2,	2	9	00
May	29	" "	2	10	25	"	16	" Field No. 3,	2	4	50
						"	19	" Field No. 4,	2	2	25
						"	23	" Field No. 5,	2	4	50
				$20	25					$20	25
Sept.	15	To Cash,	4	7	50	Aug.	5	By Fields 1 and 2,	3	4	00
						"		" Field No. 3,	3	3	50
				$7	50					$7	50

WM. WILSON (Hired Man.)

April	30	To Cash,	2	10	00	April	11	By Fields 1 and 2,	2	9	00
May	29	" "	2	10	25	"	16	" Field No. 3,	2	4	50
						"	19	" Field No. 4,	2	2	25
						"	23	" Field No. 5,	2	4	50
				$20	25					$20	25
Sept.	15	To Cash,	4	6	50	Aug.	5	By Fields 1 and 2,	3	3	00
						"	5	" Field No. 3,	3	3	50
				$6	50					$6	50

Dr.   GARDEN AND ORCHARD.   Cr.

1880							1880					
April	28	To Cash,	2	$6	00	Sept.	30	By Cash,		4	$595	00
"	"	" "	2	9	00	March	31	" Cows,		5	10	00
Sept.	30	" "	4	50	00							
April	1	" Loss and Gain,	6	530	00							
				$595	00						$595	00

COWS.

March	31	To Sundries,	5	95	00	May	5	By Cash,		2	15	70
April	1	" Loss and Gain,	6	60	60	Aug.	30	" "		4	62	80
						Nov.	30	" "		4	47	10
						1881						
						March	31	" House Expenses.		5	30	00
				$155	60						$155	

HOUSE EXPENSES.

						1881						
June	1	To Cash,	3	24	50	April	1	By Loss and Gain,	6		359	20
Sept.	15	" "	4	47	50							
Nov.	30	" "	4	15	20							
1881												
Jan.	20	" "	5	20	00							
March	31	" "	5	18	90							
"	31	" "	5	138	10							
"	31	" Cows,	5	30	00							
"	31	" Farm Produce,	5	65	00							
				$359	20						$359	0

SHEEP.

March	31	To Field No. 7,	5	5	00	June	30	By Cash,		3	43	00
"	31	" Farm Produce,	5	10	00							
April	1	" Loss and Gain,	6	28	00							
				$43	00						$43	00

HORSE KEEP.

						1881						
March	31	To Farm Produce,	5	$210	00	April	1	By Loss and Gain,	6		$210	00

FIELD No. 7.
(Pasture.)

						1881						
April	1	To Loss and Gain,	6	30	00	March	31	By Cows,		5	25	00
						"	31	" Sheep,		5	5	00
				30	00						$30	00

Dr. LOSS AND GAIN, *Cr.*

1881						1881					
March	31	To Plant,	5	$ 89	00	April	1	By Fields 1 and 2,	3	$343	00
April	1	" House Expenses,	6	359	20	"	1	" Field No. 3,	3	264	40
"	1	" Horse Keep,	5	210	00	"	1	" Field No 4,	3	61	70
"	1	" *Capital,*	1	955	50	"	1	" Field No. 5,	3	113	00
						"	1	" Field No. 6,	3	183	00
						"	1	" Field No. 7,	6	30	00
						"	1	" Gard. & Orch'd.	4	530	00
						"	1	" Cows,	5	60	60
						"	1	" Sheep,	5	28	00
				$1613	70					$1613	70

BALANCE.

1881						1881					
April	1	To Real Estate,	1	3750	00	April	1	By *Capital,*	1.	$7185	50
"	1	" Furniture,	1	520	00						
"	1	" Plant,	1	801	00						
"	1	" Live Stock,	1	215	00						
"	1	" Cash,	2	1503	70						
"	1	" Farm Produce,	2	395	80						
				$7185	50					$7185	50

TRIAL BALANCE.

April 1st, 1881.

Dr. *Cr.*

Folio									
1	Capital,	.....	......	......	......			$6230	00
1	Real Estate,	......	......	......	......	$3750	00		
1	Furniture,	.. ...	......	......	......	520	00		
1	Plant,	......	......	......	......	801	00		
1	Live Stock,	......	......	......	......	215	00		
2	Cash,	......	......	......	......	1503	70		
2	Farm Produce,	......	......	......	......	395	80		
3	Field No. 6,	......	......	......	......			183	00
3	Fields Nos. 1 and 2,	......	......	......	......			343	00
3	Field No. 3,	.... .	.....	......	......			264	40
3	Field No. 4,	......	......	......	......			61	70
3	Field No. 5,	......	......	......	......			113	00
4	Garden and Orchard,	......	......	......	......			530	00
5	Cows,	......	......	......	.....			60	60
5	House Expenses,	......	......	......	......	359	20		
5	Sheep,	......	......	.....	......			28	00
5	Horse Keep,	......	......	......	......	210	00		
6	Field No. 7,	......	......	......	......			30	00
6	Loss and Gain,	......	......	......	......	89	00		
						$7843	70	$7843	70

LOSS AND GAIN STATEMENT.

April 1st, 1881.

Folio.		Losses.		Gains.	
3	Fields Nos. 1 and 2, 16 acres sown in Barley,			$343	00
3	Field No. 3, 8 acres sown in Wheat,			264	40
3	Field No. 4, 4 acres sown in Oats,			61	70
3	Field No. 5, 4 acres sown in Corn and Potatoes,			113	00
3	Field No. 6, 8 acres Grass,			183	00
6	Field No. 7. 6 acres Pasture,			30	00
4	Garden and Orchard, 4 acres,			530	00
5	Cows, 5,			60	60
5	Sheep, 10,			28	00
5	House Expenses:	$359	20		
5	Horse Keep.	210	00		
1	Plant, 10 per cent. written off for wear and tear,	89	00		
	Net Gain,	955	50		
		$1613	70	$1613	70

ASSET AND LIABILITY STATEMENT.

April 1st, 1881.

Folio.		Assets.		Liabilities.	
1	Real Estate, 50 acres, including Buildings,	$3750	00		
1	Furniture, Contained in House,	520	00		
1	Plant, as per list of a year ago, less 10 per cent. written off for wear and tear,	801	00		
1	Live Stock, as per list of a year ago,	215	00		
2	Cash, In Bank $1490, in hand $13.70,	1503	70		
2	Farm Produce, Various crops unsold and unused now in Barn,	395	80		
1	*John Roblin's Capital one year ago,* ...... 6230.00 *Gain as per statement,* ...... 955.50 *Worth 1st April,* 1881.			7185	50
		$7185	50	$7185	50

MARKING COST AND RETAIL PRICE ON GOODS.

In such a business as Dry goods and Hardware the *Cost* price, as well as the retail price, should be marked on each piece of goods. The principal object in view in marking the cost price is, that when an Inventory of Stock is being taken you may know what each piece of goods cost.

Some merchants mark the retail price in plain figures, and the cost in letters; others mark the former in letters and the latter in characters. The following will illustrate the method of marking goods:

COST MARK.

1 2 3 4 5 6 7 8 9 10 11 12 cipher. repeater. adds ten.

⊔ o \ ⊓ ⊃ V ⊓ ơ /V ⊥ ⊔ ⊋ x θ —

RETAIL MARK.

1 2 3 4 5 6 7 8 9 10 cipher. repeater.
d o n t g i v e u p x z.

EXAMPLE.

Suppose goods cost $6 a dozen, and you intend to retail them at an advance of 50 per cent., mark the cost by the character representing 6 (which is V), and follow it with the character representing the cipher, and follow this with the repeater; then mark the retail price for the sigle article directly under the cost, in this case the price would be 75c., which would be written .vg. Then the goods would be marked thus ; V. Xo.

.VG

TRADE AND CASH DISCOUNTS.

A TRADE DISCOUNT is a discount off a nominal list price, as, for instance, hardware manufacturers quote the prices of some goods at say $9.00 a dozen and 25 per cent. off; the real price being $6.75. When they desire to raise the price of particular lines of goods they don't alter the list, or nominal price, but lower the discount; and if they desire to lower the price they raise the discount. See form of invoice page 57. Sometimes discounts such as 10 and 10 and 5 are allowed. This, it will be seen, is less than 25 per cent. off the face of the invoice.

A CASH DISCOUNT is an allowance made for the prompt payment of goods, instead of a term of credit being taken. It will be well to bear in mind that when paying duty on importations the Customs authorities will not allow any deduction of duty from the face of an invoice for Cash discounts.

BOOK-KEEPING FOR CHURCHES OR OTHER PUBLIC INSTITUTIONS.

If the accounts of public institutions were kept by an efficient method and audited by competent men, a vast amount of trouble and scandal would often be saved. Many a good man has undertaken to be honorary treasurer and to keep the books of a church without any knowledge whatever of even the simplest book-keeping methods, or without knowing on what side of the Cash account he should place the entries for receipts of money; the result being a "muddle" of the church's affairs, perplexity and trouble to the man, and a cry of dishonesty on the part of the other people interested. We shall suggest a system by which the accounts of such institutions may be kept, that will require on the part of the individual whose business it will be to keep the books a knowledge of only the first principles of the double entry method.

We will suppose that an individual is appointed treasurer for a public institution, say a church, as being an institution universal in this country. He takes office and finds the accounts in an unsatisfactory state, kept by a bad method, or by no method at all. He concludes that it is best to open a new set of accounts and keep them on the double entry system.

He should do first what the skilled accountant will always do where he is called upon to bring order out of confusion or change single entry books to double entry—ascertain the resources and liabilities wherever they can be found, make out a statement of them, and by subtracting the one from the other he will determine whether the institution possesses capital, or is insolvent.

BOOKS TO BE USED.

The books will be the Cash Book, Journal, Pew Rent Receipt Book with stubs, and Ledger, and if there are a large number of pew holders it will probably be desirable to keep a

SUBSIDIARY LEDGER.

in which to keep the individual pew holder's accounts, and keep one account in the General Ledger called "Pew Holders'," the debit balance of which would always be the same as the debit balances of the individual accounts in the Subsidiary Ledger. Pew rents would be journalized say every six months as follows:—

Pew Holders,
      To Pew Rents,

following which the names, numbers of pews, and amount of rent due by each individual would be given; the sum total being posted to the debit of the account in the General Ledger called "Pew Holders," and the respective amounts to the debit of each pew holders' account in the Subsidiary Ledger, and "Pew Rent" account would receive credit.

In the Cash Book special columns should be ruled on each side, that on the debtor side for "Pew Holders." When posting, credit "Pew Holders" account in the General Ledger with the monthly total, and post to the credit of the respective pew holders' accounts in the Subsidiary Ledger the amounts paid by them. Another special column on the debtor side might be kept for collections. On the credit side the special columns, would be devoted to those accounts for which disbursements are most frequently made.

SHORT ILLUSTRATION OF THE METHOD.
JOURNAL.

To open the books journalize the resources and liabilities from the statement. The

200

account to represent capital or insolvency (similar to stock in a merchant's ledger) will be Church account.

Folio Pew Holders Ledger	Folio General Ledger	RESOURCES.					
	1	Sundries to Church account, ...				$19708	50
	1	Real Estate, ...			$15000	00	
	1	Organ, ...			3000	00	
	1	Cash, ...			120	00	
	2	Furniture, ...			1500	00	
	2	Pew Holders, due at this date as below, ...			88	50	
1		John Robinson, Pew No. 9, 6 mos.,	$6.00				
1		S. Johnson, " 28, 1 yr.,	15.00				
1		J. T. Reaves, " 115, 6 mos.,	8.00				
1		R. H. Garratt, " 89, 1 yr.,	10.00				
1		N. Yeomans, " 58, 6 mos.,	7.00				
2		R. Flint, " 79, 1 yr.,	15.00				
2		S. Donnelly, " 61, 6 mos.,	7.50				
2		J. H. Ritchie, " 71, 18 mos.,	20.00				
			$88 50				

LIABILITIES.

	1	Church account to Sundries, ...			3447	10		
	2	Mortgage Payable, ...					3000	00
	2	J. Neil & Co., ...					159	50
	3	Geo. Wallace, ...					58	70
	3	Jas. Lobb, ...					78	90
	3	Rev. H. Lord, ...					150	00

NOTE :— *When the above resource and liability entries have been posted to the Ledger, the difference between the two sides of the Church Account will show the capital, and to the debit of their respective accounts you will have placed the resources, and to the credit of their respective accounts the liabilities.*

There will be very few entries required in the Journal, as cash is almost the only element in the transactions. The crediting of salaries and the debiting of pew rents every six months will be about the only ones, except at the end of the financial year. We will therefore, to illustrate, suppose that six months have elapsed since the opening Journal entries were made.

Folio Pew Holders Ledger.	Folio General Ledger.							
	2	Pew Holders Dr.			70	50		
	3	To Pew Rents, ...					70	50
		For 6 mos rent as below :						
1		John Robinson, pew No. 9,	$6.00					
1		S. Johnson, " 28,	7.50					
1		J. T. Reaves, " 115,	8.00					
1		R. H. Garratt, " 89,	5.00					
1		N. Yeomans, " 58,	7.00					
2		R. Flint, " 79,	7.50					
2		S. Donnelly, " 61,	7.50					
2		J. H. Ritchie, " 71,	6.50					
2		Jno. Gillis, " 9,	7.50					
2		W. Buntin, " 15,	8·00					
			$70.50					

NOTE.—*Post to debit of Pew Holders' Account in General Ledger the sum total, and to the debit of the individual pew holders in subsidiary Ledger their respective amounts, and to the credit of Pew Rents' Account the sum total.*

	2	Salaries acct. Dr. to Sundries, For 6 mos. salary,			575	00		
	3	Rev. H. Lord, ...					400	00
	4	Miss Bowman, ...					75	00
	4	John Harris, ...					100	00

NOTE.—*Make Salary Account debtor for the total of the salaries for the 6 mos., and give each individual credit for his and her own amount.*

At this point also make entries for any debts contracted since the last closing of the books that have not already been placed to the credit of the parties.

Date	Fol. Led.	Fol. Gen. Led.	Fol. Sub. Led.		Collec'ns		Pew Holders		Sundries		Date	L.F.		Expense		Sundries	
				Dr. CASH.							CASH. Cr.						
				*To balance in hand,	$120								By Expense, as per receipt No. 1.	$2	50	10	00
			1	" Collections, Sundays in Jan'y,	$157	20						4	" John Harris, on acct. of salary.			150	00
			1	" J. Robinson, Pew R't in full, Stub 1			$12	00				3	" Rev. H. Lord " " "				
			2	" J. H. Ritchie, " " " " 2			26	50				4	" Expense, as per receipt No. 2,	3	90		
			1	" Collections, Sundays in February	161	90						4	" Fuel acct., Coal " " " 3.			40	00
			2	" S. Donnelly, Pew R't in full, Stub 3			15	00				4	" Lighting acct., Gas Bill " 4.			76	20
			1	" N. Yeomans, " " " " 4			14	00				4	" Expense, as per receipt " 5.			50	00
			2	" R. Flint, " in part.			12	00				4	" Miss Bowman, on acct. of salary.	6	35	35	00
			1	" Collections, Anniversary and N'ch.	250	60						3	" Rev. H. Lord, " " "			80	00
			1	" J. T. Reaves, Pew R't in full, Stub 5.			16	00				4	" John Harris, " " "				
				" Collections, Sundays in April,	190	60						4	" Interest, six mos. int. on mortgage as per receipt No. 6.			180	00
				" S. Johnson, Pew Rent in full, Stub 6			22	50				3	Expense to Cash,			12	75
				" Collections, Sundays in May,	189	20						1	Cash by Sundries,			948	95
				" Collections, Sundays in June,	174	80							Balance on hand,			313	35
				Total credit to Collections acct.	$1124	30											
				" " " Pew Holders acct.			$118	00									
				" to debit of Cash,					1124	30							
									118	00							
									1242	30							
									120	00							
				* Balance on hand at opening books.					$1262	30						$1262	30

The Stubs referred to above are the Stubs of the book from which receipts for pew rents are given, and it would be from these that the auditors would check that part of the income.

It will be well to have receipts for all payments made, and to number them to correspond with the entries as in examples above. This will simplify the work of auditing.

GENERAL LEDGER.
CHURCH ACCOUNT.

Dr. (*Capital.*) *Cr.*

Date		J.F.			Date		J.F.		
	To Sundries,		3447	10		By Sundries,		19708	50
	" Balance,		16572	25		" Working acct.		310	85
			$20019	35				$20019	35
						By Balance,		$16572	25

REAL ESTATE.

	To Church acct.,		15000	00					

ORGAN.

	To Church acct.,		3000						

CASH.

	To Church acct.,		120	00		By Sundries,		948	95
	" Sundries,		1242	30		" Balance,		413	35
			$1362	30				$1362	30
	To Balance,		413	35					

FURNITURE.

	To Church acct.,		1500						

PEW HOLDERS.

	To Church acct.,		88	50		By Cash,		118	00
	" Pew Rents,		70	50		" Balance,		41	00
			$159	00				$159	00
	* To Balance,		41	00					

MORTGAGE PAYABLE.

						By Church acct.,		3000	00

J. NEILL & CO.

						By Church acct.,		159	50

* This balance is the total indebtedness of Pew Holders at the yearly closing of the books, and agrees with the total debit balances in the Subsidiary Ledger.

Dr.   SALARIES.   Cr.

Date	To Sundries,	J.F.	$575	00	Date	By Working acct.,	J.F.	$575	00

GEO. WALLACE.

						By Church acct.,		58	70

JAS. LOBB.

						By Church acct.,		78	90

REV. H. LORD.

To Cash,		150	00	By Church acct.,		150	00
" "		350	00	" Salaries,		400	00
" Balance,		50	00				
		550	00			550	00
				By Balance.		50	00

COLLECTIONS.

To Working acct.,		1124	30	By Cash,		1124	30

EXPENSE.

To Cash,		12	75	By Working acct.,		12	75

PEW RENTS.

To Working acct.,		70	50	By Pew Holders,		70	50

FUEL.

To Cash,		40	00	By Working acct.,		40	00

LIGHTING.

To Cash,		76	20	By Working acct.,		76	20

Dr. MISS BOWMAN (*Organist.*) *Cr.*

Date		J.F.			Date		L.F.		
	To Cash,		50	00		By Salaries acct.,		75	00
	" Balance,		25	00					
			75	00				75	00
						By Balance,		25	00

JOHN HARRIS (*Sexton.*)

	To Cash,		10	00		By Salaries acct.,		100	00
	" "		80	00					
	" Balance,		10	00					
			100	00				100	00
						By Balance,		10	00

INTEREST.

	To Cash,		180	00		By Working acct.,		180	00

WORKING ACCOUNT.

	To Salaries,		575	00		By Collections,		1124	30
	" Expense,		12	75		" Pew Rents,		70	50
	" Fuel,		40	00					
	" Lighting,		76	20					
	" Interest,		180	00					
	" *Church acct.,		310	85					
			$1194	80				$1194	80

SUBSIDIARY LEDGER.

For Pew Holders' personal accounts.

Dr. JOHN ROBINSON (*Pew No. 9.*) *Cr.*

Date		J.F.			Date		C.B.F.		
	To six mos' Rent,		6	00		By Cash,		12	00
	" " "		6	00					
			$12	00				$12	00

S. JOHNSON (*Pew No. 28*).

	To 1 yr's Rent,		15	00		By Cash,		22	50
	" 6 mos.' Rent,		7	50					
			$22	50				$22	50

J. T. REEVES (*Pew No. 115*).

	To 6 mos.' Rent,		8	00		By Cash,		16	00
	" 6 " "		8	00					
			$16	00				$16	00

*This balance, which goes to Credit of Church account, is the difference between the income and expenditure of the year, or, if we may so speak in connection with a church, the year's gain. The working account is the same as Loss and Gain account in a business.

205

Dr.   R. H. GARRATT (*Pew No.* 89).   Cr.

Date		J.F.			Date		C.B.F		
	To 1 year's Rent,		$10	00		Balance,		$15	00
	" 6 mos.' "		5	00					
			$15	00				$15	00
	To Balance,		$15	00					

N. YEOMANS (*Pew No.* 58).

	To 6 mos.' Rent,		7	00		By Cash,		14	00
	" " " "		7	00					
			$14	00				$14	00

R. FLINT (*Pew No.* 79).

	To 1 year's Rent,		15	00		By Cash,		12	00
	" 6 mos.' "		7	50		" Balance,		10	50
			$22	50				$22	50
	To Balance,		$10	50					

S. DONNELLY (*Pew No.* 61).

	To 6 mos.' Rent,		7	50		By Cash,		15	00
	" " " "		7	50					
			$15	00				$15	00

J. H. RITCHIE (*Pew No.* 17).

	To 18 mos.' Rent,		20	00		By Cash,		26	50
	" 6 " "		6	50					
			$26	50				$26	50

J. McGILLIS (*Pew No.* 9).

	To 6 mos.' Rent,		7	50					

W. BUNTIN (*Pew No.* 15).

	To 6 mos.' Rent,		8	00					

P

TRIAL BALANCE.

L.F.	ACCOUNTS.	Dr. Balances		Cr. Balances	
1	Church,			16261	40
1	Real Estate,	15000	00		
1	Organ,	3000	00		
1	Cash,	413	35		
2	Furniture,	1500	00		
2	Pew Holders,	41	00		
2	Mortgage Payable,			3000	00
2	J. Neill & Co.,			159	50
2	Salaries,	575	00		
3	Geo. Wallace,			58	70
3	Jas. Lobb,			78	90
3	Rev. H. Lord,			50	00
3	Collections,			1124	30
3	Expense,	12	75		
3	Pew Rents,			70	50
4	Fuel,	40	00		
4	Lighting,	76	20		
4	Miss Bowman,			25	00
4	John Harris,			10	00
4	Interest,	180	00		
		$20838	30	$20838	30

WORKING ACCOUNT STATEMENT.

(Similar to Loss and Gain Statement of a business.)

L.F.	Dr.			L.F.	Cr.		
2	To Salaries,	575	00	3	By Collections,	1124	30
3	" Expense,	12	75	3	" Pew Rents,	70	50
4	" Fuel,	40	00				
4	" Lighting,	76	20				
4	" Interest,	180	00				
	Balance, showing a gain as the result of the ½ year's operations,	310	85				
		$1194	80			$1194	80

STATEMENT OF ASSETS AND LIABILITIES.

L.F.	Assets.			L.F.	Liabilities.		
1	Real Estate,	15000	00	2	Mortgage Payable,	3000	00
1	Organ,	3000	00	2	J. Neill & Co.,	159	50
1	Cash,	413	35	2	Geo. Wallace,	58	70
2	Furniture,	1500	00	3	Jas. Lobb,	78	90
2	Pew Holders,	41	00	3	Rev. H. Lord,	50	00
				4	Miss Bowman,	25	00
				4	John Harris,	10	00
					Net capital at date, being the worth when the books were opened, as shown in Church account, 16261.40 and the gain as shown in working acct. and statement, 310.85	16572	25
						$16572.25	
		$19954	35			$19954	35

JOINT STOCK COMPANIES.

A PAPER PREPARED FOR AND READ BEFORE THE INSTITUTE OF CHARTERED
ACCOUNTANTS AT TORONTO, BY J. W. JOHNSON, F. C. A., JANUARY 21, 1886.

JOINT STOCK COMPANY.—A Joint Stock Company is an association of individuals, who have united and have become incorporated for the purpose of carrying out an undertaking, which would require a greater amount of capital than any single person would be able or willing to risk. Each member subscribes and pays for shares in the capital stock. The object may be to mine or manufacture, to trade, to print, to carry on a banking, loan, or insurance business, or, in general, to do what an individual may do.

The extent to which the resources of Canada have been developed is largely owing to the efforts of joint stock companies, acting under letters patent from the crown, or under the authority of special Acts of Parliament, upon the limited liability principle.

LIMITED LIABILITY.—The term "limited liability" expresses the position of shareholders in joint stock companies other than banks. It means that the responsibility of shareholders for the liabilities of a company does not extend beyond the amount of stock subscribed for. If that has been fully paid up, no further calls can be made; but if it has not, then, in the event of its being required, shareholders must pay in full the sum of the shares taken. Individuals will contribute of their means, and become partners in a concern formed to develop a local or general industry, that will benefit the community, when doing so will involve no risk beyond a definite sum, while they would refuse to join an ordinary partnership, with its attendant risks and unlimited liability, formed to effect the same purpose.

While the law thus limits the liability of shareholders in joint stock companies, it requires, under a penalty of twenty dollars per day for neglect, that the public shall be informed that they are dealing with a partnership possessing exceptional privileges as to the liability of the members, and it is incumbent upon every company to affix the word " Limited " after its name on its sign over its place of business, on its seal, on its advertisements, on its business papers, and, in short, whenever its name is used.

DOUBLE LIABILITY.—The term " Double Liability " expresses the position of shareholders in banks. In order to afford security to billholders and depositors, the law makes the liability of stockholders double the amount of the subscribed capital. For instance, the owner of ten paid-up shares of one hundred dollars each would be liable, in the event of the bank's failure, to be called upon to pay in one thousand dollars, as well as lose the money already invested. Except in the recent case of the Exchange Bank, this protection has always been ample. The only fault to be found with this method of securing the currency of the banks is, that billholders may be inconvenienced by delay in payment, owing to the length of time necessarily taken to liquidate the affairs of the suspended bank. I may add here that neither delay nor loss can be experienced by holders of bills issued by American banks, as their notes are secured by deposits of United States' bonds with the National Government.

UNLIMITED LIABILITY.—Unlimited liability in connection with joint stock companies is unknown in Canada, but it is quite common in Great Britain. The failure, about five years ago, of the City of Glasgow Bank was an illustration of the utter ruin that may come to the holders of shares in an unlimited liability company.

INCORPORATION.—The incorporation of joint stock companies may, under Dominion legislation, be effected in two ways, either by obtaining a special Act of Parliament, or by letters patent under the General Joint Stock Companies' Act. Banking, Insurance, and Railway Companies must be incorporated by special Act, as their requirements are such, and the powers which they seek are so extensive, that special legislation determining their limit and scope is absolutely necessary. For all ordinary undertakings, incorporation under the general Act is amply sufficient. The general Dominion Act now in force is "The Canada Joint Stock Companies' Act, 1877," to be found at chap. 43, Statutes of Canada, 40 Victoria, 1877.

Under Ontario legislation incorporation may be effected, either by a special Act of the legislature, or under "The Ontario Joint Stock Companies' Letters Patent Act," to be found at chap. 150, page 1320, of the Revised Statutes of Ontario.

PROSPECTUS.—A number of individuals having agreed to form a joint stock company, under the Dominion Joint Stock Companies' Act, issue a prospectus, setting forth the proposed name of the Company (which must not be the same or similar to that of any other incorporated or unincorporated company), the number of shares, the amount of each, and the capital, the names of the provisional directors, the bank at which it is proposed to keep their account, and generally stating the business to be carried on, and the probable profits to be derived from it.

STOCK BOOK.—A stock book is prepared, in which each of the subscribers for shares writes the number he is willing to take and affixes his signature, seal and residence. This is a binding and solemn contract to pay the calls upon the stock as they shall severally become due. Having obtained subscriptions to the amount of at least one half of the total amount of the stock of the company, and not less than ten per cent. thereof having been paid in and deposited to such credit in some chartered bank (unless the object of the company is one requiring that it should own real estate), application may be made to the Governor-General through the Secretary of State of Canada, for the issue of letters patent, the applicants being in number not less than five. Prior to the application, at least one month's notice must have been given in the *Canada Gazette* of the intention to apply for the same, stating therein the proposed name of the company, its purposes, place of business, amount of capital, number of shares, the name, address and calling of each of the applicants, and the names of those who are to be the provisional directors. Notice of the granting of letters patent will be given forthwith by the Secretary of State in the *Canada Gazette*, and, thereupon, from the date of the letters patent, the persons therein named, and their successors, shall be a body corporate and politic by the name mentioned therein. The fees charged are, when the capital is $500,000 or upwards, $200; between $200,000 and $500,000, $150; between $100,000 and $200,000, $100; between $40,000, and $100,000, $50; less than $40,000, $30. A change of name may be obtained subsequently, if it is not sought for an improper purpose.

INCREASE OF STOCK.—The directors of a company may at any time, after the whole capital stock has been taken up, and fifty per cent. thereon paid in, make a by-law for increasing the capital stock, and they may also in the same way decrease the capital stock, but their action in this regard must be sanctioned by a vote of not less than two-thirds in value of all the shareholders of the company, at a general meeting called for considering the same, and confirmed by supplementary letters patent.

DIRECTORS.—The affairs of the company are managed by a board of directors, which may consist of not less than three nor more than fifteen. They are usually elected annually at the annual general meeting, and they must be shareholders in their own right to the amount required by the company's by-law, and not in arrears in respect of any call upon stock. Each shareholder is entitled to give one vote for each share held by him ; such votes may be given in person or by proxy—the holder of any such proxy being himself a shareholder.

OFFICERS.—The president and permanent officers of the company are elected by the directors ; but the auditors should be appointed at the annual meeting of the shareholders, for the reason that the officers of the company are largely controlled by the directors, and the audit being, as far as this connection goes, an examination of the faithfulness to the shareholders of both the officers and directors, it is necessary that the stockholders themselves should appoint the auditors.

SECRETARY.—The secretary, who is frequently the responsible bookkeeper also, should be a skilled accountant. In my own experience I have been called upon to audit the books of companies that had at their inception appointed as secretary and accountant a " friend of the president," or a lawyer, or some " young gentleman," whose father was a large stockholder, and the books, or to be more accurate, the memoranda, kept by such men have always been mixed and muddled. You can no more expect a man to perform the work of an accountant who has never thoroughly and patiently learned his business than you can look for reliable building plans from a man who has never studied architecture. It is hardly necessary to point out how much the success of the business of an individual, or firm, or a company, depends upon sound and accurate bookkeeping, and yet the lessons taught by the failures confessedly brought about by the absence of it are often neglected. No man or number of men should attempt to conduct a business without the knowledge of bookkeeping themselves, or the employment of those who are possessed of it; and what is essential in this respect with individuals or firms is indispensable in connection with joint stock companies, the affairs of which are usually of magnitude, and affect a wide circle.

CALLS ON STOCK.—For the first and each subsequent call upon stock an instalment list will be made out, and the payments will be acknowledged by issuing to each shareholder instalment scrip. When the last call has been paid the instalment scrip will be called in, and in place of it stock certificates will be issued.

BOOKKEEPING.—There are certain books that are required by law to be kept by all companies, and which shall be kept open for the inspection of shareholders and creditors of the company, and from which they may make extracts. One of these is called the Reference Book, which shall contain :—

1. A copy of the Letters Patent incorporating the Company and the by-laws thereof.

2. The names, alphabetically arranged, of all the persons who are or have been shareholders, with their address and calling.

3. The number of shares held by each shareholder.

4. The amount paid in and remaining unpaid, respectively, on the stock of each shareholder.

5. The names, addresses and calling of all persons, who are or have been directors of the Company, with the several dates at which each became or ceased to be such director.

A book, called the Register of Transfers, shall be provided, and in such book shall be entered the particulars of every transfer of shares.

The penalty for neglecting to keep such books is the forfeiture of the Company's Corporate rights. For the bookkeeping proper, all Companies will at least have a Cash Book, Journal, General Ledger and Stock Ledger; such auxiliary books will be used as the nature of the business may demand.

STOCK LEDGER.—The use of a stock ledger will be apparent, if you consider how troublesome and inconvenient it would be to keep an account in the general ledger, with the numerous individual stockholders of a company, who hold stock to day and may part with it to-morrow, as is done with the individual partners of an ordinary partnership, whose interest is permanent. This book contains an account with each shareholder, in which are recorded his name and address, the number of shares of the capital stock of the Company held by each, and the instalments that have been paid upon them. A moment's reflection will make it apparent how easily transfers of stock are posted in this book, without affecting the general ledger. For instance, there stands at the credit of A 10 paid up shares, which he sells to-day to B. They go to the office of the company, where A signs a transfer on the company's transfer book, and delivers up his certificate, which is cancelled. A new one is issued to B, and from the stub of the transfer book A is made debtor to B in the stock ledger. Such transfers may be made through the medium of stock-brokers, acting for both buyer and seller. No restrictions can be placed upon the transfer of fully paid up stock, but the directors of a company must sanction the transfer of stock that is not fully paid up in order to prevent holders from getting rid of the liability to pay, by transferring it to people who are not worth anything.

OPENING.—In opening the books of a company, there are two ways of dealing with the stock subscribed for: you may debit the original subscribers for stock in the general ledger with the amount of their subscriptions, and place at the credit of the capital Stock account the total of these, which is the nominal capital of the Company, until the stock has been fully paid up, when it becomes the real capital. It is a permanent credit on the ledger, only affected when the capital stock is either increased or diminished or watered. As calls upon stock are paid, credit the shareholders' accounts in the general ledger from the cash book, and at the same time credit their accounts in the stock ledger, which will be opened when the first call is paid. When stock has been fully paid up the shareholders' accounts in the general ledger will be closed, after which the stock ledger only will show their accounts. In the event of the ledger being closed before stock is fully paid up, close the accounts of shareholders " By Balance," as you would any other personal accounts, showing a debit to the Company. In the balance sheet put the matter thus:

Capital Stock subscribed (say)....$50,000
"   "   unpaid, 60₀/°......30,000
"   "   paid up..........20,000

Capital Stock account in the general ledger will agree with the first figures; the total debit balances against the shareholders in the general ledger will agree with the second figures, and the total of the amounts credited to shareholders in the stock ledger will agree with the last.

Another way of dealing with the Capital Stock is to credit the account as instalments are paid, crediting the payments to the shareholders in the stock ledger at the same time, without opening accounts for the shareholders in the general ledger at all. This is the simpler way; the argument for the first is that as the unpaid stock is a liability to the company, it should be shown in the general ledger at the debit of the individuals.

PRICES OF SHARES.—Whether a company's share are being sold at par, that is, the face value, at a premium or a discount, they are always at par in the company's books. The first issue of shares at the inception of a company will always be at par. Subsequent issues may be offered at a premium, if the old stock is above par in the market. After the stock authorized by the charter has been taken by subscribers, a company's shares are no longer within its own control. It has none to sell, and their real value will be the investing public's estimation of them, based upon the efficiency of the company's management, the past earnings and an estimate of its powers in that direction in the future. If you desire to buy stock in a company, whose shares have all been taken up, you must find some holder willing to sell, either by your own seeking, or the employment of a stock broker. What you pay for the shares is a private bargain between yourself and the holder, with which the company cannot interfere. If the company whose shares you buy is a large and important concern, like a loan company or a bank, the stock will be quoted on the stock exchange, and you will be guided in your purchase by the latest quotations.

DIVIDENDS AND RESTS.—It seldom occurs that any properly managed company declares a dividend (division of profits) amounting to the full sum of its earnings. The proper course is to reserve a certain sum annually, to provide against possible future contingencies. Our chartered banks have a Rest Account to the credit of which a certain sum is carried annually from the profit and loss account, until it reaches a certain proportion of the Capital Stock; and it is customary also with them to leave a certain amount at the credit of profit and loss.. The prosperity of the Bank of Montreal, selecting it as the most prominent example, is, in a large measure, due to following this wise course. Its "rest" now amounts to six millions of dollars; that is, out of its earnings, it has set aside from year to year sums that now amount to this figure. The bank would have to lose in bad debts the sum of six millions before its capital could be impaired. Besides the provision which the possession of a "rest" makes against unforeseen contingencies and bad debts, it serves the exceedingly useful purpose of enabling the company to pay as nearly as possible a uniform dividend from year to year. In any one year the profits of a company will not be precisely the same as those of a previous year, but the possession of a rest will enable the directors to equalize the dividend, and preserve the stock of the company from the fluctations in price, to which a constantly changing rate of dividend would subject it.

DIVIDEND STOCK.—Dividend Stock will be most easily explained by giving an example: We will suppose that a certain gas company has been in existence a score of years in a prosperous community, enjoying the monopoly of supplying it with light. The price charged is high, and in consequence the company is making large profits; so large indeed, that the directors fear that if the facts should become known, they will be confronted either with a demand for a reduction in the price, or the formation of a rival company. In order, therefore, to make it appear to the consumers that the profits are not excessive, they declare a reasonable dividend in cash, and place a certain amount to the credit of the "rest" account, of which the public are informed, and they also distribute a dividend in stock, of which the public are kept in ignorance.

When this has been done for a number of years, the capital stock will have greatly increased. We will say, for the purpose of illustration, to double the original money paid in. Now, while the annual profit upon the original capital, if it were known to the public, would appear excessive, the profit upon both the original stock and dividend stock combined is reasonable, and the directors say—" Why, we are only making eight per cent of profit on our capital, and cannot afford to sell gas for less than we are now charging."

The entries in the books of so fortunate a conpany, for distributing the profits, as indicated above, would be as follows: —

At the credit of profit and loss account there stands—say the sum of $16,000, as the net profit for the year upon a capital of $100,000 ; this is 16 per cent. A dividend of 7 per cent. in cash is to be paid, 2 per cent. is to be placed to the credit of rest account, and the balance is to be paid in stock.

Pofit and Loss, Dr. $16,000.

To Dividend	$7,000
" Rest	2,000
" Capital Stock	7,000

When the dividend has been paid that account will close. In the stock ledger credit each shareholder with his proportion of the $7,000, and issue certificates. In doing this, of course, there will be fractions of shares to be credited in some cases.

The above mode of creating stock is simply equivalent to the existing shareholders subscribing for new stock and paying for it out of the earnings of the old stock. The only objection that can be urged against it is that it deceives the public regarding the company's profits, and by the manipulation the company maintains excessive prices for its wares. In the case of a company in which the public has no interest, there can be no objection at all to the payment of stock dividends.

WATERED STOCK.—There is another method of creating stock, called watering, to which serious objection may be urged. It is the writing up of the value of assets beyond their cost or worth, the crediting of capital stock with the amount, and the issuing of shares to the extent of the inflation. I can only suppose a very few instances where such a course would be honest or justifiable. One would be the case of a mine, for which say $100,000 had been paid, but which proved, by the operation for years, to be worth a much larger sum.

CONVERSION OF PRIVATE PARTNERSHIPS INTO JOINT STOCK COMPANIES.— In Great Britain within the last twenty-five years, and latterly to some extent in Canada, the conversion of private partnerships into joint stock companies has become very general. In all branches of commerce you will observe such signs as "John Arnott & Co. (Limited)," and on making inquiry regarding the change, it will generally be found that it was effected at the death of some of the original partners, whose interest in the concern has been inherited by a number of heirs who desire to retain the interest in the business, but take no part in its management, nor incur any responsibility for its liabilities. An old-established firm that might otherwise cease to exist, for death dissolves a partnership, is thus preserved, the management remains undisturbed, the shares are in the hands of the families of the original partners, who, without risk or anxiety, enjoy the fruits of the labors of those whose heirs they are. When any of these desire to sell their shares, they have simply to find a purchaser at will. During a visit to Ireland three years ago, I found that the old Belfast house of Hawkins, Robertson, Ferguson & Co., with whom I served an apprenticeship of four years, had become a joint stock company under the name of Robertson, Ferguson, Ledlie, & Co, (Limited), at the death of the senior partner, and for the reasons that I have mentioned. It has latterly become quite common for manufacturers in the Dominion to convert their concerns into joint stock companies ; the object being to extend their trade by the introduction of new capital, which could not be obtained on the ordinary partnership or special partnership principle, but only on that of limited liability. The former owner will take the price of the property in paid-up stock. In opening the books under such circumstances, make the plant and other property accounts debtor for their respective values to capital stock ; credit the man in the stock ledger, and give him a stock certificate for the number of shares. The new stock and stockholders will be dealt with as before described.

SERVICES PAID IN STOCK.—Services are sometimes paid for by the issue of stock. A company which had not issued all the stock authorized by its charter, being desirous to reward a president for his services, might do so by giving him say ten shares of paid-up stock. The journal entry would be:—

Expense, Dr.
To Capital Stock,

and in the stock ledger the president would be credited with ten shares, and he would receive a certificate for that number.

SUBSCRIBED, BUT UNPAID STOCK A RESOURCE.—It is not unusual for companies, other than banks, which desire to secure public confidence, without which they could not exist, to obtain subscriptions for stock to a much larger amount than the capital necessary to carry on their affairs. To illustrate—a life insurance company must command public confidence to be successful. The capital required to carry on its operations beyond the amount deposited with the Dominion Government, in the interest and for the security of policy holders, is small in comparison with that of a bank, or an important manufacturing concern; but the permanence of the company and the ability to pay its liabilities to the widows and orphans, who will be its chief creditors, is of vital importance. By obtaining subscriptions for stock to an amount much larger than the capital required, and calling up say only a fourth of the amount, it has a reserve which, in the event of its being required, can be called for any time. This reserve in the case of life insurance companies, is as tangible an asset as the double liability resource of a bank.

BONDS OR DEBENTURES.—When joint stock companies borrow money for a long period, they do so by the issuing and disposing of bonds or debentures, which are negotiable instruments, payable to the bearer, and attached to which are interest coupons, usually two for each year of the time for which the bonds are to run. The bonds of a railway or mining company are usually secured by a mortgage upon its property held by trustees for the bondholders, and they are called first mortgage bonds, if the mortgage is the first lien upon the property. Loan companies borrow money upon their bonds, not, as in the case of the railway or mining company, because they are hard up, but to obtain money at a cheap rate to lend at a high rate. If the company be an old and sound one it could probably borrow at par in England upon its bonds at four per cent. The proceeds would be brought to Canada and loaned at say seven or eight per cent., the result being a handsome profit upon funds not contributed by its shareholders, just as the banks make a profit by loaning the funds left with them on deposit.

The difference between a stockholder and bondholder of a company will, of course, be apparent—the stockholder is a partner, the bondholder is a creditor. Governments and municipalities also borrow upon debentures or bonds. The bonds of the Government of England are called " Consols, " which is an abbrevation of the term " consolidated bonds."

SPECULATION IN STOCKS.—The purchase and transfers of stock, to which I have hitherto alluded, have been genuine sales and can be easily understood. There is a large amount of speculation in stocks, however, in which there is no intention actually to deliver and receive them. This is called "buying on margin," which, with the particular jargon used in connection with it, is not easily understood by the unitiated. A contract is made through a broker to buy a certain number of shares of some particular stock at a fixed price, within so many days—a margin, say five per cent. of the amount, being placed in the hands of the broker. Should the stock rise in the market, the speculator may order his broker to sell, and after paying him his commission pocket a handsome profit; on the other hand, should the stock decline, the speculator must keep up his margin by making further payments, and it may be that, no favorable turn taking place immediately, he is unable to continue to carry the stock, and loses all he has invested. It will be seen that this kind of speculation simply amounts to a bet that a particular stock will be above a certain figure in the future. If it prove to be, the speculator wins; if not, he loses. Some curious phrases are used on 'change (This is an abbrevation of Stock Exchange, where the brokers carry on their operations), such as " bulls " and " bears, " " corner," " short," " long, " " put " or "call." The name " bulls " is given to those dealers who are endeavoring to force up the price of certain shares, and those are called " bears " whose object it is to lower them. A " corner " is the result of certain operations between these opposing forces. When it becomes known that there is a large number of " short contracts" out in a certain stock, advantage is taken of the fact by the buyers, who purchase all the shares they can get hold of, so that when the time arrives for the fulfilment of their contracts the holders have the " shorts " at their mercy. The latter are compelled to purchase at greatly advanced prices, and are "cornered " unless they can break down the corner, when the tables may be turned upon the "longs." A " put " or "call " is a contract whereby, for the payment of a small sum of money, one dealer may require another to take or deliver within a limited time, say one day, a certain amount of stock at a stated price.

LIQUIDATION.—A Joint Stock Company, upon which a demand has been made for a debt amounting to $200, and which remains unpaid after 60 days, may be forced into liquidation by its creditors. Application is made to the Court for a winding up order, after four days' notice to the Company. The Court may, in its discretion, grant the order forthwith, or adjourn to make inquiry. The Company must show its books. After the order has been made, and a liquidator appointed, no transfer of stock can be effected, and the business of the Company must cease unless the liquidator deems it best that it should go on. With the appointment of the liquidator, the functions of the directors cease, for in him is vested full power to do all things necessary to wind up. He may appoint a solicitor to assist him. An execution cannot be enforced against a company in liquidation, and remedy against it cannot be obtained by suit, but by an order of the Court. The liquidator is subject to the Court. He must not deposit the company's money in the bank in his own name only, but in his official capacity, and he must produce the bank pass book at meetings. He is paid as the Court directs. After the final order is made. the money in hand is deposited and left for three years, subject to any legitimate call, and at the end of that time it is paid over to the Receiver-General. The Statute of Liquidation in force is that of 1882.

For Joint Stock Company Book-Keeping, see J. W. Johnson's work: "JOHNSON'S JOINT STOCK COMPANY BOOK-KEEPING," *published by Ontario Business College, Belleville.*

THE

CANADIAN ACCOUNTANT

PART III.

CONTAINING A COMPREHENSIVE SUMMARY OF ONTARIO LAW,
FORMS OF BUSINESS PAPERS, COMMERCIAL
CORRESPONDENCE,

AND

COMMERCIAL CALCULATIONS,

COMPREHENDING

*ABBREVIATED METHODS OF PRACTICAL COMPUTATION,
SETTLEMENT OF ACCOUNTS, &c., NOT FOUND
IN COMMON ARITHMETICS.*

SUMMARY OF ONTARIO LAW.

Prepared by WILLIAM N. PONTON, M.A., Barrister and Solicitor, Belleville, lecturer on Commercial Law at Ontario Business College.

ACTIONS.—An entire change in the procedure and practice of the Courts was affected by the Ontario Judicature Act 1881. Law and Equity are administered concurrently. All the Superior Courts were consolidated together to form the Supreme Court of Judicature for Ontario, which consists of two permanent divisions, "The Court of Appeal for Ontario" and "The High Court of Justice for Ontario."

All actions in the Supreme Court are commenced by a writ indorsed with a statement of the claim made, or of the relief or remedy sought. The writ requires the defendant, if served in Ontario, to enter an appearance within ten days after service. The defendant may set off or set up by way of counter-claim, any claim which he has against the plaintiff. If the defendant claims indemnity or contribution or other remedy over or against any third person, provision is made for service of notice on such third person. Speedy judgment can be applied for after a writ of summons has been issued, when it is made to appear to the Court that it will be conducive to the ends of justice. Inferior jurisdiction is exercised by County and Division Courts. County Courts have no jurisdiction in actions where the title to land is in question, or where the validity of any devise is disputed, nor in actions of libel or slander. County Courts have jurisdiction in personal actions, where claim does not exceed $200. In all actions of debt and contract, where amount is liquidated or ascertained they have jurisdiction up to $400.

Division Courts are held frequently, and are presided over by the County Court judges. There are twelve Division Courts in the County of Hastings, and ten in the County of York. The scale of costs is very low, and the Court has been called the poor man's Court, which it is in more senses than one. The action should be brought where the Defendant resides or where the cause of action arose. The Court has jurisdiction in all personal actions to $60, in all claims of debt or breach of contract to $100, and where the amount is ascertained by the signature of the Defendant to $200. The Judge may commit a Judgment Debtor to gaol for the several causes set out in Sec. 240 of the Division Courts Act, R. S. O., cap. 51 and amendments thereto.

ADMINISTRATION.—See page 120.

AFFIDAVIT.—See Registration.

APPEAL.—There is (except in matters of discretion) an appeal allowed from a single judge of the High Court to the full Court, and thence to the Court of Appeal for Ontario, thence in some cases to the Supreme Court of Canada, which sits at Ottawa ; and in very important cases to the Judicial Committee of the Privy Council in England. An appeal is also allowed from the judges of the County Court to the Court of Appeal, and in those Division Court actions where the amount involved exceeds $100.

APPROPRIATION OF PAYMENTS.—The buyer or debtor has the right to appropriate the payments made by him to whatever items he chooses. If he does not so appropriate, the person receiving the money may apply the payment even to reduce a debt barred by the Statute of Limitations. (See Limitations below.)

ALIENS may hold real and personal property as freely as natural born subjects, but labor under disability as to the franchise.

Aliens may become naturalized by taking the oath of allegiance to the Sovereign, and obtaining the sanction of a Judge in open Court.

ARBITRATIONS are more frequently adopted for the settlement of disputes than formerly ; while they are sometimes more expeditious, they are not always more inexpensive than ordinary law suits. Arbitrations may grow out of law suits, the Judge having power to refer the matters in question before him to one or more referees, especially where there are involved accounts. Nearly all Insurance Companies require claims to be arbitrated when they are disputed. The price of lands expropriated by Railway Companies or by Municipalities for rights of way, is generally ascertained by arbitration. An award should generally be under seal, and signed by all the arbitrators in presence of each other. Some references provide that the award signed by two out of three arbitrators shall be binding. The award may be made a rule of Court, and afterwards enforced by judicial process. Care should be taken that the arbitrators do not exceed their powers under the reference, and provision should be made for disposing of the cost of the arbitration and award. The Statutes provide for arbitration in the cases of disputes between masters and workmen, injuries to employees, etc., etc. Professional arbitrators are entitled to from $10 to $20 per day. Non professional arbitrators are allowed from $5 to $10 per day or as may agreed. Formerly war was the only arbiter of nations; now International Arbitration rather that bloodshed is the basis of Treaties.

ARREST for debt has been abolished, except in cases of fraudulent disposal or concealment of property liable for debt, and refusal to give proper answers on examination as a Judgment Debtor. In these cases, however, it is rather for contempt of Court and refusal to obey its orders, than for debt that imprisonment is decreed. Debtors may also be arrested on capias and held to bail, if it be proved to the satisfaction of the judge, on behalf of a bona fide creditor, that the debtor is about to leave the jurisdiction with the design of defrauding creditors.

ASSIGNMENTS made on the eve of insolvency, with intent to prefer a creditor or benefit a relative or friend, to the prejudice of creditors generally, are null and void, and will be set aside by the Court. Assignments in trust should be made to the Sheriff, or with the consent of the majority of creditors to some other responsible person. While the Statute forbirds any perferential security being given for a debt, where assets are deficient, it does not invalidate or make void any deed of assignment made by any debtor, for the purpose of paying and satisfying rateably and proportionably, and without preference or priority, all the creditors of such debtor, their just debts; or any bona fide sale of goods in the ordinary course of trade or calling to innocent purchasers. See R. S. O. cap. 124 and amendments.

ATTACHMENT OF GOODS.—If any person resident in Ontario, indebted to any other person, departs from Ontario with intent to defraud his creditors, and at the time of his so departing is possessed of any property, he shall be deemed an absconding debtor, and his property may be seized for his debts by a writ of attachment. Upon affidavit made by any plaintiff, that any such person so departing is indebted to such plaintiff in a sum exceeding $100.00, and stating the cause of action and that deponent has good reason to believe, and does verily believe, that such person has departed from Ontario, and has gone with intent to defraud the plaintiff of his just dues, or to avoid, being arrested or served, and was at the time possessed of real or personal property, not exempt by law from seizure, in this Province, and upon the further affidavit of two other credible persons, that they are well acquainted with the debtor, and have good reason to believe and do believe that such debtor has departed from Ontario with intent to defraud the said plaintiff, or to avoid being arrested or served, either the High Court or the Judge of any County Court may direct a writ of attachment to issue, and may appoint the time for the defendant's putting in special bail.

BILL OF EXCHANGE AND PROMISSORY NOTES.—See page 224.

BILLS OF SALE AND CHATTEL MORTGAGES.—Every mortgage or sale of goods and chattels, not accompanied by an immediate delivery and followed by an actual and continued *change of possession*, must be in writing, and be accompanied by an affidavit of execution, and also by an affidavit by the mortgagee or bargainee, or his agent (if such agent is aware of the circumstances connected therewith, and is properly authorized in writing to take such mortgage) as to the *bona fides* of such mortgage or bill of sale, and must be filed in the office of the Clerk of the County Court of the county where the goods are situated, within five days from its execution, otherwise such mortgage or sale will be void as against creditors of the mortgagor or bargainor, and as against subsequent purchasers or mortgagees in good faith for valuable consideration. A chattel mortgage will cease to be valid after the expiration of one year from the filing, as against creditors or subsequent mortgagees, unless within thirty days preceding the expiration of the year, and so on from year to year, a statement is filed in the office of the Clerk of the County Court of the county where such goods and articles are then situate, stating the interest of the mortgagee, and showing the payments made on account and the amount still due, accompanied by an affidavit by the mortgagee or his agent (authorized in writing,) swearing to the truth of the statements, and that the mortgage is not kept on foot for any fraudulent purpose. Where goods are actually delivered and handed over to the purchaser a Bill of sale is not necessary, but is always advisable as evidence of the transaction. The goods should be described distinctly so as to be readily identified, and great care should be exercised in observing all the formalities required by the Act, R. S. O. cap. 125, and amendments thereto. Chattel mortgages are often taken as collateral (additional and contemporaneous) security to Bills and Notes, and if so, the fact should always be so expressed in such security.

BONDS are obligations under seal, wherein the obligors and sureties are bound on certain penal sums to the performance of certain conditions. If sureties are obliged to pay they must contribute proportionately. Bonds of indemnity are required by Banks when deposit receipts are lost, and by the Courts when a lost note is sued on.

CONTRACTS may be made by letters, telegrams, and detached papers, as well as by a formal instrument. Contracts made on Sunday are void, but may be ratified on a week day. Contracts are construed by the law of the place where made, and the *whole* contract including recitals is considered; the *custom of merchants* plays an important part in the decision of commercial cases. Specialty contracts are contracts under seal, which do not require any consideration to be expressed. Simple contracts are those not under seal, whether verbal or written.
A minor or infant may contract for necessaries consistent with the minor's station in life. An infant may, after attaining 21, ratify *in writing* a contract made during minority. A will is not a contract, being always revocable by the testator.* A contract, to be valid, requires the mutual assent of competent contracting parties; a good and valid consideration; something to be done or omitted, and a legal object. Contracts in absolute restraint of trade are held void by reason of Public Policy. The Statute of Frauds requires all contracts regarding lands (except leases for 3 years), all contracts not to be performed within one year, all guarantees for the debt of another, and all contracts for sale of goods over the value of $40 (unless partly executed and performed), to be in writing. The contract is not the writing. The writing is the evidence of what the contract is.

COMMON CARRIERS, TRAVELLERS, etc.

The liability of Railway Companies, both as to freight and passengers and baggage, is very stringent, and they cannot avoid their responsibility by any conditions endorsed on tickets or shipping receipts, which would tend to render nugatory the whole contract, or would excuse the negligence of their employees or agents. All conditions must be reasonable.

If baggage is left at the station of destination an unusual time, the liability of the company is only that of warehousemen, not of common carriers, so that if a fire should accidentally destroy the baggage room and goods, the company would not be liable. An insurance policy against accidents, while travelling in a public conveyance, is always construed in favor of the insured, and covers accidents which occur when alighting, or changing cars. A ticket is a contract, and a time-table is a representation. Railway Companies are not liable for mere loss of time occasioned by delay of trains, but are liable for actual pecuniary special damage, which can be proved to have directly been incurred from such delay. A traveller who refuses to pay his fare to an official authorized to receive it (and wearing on his cap the badge of such authority), may be put off the train, but only near some dwelling house or at a usual stopping place.

The company is responsible for the act of a servant acting within the scope of his employment, even when disobeying orders. A railway track *per se* is a warning of danger. If one employee is injured through the negligence of a fellow employee, the employer is not liable. Usually a servant accepts the risks of his employment, but see now the recent Employees Liability Act.

Common carriers are bound to use the highest degree of care that a reasonable man would use for himself, and to secure safety consistently with the mode of transportation.

Shipowners are bound to furnish a vessel sea-worthy and well equipped, with adequate crew, and competent master. Owners of stages are responsible that all equipments of conveyance, drivers, horses and harness are fit and suitable.

Carriers are not liable, where, by the exercise of reasonable care on the part of the injured, the accident might have been avoided, i. e., where there was "legal" contributory negligence.

CONVEYANCES OF LANDS are made by Deeds which are instruments under seal, executed by the vendor (grantor) to the purchaser (grantee). It is most important that the lands intended to be conveyed should be clearly defined, otherwise the deed cannot be registered.

COURTS—See Actions.

DOWER is the right of a widow to a one-third interest for life in the lands of her deceased husband, or in the rents and profits thereof. Under a recent statute on the devolution of estates a widow may take an absolute interest in the one-third, in the same way as in personal estate. In the N.W. Territories Dower, as dower, is not recognized in real estate property law.
A widow is entitled to dower in lands (except in cases mentioned in statute) of which her husband was seized during the marriage. A married woman may bar her dower in any lands or hereditaments, by joining with her husband in a deed or conveyance thereof, in which a release of dower is contained.

DECLARATIONS—Statutory declarations are allowed as evidence in cases where extra-judicial oaths are forbidden. They should always be made before a Notary Public or Justice of the Peace.

EVIDENCE—In civil proceedings the evidence of all parties is admissible, and there is no incompetence on the ground of interest as a party or otherwise. In Quebec, however, parties cannot give evidence on their own behalf.

In a suit by or against representatives of a deceased person, an opposite or interested party to the suit cannot obtain a judgment on his own evidence, as to any matter occurring before the death of the deceased, unless such evidence is corroborated. The onus of proof is on that party who asserts the virtual affirmative.

In giving evidence, a witness is not bound to answer any questions, the answers to which would tend to criminate himself.

In criminal courts (except in some few cases, such as common assaults and liquor prosecutions) the accused is not competent or compellable to give evidence on his own behalf. A person is presumed to be innocent until proved to be guilty, and the jury is always directed to give a prisoner the benefit of any reasonable doubt. Quakers, and those who believe it unlawful to take an oath, and those on whose conscience an oath has no effect, affirm and declare, and do not swear. Evidence may be taken out of the Province, on commission issued by the Courts.

EXECUTION—Judgments do not of themselves bind the property of debtors. Writs of execution must issue and bind the property of the debtor, from the time of the receipt thereof by the sheriff of the county where such property is situated. Lands cannot be sold by sheriff till after the lapse of twelve months.—See *Actions*.

EXEMPTION.—The following chattels are exempt from seizure under writ of execution.

1. The bed, bedding and bedsteads in ordinary use by the debtor and his family.
2. The necessary and ordinary wearing apparel of the debtor and his family.
3. One cooking stove with pipes and furnishings, one other heating stove with pipes, etc., one set of cooking utensils, one pair of tongs and shovel, one coal scuttle, one lamp, one table, six chairs, one washstand with furnishings, six towels, one looking glass, etc., one bureau, one clothes press, one clock, one carpet, one cupboard, one broom, twelve knives and forks, twelve plates, etc., two pails, one washtub, etc., all spinning wheels and weaving looms in domestic use, one sewing machine and attachments in domestic use, thirty volumes of books, one axe, one saw, one gun, etc., the articles in this subdivision enumerated not exceeding in *value* $150.00.
4. All necessary fuel, meat, fish, flour and vegetables actually provided for family use of the debtor and his family, for thirty days, and not exceeding in *value* $40.
5. One cow, six sheep, four hogs, and twelve hens, in all not exceeding the *value of* $75, and food for thirty days, and one dog.
6. Tools and implements of or chattels ordinarily used in the debtor's occupation to the value of $100. (Or if so elected proceeds of sale thereof up to $100.)
7. Bees, fifteen hives. See R. S. O., 1887, cap. 64.

The debtor, his widow and family, or in case of infants, their guardian, may select out of any larger number the several chattels exempt from seizure.

Lands taken up under the free grant and homestead act are exempt from execution for twenty years from the location of the land being made by the locatee. While the above goods are exempt from seizure under ordinary process of law, they are not all exempt from the summary right of distress possessed by a landlord against his tenant for arrears of rent, nor are they exempt at law if the debt, for which execution issued, was contracted for the identical chattel with reference to which exemption is claimed. Exemptions in Manitoba are far more extensive.

FEME COVERTE —A married woman may now hold her separate property as though she were a *feme sole* (spinster). In deeds of lands it is always better, however, to get the husband to join, so as to get rid of his possible claim to a tenancy by the curtesy (Life Estate).

INSURANCE.—A fire insurance policy is a contract of indemnity. Nothing should be concealed from the Company which is material to the risk, whether as to ownership, incumbrances, value, location, occupation, or prior or other insurance. A personal debt of the agent cannot be set off as against a premium on a policy. If insurance is assigned, the Head Office of the Company should ratify the assignment. Life insurance may be effected in favor of wife and children, and creditors cannot touch proceeds. It is always advisable to get an admission of age when effecting insurance. Concealment even without fraud has been held to vitiate a policy.

INSOLVENCY.—The Insolvent Acts have been repealed, and a bankrupt cannot now obtain an absolute discharge without the consent of creditors. The Creditor's Relief Act abolishes priority among creditors, and provides for the rateable distribution of assets in the sheriff's hands, among those who have obtained judgment within a limited time. The act does not interfere, however, with those creditors who hold valid special securities.—*See Assignment.*

INTEREST.—Where no rate is stipulated for by agreement, only six per cent. per annum can be recovered, calculated from the time the debt was due and demanded. There are no usury laws in force in Ontario, but loan companies and money lenders are not allowed to charge a higher rate on default of payment than they would have charged had payment been regularly made. If a mortgage is in default, the mortgagee is entitled to six months' interest as bonus, before the mortgagor can redeem, unless the mortgage has run for five years, and was made after the Statute in that behalf, in which case the mortgagee is obliged to take his money in full on being paid three months' interest in advance by way of bonus. Interest does not run on an open overdue account unless demanded. The Courts regard interest as damages for detention of money. Instruments drawing interest at a higher rate than 6 per cent. should be expressed to bear interest at that rate as well after as before maturity.

JOINT STOCK COMPANIES.—See after *Partnership*.

LANDLORD AND TENANT.—See *Mortgages, Taxes* and *Exemptions*.

A yearly tenant requires a full 6 months (183 days,) notice to quit, expiring at the end of a year. A monthly tenant requires a full month's notice to quit. Tenants desiring to leave should give the same notice. Goods distrained for rent can be sold after five days from seizure and demand.

Leases for three years and shorter periods are valid even though not in writing.

LIMITATION.—Actions on simple contracts, notes, instruments not under seal, and money demands must be brought within six years from the time the cause of action accrues. When plaintiff is under disability by reason of infancy or lunacy, the statute runs from the removal of the disability. Actions to recover lands must be brought within ten years after the right of action accrued ; that is to say, if A enters on B's cultivated lands, and stays there in open, peaceable, continuous possession for upwards of ten years, not as a tenant or caretaker, he acquires a title by possession to the land so trespassed on, and can successfully resist an action of ejectment. A mortgage is outlawed in ten years from the last payment of interest or acknowledgment, so far as the land security is concerned. Covenants are good for 20 years.

MECHANICS' AND OTHER LIENS.—Every mechanic, machinist, builder, laborer, contractor, sub-contractor or other person doing work upon or furnishing materials to be used in any building or machinery in connection with any building, has a lien for the price of the work, etc., on such building, mines, erection, and the land occupied thereby and enjoyed therewith. The lien will be lost if a claim be not filed in the Registry Office within 30 days from completion of work or supplying of materials, and legal proceedings to enforce the lien must be taken within 90 days.

A solicitor has a lien on his client's papers for costs incurred. A workman has a lien on a chattel for cost of repairs and improvements done by him. An inn-keeper has a lien on the goods of his guest for unpaid board and lodging. A pawnee has a lien on goods for money advanced by him. A lien is a right to possession ; possession being given up, the lien is gone.

MORTGAGE OF LANDS.—A mortgage must be made under seal, and to be valid against subsequent purchasers or mortgagees for value without notice, should be registered in the registry office for the county in which the lands are situate. A short statutory form for mortgages is provided by the Revised Statutes of Ontario, Cap 107. The usual remedies of the mortgagee in default of payment, are by sale under power of sale in the mortgage, or obtaining foreclosure by an action at law, in conjunction with which and in the same action, an order for possession of the land and a judgment and execution on the *personal* covenant against the mortgagor generally, may be obtained. The mortgagee has also the right to distrain on the goods *of the mortgagor* (not of any third person), for arrears of interest. When mortgages are paid a formal discharge, which when registered reconveys the land to the mortgagor, should be obtained. A receipt is not sufficient. See *Interest*.

PARTNERSHIPS.—A partnership may be legally defined as a voluntary unincorporated association of individuals as principals for the carrying out of a joint operation or undertaking for the purpose of joint profit. A part owner is not necessarily a partner; nor is a servant a partner of his master, even where for his trouble and labor he gets part of the profits, or wages in proportion to the profits, he not being liable for losses. A dormant or sleeping partner is, when discovered, equally liable with those held out to the world as partners. The liability of partners to third parties may be illustrated by the case of two horse dealers, who agreed in their articles of partnership, each with the other, that they would not warrant any horse that they might sell ; one did warrant a horse sound, and the horse being unsound, *both* partners were held liable to the victim, despite their agreement, because such warranty was within the scope of and incidental to their business.

The most stringent good faith, *uberrima fides*, is required of partners. Each partner has a right to an account at any time. A partnership may be dissolved by the death of one of the partners; by mutual consent; or by effluxion of time. Dissolution will be decreed by the Court on the insanity of one partner, or where there has been wilful fraud, or where the particular object of the partnership becomes impracticable. A partnership becomes dissolved by act of law on bankruptcy. Each partner's individual property is liable to the fullest extent for partnership debts, if the assets of the firm are insufficient to pay them. The importance of articles of partnership properly drawn up, providing for duration, division and dissolution, cannot be too strongly urged. Declarations of co-partnership should be registered within six months in the County Registry Office. *See R. S. O., cap.* 130; and see *Joint Stock Companies* below.

SPECIAL OR LIMITED PARTNERSHIPS may be formed under *Revised Statutes Ontario*, Chapter 129, where there are one or more general partners whose names are public, and who are liable to the full extent of their means, and whose death involves dissolution (unlike Joint Stock Companies); but also one or more special contributors to capital, who must not interfere in the active management, and who must be registered as *special*, and whose liability in such case is limited to the amounts by them contributed to the capital.

JOINT STOCK COMPANIES (Limited).—A Joint Stock Company (Limited) is a body corporate, created by letters patent, having a common seal, with a capital stock usually divided into shares, which are subscribed for by those desiring to become stockholders, and who are liable to creditors of the company only to the extent of the respective amounts remaining unpaid on the stock subscribed by them. Thus if A, B, C and D agree to enter into an ordinary partnership with a capital of $10,000, and the business fails, each is liable personally to the full extent of the deficiency of assets; but if these same men form a limited company under *R. S. O., cap.* 157, or under the Dominion Statute, for the same purpose, and with the same capital, and the business fail, and all of them but A have paid up their subscribed shares of the capital in full and A has paid all but $100, then A alone is *personally* liable to creditors of the company, and that only to the extent of $100. A company has an existence apart from the members comprising it and is a sort of anonymous statutory partnership. Companies usually speak and act through their directors and authorized officers with their seal; but contracts, bills, notes, cheques etc., made by an agent or officer of the company, on behalf of the company, in general accordance with his powers, under the by-laws or charter of the company, are binding without the seal. For general and comprehensive information on this subject, see J. W. Johnson's "Joint Stock Company Book-keeping," and his pamphlet on the same subject reprinted in this volume. See also *Partnerships* above.

REGISTRATION.—All instruments, deeds, mortgages, etc., affecting lands should be registered promptly in the Registry Office of the County where the lands lie; otherwise they will not retain priority as against subsequent purchasers or mortgagees for value in good faith without notice. Unregistered instruments are good and effectual *as between the actual parties* to those instruments, but not as against innocent third parties who may obtain priority by prior registration, even though the grantor or mortgagor may be guilty of fraud. Leases unless for seven years and upwards need not be registered. Wills and grants from the Crown are registered in the manner set out in the *Registry Act R. S. O., cap.* 114. All other instruments (including Powers of Attorney) are registered by the production of the original (generally in duplicate), with an affidavit of execution made by a subscribing witness attached to each duplicate, care being taken that the witness gives his *full* name, residence, *and occupation*, and takes the oath before a competent officer, who is usually in Ontario, a Commissioner, or Notary Public, or the Registrar; in other Provinces, a Notary Public (with seal,) or a Commissioner for Ontario; and in Foreign countries a Mayor, Notary Public or British Consul, in all these latter cases the official seal being attached to the jurat of the affidavit.

The following is a

FORM OF AN AFFIDAVIT OF EXECUTION.

COUNTY OF HASTINGS, } I, WILLIAM NISBET PONTON, *of the City of Belleville, in the County of*
To wit: } *Hastings, Barrister-at-law, make oath and say.*

1. THAT *I was personally present, and did see the within Instrument and Duplicate duly signed, sealed and executed by* JOHN WESLEY JOHNSON AND WILLIAM BYRON ROBINSON, *two of the parties thereto.*
2. THAT *the said Instrument and Duplicate were executed at the City of Belleville.*
3. THAT *I personally know the said parties.*
4. THAT *I am a subscribing Witness to the said Instrument and Duplicate.*

Jurat { SWORN *before me at the city* }
{ *of Belleville, in the County of* } (Signed), W. N. PONTON.
{ *Hastings, this —— day of May,* }
{ *in the year of our Lord* 1889. }

(Signed) WM. HAMILTON PONTON,

Registrar Co. Hastings,

(or) *A Commissioner for taking affidavits,* H. C. J.

(or) *Notary Public,* (or) J. P.

REPLEVIN.—When goods have been wrongfully distrained or taken, they may be replevied upon giving to the sheriff security in treble the value of the property to be replevied. This is the remedy sought where the object is speedily to recover the specific goods and not merely damages for their loss.

SECURITY FOR COSTS.—Where the plaintiff is resident out of the jurisdiction, and has not sufficient property in the jurisdiction, the defendant can require him to give security for the costs of the action in the sum of $400.00. So also where the plaintiff is suing for a penalty, and where a "man of straw" or nominal plaintiff acts for another without having any real interest in the cause of action.

STOPPAGE *in transitu.* When it is ascertained by a consignor that a consignee, to whom he has sold and shipped goods, has become insolvent, he may at any time, during transport and before delivery to the consignee or his assignee or agent, stop the delivery of such goods, and so avoid being obliged to rank on the insolvent estate with the general creditors at so much on the dollar.

SUBROGATION.—The right to stand in the place of another to or for whom money has been paid.

TAXES are a charge on Real Estate, and the collector has the power to levy the amount by distraining on goods on the premises, or on the goods of the person assessed within the municipality. Great care should be taken in drawing a lease to provide clearly whether the landlord or tenant is to pay taxes, and what taxes. In purchasing land arrears of taxes should be paid, and the Treasurer's certificate obtained before accepting title. Lands may be sold for taxes which are in arrear for the third year provided there is no sufficient distress on the premises. The right of the tax collector to distrain has been limited by recent statutes.

TENDER.—The definite and actual offer of a specific sum of money in payment of a debt, made directly to the creditor in proper form.

TITLE.—In investigating titles searches should be made at the Registry Office, the Sheriff's office, the Treasurer's office, and the Collector's office, and in the opinion of the writer *no one but a trained solicitor is competent to search a Title.*

TRAVELLERS.—See *Common Carriers.*

WILLS.—Wills may be made by any person married or single, male or female, of the full age of twenty-one years. No will is valid unless it is in writing, signed by the testator at the foot or end thereof, or by some other person in his presence, and by his direction, and such signature must be made or acknowledge in the presence of two or more witnesses, present at the same time, and such witnesses shall subscribe such will in the presence of the testator. No form of attestation is necessary. Creditors and executors are competent witnesses, but if any person attests the execution of any will, to whom or to whose wife or husband any bequest or devise is given, such bequest or devise shall be void, though such person shall be a competent person to prove the will. A will may be registered by production of the original will, and a true copy thereof, with an affidavit of a subscribing witness to the will as to its due execution, as to the death of the testator or testatrix, and as to the annexed copy being a true copy of the original, or by the production of the probate of the will with a verified copy. A will speaks only from the death of the Testator. If no executor is named in the will, the court will appoint an administrator with the will annexed. If a person die without a will he is called an Intestate, and an administrator will be appointed by the Surrogate Court to wind up the estate. A will is revoked by marriage, by cancellation and destruction, and by a subsequent will. A codicil or supplementary will requires to be executed with the same formalities, and all alterations and interlineations should be executed and witnessed in the same way as the will itself. See page 120.

This summary is not intended to be exhaustive, nor to take the place of large treatises or legal counsel, but rather to suggest points of practical importance to the student, and to form a basis for examination on subjects which are more elaborately treated in the lectures at the College. In all cases of doubt consult a lawyer, whose business it should be to prevent rather than to create lawsuits, and tell him as much about your opponent's contention and position as you do about your own side of the question. "Nothing extenuate nor set down aught in malice," and you will get better advice and sounder sleep and have a more satisfactory balance sheet. A litigious merchant commits mercantile suicide.

You are invited to make application at any time to the lecturer for information on any point of law.

FORMS OF BUSINESS PAPERS;

AND EXPLANATIONS THEREON.

The student will find it to his advantage to learn thoroughly the general laws which govern Bills of Exchange, Notes, Drafts, etc., and to note closely the wording and form of all Business and Commercial Papers, as they represent, to a certain degree, the language of trade.

BILLS OF EXCHANGE.

A BILL OF EXCHANGE *is a written order from one person to another, directing him to pay a third a sum of money therein named, and usually the bill is made payable, not to the payee alone, but also to his order or to the bearer.*

The person who makes the bill is called the DRAWER; the person to whom it is addressed the DRAWEE, and the person to whom it is ordered to be paid the PAYEE. When the drawee undertakes to pay the amount, he is then called the ACCEPTOR.

If the bill is made payable to the payee, or BEARER it may be transferred to a fourth party by merely delivering it into his hands, and the fourth party will stand in the same situation as the original payee did. If the bill be payable to the payee, OR ORDER, he cannot transfer it except by a written order usually on the back of the bill, called an indorsement, after which the payee is called the INDORSER, and the person to whom it is transferred the INDORSEE. HOLDER is a general word, applied to any one of the parties in possession of the bill, and entitled at law to receive its contents from another.

A bill is either FOREIGN or INLAND. It is called foreign when drawn by a person in one country upon a person in another country; and inland, when both drawer and drawee reside in the same country. The latter are usually termed drafts. See page 62.

Foreign bills are usually drawn in sets; that is, copies of the bills are made separately, each part containing a condition that it shall continue payable only so long as the others remain unpaid. Whenever any one of a set is paid, the others are void; for the whole set constitutes but one bill. The object in drawing them in sets is, that they may be sent at different dates, or by separate conveyances, that time may be saved should one or more be lost. A LETTER OF CREDIT, sometimes called a Circular Letter of Credit, is a Bill of Exchange carried by travellers on which they can obtain money in different countries.

FORM OF SET OF BILLS OF EXCHANGE.

1st BILL OF EXCHANGE.

Belleville, 12th May, 1889.

Exchange for £85.

Three days after sight of this my first of exchange (second and third of same date and tenor unpaid), pay to S. G. Beatty, or order, Eighty-five Pounds Sterling, value received, and charge the same to the account of

W. B. ROBINSON.

To GEORGE H. SIMPSON,
    Banker, London.

2ND BILL OF EXCHANGE.

Exchange for £85.   *Belleville*, 12*th May*, 1889.

Three days after sight of this my second of exchange (first and third of same date and tenor unpaid), pay to S. G. Beaty, or order, Eighty-five Pounds Sterling, value received, and charge the same to the account of

                                          W. B. ROBINSON.

To GEORGE H. SIMPSON,
    Banker, London.

3RD BILL OF EXCHANGE.

Exchange for £85.   *Belleville*, 12th *May*, 1889.

Three days after sight of this my third of exchange (first and second of same date and tenor unpaid), pay to S. G, Beaty, or order, Eighty-five Pounds Sterling, value received, and charge the same to the account of

                                          W. B. ROBINSON.

To GEORGE H. SIMPSON,
    Banker, London.

The par value of Sterling Exchange is 4.86\frac{2}{3}$, or $9\frac{1}{2}$ per cent. over the old par which was 4.44\frac{4}{9}$. The rate of exchange is the price at which it is being bought and sold daily.

PROMISSORY NOTES.

A PROMISSORY NOTE is a written promise to pay unconditionally, and at all events, a specified sum of money. The person who makes the note is called the MAKER, and the person to whom it is payable the payee. A note, while in the hands of the payee, has this resemblance to a bill, that it is for the payment of money absolutely and at all events, and when indorsed and transferred it is exactly similar to a bill of exchange. The resemblance begins as soon as the indorsement is made; for then it is an order of the indorser upon the maker to pay the indorsee, which is the very definition of a bill of exchange; the indorser on a note is the same as the drawer of a draft, the maker of a note the same as the acceptor of a draft, and the indorsee the person to whom it is made payable. See forms of notes, page 65.

REQUISITES OF A BILL OR NOTE.

No particular words are necessary to make a bill or note; but it must be a WRITTEN order or promise, which, from the time of making it, cannot be complied with or performed without the payment of MONEY. Though a bill or note, or an indorsement thereon, must be in writing, such writing need not be in ink. A writing in pencil is sufficient; ink, however, is obviously more desirable.

The exact sum for which a bill or note is given must be inserted, and it must be for the payment of MONEY, and money only, and the sum to be paid must be payable absolutely, and must not depend upon any circumstances which may or may not happen.

A bill or note drawn for a given sum, " and all other sums that may be due to the payee," is not, even between the original parties, a bill or note. Nor is it good for the sum it specifies, except as evidence of a debt.

A variance between the sum superscribed in figures, and that mentioned in the body of the bill in words at length, will not render it uncertain, but the latter will prevail.

The place where a bill is drawn should, in general, appear upon it; it should also be dated, though the omission of either, or both, does not render the paper invalid.

Any date may be inserted by the maker of a bill, or negotiable instrument, whether past, present, or future; and the instrument is not invalidated by his incapacity at the time of the nominal date.

If a bill or note is dated forward of a day not arrived, and any of the parties die before that day, such death will be no bar to the remedy of a BONA FIDE holder.

It is no objection to a bill or note that it is dated on Sunday, for it does not follow that it was made on that day. A bill drawn on Sunday, founded upon a contract made on that day in the ordinary calling of a person making it, is void in the hands of a person who, with knowledge of the circumstance, took it from the person to whom it was given; but it holds good in the hands of an innocent indorsee for value.

Every bill or note must be signed by the person making it, or some one authorized by him for that purpose.

It is not essential to the validity of a bill that it be negotiable, or that it contain the words "value received," although in many (indeed in most) cases it is highly important words be inserted.

A bill or note may be issued with a blank for the payee's name, and any BONA FIDE holder may insert his own name as payee. But until the blank is filled up it is not a bill or note.

A memorandum on a bill or note made before it is issued may, in some instances, be considered as part of the bill or note, and control its operation; as a memorandum, that if any dispute shall arise respecting the consideration, the bill or note shall be void.

PARTIES TO A BILL OR NOTE.

A bill or note cannot properly be made or indorsed by, nor can a BILL be properly addressed to, any person incapable of making himself responsible for the payment, nor can it be properly made payable or indorsed to any person incapable of suing.

Therefore, a bill or note cannot properly be made or indorsed by, nor can a bill be properly addressed to an infant (a person under age); except perhaps where it is drawn, indorsed or accepted for necessaries.

As an infant is capable of suing, he may be payee or indorsee. But it may be questionable, in some cases, whether payment should not be made to his guardian.

Bills or notes cannot properly be made, indorsed or accepted by a married woman, unless under peculiar circumstances, where she holds property of her own, or acts by authority from her husband; or where she resides here, and he is under a civil incapacity of being in this country.

Where a bill or note is given to a single woman, and she marries, the property vests in her husband; and husband and wife must usually join in the action upon it. If a note be made to a woman AFTER MARRIAGE, the interest vests in the husband. If a single woman, being a party liable on a note, marries, her husband becomes responsible to the extent of the property which has come from her into his hands, and they should be sued jointly. If (the debt being still unsatisfied) he dies, she is liable, and not his executors; if she dies, her representatives are liable if there be assets, but not her husband. In Ontario, under the Act of 1884, married women can deal with their separate estate as though they were single.

The contracts of a lunatic, an idiot, or other person *non compos mentis* from age or personal infirmity, are utterly void.

A note obtained by fraud, or from a person in a state of TOTAL drunkenness, cannot be collected by a party who knew the circumstances when he took it.

If persons who fill official situations, as churchwardens, overseers, surveyors, commissioners, managers of joint stock companies, and the like, give bills or notes on which they describe themselves in their official capacity, they are nevertheless personally liable, unless exempted from liability by statute, or by the charter of the Company.

JOINT NOTES.

A note by two or more makers may be either joint, or joint and several, according to its form. The makers of a joint note should be sued jointly ; for if sued separately the action may be defeated or delayed, owing to the non-joinder of the other maker or makers. If one of the parties to a joint note be insolvent, or out of the country when the note falls due, it may be collected from the other. The makers of a joint and several note may be sued upon it, either jointly or separately ; and if sued separately a recovery of judgment (without satisfaction) against one will not be a bar to recovery against another maker.

A note signed by more than one person, and beginning, "We promise," &c., is a joint note only. A joint and several note usually expresses that the makers jointly and severally promise. But a note signed by more than one person, and beginning. "I promise," &c., is several as well as joint. So a note beginning in the singular, " I promise," &c., and signed by one partner for his co-partners, is the joint note of all, and has been held to be also the several note of the signing party.

A joint and several note, though on one piece of paper, comprises in reality, and in legal effect, several notes. Thus if A, B and C join in making a joint and several note, there are, in effect, four notes. There is the joint note of the three makers, and also the several notes of each.

OF THE ALTERATION OF BILLS OR NOTES.

Correcting the date, or the mode of its negotiability, to make it what it was intended, will not affect a bill or note, if done by the maker.

An alteration of a bill or note in a material part invalidates the bill or note, except as between the parties consenting to such alteration.

Inserting a mere memorandum to say where the bill or note is to be payable, if it give a right direction in that respect, or correcting the address or style of the drawee, so as to make it accord with the acceptance, will not affect a bill. But altering an acceptance so as to give an unwarranted place for payment invalidates the acceptance.

Altering a place where a bill or note is payable, if for a fraudulent purpose, may be punishable as a forgery.

Cutting off from a joint and several note the name of one of the parties who has executed it will invalidate the note.

If a bill or note appear upon the face of it to have been altered, it is for the holder to prove that it was altered under circumstances which make it still available. The payment of interest upon it by the party chargeable will suffice for this purpose.

When paying a note or acceptance you should, if it has not been done already, obtain the indorsation of the payee upon it, as proof that you both gave the note and paid it.

OF THE OBLIGATIONS OF PARTIES.

The drawer's undertaking in a bill of exchange is that the drawee, upon due presentment to him, shall accept such bill, and pay the same when due; and that if the drawee do not accept it, or pay it when due, he will pay the amount of the bill, together with certain damages allowed by law; provided he is duly notified of such non-payment.

It is the payee's duty, if the bill remain in his possession, to present it to the drawee for acceptance and for payment at the proper time and place; and in case the drawee refuse to accept, or pay, to give notice without delay, to the drawer, of such refusal.

The acceptor undertakes, and is bound to pay the bill, according to the tenor of the acceptance, when it becomes due, and upon due presentment thereof. In short, all those who have signed accepted, or indorsed a bill of exchange, are jointly and severally liable upon it to the holder. The acceptor is considered, in all cases, as the party primarily liable on the bill. He is to be treated as the principal debtor to the holder, and the other parties as sureties liable on his default.

The acceptor of a bill stands, for most purposes, in the same situation as the maker of a note, and the maker of a bill in the situation of the indorser of a note.

The acceptor's liability can only be discharged by payment, or other satisfaction, by release, or by waiver.

INDORSEMENT.

A person who writes his name upon a bill or note [otherwise than as a maker or acceptor, and delivers it with his name thereon to another person, is called an indorser, and his act is called an indorsement.

Indorsements are of two sorts: BLANK, and FULL OR SPECIAL indorsements, and are always written upon the back.

Special indorsements are modified in different ways, as shown in the following:

FORMS OF INDORSEMENT.

1.—Indorsement in blank.
John A. Fraser.
2.—Indorsement in full.
Pay to John A. Fraser, or order.
S. G. Baker.
3.—Qualified Indorsement.
Without recourse to me.
S. G. Baker.
4.—Restrictive indorsement.
Pay to John Smith only.
S. G. Baker.

Or the following may be used:
Pay to John Smith or order for my use.
Pay to John Smith for my account.
5.—Guarantee on a note.
For value received I hereby guarantee the payment of the within note.
S. G. Baker.
6.—Indorsing partial payments on a note.
Date.
Received on the within note the sum of Twenty-five Dollars.

When sending cheques to the bank for deposit by a clerk, write "*For Deposit only*" above the signature when endorsing. This will prevent a possible attempt to draw the money.

No particular form of words is essential to any indorsement. A BLANK INDORSEMENT is made by the mere signature of the indorser on the back of the bill, as above: its effect is to make the instrument thereafter payable to bearer, and it places the indorser in the position of surety for the maker.

When several persons separately indorse a bill, in blank, and it is dishonored by the drawer, the payee or holder has a right of action against all the indorsers, and he may sue and recover the amount from any one of them.

229

The maker of a note is the principal debtor, and all the indorsers are sureties for him, liable on his default. But though all the indorsers are, IN RESPECT OF THE MAKER, sureties, they are not, as BETWEEN THEMSELVES, merely co-sureties, but each prior party is a principal in respect of each subsequent party. For example, suppose a note to be indorsed by the payee and two subsequent indorsers, as between the holder and maker, the maker is the principal debtor, and the indorsers are his sureties. But as between the indorsers, the first indorser is the principal debtor, and the subsequent indorsers are his sureties. A discharge, therefore, to the prior parties is a discharge to the subsequent parties, but a discharge to the subsequent parties is not a discharge to the prior parties.

In case of an indorsement where parties become co-sureties, an indorser who pays a bill has a right to reimbursement from his co-sureties, in proportion to their number. Thus if A, B and C be co-sureties, A, having paid the debt, would be entitled to recover AT LAW a third from each of the others.

An INDORSEMENT IN FULL makes the instrument payable to the payee or his order only; and he cannot transfer it otherwise than by indorsement.

A QUALIFIED INDORSEMENT is given to make a bill negotiable, without incurring personal responsibility on the part of the indorser.

A RESTRICTIVE INDORSEMENT is a restrictive direction appended to the payee's name, so that, into whose hands soever the bill may fall, it will carry a trust on the face of it.

If a person, at the time a note is made, write on the back of it, " I guarantee the payment of the within note," he will be treated as a joint and several promissor with the maker thereof, and not as mere guarantor. But if the indorsement be made at a subsequent time, or be a guarantee of COLLECTION instead of PAYMENT, the indorser would be considered as a guarantor; a consideration, however, in these last cases should be expressed. If a note be indorsed thus, " For value received I guarantee the collection of the within note," the guarantor would not be liable upon it unless the holder showed a diligent atttempt to collect it.

A bill or note cannot be indorsed for part of the sum remaining due upon it. If the bill has been partly paid, it may be specially indorsed for the part remaining due upon it.

An indorsee has a right to convert a blank indorsement into a special one, by writing over the signature the necessary words.

OF THE TRANSFER OF BILLS AND NOTES.

Bills and notes are divided into two classes—Negotiable and Non-negotiable.

Negotiable paper is that, the ownership of which may be freely transferred from one to another, giving the holder the right of action, without being subject to any offsets or legal defences existing between the original parties, if transferred before maturity for a valuable consideration, and received without any defect therein.

Negotiable paper is made payable to the order of the payee, to the payee or order, to the payee or bearer, or to the bearer, or some other term of similar import, showing that the maker intends to give the payee the right of transfer.

Non-negotiable paper is that which is made payable to the person therein named, without authority to transfer it to a third party.

It may be transferred from one to another by assignment, or indorsement, but it remains subject to all offsets and legal defences existing between the original parties.

The title to negotiable paper passes from one to another by delivery, if made payable to the payee or bearer, or to the bearer; and by indorsement and delivery, if made payable to order of payee, or to payee or order. The title to non-negotiable paper passes by assignment, or indorsement and delivery.

A transfer by mere delivery, without indorsement of a bill or note made payable to the bearer, does not render the transferer liable. A transfer by delivery, however, warrants that the bill or note is not forged or fictitious.

PRESENTMENT OF A BILL FOR ACCEPTANCE.

Presentment for acceptance is necessary, if the bill be drawn payable at sight or at a certain period after sight or after demand. Till such presentment, there is no right of action against any party; and generally, unless it be made within a reasonable time, the holder loses his remedy against the antecedent parties.

Presentment should be made during the usual hours of business.

OF ACCEPTANCE.

ACCEPTANCE, in its ordinary signification, is an engagement by the drawee to pay the bill when due, in money. It must be in writing, though no precise form is necessary; any written words clearly denoting an intention to accept the bill are sufficient. See page 63.

An instrument drawn by A upon B, requiring him to pay to the order of C a certain sum at a certain time, is a BILL OF EXCHANGE OR DRAFT, but after its acceptance by B it is usually called an ACCEPTANCE.

A bill is said to be honored when it is duly accepted or paid; and when acceptance or payment is refused, it is said to be dishonored.

The holder is entitled to require from the drawee an absolute engagement to pay according to the tenor of the bill, unincumbered with any condition or qualification. If the drawee refuse to give the holder a general and unqualified acceptance, he may treat the bill as dishonored. Notice must be given of a failure in the attempt to procure an acceptance; otherwise, the person guilty of neglect may lose his remedy upon the bill.

ON PRESENTMENT FOR PAYMENT.

The contract of the acceptor of a bill, or the maker of a note, being to pay the amount upon due presentment at maturity, in order to charge the indorsers, it is the duty of the holder to demand payment of the maker on the very day on which, by law, the bill becomes due; and unless the demand be so made, the holder loses his remedy against the indorsers, although the maker would still be liable.

If a bill or note be made payable at a particular place, the holder is bound to make a demand of payment at that place. In determining when a bill or note becomes due, days of grace, as they are called, must be allowed. These days in different countries are as follows: In Canada, the United States, Great Britain and Australia, 3; in the Netherlands, none; in Hamburg and Altona, 12; in Frankfort-on-the-Main, 4; in Paris, Bordeaux, Dantzic and Russia, 10; in Geneva, 5; in Bremen, 8; in Antwerp, Amsterdam, Cadiz, Lisbon, Oporto, Rio Janeiro, Rotterdam and Venice, 6; in Russia, 3 days are allowed on all bills payable after sight.

When a bill is drawn "on demand," or if no time of payment be specified upon its face, it must be paid on presentation, no grace being allowed. If the last day of grace falls on Sunday, or a legal holiday, the bill is payable the day after.

Bills or notes made payable at a bank are generally left with that bank for collection. If a bill or note is payable generally, without any specification of place, the holder may present it for payment to the acceptor or maker, wherever he may be found.

A notice stating that a bill or note has been dishonored is effectual. Sending a verbal notice to a merchant's counting house in the ordinary hours of business, or to the house of a person not a merchant, is sufficient, though he be not at home.

Sending notice by the post is sufficient, though it be delayed or be not received through the fault of the post.

PROCEEDINGS ON NON-PAYMENT.

* No protest is required to be made upon the dishonor of a bill or note, although it is common to protest them for non-payment, especially in commercial towns. But in every case of the dishonor of a bill or note, it is the duty of the holder to give due notice thereof to all the prior parties on the note to whom he means to look for payment; for the holder cannot recover against a party to whom he has failed to give due notice of the dishonor.

OF PAYMENT.

If the maker makes due payment of a bill or note to a BONA FIDE holder it will amount to a complete discharge of all other parties thereon. But when payment is made by an indorser, such indorser, as a general rule, will retain his right to recover over against all the antecedent parties to the instrument until he has received a full indemnity; such payment, generally, discharges all the indorsers subsequent to himself.

The party paying a bill or note has a right to insist on its being delivered up to him. But when the bill or note is not negotiable, he cannot refuse to pay it until it is delivered up.

A party paying any debt has a right to demand a receipt for the same, and the party to whom money has been paid is bound to give a receipt, when properly tendered to him for signature.

OF INTEREST

Interest is recoverable on a promissory note in which there is no special agreement to pay interest, from the time when the principal becomes due, or ought to have been paid. A note payable on demand carries no interest till a demand is made, either by suit or otherwise, unless there is an agreement to pay interest. A note not on demand, in which no time of payment is mentioned, draws interest from date.

Whenever there is a special agreement to pay interest, that is when the words " with interest," &c., are contained in the note, it draws interest, of course, according to such agreement of contract.

A note is said to be outlawed in six years from the time it becomes due. The statute requires that all actions founded upon any instrument or contract not under seal, must be commenced within six years next after the cause of action accrued, and not after.

Interest ceases to run after a tender is made, providing the bill or note is already due.

Any rate of interest agreed to by the parties to a bill or note, and inserted therein, may be collected.

---
* See Index for Protests.

In cases where interest is allowable on a bill or note, and no rate is specified, six per cent. per annum may be collected.

OF A LOST BILL OR NOTE.

If a bill or note be destroyed by fire or other accident, an action may, perhaps, be brought thereon. But if a bill or note be lost, there can be no remedy upon it at law, unless it was in such a state when lost, that no person but the plaintiff could have acquired a right to sue thereon, or the payee give the maker sufficient security to indemnify him in case the note turns up.

Losing a bill implies negligence in the loser, and the results of negligence ought to fall upon him.

It is advisable in case of a lost bill or note that the loser immediately give notice of the loss to the parties liable on the bill; for they will thereby be prevented from taking it up without due inquiry.

Public advertisement of the loss should also be given; for, if any person discounts it with notice of the loss, that will be such strong evidence of fraud that he can acquire no property in it.

OF COMMERCIAL PAPERS.

Some of the different papers used in business are, Receipts, Drafts, Checks, Due Bills, Orders, Bills, Invoices, Account Sales, Leases, Bonds and Mortgages, Protests, Manifests, Bills of Lading, Releases, Contracts, Debentures, etc., etc.

Definitions and forms of a number of these are given in a previous part of the work, beginning at page 56.

AN ACCOUNT SALES is an exhibit of the sales of goods disposed of on commission, with the charges incurred thereon.

A LEASE is the written contract of agreement between landlord and tenant.

A BOND is a legal instrument by which the giver binds himself to do, perform, or fill a certain contract by a stated time. When in your favor it is called a Bond Receivable, and when against you, a Bond Payable.

A MORTGAGE is a pledge of property, either real or personal, by a debtor to a creditor.

A PROTEST of a note or a bill of exchange is a formal declaration made by a notary public under hand and seal, at the request of the holder, for non-acceptance or non-payment.

A MANIFEST is a list of the cargo of a ship, with the mark, number, or description of each article or package, to be exhibited at the custom-house.

A BILL OF LADING is a formal receipt subscribed to by the master of a ship, or other common carrier, acknowledging the receipt of goods intrusted to him for transportation, and binding himself, under certain exceptions, to deliver them in like condition as received at the place and to the person named in the bill, or his assigns, for a remuneration of freightage.

DEBENTURES are promises to pay of the nature of notes, but under seal. They are issued by Municipalities as security for loans.

COUPONS are promises to pay interest, and are attached to Debentures and Bonds.

REMITTANCE BLANK WITH RECEIPT (TO BE RETURNED) ATTACHED.

_____ 188

M _____

_____

_____

Inclosed please find _____

_____ *Dollars,*

In settlement of _____

_____

Please sign receipt attached, and return, and oblige

Yours respectfully,

_____ 188

Received from _____

_____ *Dollars,*

For _____

$ _____

The above will be found very convenient as a form to be used in making remittances. It saves the writing of a formal letter. The receipt being attached, the person receiving the money can hardly fail to acknowledge the amount at once by returning it completed. Have them printed in copying ink, and put in pads.

RECEIPT.

A receipt in full, though strong evidence, is not conclusive; and a party signing such receipt will be permitted to show a mistake or error therein, if any exist.

Receipts for the payment of money are open to examination, and may be varied, explained, or contradicted, by parole testimony. SEE FORMS OF RECEIPTS, PAGE 61.

FORM OF LEASE.

This Indenture, made the first day of September, in the year of Our Lord one thousand eight hundred and seventy-four, IN PURSUANCE OF THE ACT RESPECTING SHORT FORMS OF LEASES :

Between GEORGE PATTERSON, of the Town of Belleville, in the county of Hastings, Province of Ontario, Gentleman, hereinafter called the Lessor;

And ROBERT HENRY PORTER, of the same place, yeoman, hereinafter called the Lessee:

Witnesseth, that in consideration of the Rent, Covenants and Agreements hereinafter reserved and contained, by the said Lessee, HIS executors, administrators and assigns, to be paid, observed, and performed, the said Lessor hath demised and leased, and, by these Presents, DOTH demise and LEASE unto the said Lessee, HIS executors, administrators, and assigns, ALL that certain farm, piece or parcel of land, situate, lying and being in the Township of Sidney, in the County of Hastings and Province of Ontario, and described as the SOUTH HALF of lot number six in the First Concession of the Township of Sidney aforesaid, containing by admeasurement, one hundred acres, be the same more or less.

Together with all the rights, members, and appurtenances whatsoever to the said premises belonging or appertaining, TO HAVE AND TO HOLD the said hereby demised premises, with their appurtenances, unto the said Lessee, his executors, administrators, and assigns, for and during the term of five years, to be computed from the first day of September, one thousand eight hundred and seventy-four, and from thenceforth next ensuing and fully to be complete and ended, YIELDING AND PAYING therefor unto the said Lessor, his heirs, executors, administrators, or assigns, the clear yearly rent or sum of Two Hundred Dollars of lawful money of Canada, to be payable on the following days and times, that is to say : in equal half yearly instalments on the first days of the months of March and September, in each and every year during the continuance of this lease.

The first of such payments to become due and be made on the first day of March next, and the last of such payments to be made in advance on the first day of March preceding the expiration of the said term.

And the said Lessee, for himself, his heirs, executors, administrators, and assigns, hereby covenants with the said Lessor, his heirs, executors, administrators, and assigns, in form and manner following, that is to say :—To pay rent; And to pay taxes : And to repair reasonable wear and tear, accidents by fire or tempest excepted : AND to keep up fences and not to cut down timber : And that the said Lessor may enter and view state of repair, and that the said Lessee will repair according to notice : AND will not assign or sublet, without leave : AND will not carry on any business that shall be deemed a nuisance on said premises: And that the said Lessee will leave the premises in good repair : AND ALSO, that if the term hereby granted shall be at any time seized, or taken in execution, or in attachment, by any creditor of the said Lessee, or if the said Lessee shall make any assignment for the benefit of his creditors, or becoming bankrupt or insolvent shall take the benefit of any Act that may be in force for bankrupt or insolvent debtors, the then current half-year's rent shall immediately become due and payable, and the said term shall immediately become forfeited and void, but the next current half-year's rent shall, nevertheless, be at once due and payable.

Proviso for re-entry by the said Lessor, on non-payment of rent, or non-performance of covenants, or seizure of the said term for any of the causes aforesaid : THE said Lessor covenants, with the said Lessee for quiet enjoyment.

In Witness Whereof, the said parties to these presents have hereunto set their Hands and Seals, the day and the year first above written.

Signed, sealed and delivered
in the presence of
W. B. SMITH.

GEO. PATTERSON.   SEAL.

ROBT. H. PORTER.   SEAL.

SHORT FORM OF LEASE NOT UNDER SEAL.

This instrument witnesseth, that Robert Brown, of the city of Toronto, has let and rented to Thomas North, for the term of one year, to commence on the———day of——— all that certain house and lot in the town of Whitby, on the north side of Main Street, lately occupied by Henry South, with the appurtenances, for the yearly rent of one hundred dollars in quarterly-payments of twenty-five dollars, to be made on the first days of the months of———. The taxes are to be paid by the said———.

And the said Thomas North agrees to pay the said rent (and the taxes if so agreed), and to quit and surrender the premises at the expiration of the said term in as good condition as reasonable use thereof will permit, damages by the elements excepted.

Dated at Whitby this———day of———, 1878.

Witness :   ROBERT BROWN.
PETER COOPER.   THOMAS NORTH.

AN ASSIGNMENT OF A LEASE BY WAY OF ENDORSEMENT.

I, Robert Henry Porter, of, etc., in consideration of———, to me in hand paid by William Henry, the receipt whereof I do hereby acknowledge, have bargained, sold, assigned and set over, and do hereby bargain, sell, assign and set over unto the said William Henry, his executors, administrators and assigns [or, if a durable lease, say his heirs, etc.], as well the written indenture, as also the term and interest in all and singular the lands, tenements, hereditaments and premises within mentioned, yet remaining under and by virtue of the said indenture, and likewise all my estate, right, title, interest, claim, property and demand, of, in, or to the same lands, tenements, hereditaments and premises, which I now have, either by means of the within indenture, or otherwise howsoever ; subject, nevertheless, to the rents and covenants in the said indenture contained.

IN WITNESS WHEREOF, ETC.

FORM OF A BOND.*

Know all Men by these Presents:

That, I, JOHN SMITH, of the town of ——, in the county of ——, and Province of Ontario, am held and firmly bound unto Robert Jones, of the town of, etc., in the penal sum of twelve hundred dollars of lawful money of Canada, to be paid to the said Robert Jones or his certain Attorney, executors, administrators or assigns, for which payment well and truly to be made I bind myself, my heirs, executors and administrators for ever firmly by these Presents. Sealed with my seal and dated this first day of December, in the year of Our Lord one thousand eight hundred and seventy-eight.

The condition of the above written bond or obligation is such that if the above bounden John Smith, his heirs, executors and administrators do and shall well and truly pay or cause to be paid unto the above named Robert Jones, his executors, administrators, or assigns, the just and full sum of six hundred dollars, in three annual payments from the date hereof, with annual interest at nine per cent., then the above obligation to be void; otherwise to remain in full force and virtue.

Signed, sealed and delivered
in the presence of
GEO. SHERRY.
    JOHN SMITH.   : SEAL. :

STATUTORY MORTGAGE.

This Indenture, made (in duplicate) the first day of July, one thousand eight hundred and seventy-four, in pursuance of the Act respecting Short Forms of Mortgages:

Between Mary Wilson, of the village of Marmora, in the county of Hastings, wife of Robert Wilson, and Robert Wilson, of the said village of Marmora, yeoman, hereinafter called the mortgagors, of the first part, and John Smith, of the town of Picton, in the county of Prince Edward, merchant, hereinafter called the mortgagee, of the second part.

Witnesseth, that in consideration of one thousand dollars of lawful money of Canada, now paid by the said mortgagee to the said mortgagors (the receipt whereof is hereby acknowledged), the said mortgagors do grant and mortgage unto the said mortgagee, his heirs and assigns for ever:

All and Singular, that certain parcel or tract of land and premises situate, lying and being in the township of Marmora, in the county of Hastings, Province of Ontario, being the east half of lot number eight, in the fourth concession of the township of Marmora aforesaid, containing by admeasurement One Hundred Acres, be the same more or less.

Provided, this mortgage to be void on payment of one thousand dollars of lawful money of Canada, with interest at eight per cent. per annum, as follows: the said principal sum of one thousand dollars to be due and payable in three years from the date hereof with interest thereon from the date at eight per centum per annum, as aforesaid, payable yearly, and taxes and performance of statute labor.

The said mortgagors covenant with the said mortgagee, that the mortgagors will pay the mortgage money and interest, and observe the above proviso.

That the mortgagors have a good title in fee simple to the said lands; and that they have the right to convey the said lands to the said mortgagee: And that on default the

---

* Debentures, see page 259, also get the name of Bonds.

mortgagee shall have quiet possession of the said lands free from all encumbrances : And that the mortgagors will execute such further assurances of the said lands as may be requisite : And that the said mortgagors have done no act to incumber the said lands: And that the mortgagors will insure the buildings on the said lands to the amount of not less than nine hundred dollars currency : And the said mortgagors do release to the said mortgagee all claims upon the said lands, subject to the said proviso.

Provided, that the said mortgagee on default of payment for three months, may, upon giving one month's notice, enter on and lease or sell the said lands : Provided that the mortgagee may distrain for arrears of interest: Provided, that in default of payment of the interest hereby secured, the principal hereby secured shall become payable : Provided, that until default of payment the mortgagors shall have quiet possession of the said lands :

In witness whereof the said parties hereto have hereunto set their hands and seals.

Signed, sealed and delivered
in the presence of
THOMAS BROWN.

MARY WILSON.   SEAL.

ROBERT WILSON. SEAL.

ASSIGNMENT OF MORTGAGE.

This Indenture, made (in duplicate) the first day of September, one thousand eight hundred and seventy-four.

Between, A. B., of the, &c.,——hereinafter called the ASSIGNOR, of the first part, and C. D. of the, &c.,——hereinafter called the ASSIGNEE, of the second part.

Whereas, by a Mortgage dated on the fourth day of January, one thousand eight hundred and seventy-two, E. F.* did grant and mortgage the lands and premises therein described to me, my heirs and assigns, for securing the payment of (HERE INSERT THE AMOUNT), and there is now owing upon the said Mortgage (here insert the amount yet owing upon it).

Now this Indenture Witnesseth, that in consideration of——of lawful money of Canada, now paid by the said Assignee to the said Assignor (THE RECEIPT WHEREOF IS HEREBY ACKNOWLEDGED), THE said Assignor DOTH HEREBY ASSIGN and set over unto the said Assignee, his executors, administrators and assigns, ALL that the said before in part recited Mortgage, and also the said sum of——now owing as aforesaid.

Together with all moneys that may hereafter become due or owing in respect of said Mortgage, and the full benefit of all powers and of all covenants and provisoes contained in said Mortgage. And also full power and authority to use the name or names of the said Assignor, his heirs, executors, administrators or assigns, for enforcing the performance of the covenants and other matters and things contained in the said Mortgage.

And the said Assignor DOTH HEREBY GRANT and convey unto the said Assignee, his heirs and assigns, ALL AND SINGULAR, that certain piece (here describe the property as described in Mortgage).

To have and to Hold the said Mortgage and all moneys arising in respect of the same, and to accrue thereon, and also the said lands and premises thereby granted and

---
* If the mortgage has been assigned, here mention the day and date of registration of each assignment thereof, and the names of the parties.

R

mortgaged, To THE USE of the said Assignee, his heirs, executors, administrators and assigns, absolutely for ever; but subject to the terms contained in such Mortgage.

And the said Assignor, for his heirs, executors, administrators and assigns, DOTH HEREBY COVENANT with the Assignee, his heirs, executors, administrators and assigns, that the said Mortgage hereby assigned is a good and valid security, and that the said sum of $——is now owing and unpaid, and that he has not done, or permitted any act, matter or thing whereby the said Mortgage has been released or discharged, either partly or in entirety; and that he will, upon request, do, perform and execute every act necessary to enforce the full performance of the covenants and other matter contained therein.

In Witness Whereof, the said parties have hereunto set their hands and seals, the day and year first above written.

Signed, sealed and delivered }

PROVINCE OF ONTARIO, } DISCHARGE OF MORTGAGE.
To wit:

To the Registrar of the County of Hastings.

I, James Williams, do certify that Peter Henry Cooper, merchant, of the town of Napanee, has satisfied all money due on or to grow due on a certain mortgage made by the said Peter Henry Cooper to me, James Williams, yeoman, of the same place, which mortgage bears date the first day of November, A. D. 1870, and was registered in the Registry Office for the County of Hastings, on the second day of November, A. D. 1870, at twenty minutes past eleven o'clock, forenoon, in Liber B., for Thurlow, as No. 1765, and that said mortgage has not been assigned.*

And that I am the person entitled by law to receive the money; and such mortgage is therefore DISCHARGED.

Witness my hand this first day of November, 1878.

Witness: JAMES WILLIAMS.
    ROBERT DOYLE.

PROTESTS.

The holder of a Promissory Note, Draft or Bill of Exchange, which has not been paid at maturity, and on which there is an indorser's name, should have it immediately protested by a Notary Public, who will notify such indorser by depositing to his address *in the post office of the place where the note or bill was due and payable* a notice of the protest. Should the holder neglect to notify the indorser immediately (or, if more than one indorser, all the indorsers) he will lose recourse against him.

Drafts and Bills are also protested for non-acceptance, unless instructions to the contrary have been given by the drawer (see page 141).

---

* If the mortgage has been assigned here mention the day and date of registration of each assignment thereof, and the names of the parties.

WAIVE PROTEST.—This is the act of the indorser, who consents that the holder need not protest a note, and he writes on the back of note:
" I hereby accept notice of non-payment, and waive protest.

JOHN BROWN."

1. *Promissory Note for non-payment.*

On this first day of September, in the year of Our Lord one thousand eight hundred and seventy-seven, at the request of the MERCHANTS BANK OF CANADA, holder of the Promissory Note hereunto annexed, I, GEORGE DEAN DICKSON, a Notary Public for Ontario, by Royal authority duly appointed, did exhibit the said Note unto a Clerk at the office of the MERCHANTS BANK OF CANADA, at Belleville, where the same is payable, and there speaking to him, did demand payment of the said note, to which demand he answered.

" No FUNDS."

Notices mailed the
1st day of September,
A.D. 1877.
P.Q.

Protest, .. 50 Cts.
Postage, .. 04 "
Notices, .. 50 "
―――――
$1 04

Wherefore I, the said Notary, at the request aforesaid, have protested, and do hereby solemnly protest, as well against all the parties to the said Note, as against all other persons to whom it may concern, for all interest, damages, costs, charges, expenses, and other losses suffered or to be suffered for want of payment of the said Note; and afterwards, on the day and year mentioned in the margin, I, the said Notary Public, did serve due notice according to law, of the said presentment, non-payment, and protest of the said note, upon the several parties thereto, by depositing in Her Majesty's Post Office at Belleville, being the nearest Post Office to the place of the said presentment, letters containing such notice, one of which letters was addressed to each of the said parties severally, the superscription and address of which letters are respectively copied below as follows, that is to say:
PAID, John Smith, Esq., Belleville.
PAID, Messrs. J. McKay & Co., Montreal.
PAID, ...
PAID, ...

In testimony whereof, I have hereunto set my hand and affixed my Seal of Office the day and year first above written.

GEORGE D. DICKSON,
Notary Public.   [SEAL]

2. *A Bill for Non-Acceptance.*

On this first day of September, in the year of Our Lord one thousand eight hundred and seventy-four, at the request of THE BANK OF MONTREAL, holders of the BILL OF EXCHANGE hereunto annexed, I, Charles William Brown, a Notary Public for Ontario, by Royal authority duly appointed, did exhibit the said Bill unto John Smith, Esq., at his place of business at Belleville, and there speaking to him did demand acceptance of the said Bill, to which demand he answered:

"I WILL NOT ACCEPT."

Notices mailed the 1st day of September, A. D. 1874. P.Q. Protest, . . 50cts. Postage, . . 04 " Notices, . . 50 " $1 04	Wherefore I, the said Notary, at the request aforesaid, have protested, and do hereby solemnly protest, as well against all the parties to the said Bill, as against all other parties whom it may concern, for all interest, damages, costs, charges, expenses, and other losses suffered or to be suffered for want of acceptance of the said Bill; and afterwards, on the day and year mentioned in the margin, I, the said Notary Public, did serve due Notice according to law, of the said presentment, non-acceptance and protest of the said Bill upon the several parties thereto, by depositing in Her Majesty's Post Office at Belleville, being the nearest Post Office to the place of the said presentment, Letters containing such notice, one of which Letters was addressed to each of the said parties severally, the Superscription and Address of which Letters are respectively copied below as follows, that is to say : PAID, John Smith, Esq., Belleville. PAID, Messrs. J. McKay & Co., Montreal. PAID, ... PAID, ...

In testimony whereof, I have hereunto set my hand and affixed my Seal of Office, the day and year first above written.

          CHAS. W. BROWN.
            Notary Public. : SEAL :

---

3. *A Bill for Non-Payment.*

On this first day of September, in the year of Our Lord, one thousand eight hundred and seventy-four, at the request of the BANK OF MONTREAL, holders of the BILL OF EXCHANGE hereunto annexed, I, CHARLES WILLIAM BROWN, a Notary Public for Ontario, by Royal authority duly appointed, did exhibit the said bill unto a clerk in the office of the Bank of Montreal, at Belleville where the same is payable, and there speaking to him, did demand payment of the said Bill, to which demand he answered,

"No FUNDS."

Notices mailed the	Wherefore, I, the said Notary, at the request aforesaid, have protested, and do hereby solemnly protest as well against all the parties to the said Bill as against all other persons whom it may concern, for all interest, damages, costs, charges, expenses, and other losses suffered or to be suffered for want of payment of the said

1st day of September,		Bill; and afterwards, on the day and year mentioned in the margin, I, the said Notary Public, did serve due notice, according to law, of the said presentment, non-payment and protest of the said Bill upon the several parties thereto, by depositing in Her Majesty's Post Office at Belleville, being the nearest Post Office to the place of the said presentment, Letters containing such notice, one of which Letters was addressed to each of the said parties severally, the Superscription and Address of which Letters are respectively copied below as follows, that is to say :
A.D. 1874,		
	P.Q.	
Protest,	50 cts.	
Postage,	04 "	
Notices,	50 "	PAID, John Smith, Esq., Belleville.
	$1 04	PAID, Messrs. J. McKay & Co., Montreal.
		PAID, ...
		PAID, ...

In testimony whereof I have hereunto set my hand and affixed my Seal of Office, the day and year first above written.

CHAS. W. BROWN,
Notary Public.   SEAL.

NOTICE OF PROTEST.

Belleville, September 1, 1878.

To John Smith, Esq.,
Belleville.

Take notice that a PROMISSORY NOTE, dated on the twenty-ninth day of August, 1877, for the sum of $400, drawn by yourself in favor of J. MCKAY & Co., or order, payable one year after the date thereof, at the office of the MERCHANTS BANK, in Belleville, and endorsed by J. MCKAY & Co., was this day presented by me for payment at the said Bank, and that payment thereof was refused ; and that the MERCHANTS BANK, the holders of the said Promissory Note, look to you for payment. Also, take notice that the same was PROTESTED this day by me for non-payment.

Your obedient servant,

GEORGE D. DICKSON,

Notary Public.

MANIFEST OF STEAMER "PASSPORT," THOMAS SMITH, MASTER, FROM HAMILTON TO MONTREAL, JUNE 1, 1877.

Consignees.	Destination.	Marks.	Articles.
J. Taylor & Co.,	Montreal,	J. T. & Co.	35 boxes and 46 bales.
" "	"	J. T.	600 barrels of Salt.
J. C. Towers,	"	J. C. T.	100 " Pork.
S. Sands & Co.,	"	S. S.	Furniture.
Wilson & Co.,	"	W. & Co.	25 boxes and 10 trunks.
J. Landis & Co.,	"	J. L.	120 barrels Apples.
D. B. Carrell,	"	D. B. C.	4 Trunks.
C. K. Hamilton,	"	. H.	100 bbls. Pork and 200 bbls. Salt.
Ourselves,	"	S. B. H.	500 bbls. Flour.
Ferguson & Reid,	"	F. R.	47 Bales.
" "	"	W. M.	200 bbls. Pork and 150 Salt.
Willis & Webb,	Kingston,	W. & W.	Furniture.
" "	"	"	50 barrels Flour.
J. Jordon,	Brockville,	J. Jordon.	500 barrels Flour.
T. Cope,	"	T. C.	Furniture.
R. Ross,	Montreal,	R. Ross.	58 barrels Flour.

The above is the simplest possible form of a manifest; it is made out on a large sheet ruled for the purpose, and placed in a conspicuous place for the inspection of consignees inquiring for their freight. When vessels are plying between different countries, a copy of the manifest is required to be exhibited at the Custom-House. Way-freight may be inserted or left out, as the clerk pleases, and a list of the names of the passengers appended when desirable.

BILL OF LADING.

SHIPPED in apparent good order by S. G. BEATTY, *Hamilton, Ontario*, and consigned to the order of Messrs. J. TAYLOR & Co., *Montreal*, in and upon the *Steamer Passport*, whereof *Thomas Smith* is master or agent for the present voyage, and now lying in the port of *Hamilton*, viz.:

Ma and Numbers.	ARTICLE.	WEIGHT.
J. T. & Co. M. 139	Thirty-five Boxes Tea, Forty-six Bales Paper Bags,	2100

Being marked and numbered as per margin; and are to be delivered in like good order and condition, at the Port of *Montreal, in the Province of Quebec* (the Act of God, the Queen's enemies, Fire, and all and every the dangers and accidents of the Seas and Navigation, of whatever nature and kind excepted), he or they paying freight for the said goods at the rate of two dollars per cwt.

In witness whereof, the Master or Purser of said vessel hath affirmed to THREE Bills of Lading, all of this tenor and date; one of which being accomplished. the rest to stand void

Dated at Hamilton, this 21st day of June, 1874,

C. PORTER, Purser.

DEEDS.

A deed is a writing sealed and delivered, to testify the agreement of the parties to the thing contained in the deed. All instruments under seal are in law deeds; but in common acceptation a deed is a conveyance of lands. The consideration of a deed may either be GOOD or VALUABLE. A GOOD consideration is founded on natural love and affection between near relations by blood; a VALUABLE consideration is founded on something deemed valuable, as money, goods, service, or marriage.

Every deed or contract is void when made for any fraudulent purpose, or in violation of law, such as a deed given in preference of one creditor unjustly over others.

1. SIMPLE DEED.

This Indenture made (in duplicate) the ―――day of―――, in the year of Our Lord one thousand eight hundred and―――, in pursuance of the Act respecting Short Forms of Conveyances:

Between STEPHEN HAMILTON LEPP, of (here insert place of residence, &c.), of the first part, and ALBERT INGERSOLL, of, etc., of the second part.

Witnesseth, that in consideration of the sum of―――of lawful money of Canada, now paid by the said party of the second part to the said party of the first part (the receipt whereof is hereby by him acknowledged), the said party of the first part doth grant unto the said party of the second part, his heirs and assigns for ever, all and singular that certain parcel or tract of land and premises situate, lying and being (here describe the premises).

To have and to hold unto the said party of the second part, his heirs and assigns, to and for his and their sole and only use for ever; subject, nevertheless, to the reservations, limitations, provisoes and conditions expressed in the original grant from the Crown.

The said party of the first part covenants with the said party of the second part, that he hath the right to convey the said lands to the said party of the second part, notwithstanding any act of the said party of the first part. And that the said party of the second part shall have quiet possession of the said lands free from all encumbrances. And that the said party of the first part will execute such further assurances of the said lands as may be requisite. And that the said party of the first part has done no act to encumber the said lands.

And that the said party of the first part releases to the said party of the second part all his claims upon the said lands.

In Witness whereof, the said parties to these presents have (here insert date, affix seal, sign, &c.

2. QUIT CLAIM DEED.

This Indenture, made (in duplicate) the first day of September, in the year of Our Lord one thousand eight hundred and seventy-seven. *Between* George West, of the town of, etc., and Mary West, the wife of the said George West, of the first part, and James East, of the, &c., of the second part.

Witnesseth, that the said parties of the first part, for and in consideration of (HERE INSERT THE AMOUNT) of lawful money of Canada, to them in hand paid by the said party of the second part at or before the sealing and delivery of these presents (the receipt whereof is hereby acknowledged), have granted, released and quitted claim, and by these presents do grant, release and quit claim unto the said party of the second part, his heirs and assigns for ever, all the estate, right, title, interest, claim and demand, whatsoever, both at law and in equity, or otherwise howsoever, and whether possession or expectancy, of, in, and to, all and singular that certain parcel or tract of land and premises situate, lying and being, etc. (HERE DESCRIBE THE PROPERTY). Together with the appurtenances thereto belonging or appertaining ; to have and to hold the aforesaid land and premises, with all and singular the appurtenances thereto belonging or appertaining, unto and to the use of the said party of the second part, his heirs and assigns for ever ; subject, nevertheless, to the reservations, limitations, provisoes, and conditions expressed in the original grant thereof from the Crown.

In witness whereof, the said parties to these presents have hereunto set their hands and seals the day and year first above written.

Signed, Sealed and Delivered
  in the presence of   GEORGE WEST.   SEAL.
    E. B. SAMPLE.

                                    MARY WEST.   SEAL.

INDENTURE OR ARTICLES OF CO-PARTNERSHIP.

This Indenture, made this 14th day of May, in the year of Our Lord one thousand eight hundred and seventy-seven, between Henry Smith, of the first part, Robert Bruce, of the second part, and Robert Jones, of the third part.

Witnesseth, that in consideration of the mutual trust and confidence which the said parties have in each other, each doth for himself, his heirs, executors and administrators, covenant with the other, his heirs, executors and administrators, by these presents, in manner following, to wit:

I. That the said parties hereto will be partners in the business of buying and selling dry goods and groceries at wholesale, and in the business of shipping and forwarding goods of other parties to such points as may be required of said co-partnership. Such partnership to extend for the period of three years from this date.

The name and style of such co-partnership shall be Henry Smith & Co., and the business shall be carried on at Oshawa, Ontario.

II. The Capital of the said firm shall consist of   , to be put into the said business by the said partners as follows :

Said Henry Smith shall invest —— in Cash, and —— in Merchandise, Notes and Book Accounts to the value of

Said Robert Jones shall invest in Cash Two Thousand Dollars, and Merchandise to the value of Two Thousand Dollars ; but it is understood that the said Henry Smith and the said Robert Jones are not required to reside at Oshawa, or have any actual concern in such business, which will be personally attended to by said Robert Bruce, but in the division of losses and profits in such business the same shall be apportioned as follows : to the said Robert Jones two-sevenths, and to the said Henry Smith and said Robert Bruce the remainder in equal shares.

NOTE—No two articles of co-partnership will be alike. This is given to indicate the form that would be followed, and the probable facts to be stated. The arrangement that should be made for an equitable distribution of gains and losses where there is an unequal investment of capital, but equal skill and time, is stated at page 80. Also at the same page will be found the manner of adjusting inequality in time and skill. A declaration of partnership in Ontario must be filed at the Registry Office within six months from its formation.

The said parties hereto may each draw out of said business a sum in cash or stock not exceeding Fifty Dollars per month, for his separate use ; but in case, at the end of each year, on taking a general annual account, it shall appear that the net profits of such year shall not amount to the gross sum so drawn out of the business by all the partners, then each partner shall immediately repay to said partnership the excess, if any, of the sums which he shall have so drawn out of said business over the sum which he shall be entitled to receive as his share of the net profits of said business during the year.

And in case there shall have been a loss in the business of any year, then, at the beginning of the next ensuing year, the several partners shall contribute a PRO RATA sum (taking into account the state of the account of each partner with said partnership), which shall restore the original capital of said partnership.

III. The said Robert Bruce shall have the right to hire and dismiss all clerks and other employees of said firm, and shall give his sole and exclusive attention to the conduct of the aforesaid business ; but no bill, note of hand, or other evidence of debt, shall ever be issued or put in circulation by him in the name of said firm, but every such evidence of indebtedness shall be deemed the individual obligation of the partner who shall sign such firm name, and shall be charged to him as such in the accounts of such firm.

No member of said firm shall have power to sign the partnership name as surety.

IV. All goods shall be sold for cash, unless a credit is given by the concurrence of all the members of the firm, and books of account shall be kept by said Bruce, and proper entries made therein of all the moneys, goods, effects, debts, sales, purchases, receipts, payments and other transactions of said partnership, which books, together with all cash securities and assets of said firm, shall at all times be accessible at said Oshawa for the inspection of all partners, and to take copies of the same if required ; at the end of each year hereafter there shall be a full and particular account, in writing, taken by the said Bruce, of all the stock in trade, money and assets of said firm, and of all debts due and owing by and from the same, and a just valuation or appraisement made of such assets and liabilities, which account shall immediately, on being completed, be shown by the said Bruce to the said Smith and the said Jones, at the place of business of said firm in Oshawa aforesaid.

In case disputes shall arise between parties hereto, or any two of them, growing out of said business, and before the expiration of said co-partnership, no attempt shall be made to interfere with the ordinary conduct of such business by injunctions and receivers, or by any proceedings at law or equity; but all such disputes shall be determined by arbitration in the manner pointed out in the Statutes relating to arbitrations.

In witness whereof, the parties to these presents have hereunto set their hands and seals the day and year first above written.

Signed, Sealed and Delivered ⎫   HENRY SMITH.   [L.S.]
    in the presence of   ⎬   ROBERT T. BRUCE. [L.S.]
      S. G. BEATTY.   ⎭   ROBERT JONES.   [L.S.]

AGREEMENT FOR BUILDING A HOUSE.

This Indenture made (in duplicate) this   day of   , in the year of Our Lord one thousand eight hundred and seventy-seven, between A. B., of, etc., and C. D. of, etc.

Witnesseth, that the said C. D., for the consideration hereinafter mentioned, doth for himself, his heirs, executors and administrators, covenant with the said A. B., his executors, administrators and assigns, shall and will within the space of (here insert the time) next after the date hereof, in a good and workmanlike manner, and at his own proper charge and expense, at (here insert the place), well and substantially erect, build and finish one house, according to the draught, scheme and explanation hereunto annexed with such stone, brick, timber and other materials, as the said A. B. or his assigns shall find or provide for the same.

In CONSIDERATION whereof the said A. B. doth, for himself, his executors and administrators, covenant with the said C. D., his executors and assigns, well and truly to pay unto the said C. D., his executors and assigns, the sum of———of lawful money of Canada, in manner following, viz. :———part thereof at the beginning of said work,———more, another part thereof, when the said work shall be half done, and the remaining———, in ful for the said work when the same shall be completely finished : And also, that he, the said A. B., his executors, administrators or assigns, shall and will, from time to time, as the same shall be required, at his and their own expense, provide stone, brick, timber and other materials necessary for making, building and finishing the said house. And for the performance of all and every the articles and agreements above mentioned, the said A. B. and C. D. do hereby bind themselves, their executors, administrators and assigns, each to the other, in the penal sum of———firmly, by these presents.

IN WITNESS WHEREOF, &c.

WILL.

When it is convenient to employ a lawyer, or some one acquainted with legal forms, to write a will, the services of such a person should be procured. But this is not always convenient. Therefore, every person who can write a legible hand should learn to draw a will in proper form. If he never has occasion to use this knowledge for himself, he may be called on to perform this kind office for a friend or neighbor suddenly thrown upon a bed of death.

Every pupil, before leaving the public school, should be taught the form and legal requisites of a will.

The TESTATOR is the person who makes and signs the will.

The DONEE, also called LEGATEE or DEVISEE is the one who receives property by the will. He should not write it, nor in any way procure the writing of it, nor be a subscribing witness to it.

The EXECUTOR is the person to whom the execution of the will is intrusted by the testator.

A will requires two subscribing witnesses, and they should sign their names in the presence of each other, and in the presence of the testator, and at his request.

The witnesses to a will should write their several places of residence opposite their respective names.

The signature of the testator must be at the foot or end of the will, and where there are several sheets of paper it is better for the testator and witnesses to sign every sheet.

A seal is not essential, though the practice is to put a seal to the testator's signature.

The date should never be omitted ; for, though it is not essential to the validity of a will, it is evidence of the time of its execution in case another will should be found.

A will made by a person under twenty-one years of age is invalid. The marriage of the testator generally revokes a will.

FORM OF WILL.

I, WILLIAM HENRY BROWN, of the City of Belleville, in the County of Hasting and Province of Ontario, Canada, being of sound mind and memory, and considering the uncertainty of this frail and transitory life, do therefore make, and declare this to be, my last WILL AND TESTAMENT, that is to say:

First.—After all my lawful debts and funeral and testamentary expenses are paid and discharged, I BEQUEATH to my wife, Laura Brown, the dwelling house and land connected therewith, which we now occupy as a homestead; and all the furniture and household goods, including pictures, books, linen, china, plate, provisions, chattels, and effects (other than money or securities for money), which shall at my death be in or about my dwellin house, or the out-buildings or grounds thereof. I also bequeath to my said wife the sum of six thousand dollars cash, to be paid to her within one calendar month after my death without interest.

Second—I give to my daughter Jane, four thousand dollars cash, and thirty shares in the BANK OF MONTREAL, for her sole use and for the use of her heirs at her discretion.

Third.—I give to my son William all my real estate in the Township of Thurlow, County of Hastings, Province of Ontario, and all the live stock and implements used for farming purposes in connection with the same.

Fourth.—The residue of my property, real and personal, I giv and bequeath to my son Thomas.

Fifth.—I hereby appoint my son WILLIAM to be executor and my wife LAURA execu trix of this, my last will and testament, hereby revoking all former wills by me made. AND I APPOINT my said wife and Robert Henry Smith, of the City of Belleville, afore said, guardians of my infant children.

IN WITNESS WHEREOF, I, the testator, have hereunto set my hand and seal, this first day of December, in the year of Our Lord one thousand eight hundred and seventy-seven.

Signed, sealed and delivered by the testator, in the presence of us, who (in his presence), at his request, and in the presence of each other, have hereunto subscribed our names as witnesses.

WILLIAM H. BROWN. [SEAL]

THOMAS STRONG,
 of Cobourg, Ontario,
PETER FARNOR,
 of Belleville, Ontario.

POWER OF ATTORNEY.

Know all men by these Presents, that I (insert name here), of in the County of and Province of Ontario, for divers good causes and considerations me thereunto moving, have nominated, constituted and appointed, and by these presents do nominate, constitute and appoint (insert name here) my true and lawful Attorney, for me and in my name and on my behalf, and for my sole and exclusive use and benefit, to demand, recover and receive from all and every or any person or persons whomsoever all and every sum and sums of money, goods, chattels, effects, and things whatsoever which now are or is, or which shall or may hereafter appear to be due, owing, payable or belonging to me, whether for rent or arrears of rent, or otherwise in respect of my real estate, or for the principal money and interest now or hereafter to become payable to me upon or in respect of any mortgage or other security, or for the interest or dividends to accrue or become payable to me for or in respect of any shares, stock or interest which I may now or hereafter hold in any Joint Stock or Incorporated Company or companies, or for any moneys or securities for money which are now or hereafter may be due or owing or belonging to me upon any Bond, Note, Bill, or Bills of Exchange, balance of Account Current, consignment, contract, decree, judgment, order or execution, or upon any other account.

And to examine, state, settle, liquidate and adjust all or any account or accounts depending between me and any person or persons whomspver. And to sign, draw, make, or indorse my name to any Cheque or Cheques or orders for the payment of money, Bill, or Bills of Exchange, or Note or Notes of Hand, in which I shall be interested or concerned, which shall be requisite. And also in my name to draw upon any Bank or Banks, Individual or Individuals, for any sum or sums of money that is or are or may be to my credit, or which I am or may be entitled to receive, and the same to deposit in any Bank or other place, and again at pleasure to draw for from time to time as I myself could do. And upon the recovery or receipt of all and every or any sum or sums of money, goods, chattels, effects or things due, owing, payable or belonging to me, for me and in my name and as my act and deed to sign, execute and deliver such good and sufficient receipts releases and acquittances, certificates, reconveyances, surrenders, assignments, memorials or other good and effectual discharges as may be requisite.

Also in case of neglect, refusal, or delay on the part of any person or persons to make, and render just, true and full account, payment, delivery and satisfaction in the premises, him, them or any of them thereunto to compel, and for that purpose for me in my name to make such claims and demands, arrests, seizures, levies, attachments, distraints and sequestrations, or to commence, institute, sue and prosecute to judgment and execution such actions, ejectments and suits at law or in equity as my said attorney or attorneys shall think fit; also to appear before all or any Judges, Magistrates or other Officers of the Courts of law or Equity, and then and there to sue, plead, answer, defend and reply in all matters and causes concerning the premises; And also to exercise and execute all Powers of Sale or Foreclosure, and all other powers and authorities vested in me by any mortgage or mortgages belonging to me as mortgagee.

And also, in case of any difference or dispute with any person or persons concerning any of the matters aforesaid, to submit any such differences and disputes to arbitration or umpirage, in such manner as my said attorney, attorneys shall see fit; And to compound, compromise and to accept part in satisfaction for the payment of the whole of any debt or sum of money payable to me, or to grant an extension of time for the payment of the same, either with or without taking security, or otherwise to act in respect of the same as to my said attorney or attorneys shall appear most expedient.

And also, for me and in my name, or otherwise on my behalf, to take possession of, and to let, set, manage and improve my real estate, lands, messuages and hereditaments whatsoever and wheresoever, and from time to time to appoint any agents or servants, to assist him or them in managing the same, and to displace or remove such agents or servants, and appoint others, using therein the same power and discretion as I might do.

And also, as and when my said attorney or attorneys shall think fit, to sell and absolutely dispose of my said real estate, land and hereditaments, and also such shares, stocks, bonds, mortgages, and other securities for money as hereinbefore mentioned, either together or in parcels, for such price or prices, and by public auction or private contract as to my said attorney or attorneys shall seem reasonable or expedient; And to convey, assign, transfer, and make over the same respectively to the purchaser or purchasers thereof, with power to give credit for the whole or any part of the purchase money thereof; And to permit the same to remain unpaid for whatever time and upon whatever security, real or personal, either comprehending the purchased property or not, as my said attorney or attorneys shall think safe and proper.

And further, for me and in my name and as my act and deed, to execute and do all such assurances, deeds, covenants and things as shall be required, and my said attorney or attorneys shall see fit, for all or any of the purposes aforesaid; and to sign and give receipts and discharges for all or any of the sum or sums of money which shall come to his or their hands by virtue of the powers herein contained, and which receipts, whether given in my name or that of my said attorney or attorneys, shall exempt the person or persons paying such sum or sums of money from all responsibility of seeing to the application thereof.

And also, for me and in my name, or otherwise, and on my behalf, to enter into any agreement or arrangement with every or any person to whom I am or shall be indebted touching the payment or satisfaction of his demand, or any part thereof; And generally to act in relation to my estate and effects, real and personal, as fully and effectually, in all respects, as I myself could do if personally present.

And I hereby grant full power to my said attorney to substitute and appoint one or more attorney or attorneys under him with the same or more limited powers, and such substitute and substitutes at pleasure to remove, and others to appoint, I the said (here insert name), hereby agreeing and covenanting for myself, my heirs, executors and administrators, to allow ratify, and confirm whatsoever my said attorney or his substitute or substitutes shall do or cause to be done in the premises by virtue of these Presents; including in such confirmation whatsoever shall be done between the time of my decease or of the revocation of these Presents, and the time of such decease or revocation becoming known to my said attorney or attorneys, or such substitute or substitutes.

As witness my hand and seal, this   day of   in the year of our Lord one thousand eight hundred and eighty-

Signed, sealed and delivered }
in the presence of }

NOTE.—The above is a General Power of Attorney, a Special Power of Attorney would confer limited power, for instance, to perform one act or a limited number of acts only.

$1,000.   PROVINCE OF ONTARIO.   L No. 1.

DEBENTURE OF THE CITY OF BELLEVILLE.

Under the Authority of the Acts of the Legislature of the Province of Ontario, and in accordance with the provisions of By-Law No. 462, of the Corporation of the City of Belleville, the said The Corporation of the City of Belleville promise to pay the Bearer, at the Merchants Bank of Canada, in the City of Belleville, aforesaid, the sum of one thousand dollars of lawful money of Canada, on the sixteenth day of November, One Thousand Nine Hundred, and will also pay the Coupons hereunto attached, as the same shall severally become due.

In testimony whereof, the Mayor of the said City has signed and sealed, and the Treasurer thereof has countersigned these Presents at Belleville, the Sixteenth day of November, 1880.

_____ Treasurer City of Belleville.   _____ Mayor City of Belleville.

PROVINCE OF ONTARIO. The Corporation of the City of Belleville will pay the Bearer at the Merchants Bank of Canada at Belleville, Thirty Dollars, for one-half year's interest on Debenture L No. 1, Coupon No. 40, on the Sixteenth day of November, 1900. _____ Treasurer. _____ Mayor.	PROVINCE OF ONTARIO. The Corporation of the City of Belleville will pay the Bearer at the Merchants Bank of Canada at Belleville, Thirty Dollars, for one-half year's interest on Debenture L No. 1, Coupon No. 39, on the Sixteenth day of May, 1900. _____ Treasurer. _____ Mayor.	PROVINCE OF ONTARIO. The Corporation of the City of Belleville will pay the Bearer at the Merchants Bank of Canada at Belleville, Thirty Dollars, for one-half year's interest on Debenture L No. 1, Coupon No. 38, on the Sixteenth day of November, 1899. _____ Treasurer. _____ Mayor.	PROVINCE OF ONTARIO. The Corporation of the City of Belleville will pay the Bearer at the Merchants Bank of Canada at Belleville, Thirty Dollars, for one-half year's interest on Debenture L No. 1, Coupon No. 37, on the Sixteenth day of May, 1899. _____ Treasurer. _____ Mayor.	PROVINCE OF ONTARIO. The Corporation of the City of Belleville will pay the Bearer at the Merchants Bank of Canada at Belleville, Thirty Dollars, for one-half year's interest on Debenture L No. 1, Coupon No. 36, on the Sixteenth day of November, 1898. _____ Treasurer. _____ Mayor.
PROVINCE OF ONTARIO. The Corporation of the City of Belleville will pay the Bearer at the Merchants Bank of Canada at Belleville, Thirty Dollars, for one-half year's interest on Debenture L No. 1, Coupon No. 35, on the Sixteenth day of May, 1898. _____ Treasurer. _____ Mayor.	PROVINCE OF ONTARIO. The Corporation of the City of Belleville will pay the Bearer at the Merchants Bank of Canada at Belleville, Thirty Dollars, for one-half year's interest on Debenture L No. 1, Coupon No. 34, on the Sixteenth day of November, 1897. _____ Treasurer. _____ Mayor.	PROVINCE OF ONTARIO. The Corporation of the City of Belleville will pay the Bearer at the Merchants Bank of Canada at Belleville, Thirty Dollars, for one-half year's interest on Debenture L No. 1, Coupon No. 33, on the Sixteenth day of May, 1897. _____ Treasurer. _____ Mayor.	PROVINCE OF ONTARIO. The Corporation of the City of Belleville will pay the Bearer at the Merchants Bank of Canada at Belleville, Thirty Dollars, for one-half year's interest on Debenture L No. 1, Coupon No. 32, on the Sixteenth day of November, 1896. _____ Treasurer. _____ Mayor.	PROVINCE OF ONTARIO. The Corporation of the City of Belleville will pay the Bearer at the Merchants Bank of Canada at Belleville, Thirty Dollars, for one-half year's interest on Debenture L No. 1, Coupon No. 31, on the Sixteenth day of May, 1896. _____ Treasurer. _____ Mayor.
PROVINCE OF ONTARIO. The Corporation of the City of Belleville will pay the Bearer at the Merchants Bank of Canada at Belleville, Thirty Dollars, for one-half year's interest on Debenture L No. 1, Coupon No. 30, n the Sixteenth day of November, 1895. _____ Treasurer. _____ Mayor.	PROVINCE OF ONTARIO. The Corporation of the City of Belleville will pay the Bearer at the Merchants Bank of Canada at Belleville, Thirty Dollars, for one-half year's interest on Debenture L No. 1, Coupon No. 29, on the Sixteenth day of May, 1895. _____ Treasurer. _____ Mayor.	PROVINCE OF ONTARIO. The Corporation of the City of Belleville will pay the Bearer at the Merchants Bank of Canada at Belleville, Thirty Dollars, for one-half year's interest on Debenture L No. 1, Coupon No. 28, on the Sixteenth day of November, 1894. _____ Treasurer. _____ Mayor.	PROVINCE OF ONTARIO. The Corporation of the City of Belleville will pay the Bearer at the Merchants Bank of Canada at Belleville, Thirty Dollars, for one-half year's interest on Debenture L No. 1, Coupon No. 26, on the Sixteenth day of May, 1894. _____ Treasurer. _____ Mayor.	PROVINCE OF ONTARIO. The Corporation of the City of Belleville will pay the Bearer at the Merchants Bank of Canada at Belleville, Thirty Dollars, for one-half year's interest on Debenture L No. 1, Coupon No. 29, on the Sixteenth day of November, 1893. _____ Treasurer. _____ Mayor.

251

PROVINCE OF ONTARIO. The Corporation of the City of Belleville will pay the Bearer at the Merchants Bank of Canada at Belleville, Thirty Dollars, for one-half year's interest on Debenture £ No. 1, Coupon No. 21, on the Sixteenth day of May, 1891. *Treasurer.* *Mayor.*	PROVINCE OF ONTARIO. The Corporation of the City of Belleville will pay the Bearer at the Merchants Bank of Canada at Belleville, Thirty Dollars, for one-half year's interest on Debenture £ No. 1, Coupon No. 16, on the Sixteenth day of November, 1888. *Treasurer.* *Mayor.*	PROVINCE OF ONTARIO. The Corporation of the City of Belleville will pay the Bearer at the Merchants Bank of Canada at Belleville, Thirty Dollars, for one-half year's interest on Debenture £ No. 1, Coupon No. 11, on the Sixteenth day of May, 1886. *Treasurer.* *Mayor.*	PROVINCE OF ONTARIO. The Corporation of the City of Belleville will pay the Bearer at the Merchants Bank of Canada at Belleville, Thirty Dollars, for one-half year's interest on Debenture £ No. 1, Coupon No. 6, on the Fifteenth day of November, 1883. *Treasurer.* *Mayor.*
PROVINCE OF ONTARIO. The Corporation of the City of Belleville will pay the Bearer at the Merchants Bank of Canada at Belleville, Thirty Dollars, for one-half year's interest on Debenture £ No. 1, Coupon No. 22, on the Sixteenth day of November, 1891. *Treasurer.* *Mayor.*	PROVINCE OF ONTARIO. The Corporation of the City of Belleville will pay the Bearer at the Merchants Bank of Canada at Belleville, Thirty Dollars, for one-half year's interest on Debenture £ No. 1, Coupon No. 17, on the Sixteenth day of May, 1889. *Treasurer.* *Mayor.*	PROVINCE OF ONTARIO. The Corporation of the City of Belleville will pay the Bearer at the Merchants Bank of Canada at Belleville, Thirty Dollars, for one-half year's interest on Debenture £ No. 1, Coupon No. 12, on the Sixteenth day of November, 1886. *Treasurer.* *Mayor.*	PROVINCE OF ONTARIO. The Corporation of the City of Belleville will pay the Bearer at the Merchants Bank of Canada at Belleville, Thirty Dollars, for one-half year's interest on Debenture £ No. 1, Coupon No. 7, on the Sixteenth day of May, 1884. *Treasurer.* *Mayor.*
PROVINCE OF ONTARIO. The Corporation of the City of Belleville will pay the Bearer at the Merchants Bank of Canada at Belleville, Thirty Dollars, for one-half year's interest on Debenture £ No. 1, Coupon No. 23, on the Sixteenth day of May, 1892. *Treasurer.* *Mayor.*	PROVINCE OF ONTARIO. The Corporation of the City of Belleville will pay the Bearer at the Merchants Bank of Canada at Belleville, Thirty Dollars, for one-half year's interest on Debenture £ No. 1, Coupon No. 18, on the Sixteenth day of November, 1889. *Treasurer.* *Mayor.*	PROVINCE OF ONTARIO. The Corporation of the City of Belleville will pay the Bearer at the Merchants Bank of Canada at Belleville, Thirty Dollars, for one-half year's interest on Debenture £ No. 1, Coupon No. 13, on the Sixteenth day of May, 1887. *Treasurer.* *Mayor.*	PROVINCE OF ONTARIO. The Corporation of the City of Belleville will pay the Bearer at the Merchants Bank of Canada at Belleville, Thirty Dollars, for one-half year's interest on Debenture £ No. 1, Coupon No. 8, on the Sixteenth day of November, 1884. *Treasurer.* *Mayor.*
PROVINCE OF ONTARIO. The Corporation of the City of Belleville will pay the Bearer at the Merchants Bank of Canada at Belleville, Thirty Dollars, for one-half year's interest on Debenture £ No. 1, Coupon No. 24, on the Sixteenth day of November, 1892. *Treasurer.* *Mayor.*	PROVINCE OF ONTARIO. The Corporation of the City of Belleville will pay the Bearer at the Merchants Bank of Canada at Belleville, Thirty Dollars, for one-half year's interest on Debenture £ No. 1, Coupon No. 19, on the Sixteenth day of May, 1890. *Treasurer.* *Mayor.*	PROVINCE OF ONTARIO. The Corporation of the City of Belleville will pay the Bearer at the Merchants Bank of Canada at Belleville, Thirty Dollars, for one-half year's interest on Debenture £ No. 1, Coupon No. 14, on the Sixteenth day of November, 1887. *Treasurer.* *Mayor.*	PROVINCE OF ONTARIO. The Corporation of the City of Belleville will pay the Bearer at the Merchants Bank of Canada at Belleville, Thirty Dollars, for one-half year's interest on Debenture £ No. 1, Coupon No. 9, on the Sixteenth day of May, 1885. *Treasurer.* *Mayor.*
PROVINCE OF ONTARIO. The Corporation of the City of Belleville will pay the Bearer at the Merchants Bank of Canada at Belleville, Thirty Dollars, for one-half year's interest on Debenture £ No. 1, Coupon No. 25, on the Sixteenth day of May, 1893. *Treasurer.* *Mayor.*	PROVINCE OF ONTARIO. The Corporation of the City of Belleville will pay the Bearer at the Merchants Bank of Canada at Belleville, Thirty Dollars, for one-half year's interest on Debenture £ No. 1, Coupon No. 20, on the Sixteenth day of November, 1890. *Treasurer.* *Mayor.*	PROVINCE OF ONTARIO. The Corporation of the City of Belleville will pay the Bearer at the Merchants Bank of Canada at Belleville, Thirty Dollars, for one-half year's interest on Debenture £ No. 1, Coupon No. 15, on the Sixteenth day of May, 1888. *Treasurer.* *Mayor.*	PROVINCE OF ONTARIO. The Corporation of the City of Belleville will pay the Bearer at the Merchants Bank of Canada at Belleville, Thirty Dollars, for one-half year's interest on Debenture £ No. 1, Coupon No. 10, on the Sixteenth day of November, 1885. *Treasurer.* *Mayor.*

Debentures (or Bonds) are securities upon which Governments, Municipalities and Incorporated Companies (that have the power) borrow money for long periods.

QUESTIONS FOR REVIEW.—BUSINESS PAPERS.

What is a Bill of Exchange? How many persons are interested therein? When the drawee of a bill undertakes to pay it, what is he then called? Describe what is necessary in order to transfer bills of different kinds. Bills of Exchange are of how many kinds? How are foreign Bills usually drawn? What is the object of drawing them in sets?

Give the form of a set of Exchange.

What is a Promissory Note? What resemblance is there between a Note and a Bill of Exchange?

Must a Bill or Note, or an indorsement thereon, necessarily be in ink? If there should be a variance between the sum superscribed in figures and that mentioned in the body of the note, which will prevail? Does the omission of the place where the note is made, the date, or the words "value received," invalidate it. Under what circumstances does the dating of a note on Sunday render it void? Can a note made by an infant be collected under any circumstances?

Has a married woman power to issue a note or bill? Relate the laws that governs notes issued by women. What persons are, by law, considered incompetent to make a contract? Can a note be collected if obtained by fraud or from a person in a state of drunkenness? What is a joint note? How should the makers of a joint note be sued? What is a joint and several note? What is the distinction between a joint note and a joint and several note? What effect has an alteration of a bill or note, after it has once been issued, upon it?

What is the drawer's undertaking in a Bill of Exchange? What is the duty of the payee, if the bill remain in his possession? What is the acceptor's undertaking? How is the acceptor's liability discharged? What is an indorsement? Name five different forms of indorsement, and give an example of each. If a note indorsed by several parties be dis_honored, against whom has the holder a right of action. If the note be paid by the first indorser, to whom must he look for the recovery of the amount? Has the first indorser, under any circumstance, a right of action against the subsequent indorsers? What is the object of the several forms of indorsement? What is the distinction between negotiable and non-negotiable paper? How is negotiable paper transferred in order to give the holder the right of action.

Is it necessary to present a bill for acceptance? What is understood by a bill being honored and dishonored?

Why is it necessary to give notice of a bill being dishonored? What is necessary in order to hold the indorser of a bill or note? When is a note drawn on demand or without a specified time, payable? If a note is dishonored how should notice be given? Has the party paying a bill or any other debt a right to demand a receipt?

Under what circumstances may interest be collected on a note? How many years has a note or other debt to run before it becomes outlawed?

Can the amount of a lost bill or note be recovered, under any circumstances? Name some of the different papers used in business, aside from bills or notes. Define some of these papers. If a receipt be given in mistake, does it necessarily bind the giver? Name the different forms of time drafts. What is necessary before a draft becomes the obligation of the person on whom it is drawn?

In what cases are drafts used? What form is adopted in accepting a draft? When is the date of acceptance required? What are cheques, and wherein do they differ from bills of Exchange?

What is necessary to make a legal seal? Define the following terms used in connection with a will: TESTATOR, DONEE, LEGATEE, DEVISEE and EXECUTOR. How many sub-scribing witnesses does a will require? Where should the signature of the testator be placed? What effect has the marriage of the testator upon a will? What is said of a will made by a person under twenty-one years of age?

CORRESPONDENCE.

It should not be forgotten that a valid and binding contract can be made by the interchange of letters, if a direct offer be unconditionally accepted.

In all composition, THREE things require attention : the thoughts, their arrangement and the language employed.

Of all kinds of composition, letters are the most universal and important : yet among the millions written annually how few could bear criticism: Errors in spelling, grammar, penmanship and arrangement are generally attributed to haste, which is considered as ample apology for every fault ; when, in reality, the writer is not qualified to write a letter correctly under the most favorable circumstances.

In no way can a person so commend himself to the favorable regard of others, or impart to them so just an idea of his mental qualities, as by writing.

Says Lord Collingwood: " When you write a letter give it your greatest care, that it may be as perfect in all its parts as you can make it. Let the subject be Sense, expressed in the most plain, intelligible, and elegant language you can command. If, in a familiar epistle, you should be playful and jocular, guard carefully that your wit be not sharp so as to give pain to any person ; and before you write a sentence, examine that there be nothing vulgar or inelegant therein. Remember that your letter is a picture of your mind, and those whose minds are a compound of folly, nonsense and impertinence are to blame to exhibit them to the contempt of the world, of the pity of their friends. To write a letter with negligence, without stops, with crooked lines, and great flourishes is inelegant. It argues either great ignorance of what is proper, or great impudence towards the person to whom it is addressed. It makes no amends to add, as an apology for having scrawled a sheet of paper, that you wrote with bad pens, because you should have good ones ; or plead want of time, for nothing is more important to you, or to which your time can more properly be devoted. "

The essential requisites of any letter are : first, correct Spelling ; second, legible Writing ; third, good Grammar ; and fourth, proper Arrangement.

1. CORRECT SPELLING is a very rare accomplishment among the majority of people. Perhaps there is no part of our education, the neglect of which receives so little charity as this. Yet, when we look for that system of classification and application of general rules and principles in this, which is found in every other branch of study, we find that EXCEPTION soon becomes the rule, and the pupil is obliged to rely upon memory and unremitting practice for the orthography of almost every word.

WE SPELL ONLY WHEN WE WRITE.—Therefore, spelling is best acquired by constant practice in copying from good authors, writing from dictation, or composing and correcting original essays. These exercises are, at the same time, an efficient training in penmanship and grammar.

Copying from a printed page should form a daily exercise, until entire pages can be correctly transcribed from dictation. Such an exercise gives practice in reading, translation, spelling, punctuation and the use of capitals. It also cultivates a habit of accuracy in transcribing, which is a most desirable acquisition.

It is safe to predict that not one in fifty, who has never attempted it, can copy an entire page without a mistake. Let those who doubt, try it.

2 PENMANSHIP.—Penmanship is to a letter what dress is to the appearance of an individual; and no one can deny the deciding influence of dress. Nor does the attire of a gentleman become him less because knaves and fools sometimes assume the same. Never apologize for bad penmanship, especially where it is habitual. It is far from refreshing to the recipient to read such uninteresting commonplaces. Either write respectably, or submit to such reflections as your bad writing must inevitably suggest, whether excused or not. Culpable indifference, laziness, or, to speak a little more mildly, indolence or downright carelessness, are, in nineteen cases out of twenty, the only obstacles in the way of a good fair, legible handwriting.

A little earnestness, industry, carefulness and perseverance will overcome all difficulties. Elegant penmanship is not the subject here proposed ; but a good, readable business handwriting.

In accomplishing this, three essential particulars must be observed, viz.: Legibility. UNIFORMITY and SPACES.

3. GRAMMAR.—Remember, letter-writing is TALKING ON PAPER; but we must talk, on paper more carefully than many of us are accustomed to talk with the voice. In common conversation, redundancies, bad grammar and inelegant expressions, if they do not pass unobserved and uncriticised, may at least be excused and soon forgotten ; but in a letter they remain permament witnesses against us. Make it a rule never to commit to paper expressions you would be ashamed to acknowledge should they confront you afterwards. If spoken vulgarisms are bad, what shall we say of such expressions put upon paper and sent to one's friend ? Think of the letter you are writing as a record which may be preserved by your friends long after you have ceased to be among them ; and commit nothing to the permanence of ink and paper that can possibly throw a shade upon your memory.

4. ARRANGEMENT.—In all letters, whatever be their class or subject, attention must be paid to certain conventional forms for arranging the several parts of which they are composed.

Every letter is regarded as consisting of six essential parts: 1. The location and date. 2. The name and address of the person to whom it is written. 3. The complimentary address. 4. The body of the letter 5. Complimentary closing. 6. The signature of the writer.

The location and the date should both be written on the same line, near the RIGHT upper corner of the sheet. The name and title or the person to whom it is addressed follow on the next line or two below, near the LEFT side of the sheet, and the address on the line underneath a little to the right. The complimentary address follows on the line below the address, beginning a little to the left of it.

The body of the letter should be commenced very nearly under the last letter of the complimentary address.

The complimentary closing should begin very nearly under the last letter of the body ; and the signature very nearly under the last letter of the complimentary closing, as illustrated in the following :

FORM OF A LETTER.

(Location and Date.)

Belleville, Nov. 1st, 1878.

(Name and title of the person addressed.)

JOHN SMITH, ESQ.,

(Address.) *Picton, Ont.,*

(Complimentary Address.)

DEAR SIR,—

(Body of the Letter.)

We respectfully call your attention to our statement of account, rendered October 1st, a settlement of which at your earliest convenience will greatly oblige,

(Complimentary Closing.)

Yours respectfully,

(Signature.)   W. A. ROBLIN.

PUNCTUATION.

It is not intended to give in this place RULES for punctuating ; but to furnish the student with a few examples, such as, it is believed, the best usage sanctions. It may be proper to remark, however, that there is a discrepancy between the English and American style of punctuating the beginning of a letter ; but they differ only in the point placed after the NAMES, before the address : the English placing a period there, which implies that they regard the name or names grammatically in the third person, and consequently no part of the address.

Strictly speaking, the names and words of respect, whether written at the beginning or at the end of a letter, are no part of the address proper, except so far as they show who are addressed.

The names and addresses have this connection and no other. Grammatically, the names to be addressed are in the third person, governed by the proposition TO understood, and should be followed by a period. However, we shall follow the custom of this continent. The address as, *Dear Sir, Gentlemen, &c.,* are in the second person in the nominative case, independent, and should be followed by a colon, or its equivalent ; as *Dear Sir:—Gentlemen :—*etc.

The language of the names and words of respect are elliptical, and, supplying the words omitted, but understood, it would read in a single name, as *John Smith, Esq.* Toronto, Ontario, when written in full thus: *This letter is addressed to John Smith who is an Esquire, and resides in the City of Toronto, in the Province of Ontario.*

When thus written out in full, no question can arise as to the punctuation.

EXAMPLES OF PUNCTUATION.

No. 1.
John Clarke, Esq.,
        Toronto, Ont.,
Dear Sir :—
	No. 5.
	Mrs. John Smith,
	        Montreal, P.Q.,
	Madam :—

No. 2.
Messrs. Jones & Brown,
        Montreal, P.Q.,
Gentlemen :—
	No. 6.
	Rev. Dr. S. G. Smith,
	        Hamilton, Ont.,
	Rev. and Dear Sir :—

No. 3.
Hon. Robert Read,
        Belleville, Ont.,
Sir :—
	No. 7.
	Col. James Brown,
	        Ottawa, Ont.,
	Dear Col. :—

No. 4.
Drs. Dorland & Clapham,
        Belleville, Ont.,
Gentlemen :—
	No. 8.
	Prof. J. H. Brown,
	        Deaf and Dumb Institute,
	        Belleville, Ont.,
	Dear Sir :—

If the title *Mr.*, *Messrs.* or *Mrs.* be used, the period must be affixed, to show that it is an abbreviation of the word for which it stands. *Mess.* should never be used for *Messrs.* It is in bad taste. It is but an abbreviation *of* an abbreviation.

If you cannot afford to write *Gentlemen* or *Sir* in full, omit it altogether. Never write *Gent.* nor *Gents.*, nor *Sr.* for *Sir*. Although *Gent.* is used occasionally, and even justified by good authority, it is abrupt and often offends. Never write *Dr.* for *Dear*, before *Sir*. Your correspondent will hardly believe himself very dear to you, if you cannot afford to write so short a word in full

A few remarks under each of the foregoing parts will serve to develop all the mportant features relating to an ordinary letter.

MARGIN.—On the left of your page there should be given a liberal margin of say three-quarters of an inch, or a little more, with which the writing is not to interfere.

If any one thing makes a letter look mean and stingy, it is a narrow margin at the left, and if any one thing stamps the writer as a careless sloven, it is an unequal zigzag margin.

LOCATION AND DATE.—The location and date at which a letter is written is one of its most important parts. The whole legal bearing of any letter may be destroyed by the omission of this essential part: you cannot be too careful in stating it correctly and fully.

In writing from any place, care should be taken to mention the Province, and sometimes the county, as there may be more than one post office of the same name in Canada.

The order in which the words of the location and date are written varies somewhat. For instance, English letter writers generally place the day before the month, as: 1st Jan., instead of Jan. 1st.

The former is the more natural arrangement, but custom in this country generally favors the latter.

NAME AND TITLE.—1. Names. The first name of a person as; William, Robert, Jane, Mary, &c., is called the CHRISTIAN name; while the last, as: Brown, Smith, Wilson, &c., is called the SURNAME.

In addressing letters to persons, it is always best to use the same form as that adopted in their own signature, with the addition of the proper title.

When father and son have both the same name, Robert Jones, for instance, the father is addressed as Robert Jones, Sr., or Senior, meaning older, and the son as Robert Jones, Jr., or Junior, meaning younger.

There has grown up, in this country, an array of titles and addresses which, though perhaps not so numerous or cumbersome as those of Europe, are nevertheless guarded as strictly from violation by laws of etiquette. Many of these titles, or expressions of respect are clearly traceable to their foreign origin. For example, Mr. from Master; Mrs. from Mistress; Miss from the French Demoiselle; Esq. from Esquire. This a very common title of respect in this country and in the United States; it is perverted from its original signification, and applied almost indiscriminately to all classes of males. Originally a title of respect, it now signifies nothing at all. Yet its omission might, in some case, give offence, though the person addressed could lay no claim to it.

In England, several hundred years ago, there were five classes of dignitaries to whom this title belonged, viz.:

1. The oldest sons of knights, and their eldest sons in perpetual succession.
2. Such as were created Esquires by the King's letters patent, and their eldest sons.
3. The eldest son of younger sons of peers, and their eldest sons in perpetual succession.
4. Such as were Esquires by virtue of their offices, as Justices of the peace, and others who bore any office under the Crown.
5. Later than the origin of these classes, and it is said, by usurpation, the members of the legal profession were universally recognized by this title. But they have enjoyed it so long that it has become, both in England and in this country, an established distinction.

The word GENTLEMAN was originally significant of wealth and education, and signified that the bearer of the title was able to live in idleness, or, at least, without personal exertion to support himself. The historic significance of the term was long since lost through its indiscriminate application to all men, whether boors and rowdies, or persons of culture and refinement.

When a word becomes applicable to all men, it necessarily ceases to be in any sense complimentary.

This is precisely the condition of the two words *Esquire* and *Gentlemen*, as used in this country in business or other correspondence.

Titles may be divided into two classes, viz: Titles of respect as: Mrs., Miss, Mr., Esq., &c., and professional titles, as Dr., Rev., LL.D., &c.

As a general rule, two titles of the same class should not be applied to the same name. "Mr. Wm. Brown, Esq.," should be either "Mr. William Brown" or "Wm. Brown, Esq.," The first is preferable. If the profession of the person is known to the writer, the professional title alone should be used. Where there are two or more professional titles applicable to the same individual, the highest should be used in preference to the other.

Custom places mere titles of respect (except Esq.) BEFORE the name, which is not uniform in the application of professional titles, some preceding and others following it. For instance, Dr., Rev., Hon., and military titles should PRECEDE the name, while M.D., A.M., LL.D., F.C.A., &c., should follow it. It is considered more respectful to write titles of high rank in full than to abbreviate them.

ADDRESS.—The address of the person to whom you are writing should always be upon the sheet containing the body of the letter, so that, in case the letter becomes separated from the envelope, it may not be lost for want of direction. Custom has of late favored placing both the name and address at the head of the letter instead of at the close, as formerly.

This arrangement appears more sensible, as in case in is received by the wrong person through mistake, it can be discovered before reading the letter through.

This plan also facilitates addressing the envelope when several letters are written at the same time.

COMPLIMENTARY ADDRESS.—In writing to a gentleman, with whom you have little or no acquaintance, the address should be simply "Sir;" if you are on familiar terms "Dear Sir" may be used. "My Dear Sir" implies still greater intimacy.

In addressing a lady not a relative, "Madam" or "Dear Madam" may be used, according to the degree of intimacy. Unmarried ladies are sometimes addressed as "Miss" "Dear Miss," "Dear Mary," and so forth, according to the degree of intimacy.

In addressing a firm or association of individuals, comprising a Committee, Board of Trustees, or other body, "Gentlemen," or "Ladies," should be used, according to the sex of those comprising it.

You may address a man who has a right to the title as, Captain John Smith, Major Robert Brown, etc., but it would display excessive bad taste and ignorance for a man to sign his name with the title in front. The proper way is, John Smith, Captain; Robert Brown, Major. A woman should never sign, for example, Mrs. John Brown, but Mary Brown, her own name.

BODY OF THE LETTER.—The body of the letter should be made up of paragraphs. Every change of subject should be indicated by commencing a new paragraph to the left of the middle of the sheet, and about an inch farther to the right than the other lines. The opening paragraph should always be short, and unfold, if possible, the object of the letter. If it is a reply, it should announce the receipt and date of the letter to which it is an answer, and should give a brief statement of its subject matter, that all cause of misapprehension may be explained or removed, thus:

"Your favor of the 1st inst., relating to the sale of your books in this city, is received, &c."

If the letter is one of business or inquiry, dispose of the first; and unless on familiar terms, never introduce other matters. If the letter is to be short, it should be commenced so as to leave an equal space above and below.

No error is more frequent among beginners than the use of the small i instead of the capital I in writing of themselves. This pronoun occurs frequently in letter-writing, and such a display of ignorance should be carefully guarded against.

The first letter of every sentence, title, proper name, or, adjective derived from it, every name applied to the Deity; every quotation of the words of another; every line in poetry; the words I, O and Oh, the days of the week, months of the year, and the principal words in rules and headings, should be capitals.

The names of the seasons should not be commenced with a capital letter.

The tendency among beginners is to use too many capitals, especially if the writer prides himself on his dexterity in making them. Except in one of the cases above enumerated, or when in doubt, use a small letter.

Do not begin a sentence till its wording is clearly fixed in the mind. Never add clause after clause, loosely linked on with "ands" and "buts," till you are led to say what you do not mean, instead of having expressed the thought intended.

COMPLIMENTARY CLOSING.—The complimentary closing, like the complimentary address, usually consists of a phrase more or less formal in its character, regulated by the degree of familiarity between the parties. It generally consists of some such expression as: " Yours truly," " Yours respectfully," " Your sincere friend," "Yours faithfully,"&c.

The closing sentence of the body of the letter should be framed so as to connect smoothly with the complimentary closing, as : " Hoping to hear from you soon,
I am,
Yours respectfully,
JOHN SHORY."

Signatures.—The importance of an appropriate signature is much greater than is sometimes supposed.

Different tastes will suggest different styles, such as the bold, coarse hand, the condensed hand, back hand, fine hand, etc.; but it matters little what style is chosen for one's signature, if it be suited to the sex of the individual and length of the name. The liability of being counterfeited should be carefully guarded against. To this end, the signature once adopted should not vary, so that continual practice may give it a character which would be difficult for an unpracticed hand to counterfeit. Some peculiarity of combination or arrangements of the part may be observed. When the temptation to counterfeit is great, as is the case with the signatures of persons in important offices, some private mark, likely to pass unobserved by the common eye, is frequently resorted to as a security against forgery.

ETIQUETTE OF LETTER WRITING.

In general, every letter requires a reply. It is as necessary to answer when written to as when spoken to. Letters considered disrespectful or insulting should be returned at once, without a reply. Letters of business or courtesy should receive prompt attention

Two persons should not write in the same letter, unless in family letters, or when both persons are very intimate with the correspondent.

When ceremony is required, letters should be commenced a litle above the middle of the first page, and, if there is not sufficient room to finish it on the first page, without bringing the signature too near the bottom, it may be finished on the inside sheet, on the right-hand page. In such cases there should be at least two or three lines of the body of the letter upon the next page.

It is considered impolite to write other than business letters on a half sheet of paper; therefore, unless from necessity, always use a whole sheet;

In letter-writing, be particular and use a sheet appropriate in style and size to the purpose for which it is employed. For example, it would be considered bad taste to write a business letter upon colored note paper. The judicious selection and use of paper should be carefully attended to. Envelopes should be either buff, white, or some other PLAIN color, and quite thick. Avoid all fancy patterns and colors.

POSTSCRIPTS are sentences inserted after the body of the letter is finished. They indicate either haste or thoughtlessness, and should, in general, be avoided. Writing around the margin of a letter should likewise be avoided.

Letters of recommendation or introduction should not be sealed when intended to be delivered by the person to whom they relate, as he ought to know the contents.

FOLDING.—The folding of letters is a very simple operation. Whether the sheet be a single or double leaf the process is the same, viz.: 1. Turn over the bottom of the sheet till its edge lies upon the edge at the top, making a fold in the middle. 2. Bring the right end of the folded sheet to your body, and fold over about one-third of the letter towards the top. 3. Finally reverse the ends of the sheet, and fold as much of the upper part in the opposite direction.

SUPERSCRIPTIONS.—The superscription of a letter means the address of the person to whom it is sent, written upon the envelope enclosing it. The form of arrangement should correspond with the same address at the head of the letter.

Care should be taken that it is distinctly written. From neglect of this precaution, hundreds of letters are sent every month to the dead letter office. Commence the superscription about the middle, and to the left of the centre of the envelope, so as not to crowd upon the right edge or bottom.

Before writing the superscription ascertain if the envelope is right edge up. It is in this position when the part on which the gum is usually placed folds under from the top of the envelope. Never scratch or draw faint lines upon which to write the superscription.

STAMPING.—The customary spot for placing the requisite postage stamp is on the right hand upper corner of the envelope.

For business letters use No. 5½ or 6 envelope, and observed the following

FORM OF SUPERSCRIPTION.

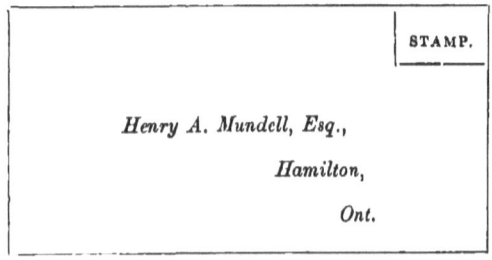

PARTICULAR LETTERS.

Letters are generally classed under two heads, viz.: Letters of Business and Letters of Friendship.

It is not our intention to treat of the latter, although the foregoing remarks apply to both classes. Limited space prevents our offering more than a few examples of the former.

LETTERS OF BUSINESS.—The characteristics of a business letter are BREVITY and CLEARNESS. Business letters are expected to be as brief as the subject will possibly allow. Unnecessary words are a waste of time to him who writes, and to him who is obliged to read them.

Few who have not had the actual experience can understand the labor of opening and reading fifty or a hundred letters; and when we consider that some large firms receive several hundred DAILY, whose contents must be read and considered, frequently through the most shocking penmanship and grammar, we can imagine why letters filling a whole sheet with business which should be despatched in a dozen lines are never read at all. In reading his correspondence, the man of business habits grasps not merely the meaning of words, but whole sentences at a glance, and extracts the important points of the letter and object of the writer almost instantaneously.

Before commencing a business letter the writer should ask himself: 1. How many different POINTS do I wish this letter to contain? 2. Can I embody all I wish to say upon each point in a single sentence? 3. If I cannot, HOW FEW SENTENCES WILL SUFFICE?

After the letter is completed, the following questions should be answered: 1. Have I included all the points or subjects I intended to write about? 2. Are they expressed in a brief and clear manner? 3. Can the language be misconstrued?

The arrangement or form of a letter should be such as will answer clearly the three questions which always arise on unsealing any letter. 1. Where is this letter from? 2. Who wrote it? 3. What does the writer want?

LETTERS OF INTRODUCTION.

A few words here may not be out of place in regard to letters of introduction. They are common,—indeed, they are becoming quiet TOO common. It may be feared they are sometimes given without due reflection and discrimination, if not for the purpose of getting rid of disagreeable importunity and of shirking an intolerable nuisance.

There are certain well-known rules, founded on good sense, that ought always to guide, not only in regard to letters of introduction, but also in reference to giving verbal introductions.

1. You should never give such a letter to be used by one in whom you have not entire confidence.

2. Having this confidence in your friend, to whom you desire to extend a favor, do not impose upon him by giving a letter directed to one who is unworthy of his confidence. He may become a sufferer in consequence of it.

3. Never accept such a letter, and be the bearer of it, from a person in whom you have not full confidence. Your own character may be suspected on account of it.

4. Be sure that your own relations to the party to whom your friend seeks an introduction are such as to warrant you in giving the letter. Otherwise that friend may find himself in an awkward predicament.

5. If the letter is of a business nature, through which pecuniary credit is sought be very careful what you write. Bear in mind that you may be held responsible before a court and jury for the contents of your letter.

6. Remember you have no right to thrust one of your acquaintances upon the attention of another, unless you are confident that it will prove mutually agreeable or advantageous.

Limited space prevents our offering more than a few forms of letters relating to business transactions of the most frequent occurrence.

The following letters are not intended to be perfectly adapted to the wants of any business man. But, taken in connection with the foregoing instructions, a few such letters may serve as general guides in the structure and literature of business epistles. The general tone, air, dress, modes of expression, complimentary terms, how to begin, how to close a letter, &c., &c., may be gleaned from them.

LETTER OF INTRODUCTION NOT INCURRING LIABILITY.

Hamilton, Oct. 29, 1889.

MESSRS. DAVID TORRANCE & CO.,
  Montreal,

GENTLEMEN :—

This will introduce to you, the bearer, Mr. H. T. Willis, a merchant of good standing in this place, who wishes to confer with you on business, the nature of which he will himself explain.

Yours respectfully,

THOMAS SMITH.

LETTER OF INTRODUCTION INCURRING LIABILITY.

London, Oct. 26, 1889.

MESSRS. GEO. WINKS & CO.,
  Montreal,

GENTLEMEN :—

Allow us to introduce to you Mr. J. B. Ashley, a merchant of this place. You may consider us responsible for goods that he may purchase from you, to any amount not exceeding four thousand dollars, on condition that you notify us immediately should default be made in payment thereof.

Yours truly,

JONES & BROWN.

INTRODUCING A FRIEND.

Belleville, Ont., Sept. 4, 1889.

HENRY BROWN ESQ.,
  Halifax, N. S.,

DEAR SIR :—

This will introduce to you the bearer, Mr. W. E. Embury, who visits your city for the purpose of engaging in the Grocery business.

I have much pleasure in assuring you that he his a young man of strict integrity, superior ability, and in every way worthy of your entire confidence.

Any assistance you may find it in your power to render him, I will regard as a personal favor to myself, which I shall be happy to reciprocate whenever an opportunity shall offer.

Yours very truly,

SAMSON SMITH.

The superscription on the envelopes enclosing letters of introduction should be thus—

```
                Henry Brown, Esq.,
                            Halifax,
   Introducing              N. S.
   Mr. W. E. Embury.
```

ENCLOSING STATEMENT OF ACCOUNT AND REQUESTING A REMITTANCE.

Toronto, Aug. 25, 1889.

Mr. Wm. Smith,
    Cobourg, Ont.,

Dear Sir :—

Your attention is called to the enclosed statement of account showing balance in our favor of one hundred dollars.

As it is long past due, an early remittance will oblige,

                Yours truly,
                          JAMES MANN & CO.

ANOTHER, IN CASE SUCH AS THE ABOVE PROVES INEFFECTIVE.

Toronto, Oct. 5, 1889.

Mr. Wm. Smith,
    Cobourg, Ont.,

Dear Sir :—

We again call your attention to the balance of your account, $100, still remaining unpaid. Your promises to remit have not been fulfilled. We trust your immediate attention to the matter will obviate the necessity of our referring to it again.

                Yours truly,
                          JAMES MANN & CO.

ANOTHER—A LAST EFFORT.

Toronto, Nov. 8, 1889.

Mr. Wm. Smith,
    Cobourg, Ont.,

Dear Sir :—

Your attention is once more called to the balance of account, $100, still unsettled. We expect a remittance of the same at once, otherwise we shall be compelled to use means to enforce collection. Trusting your prompt attention to the matter will render such a step unnecessary.

                We are, yours respectfully,
                          JAMES MANN & CO.

ANSWERS TO THE THREE FOREGOING LETTERS.

Cobourg, Aug. 29, 1889.

MESSRS. JAMES MANN & CO.,
    Toronto, Ont.,

GENTLEMEN :—

    I am in receipt of yours of the 25th inst., containing statement of account, and have to apologize for my neglect to remit the amount due you—$100. Unavoidable circumstances have prevented my doing so. You may expect an early remittance of the same.

                  Yours faithfully,
                          WM. SMITH.

Cobourg, Oct. 9, 1889.

MESSRS. JAMES MANN & CO.,
    Toronto, Ont.,

GENTLEMEN :—

    I exceedingly regret that you have once more to remind me of my account remaining unpaid, and that unexpected disappointments have caused the delay. I shall certainly remit the amount before the 15th inst.

                  Yours faithfully,
                          WM. SMITH.

Cobourg, Nov. 10, 1889.

MESSRS. JAMES MANN & CO.,
    Toronto, Ont.,

GENTLEMEN :—

    I cannot wonder at the tone of your last communication, as my conduct has been such as to justify the same. With this I remit the amount due you—$100, and much regret the long delay.

    Please acknowledge receipt by return of mail, and oblige,

                  Yours faithfully,
                          WM. SMITH.

NOTICE OF DRAFT, SENT TO DRAWEE.

Belleville, Sept. 14, 1889.

MR. WM. BROWN,
    Kingston, Ont.,

DEAR SIR:—

    We have this day drawn on you through the Bank of Montreal, at ten days' sight for the amount of your account, as per statement. Please honor, and oblige,

                  Yours respectfuly,
                          S. G. BEATTY & CO.
                                per J.

NOTE.—The last letter is written by a clerk named Jones, who places the last initial of his name under the name of the firm.

ORDER FOR GOODS.—No. 1.

Cobourg, Sept. 10, 1889.

Messrs. Geo. Ritchie & Co.,
Belleville, Ont.,
Gentlemen :—

Please forward by G.T.R., at your earliest convenience, the undermentioned articles, for which I shall remit on receipt of bill :—
1 doz. Men's Linen Collars, " Magdala," size 15¼ ins.
1 " White Neckties.
1 " pairs White Kid Gloves " Alexandres," sizes—6 & 6¼.
1 " " " " " " 7¼ & 8¼.

Yours truly,

J. WILSON.

ORDER FOR GOODS—No. 2.

Port Hope, Oct. 10, 1889.

Messrs. Alex. Urquhart & Co.,
Montreal, Que.,
Gentlemen :—

Please forward to our address per G.T.R. Freight Express :
Five (5) Half-chests Young Hyson, " Benefactor," No. 42.
Three (3) " Unc. Japan, " P. B. 132," or similar.
Two (2) Bags S. S. Almonds.
One (1) Case Eleme Figs (new).

You may draw upon us at sight for the amount of the invoice, less the usual cash discount of 3 per cent.

Yours faithfully,

PETER COOPER & CO.

REPLY TO ABOVE.

Montreal, Oct. 14, 1889.

Messrs. Peter Cooper & Co.,
Port Hope, Ont.,
Gentlemen :—

Enclosed find invoice and bill of lading of goods shipped you this day as per your valued order of the 10th. We have drawn upon you at sight, as requested, for the amount of the invoice, less 3 per cent. cash discount.

Trusting the goods will reach you in due season and prove satisfactory, and awaiting your further orders, we are,

Yours, &c.,

ALEX. URQUHART & CO.

ORDER FOR GOODS—No. 3.

Toronto, Ont., June 4, 1889.

Messrs. Jones & Brown,
  New York,

Gentlemen:—

You will please ship us at your earliest convenience, Three (3) Half-chests Imperial Tea (Andreas, 269), same as in last bill; also Two (2) Half-chests of best Imperial (Queen of the North, 179, or something better). Ship via Montreal, Que., and mark goods as follows:

A. B. CANN & Co., Toronto, Ont.

Care of J. McKay & Co., Montreal, Que.

Please write across Bill of Lading, " Insured in consignees' open policy in the Imperial Insurance Company," and send J. McKay & Co. the amount of Invoice, that they may enter it on our policy book. Your early shipment will much oblige,

Yours very truly,

A. B. CANN & CO.

RESPECTING GOODS NOT BEING SO GOOD A QUALITY AS ORDERED.

Belleville, Oct. 24, 1889.

Messrs. Jos. McKay & Bro.,
  Montreal,

Gentlemen:—

We are in receipt of the goods ordered by us through your Mr. Williams.

Upon examination of the Five pcs. Broadcloth (No. 4732), we find the quality much inferior to sample, and in our estimation worth 25 cents per yard less than Invoice price, Shall we retain them at our figures or return?

Yours faithfully,

J. A. MOORE & CO.

REPLY TO ABOVE—No. 1.

Montreal, Oct. 28, 1889.

Messrs. J. A. Moore & Co.,
  Belleville, Ont.,

Gentlemen:—

Your favor of the 24th is received. It surprises us to learn that the Five pieces of Broadcloth (No. 4732) did not prove satisfactory in regard to quality, as we supposed them to be fully equal to sample.

We are willing to accept your estimation of their value however, and have passed the difference to your credit, and herewith enclose credit note.

Yours, &c.,

JOS. McKAY & BRO.

ANOTHER.

MESSRS. J. A. MOORE & Co., Montreal, Oct. 31, 1889.
Belleville, Ont.,

GENTLEMEN :—
Your favor of the 24th is before us. We regret to learn that the 5 pcs. Broadcloth, No. 4732, are not satisfactory, as we believed them to be fully equal to the sample. The present value of the goods in this market will not allow us to make the reduction you speak of. Should you not wish to retain them at invoice price, please hold them subject to our order, and oblige,

Yours respectfully,
JOS. McKAY & BRO.

RESPECTING DIFFERENCE OF WEIGHT IN TEAS.

MESSRS. SMITH, BROWN & Co., Whitby, July 21, 1889.
Montreal,

GENTLEMEN :—
In checking over the Teas purchased from you on the 16th inst., by our Mr. Brown, we find the 5 Hlf. Chests Y. Hyson, " Benefactor 42," deficient in weight 11 lbs., as per statement below. We claim allowance for the same, and have passed the amount ($8.25) to your debit. Please send us a credit note in acknowledgment.

Yours respectfully,
JONES & BROWN.

ADVICE OF SHIPMENT.

MR. H. M. ALEXANDER, Belleville, Nov. 18, 1889.
Montreal,

DEAR SIR:—
We have this day shipped to your address, 100 Kegs Butter, as per invoice enclosed, to be sold on our account. The quality is choice, and we have no doubt it can be disposed of at good figures.

Yours truly,
ASHLEY & CO.

ANOTHER—ON JOINT ACCOUNT.

MESSRS. FLETCHER & Co., Brockville, Nov. 18, 1889.
Montreal,

GENTLEMEN :—
Your favor of the 10th inst. came duly to hand. We accept with pleasure your offer to join in shipment of Flour, and enclose invoice and shipping bill of 100 bbls. Corby's Extra Superfine, forwarded to your address this day per Str. St. Helen. We have drawn on you at 10 days' sight for one-half invoice, $250, as requested.

Trusting that the adventure will prove of mutual advantage, we are,

Yours very truly,
W. C. NUNN & CO.

ENCLOSING ACCOUNT SALES.

Montreal, Nov. 25, 1889.

MESSRS. ASHLEY & CO.,
Belleville, Ont.,

GENTLEMEN:—

Enclosed please find account sales of your shipment of the 18th inst., also sight draft on Messrs. Beatty & Wallbridge, of your town, for net proceeds, Twelve Hundred Dollars.

Trusting that the result will prove satisfactory, and soliciting further shipments, which at all times shall receive best attention, I am,

Yours very truly,

H. M. ALEXANDER.

ANOTHER.

Montreal, Nov. 28, 1889.

MESSRS. W. C. NUNN & CO.,
Brockville, Ont.,

GENTLEMEN:—

Enclosed we hand you account sales of your shipment of the 18th inst., on joint account. The net proceeds, $385, have been passed to your credit as averaging due Nov. 15th.

We feel satisfied the result will prove satisfactory, and shall be pleased to join you in any other shipments of a similar kind.

Yours very truly,

A. FLETCHER & CO.

LETTER OF RECOMMENDATION.

Belleville, May 2, 1889.

The bearer, Mr. K. MARKELL, has been in our employ for the past three years as salesman and bookkeeper, and we have ever found him diligent and faithful in the discharge of his duties, and one who always endeavored to make his employer's interest his own. He is correct and reliable in his accounts, and is well qualified for the position of bookkeeper or correspondent.

We cheerfully recommend him to any who may require the services of a trustworthy and competent person in the counting-house.

Very respectfully,

JAS. COOPER & CO.

ANSWER TO AN ADVERTISEMENT.

GENTLEMEN:— *Montreal, April 6, 1889.*

In answer to your advertisement in the "Daily Globe" of to-day, for an assistant in your counting-house, I respectfully offer my services. I am without experience in business, but I am willing to work, and have just graduated from Ontario Business College, where I have been thoroughly trained by practical accountants. If you give me a trial, I shall devote my sole attention to your interests, and endeavor to acquit myself to your entire satisfaction. For reference as to my character and ability, I would offer the names of

Mr. George Brown, 146 Jarvis Street, Toronto.
Messrs. J. E. Dwight & Co., of your city.
Should a personal interview be desired, please address as above.

Very respectfully,

ANSOM McKIM.

MESSRS. WRIGHT & CO.,
London, Ont.

APPLICATION FOR A SITUATION AS BOOKKEEPER.

Ottawa, March 1, 1889.
MESSRS. T. C. KERR & CO.,
Hamilton, Ont.

GENTLEMEN :—

Having learned from Mr. S. R. Hanson that there is a vacancy for a bookkeeper in your house, I respectfully offer my services. I have been engaged for two years in the wholesale house of A. R. McMaster & Bro., Toronto, as clerk and assistant bookkeeper, and have a good knowledge of accounts. My business acquaintance is extensive in the western part of the Province, and I could therefore influence considerable trade.

I enclose copy of testimonial from my late employers, and would also respectfully refer you, as to my character and ability, to

Messrs. Smith & Kealey, Wholesale Grocers, Toronto.
Messrs. Gordon, McKay & Co., Dry Goods, "
F. L. Biggar, Esq., City Solicitor, "

Any communication which you may be pleased to address as above will receive prompt attention.

Very respectfully yours,

J. H. BROWN.

RECOMMENDATION ENCLOSED IN THE ABOVE.

(Copy.)

Toronto, Jan. 25, 1889.

The bearer, Mr. J. H. Brown, has been in our employ as assistant bookkeeper for over two years, and we have always found him to be honest, steady and correct in his deportment, and well qualified for any position of trust in a counting house. We cheerfully recommend him as a competent bookkeeper, and one who will earnestly apply himself to promote the interests of his employers.

Respectfully,

A. R. McMASTER & BRO.

ORDER FOR A BOOK.

Hamilton, Jan. 4, 1889.

MESSRS. ROBINSON & JOHNSON,
    Belleville, Ont.,
GENTLEMEN :—

Enclosed find Two Dollars, for which please send me one copy of the "Canadian Accountant," and oblige. What trade discount will you allow on an order of say fifty copies?

                Yours truly,
                    HENRY M. CURTIS.

ORDER FOR GOODS.

Belleville, Nov. 18, 1889.

MESSRS. BRIGNALL & THOMPSON,
GENTLEMEN :—

Please deliver to Mrs. Jane Jones, goods such as she may select, to the amount of Five Dollars, and charge the same to my account.
                    JOHN JOHNSON.

ENCLOSING ADVERTISEMENT.

Picton, Nov. 5, 1889.

"INTELLIGENCER PRINTING CO."
    Belleville, Ont.,
GENTLEMEN :—

Please insert the enclosed advertisement, to occupy forty lines, for three months in weekly edition, commencing in next issue. We will remit the amount on receipt of bill.

                Yours, etc.,
                    JONES & BROWN.

ASKING REFERENCES.

Montreal, Oct. 20, 1889.

MESSRS. J. & W. CAMPION,
    Belleville, Ont.,
GENTLEMEN :—

Mr. Henry Smith is an applicant for a vacancy in our office, and refers to you (as late employers) respecting his character and ability. Will you please favor us with any information that you can give about him, and greatly oblige,

                Yours respectfully,
                  BROWN, WHITE & CO.

CIRCULAR LETTER—ENCLOSING PRICE LIST.

DEAR SIR :—

By this post we forward you our Illustrated Price List of portmanteaus, carpet bags, &c., and shall feel obliged by your perusing the same. On comparing it, you will find the prices very much lower than those previously sent. Any orders entrusted to our care shall meet with best attention, both as to quality and despatch. Trusting to have a continuance of your favors, we are,

                Your obedient servants,
                  J. LYONS & SON.

LETTER OF AUTHORITY TO SIGN BUSINESS PAPER.

SIR:—
                                                Belleville, June 1, 1889.

I have this day authorized, by Power of Attorney, my accountant, Mr. James B. West, to sign my name to Promissory Notes, Checks and Drafts; also, in like manner, to use my signature in accepting Orders, Drafts and Bills of Exchange; also, in endorsing Promissory Notes, Checks, Drafts and Bills of Exchange.

Very truly yours,

To THE   JOHN A. MILLER.
MANAGER OF THE BANK OF MONTREAL,
Belleville Ont.

The above authority must be strictly observed in form and extent, otherwise the validity of the act may be endangered.

ACKNOWLEDGING RECEIPT OF SHIPMENT.

MESSRS. JOHN JONES & Co.,   Hamilton, Nov. 1, 1889.
Napanee, Ont.

GENTLEMEN:—

We have this day received per G. T. R. freight, 500 bbls. Flour, in good order, consigned to us, to be sold for your acc't. and risk, as per your Invoice of the 13th ult.

As prices are rising, we think it advisable not to push it upon the market at present, but we shall endeavor to seize the most favorable opportunity for effecting sales to advantage.

Very respectfully,

Your ob't. servants,

THOMAS HARVEY & CO.

MESSRS. JONES & BROWN,   Toronto, Nov. 3, 1889.
Montreal, Que.,

GENTLEMEN:—

Your reply to our proposition to unite in a Company speculation of Mdse., to be sold at Kingston, came to hand on the 1st inst., and, in accordance therewith, we have this day shipped 2000 sacks Coffee, as per invoice enclosed, and consigned them to you to be sold for your and our acc't jointly. One-half of the invoice we have charged to your acc't, in accordance with the terms of our agreement—Amount, $4483.11.

A portion of the sugars consigned to us for joint acc't, of yourselves, Smith & Co., and ourselves, has been advantageously sold, and there is prospect of another sale soon.

Hoping this new adventure may prove to be for our mutual benefit,

We remain, Gentlemen,

Very respectfully yours,

DIAMOND & DAME.

PRACTICAL COMPUTATIONS.

It is not our purpose, in the small space we have to devote to the subject of Arithmetic, to present anything more than a few rules, on different subjects, that will be found practical by every business man.

By the tables, as given in most of our school arithmetics, numeration is carried only to six places, or quadrillions, running up by terms derived from the Latin numerals.

A series of units of that extent would be beyond the power of man to comprehend, or even imagine. Even millions convey a very indefinite idea, and when it rises to billions, the mind can no longer grasp the number; and though we may READ the expression, it is very much as we read sentences in an UNKNOWN LANGUAGE. We may perhaps assist the mind of the student by some little calculation. We often see MILLION spoken of in national expenditures; but the majority of the people do not even imagine the extent of the number. If a man were to count fifteen hundred dollars an hour, and work faithfully eight hours a day, it would take him nearly three months to count a MILLION dollars: and if the dollars were bank bills they would reach over one hundred and ten miles.

Dr. Thompson, Professor of Mathematics at Belfast, Ireland, very justly remarks: " Such is the facility with which large numbers are expressed, both by figures and language, that we generally have a very limited and inadequate conception of their real magnitude. The following consideration may perhaps assist in enlarging the ideas of the student on this subject:

" To count a MILLION, at one per second, would require between twenty-three and twenty-four days, of twelve hours each.

" The seconds in six thousand years are less than one-fifth of a TRILLION. A QUADRILLION of leaves of paper, each the two hundredth part of an inch in thickness, would form a pile the height of which would be three hundred and twenty times the distance of the moon from the earth. Let it also be remembered that a MILLION is equal to a thousand repeated a thousand times, and a BILLION equal to a million repeated a thousand times."

ADDITION. *

SKILL IN ADDITION is the foundation of readiness and accuracy in arithmetical computations; and this skill is to be acquired only by practice and careful attention to the principles and combinations of numbers. A clear head, quick perception, and proper cultivation, are the essential qualifications to insure success. With these, any one may place himself in the rank of experts.

Those who have already learned the rudiments of arithmetic will need, under this head, nothing more than a few practical hints. First, it is important to observe that every operation should be simplified as much as possible. The mind should be disencumbered of the clogs imposed by the school-boy rules, and trained to arrive at results in the most direct and rapid manner. Even the thought of WORDS ought to be banished.

To aid in acquiring facility and accuracy in adding short columns of figures the following is considered the best process:

```
346
534                Commence at the right hand column, and add thus:
657
436                10,23,33; carry the three tens to the next column and add:
258
632                11,19,26; carry the two hundreds to the next and add:
                   10,20,28;
2863
```

---

* See page 135 also.

In this way you name the sum of two or three figures at once with quite as much ease as you would add one figure at a time. Never permit yourself to add up a column in this manner : 2 and 8 are 10, and 6 are 16, and 7 are 23, and 4 are 27, and 6 are 33. It is just as easy, after a little practice, to name the result of two or three figures at once, and the addition can be performed at least in one-quarter of the time.

ADDITION OF LONG COLUMNS OF FIGURES.

In account books long columns of figures frequently occur, and in order to add them with certainty, and at the same time with ease and expedition, the following method is recommended :

EASY METHOD OF ADDITION.

Commence at the bottom and add as near 20 as possible, thus : $9+2+4+3=$ 7^7
18 ; place a small 8 to the right of the 3, as in example ; commence next at 6 and   4
add $6+4+8=18$; place a small 8 to the right of the 8 ; commence at $6+4+7=$ 6
17 ; place a small 7 to the right of the seven ; commence at 4 and add $4+9+3=16$; 3^8
place a small 6 to the right of the 3 ; commence at 6 and add $6+4+7=17$; place a   9
small 7 to the right of the 7 ; having now reached the top of the column, add the   4
small figures in the column thus : $7+6+7+8+8=36$; place the right hand figure of 7^7
36 under the original column as in example, and add the left hand figure to the   4
number of figures in the new column, thus the left hand figure in 36, plus 5, the number   6
of figures in the new column, stands $3+5=8$; prefix the 8 to the 6 under the original 8^8
column and you have 86, the sum of the column.   4

   6

If, upon arriving at the top of the columns, there should be one or more figures 3^8
whose sum does not equal 10, add them to the sum of the figures in the new column,   4
never placing an extra figure in the new column unless it be an excess of units above   2
ten.   9

REASONS FOR THE PRECEDING METHOD.

In the example it will be noticed that every time we placed a figure in the new column we discarded a ten, and when we set down 6 in the answer we discarded three tens; hence we add the three to 5, the number of tens discarded in forming the new columns, and we have 8 for the tens place in the answer ; on the same principle we might add between 20 and 30, always setting down a figure before adding as high as thirty ; then for every figure in the new column count 2 tens.

ADDITION OF TWO OR MORE COLUMNS.

For the addition of two or more columns, begin the same as in the preceding example, after obtaining the sum of the first column, place the right hand figure under the column and carry the remaining figures to the next column, and proceed as before, and so on with any number of columns ; thus, in the adjoining example, begin and add $2+3+5+8=$ $7{24}$
18 ; place a small 8 to the right of the 8 ; commence and add $6+7+2=15$, and so on, 26^5
until you reach the top of the column ; next add the figures in the new column together   37
with the 4 at the top, which was not included in the first addition (it being less than   43
ten), and you have 30, place the 0 under the original column ; add the 3 to the 64^7
number of figures in the new column, and you have 70 for the sum of the column ; $^5 25$
now add the 7 to the next column and proceed as before, placing the small integers to   78
the left ; after having completed the addition of the column, add together the figures   62

in the new column thus: 7 + 6 + 5 + 7 = 25; place the 5 under the tens column and add the 2 to the number of figures in the new column thus: 2 + 4 = 6; put this in the hundreds place and you have the addition completed.

This method of addition should be used only in adding very long columns of figures where the footings amount to two or three hundred and upwards, in which case it is very superior on account of its accuracy.

'47
36
28'
75
'73
42

660

MULTIPLICATION.

The process of multiplication may be greatly facilitated in many instances by a little observation and study; for instance where there are two numbers to be multiplied together, each of which consists of two figures, we have the following:

RULE.—*Set one of the numbers under the other in the form of a multiplication. Multiply the unit figure of the multiplicand by the unit figure of the multiplier. Set down the units of the result and reserve the tens to be added to the next product; next multiply the tens figure of the multiplicand by the units figure of the multiplier, and add to the product the figure reserved from the preceding multiplication; then multiply the units figure of the multiplicand by the tens figure of the multiplier; add these two results together, set down the units figure of their sum, reserving the remaining figure or figures to be added to the next product; now multiply the tens figures of the multiplicand by the tens figure of the multiplier, and to the product add the number held in reserve, place the result to the left of that part of the product previously found, and the multiplication will be completed.*

EXPLANATION.

Multiply the units of the multiplicand by the units of the multiplier, thus: $6 \times 3 = 18$; set down the eight as in example. Multiply the tens figure of the multiplicand by the units figure of the multiplier, thus: $5 \times 3 = 15$, to this add 1, the figure held in reserve from the first multiplication, which gives 16; next multiply the units figure of the multiplicand by the tens figure of the multiplier, thus: $6 \times 4 = 24$, to this add 16 and you have 40, place down the 0 and reserve the 4; next multiply the tens figures in each together, thus: $5 \times 4 = 20$, and to this product add the 4 held in reserve, which gives 24; set down the whole number and the product is complete.

56
43
——
2408

USEFUL CONTRACTIONS.

To multiply any number of two figures by 11.

RULE.—*Write the sum of the figures between them.*

1. Multiply 36 by 11. *Ans.* 396. Here 3 and 6 are 9, which write between 3 and 6.

N. B.—When the sum of the two figures is over 9, increase the left-hand figure by the one to carry. Multiply 68 by 11. *Ans.* 748.

To square any number of 9's instantaneously, without multiplying.

RULE.—*Write down as many 9's less one as there are 9's in the given number, an 8, as many 0's as 9's and a 1.*

What is the square of 9999? *Ans.* 99980001.

EXPLANATION.—We have four 9's in the given number, so we write down three 9's then an eight, three 0's, and a 1.

To square any number ending in 5.

RULE.—*Omit the 5 and multiply the number as it will then stand by the next higher number and annex 25 to the product.*

What is the square of 85? *Ans.* 7225.

EXPLANATION.—We simply say, 8 times 9 are 72, to which we annex 25.

GENERAL RULE.

To multiply any two numbers to the nearest unit.

1st. *Multiply the whole number in the multiplicand by the fraction in the multiplier to the nearest unit.*

2nd. *Multiply the whole number in the multiplier by the fraction in the multiplicand to the nearest unit.*

3rd. *Multiply the whole numbers together, and add the three products in your mind as you proceed.*

NOTE.—This rule is so simple and so true, according to all business usage, that every accountant should make himself perfectly familiar with its application. There being no such thing as a fraction to add in, there is scarcely any liability to error or mistake. By no other arithmetical process can the result be obtained by so few figures.

EXAMPLE FOR MENTAL OPERATION.

Multiply $11\frac{1}{3}$ by $8\frac{1}{4}$ by business method.

Here $\frac{1}{4}$ of 11 to the nearest unit is 3, and $\frac{1}{3}$ of 8 to the nearest unit is 3, $\qquad$ $11\frac{1}{3}$
making 6, so we simply say, 8 times 11 are 88 and 6 are 94. $\qquad$ $8\frac{1}{4}$

Answer, $\qquad$ 94

REASON.—$\frac{1}{4}$ of 11 is nearer 3 than 2, and $\frac{1}{3}$ of 8 is nearer 3 than 2. Make the nearest whole number the quotient.

A VALUABLE HINT TO MERCHANTS AND ALL RETAIL DEALERS IN FOREIGN AND DOMESTIC DRY GOODS.

Retail merchants, in buying goods by wholesale, buy a great many articles by the dozen, such as boots and shoes, hats, caps, &c. Now the merchant in buying, for instance, a dozen hats knows exactly what one of those hats will retail for in the market where he deals; and, unless he is quick at calculation, it will often take him some time to determine whether he can afford to purchase the dozen hats, and make a living profit in selling them by the single hat; and in buying his goods by auction, as the merchant often does, he has not time to make the calculation before the goods are cried off. He therefore loses the chance of making good bargains by being afraid to bid at random, or, if he bids, and the goods are cried off, he may have made a poor bargain by bidding thus at a venture. It then becomes a useful and practical problem to determine INSTANTLY what per cent. he would gain if he retailed the hats at a certain price.

RAPID PROCESS OF MARKING GOODS.

To tell what an article should retail for to make a profit of 20 per cent. is done by removing the decimal point one place to the left.

For instance, if hats cost $19.40 per dozen, remove the decimal point one place to the left, making $1.94, what they should be sold for apiece to gain 20 per cent. on the cost.

If they cost $21 per dozen, they should be sold for $2.10 each, etc. We take 20 per cent. for the following reasons, viz.: because we can determine instantly, by simply removing the decimal point, without changing a figure ; and, if the goods would not bring at least 20 per cent. profit in the home market, the merchant could not afford to purchase, and would look for goods at lower figures.

Now, as the removing the decimal point one place to the left, on the cost of a dozen articles gives the selling price of a single one, with 20 per cent. added to the cost, and, as the cost of any article is 100 per cent., it is obvious that the selling price would be 20 per cent. more, or 120 per cent.; hence, to find 50 per cent. profit, which would make the selling price 150 per cent.; we would first find 20 per cent., then add 30 per cent., by increasing it one-fourth itself; to make 40 per cent., add 20 per cent. by increasing it one-sixth itself; for 35 per cent. increase it one-eighth itself, etc. Hence to mark an article at any per cent. profit, we have the following ;

GENERAL RULE.

First find 20 per cent. profit by removing the decimal point one place to the left on the price the articles cost a dozen; then, as 20 per cent. profit is 120 per cent., add to or subtract from this amount the fractional part that the required per cent. added to 100 is more or less than 120.

TABLE FOR MARKING ARTICLES BOUGHT BY THE DOZEN.

N. B.—Most of these are used in business.

To make 20 per cent. remove the point one place to the left.
" 80 " " " and add one-half itself.
" 60 " " " " one-third "
" 50 " " " " one-fourth itself.
" 44 " " " " one-fifth "
" 40 " " " " one-sixth "
" 35 " " " " one-eighth "

GENERAL RULES FOR CANCELLATION.

RULE 1st. *Draw a prependicular line; observe this line represents the sign of equality. On the right-hand side of this line place dividends only ; on the left-hand side place divisors only.*

2nd. *Notice whether there are ciphers both on right and left of the line; if so, erase an equal number from each side.*

3rd. *Notice whether the same number stands both on the right and left of the line; if so, erase them both.*

4th. *Notice again if any number on either side of the line will divide any number on the opposite side without a remainder ; if so, divide and erase the two numbers, retaining the quotient on the side of the larger number.*

5th. *See if any two numbers, one on each side, can be divided by any assumed number without a remainder; if so, divide them by that number, and retain only their quotients. Proceed in the same manner as far as practicable.*

6th. *Multiply all the numbers remaining on the right-hand side of the line for a dividend, and those remaining on the left for a divisor.*

7th. *Divide, and the quotient will be the answer.*

SIMPLE INTEREST BY CANCELLATION.

RULE.—*Place the principal, time, and rate per cent. on the right-hand side of the line. If the time consist of years and months, reduce them to months, and place 12 (the number of months in a year) on the left-hand side of the line. Should the time consist of months and days, reduce them to days, or decimal parts of a month. If reduced to days, place 36 on the left. If to decimal parts of a month, place 12, as before.*

Point off two decimal places when the time is in months, and three decimal places when the time is in days.

EXAMPLE 1.—Find the interest on $850, for 6 months, at 7 per cent.; and for 15 months at 8 per cent.

$29.75 *Ans.* $85·00 *Ans.*

Cancel and multiply and you will obtain the answer.

EXAMPLE 2.—Find the interest on $175, for 48 days, at 7 per cent.; and on $364.50 for 19 days, at 6 per cent.

$1.63⅓ *Ans.* $1.15425 *Ans.*

EXAMPLE 3.—Find the interest on $436, for 9 months and 18 days, at 7 per cent.; and $290, for 7 months and 14 days, at 6 per cent.

$24.416 *Ans.* $10.826 *Ans.*

NOTE.—If the principal contains cents, point off four decimal places when the time is in months, and five decimal places when the time is in days.

METHOD OF COMPUTING INTEREST ON ALL NOTES THAT BEAR $12 PER ANNUM, OR ANY ALIQUOT PART OR MULTIPLE OF $12.

If a note bears $12 per annum, it will certainly bear $1 per month; hence the time in months would be the interest in $; and the decimal parts of a month would be the interest in decimal parts of a $; therefore when the note bears $12 per annum we have the following:

RULE. *Reduce the years to months, add in the given months, and place one-third of the days to the right of this number, and remove the decimal point one place to the left.* *

EXAMPLE 1.—Required the interest on $200 for three years, 7 months and 12 days, at 6 per cent.

```
   200
     6
  ─────
$12.00 = int. for yr.
```

⅓ of 12 days = 4

Yr. Mo. Ds.
3   7 12 = 43. 4 mo.
Hence 43.40 *Ans.*

---

* Remember the answer obtained by this rule is in dollars and decimals of a dollar. In the first example the years reduced to months, and one-third the number of days placed to the right give 43.4, which, reduced to dollars, is $43.40.

We see by inspection that this note bears $12 interest a year. If this note bore $6 a year instead of $12 we would take one-half of the above interest; if it bore $18, instead of $12, we would add one-half; if it bore $24, instead of $12, we would multiply by 2, &c.

EXAMPLE 2.—Required the interest on $150 for two years, 5 months and 13 days, at 8 per cent.

| 150 | ⅓ of 13 days = 4⅓ |
8	
$12.00 = int. for 1 yr.	Yr. Mo. Ds.
	2 5 13 = 29.4⅓ mo.
	Hence 29.433⅓ Ans.

We see by inspection that this note bears $12 interest a year; hence the time reduced to months, with one-third of the days placed to the right, gives the interest at once.

EXAMPLE 3.—Required the interest on $160 for 11 years 11 months and 11 days, at 7½ per cent.

| 160 | ⅓ of 11 days = 3⅔ |
7½	
$12.0 = int. for one year.	Yr. Mo. Ds.
	11 11 11 = 143.3⅔ mo.
	Hence $143.36⅔ Ans.

When the interest is more or less than $12 a year.

RULE. *First Find the interest for the given time on the base of $12 interest a year; then if the interest on the note is only $6 a year, divide by two; if $24 a year, multiply by two; if $18 a year, add on one-half, etc.*

EXAMPLE.—What is the interest on $300 for 4 years, 7 months and 18 days, at 6 per cent.

| | ⅓ of 18 days = 6. |
| 300 | 4yr. 7mo. 18ds. = 55.6 mo. |
6	
$18.00 = int. for 1 year.	2)55.6, int. at $12 a year.
$18 = 1½ times $12.	27.8
	$83.4 Ans.

If the interest were $12 a year, $55.60 would be the answer; because 55.6 is the time reduced to months; but it bears $18 a year, 1½ times 55.6 gives the interest at once.

EXAMPLE 2.—Required the interest of $150 for 3 years, 9 months and 27 days, at 4 per cent.

| | ⅓ of 27 days = 9. |
| 150 | 3yr. 9mo. 27ds. = 45.9 mo. |
4	2)45.9, int. at $12 a year.
$6.00 = int. for 1 year.	$22.95 Ans.
$6 = ½ times 12.	

If the interest had been $12 a year, $45.90 would have been the answer; because 45.9 is the time reduced to months; but it bears $6 a year, or ½ of 12; hence ½ of 45.9 gives the interest at once.

BUSINESS METHOD OF COMPUTING INTEREST AT 6 PER CENT. FOR ANY NUMBER OF DAYS.

RULE.—*Draw a perpendicular line, cutting off the two right hand figures of the $, and you have the interest of the sum for 60 days at 6 per cent.*

NOTE.—The figures on the left of the line are $' and those on the right are decimals of $.

EXAMPLE 1.—What is the interest on $520, for 60 days, at 6 per cent?

$520 = the principal.
$5 | 20cts.   Interest for 60 days.

NOTE.—When the time is more or less than 60 days, first get the interest for 60 days, and from that to the time required.

EXAMPLE 2.—What is the interest of $424, for 15 days, at 6 per cent?

         Days. Days.
         15 = ¼ of 60

$424 = principal.
4)4 | 24cts. = interest for 60 days.

1.06 cts. = interest for 15 days.

EXAMPLE 3.—What is the interest of $114.40 for 90 days, at 6 per cent?

         Days. Days. Days.
         90 = 60 + 30

$114.40 = principal.
2)1 | 1440 =interest for 60 days.
  | 5720 = interest for 30 days.

ANS. $1 | 716 = interest for 90 days.

EXAMPLE 4.—What is the interest of $824, for 75 days, at 6 per cent?

         Days. Days. Days.
         75 = 60 + 15.

$824 = principal
4)8 | 24cts. = interest for 60 days.
 2 | 06cts. = interest for 15 days.

ANS. $10.30cts. = interest for 75 days.

REMARKS.—This system of computing interest is very easy and simple, especially when the days are aliquot parts of 60, and one simple division will suffice. It is used extensively by a large majority of our most prominent business men; and taught by Commercial Colleges as the shortest system of computing interest.

METHOD OF CALCULATING AT DIFFERENT RATES PER CENT.

First Find the interest at 6 per cent., and from that any other rate per cent.

The following table shows the different rates, with the time that a given number of $ will amount to the same number of cents when placed at interest.

RULE.—*Draw a perpendicular line, cutting off two right hand figures of $, and you have the interest at the following rates per cent.*

NOTE.—This is the method in common use for computing interest for days; but since it considers the year as containing only 360 days instead of 365, the result is too large by $\frac{1}{365}$ or $\frac{1}{73}$ of itself. Hence, when perfect accuracy is desired, the interest of the days when obtained by the rule must be diminished by $\frac{1}{73}$ part of itself.

Interest at 4 per cent. for 90 days.
Interest at 5 per cent. for 72 days.
Interest at 6 per cent. for 60 days.
Interest at 7 per cent. for 52 days.
Interest at 8 per cent. for 45 days.
Interest at 9 per cent. for 40 days.
Interest at 10 per cent. for 36 days.

Interest at 12 per cent. for 30 days.
Interest at 7-30 per cent. for 50 days.
Interest at 5-20 per cent. for 70 days.
Interest at 10-40 per cent. for 35 days.
Interest at 7½ per cent. for 48 days.
Interest at 4½ per cent. for 80 days.

NOTE.—The figures on the left of the perpendicular line are dollars; and on the right decimals of $1. If the $ are less than 10, prefix a 0.

EXAMPLE 1.—What is the interest of $180, for 15 days, at 4 per cent?
                                    Days.   Days.
                                    15 = 1·6 of 90.
$180 = principal.
6)1 | 80 cts.—int. for 90 days.
    | 30 cts.—int. for 15 days.

EXAMPLE 2.—What is the interest of $182, for 13 days, at 7 per cent.?
                                    Days.   Days.
                                    13 = ¼ of 52.
$182. = principal
4)1 | 82 cts.—int. for 52 days.
    | 45½ cts.—int. for 13 days.

EXAMPLE 3.—What is the interest of $580, for 9 days, at 8 per cent.
                                    Days.   Days.
                                    9 = 1-5 of 45.
$580 = principal.
5)5 | 80 cts.—int. for 45 days.
$1 | 16 cts.—int. for 9 days.

EXAMPLE 4.—What is the interest of $462, for 64 days, at 7⅓ per cent.?
                                Days. Days. Days.
                                64 = 48 + 16.
$462 = principal.
3)4 | 62 cts.—int. for 48 days.
  1 | 54 cts.—int. for 16 days.

$6 | 16 cts.—int. for 64 days.

REMARK.—We have now illustrated several examples by the different rates per cent; if the student will study carefully the solution to the above examples, he will, in a short time, be very rapid in this mode of computing interest.

We will here illustrate an example to show the difference between this and the cancelling system: Required the interest of $420, for 49 days, at 6 per cent.

Business method.   *Cancelling method.*
2)4 | 20 cts.—int. for 60 days.   420
                                             36   6
2)2 | 10 cts.—int. for 30 days.   49
5)1 | 05 cts.—int. for 15 days.
  3 | 21 cts.—int. for 3 days.
    | 7 cts.—int. for 1 day.

$3 | 43 cts.—int. for 49 days. $3.430 Ans.

The cancelling method is much more brief; we simply cancel 6 in 36, and the quotient 6 into 420; there is no divisor left; hence 70 x 49 gives the interest at once.

If the time had been 15 or 20 days, the other method would have been equally as short, because 15 and 20 are aliquot parts of 60. The superiority the cancelling system has over all others is this: it takes advantage of the principal as well as the time.

1. What is the interest of $46.28, for 2 years, 3 months and 23 days, at 5 per cent.? Ans. $5.35.
2. What is the interest of $54.81, for 1 year, 6 months, at 5 per cent.? Ans. $4·11.
3. What is the interest of $500, for 9 months and 9 days, at 8 per cent.? Ans. $31.
4. What is the interest of $62.12, for 1 month and 20 days, at 4 per cent.? Ans. $.345.
5. What is the interest of $85, for 10 months and 15 days, at 12½ pc. cent.? Ans. $9.296
6. What is the interest of $327.825, at 8 per cent., for one year? Ans. $26.226.
7. What is the interest of $325, for 3 years, at 6 per cent.? Ans. $58.50.
8. What is the interest of $187.25, for one year and 4 months, at 6 per cent.? Ans. $14.98.
9. What is the interest of $694.84, for 9 months, at 10 per cent.? Ans. $52.113.

10. What is the interest of $57.78, for 1 year, 4 months and 17 days, at 4 per cent. ? ANS. $3.19.

11. What is the amount of $298.59, from May 19th, 1876, till August 11th, 1877, at 8 per cent. ? *

12. What is the amount of $196, from June 14th, 1876, till April 29th, 1877, at 9 per cent. ?

PROFIT AND LOSS.

Under this head we shall confine ourselves to ascertaining the gain or loss on purchasing and selling merchandise, the rules for which may be found in any ordinary arithmetic.

EXAMPLE 1.—Purchased merchandise for $15,496.80. Sales effected in eighty-four days, $13,654.20. On hand $4,295.40. Required the total gain, the average daily sales the average daily profits, and the average gain per cent.

ANS. *Total gain* $2452.80
Average daily sales,   162.55
Average daily profits,   29.20
Average gain per cent.,   .22, *nearly.*

EXAMPLE 2.—Purchased merchandise for $12,684. Sales effected in ninety days, $10,480. On hand, $3,964. Required the total gain, average daily sales, average daily profits, and average gain per cent.

ANS. *Total gain,* $1,760. *Average daily sales,* $116.44+. *Average daily profits,* $19.55+. *Average gain per cent.* $20.18+.

EXAMPLE 3.—Purchases, $6,895. Sales in thirty-six days, $4,011. On hand, $2,223. Required total gain or loss, daily sales, daily gain or loss, and the gain or loss per cent.

ANS. *Total loss,* $661. *Daily sales,* $111.416 +. *Daily loss,* $18.36 +. *Loss per cent.,* $14.12 +.

Ex. 4.—Bought molasses at 25 cents per gallon, and sold it for 23¾ cents. Required the loss per cent.   ANS. 5.

Ex. 5.—Sold merchandise for 20 per cent. advance on the first cost, and deducted 5 per cent. from the invoice for immediate payment. Required the net gain per cent.
     ANS. 14.

Ex. 6.—Sold merchandise at 25 per cent. advance, and from the invoice deducted 12½ per cent. Required the net gain per cent.   ANS. 9.375.

Ex. 7.—Sold merchandise at an advance of 50 per cent. on first cost; my customer having failed in business, I lost 40 per cent. from the selling price. Required the net gain or loss per cent.   ANS. 10 *per cent. loss.*

Ex. 8.—A merchant sold his goods to retail customers at 25 per cent. advance. He gave up the retail business, and marked his goods to sell at wholesale, 20 per cent. from the retail price. Required his gain or loss per cent.
     ANS. *No gain or loss.*

---

* The amount is the principal and interest added together.

NOTE.—The preceding mode of computing interest is derived and deduced from the cancelling system, as the ingenious student will readily see. It is a short and easy way of finding interest for days, when the days are even or aliquot parts; but when they are not, multiples and three or four divisions are necessary, the cancelling system is much more simple and easy.

PARTIAL PAYMENTS.

The method of computing interest when partial payments have been made is a subject that has given rise to much litigation. When the time of the note or obligation is more than one year the following rule has been sanctioned by a number of decisions both in law and equity:

RULE.—I. *Compute the interest on the principal to the time of the first payment, and if this payment exceed the interest then due, add the interest to the principal, and from the sum subtract the payment; the remainder will form a new principal, with which proceed as before.*

II. *But if the payment be less than the interest, compute the interest on the principal to the time when the sum of the payments shall first equal or exceed the interest due; add the interest to the principal, and from the amount subtract the sum of the payments, and treat the remainder as a new principal.*

NOTE.—This rule is based upon the principle that in all cases the payment should be applied first to interest due, then to the principal, and that the principal remains unchanged until the sum paid exceeds the accrued interest, the principal alone drawing interest.

When the computed interest exceeds the payment such interest may be added to the interest for the next interval of time, or, if estimated mentally to be less, the amounts may be computed at once up to the time when the sum paid is not less than the accrued interest.

DIFFERENCE OF TIME BETWEEN DATES.

The majority of people, in computing the difference of time between dates, count the exact number of days. Besides this plan, the two following rules are in use:

RULE I.—*By compound subtraction, reckoning 30 days for a month.*

RULE II.—*By finding the number of entire calendar months from the first date, and counting the actual number of days left.*

EXAMPLES.

	Year.	No. of months.	Day.
From August 20th, 1873, to March 10th, 1876 would be	1876 1873	3 8	10 20
according to the 1st Rule		2y 6mo	20d.
" " 2nd Rule		2y 6mo	18d.

EXAMPLES.

$4000   Toronto, June 1, 1872.

I. Two years after date I promise to pay William Smith, or order, Four Thousand Dollars. for value received, with interest at seven per cent.

RICHARD HAYWELL.

On this note were endorsed the following payments:
September 15, 1872, received ($450) Four Hundred and Fifty Dollars.
December 15, 1872, received ($50) Fifty Dollars.
March 1, 1873, received ($500) Five Hundred Dollars.
January 1, 1874, received ($1000) One Thousand Dollars.
What remained due June 4, 1874?

NOTE.—By "Calendar month" is meant the time from any day in one month to the corresponding day of the next month. If the days of the first month are a higher number than the greatest number of days in the last month, the calendar month ends with the last day. Thus, from Jan. 31st to February 28th is a calendar month

OPERATION.

Principal on interest from June 1, 1872...$4000 00
Interest to September 15, 1872, 3 mos. 14d 80 89

Amount........................... 4080 89
Less first payment............................ 450 00

Remainder for a new principal............... 3630 89
The interest from September 15 to December 15, 1872, is $63.44, which exceeds the payment.
Interest from September 15, 1872, to March 1, 1873, 5 mos. 16 d................. 117 20

Amount 3748 09
Less the sum of the second and third payments....................................... 550 00

Remainder for a new principal............... 3198 09
Interest from March 1, 1873, to January 1, 1874.................................. 186 47

Amount........... .... 3384 56
Less payment January 1, 1874............. 1000 00

Remainder for a new principal............... 2384 56
Interest from January 1 to June 4, 1874... 70 94

Balance due June 4, 1874 .... 2455 50
$1500.   *Hamilton, January* 1, 1877.
2.—One year after date, we promise to pay S. White, or order, Fifteen Hundred Dollars, with interest, value received.

GEORGE BROWN & CO.

The following payments were made on this note:—March 16, 1877, $100 ; June 13, 1877, $400; September 1, 1877, $200.
What was due January 1, 1878, interest at 6 per cent.? Ans. $870.13+.

$3500.   *Belleville, March* 15, 1876.

3. For value received, we jointly and severally promise to pay Wm. Smith, or order, Three Thousand Five Hundred Dollars, with interest.

JAMES JONES.
ROBT. BROWN.

Indorsed as follows:—June 1, 1876, received $800 ; September 1, 1876, $100; Jan. 1, 1877, $1560 ; March 1, 1877, $300.
What was due May 16, 1877, interest at 6 per cent. ? Ans. $902.753 ×.

AVERAGE OF ACCOUNTS.

AVERAGE OF ACCOUNTS OR EQUATION OF ACCOUNTS

is the process of finding the mean or average time for the payment, in one amount, of several debts due at different dates, without allowing interest to either debtor or creditor.

The time when the amount falls due by average is called the EQUATED TIME.

The different methods of averaging accounts are based upon the principle that the interest or use of any sum of money PAID BEFORE IT IS DUE, is equivalent to the interest or use of an equal sum RETAINED FOR THE SAME LENGTH OF TIME AFTER IT BECOMES DUE.

The process, therefore, consists merely in finding a point of time when the INTEREST on sums then overdue equals the DISCOUNT on the sums not due, reckoning what is here termed discount as simple interest, like bank discount.

ILLUSTRATIONS.—Suppose A owes B $100 due in one year, and $100 due in two years, without interest, the average maturity of both sums is eighteen months from the date of the first; for A will then have had the use of $100 for six months after it became due, which is equivalent to the use of $100 paid six months before it is due.

Simple average is the process of averaging an account containing debit or credit items only.

EXAMPLE.—A owes B, January 1, 1877, $1800; of which $700 is payable in six months, $300 in four months, and $800 in eighteen months; when can the whole be paid without gain or loss of interest to either party?

ANALYSIS.—It is evident that, if nothing should be paid until the maturity of the debt last due, A would owe B $1800, besides the interest of $700 for 12 months, which, at 6 per cent., is $42, and the interest of $300 for 14 months, which is $21. But the question is, when may the whole be paid without interest? Clearly, it should be paid as long prior to the expiration of 18 months as it will take $1800 to gain the interest then due, namely $42 + $21=$63. The interest of $1800, for one month, at 6 per cent., is $9; and 63 ÷ 9=7. Therefore, it will take $1800, 7 months to gain $63 interest, and the equated time is 7 months prior to July 1, 1878, or 11 (18—7) months from Jan. 1, 1877, which is Dec. 1, 1877.

PRACTICAL SOLUTION.

Product Method.

```
700 x  6 =  4200
300 x  4 =  1200
800 x 18 = 14400
────             
1800      )19800(11
           1800
           ────
            1800
            1800
```

Interest Method.

```
Int. of $700 for 6 mos.=$21.00
  "     300  "  4  "  =  6.00
  "     800  " 18  "  = 82.00
                      ──────
                   2)18.00    $99.00
                      ────
                       9)99(11
                         99
                         ──
```

EXPLANATIONS.

The USE of $700 for 6 months=the use of $1 for 4200 months.
 "   " $300 for 4 months=the use of $1 for 1200 months.
 "   " $800 for 18 months=the use of $1 for 14400 months.

 "   " $1800 for 11 months=the use of $1 for 19800 months.

The use of $1 for 19800 months is equal to the use of $1800 for as many months as 1800 is contained times in 19800=11.

By the INTEREST METHOD, the total interest of the different sums for their respective terms of credit is $99, and the interest of $1800 for one month is $9.

Therefore it will take $1800 as many months to gain $99 as 9 is contained times in 99=11. Hence, the equated time is 11 months from Jan. 1, 1877, or Dec. 1, 1877.

EXAMPLES FOR PRACTICE.

1.—Sold goods to A. as follows.—

1877, June 10, a bill at 60 days				$2500 00
Aug. 18, " " 30 "				475 32
Sept. 20, " " 90 "				500 00
Oct. 1, " " 60 "				219 75
Nov. 1, " " 30 "				150 25
				$3845 32

When will the above bill become due by average?
ANS. Sept. 11.

2.—Bought of G. C. Holton & Co., mdse. as follows :—

1877, Jan. 1, mdse., at 30 days,				$ 192 30
Feb. 13, " " 60 "				137 50
Mar. 15, " " 90 "				742 25
Apr. 11, " " 30 "				350 00
				$1422 05

When will this account average due?
ANS. May 13.

3.—Sold Smith & Co.,

1877, July 25, mdse., at 3 mos.,				$1350 00
Aug. 20, " " 2 "				463 75
Sept. 30, " " 3 "				189 25
Oct. 26, " " 2 "				300 00
				$2303 00

The purchasers propose to settle the account October 30, 1877, by giving a promissory note for the entire amount; what time should be expressed in the note to make it fall due at the average maturity of the account?

ANS. 7 days.

A merchant sold to one of his customers several bills of goods, as follows :

May 9, 1876, a bill of $940 on 4 months' credit,
June 6, " " 500 on 3 " "
July, 8, " " 945 on 5 " "
Aug. 30, " " 830 on 5 " "
Sept. 30, " " 1000 on 6 " "

What is the equated time of payment, and how much would balance the account, Jan. 1, 1877, allowing interest at 6 per cent.?

DOUBLE EQUATION OR AVERAGING OF ACCOUNTS.

There are a number of different rules for working double equation. We select the following, on account of its simplicity:

RULE.—*First find the equated time for each side of the account separately. Then multiply the amount due on that side of the account which falls due* FIRST, *by the number of days between the dates of the equated time, and divide the product by the balance of the*

U

account. The quotient will be the number of *days to be counted* FORWARD *from the* LATER DATE *when the* SMALLER *side of the account falls due* FIRST ; *and* BACKWARD *when the larger side falls due* FIRST.

EXAMPLE.

Dr.   A. IN ACCOUNT WITH B.   *Cr.*

1877				1877			
Jan.	1	To Mdse.,	500	Feb.	10	By Cash,	1000
Feb.	4	" "	600	March	4	" "	600
March	10	" "	800				

OPERATION.

DAYS.   DAYS.

Jan. 1, 500 × 00
Feb. 4, 600 × 34   20400   Feb. 10, 1000 × 00
Mar. 10, 800 × 68   54400   Mar. 4, 600 × 22 = 13200

       1900)   74800(39   1600)   13200(8¼
                  5700   12800

                  17800   400
                  17100

                    700
39 days from Jan. 1 = Feb. 9.   8 days from Feb. 10 = Feb. 18.
Due Feb. 9................ $1900   Due Feb. 18............. ....$1600
1900 side which falls due first.
9 difference between dates,

17100 ÷ 300 balance of account = 57, the number of days to count backward from Feb. 19 the latter date.   *Ans.* Dec. 24.

EXAMPLE 2,—Find the equated time for the payment of the balance of the following account:—

                                                                        Montreal, Nov. 5, 1877.
MR. JOHN SMITH,
                                                            In account with S. S. EDSALL.
Dr.   *Cr.*

1877						1877				
Aug.	18	To Mdse., 90 days,	$2500	00		Sept.	20	By Cash,	$1000	00
Sept.	20	" " 60 "	500	00		Oct.	10	" "	500	00
Oct.	1	" " 30 "	475	00		Nov.	5	" "	275	00
Nov.	5	" " 30 "	335	00				Balance,	2035	00
			$3810	00					$3810	00

First equate the debit and credit side of the account separately, by simple average. The result of the work is as follows :—

                                       Dr.   *Cr.*
               Due Nov. 16, $3810 || Due Oct. 3, $1775.

Then apply the rule as in the preceding example, and you will obtain the *Ans.* December 24.

3. When is the balance of the following accounts due per average?

---

* Fractional parts of a day not counted, unless the fraction amounts to half day or upwards ; it then counts another day.

Dr.   A, B. PERRY.   Cr.

1887						1877				
Sept.	12	To Mdse., at 30 days,		$927	30	Oct.	10	By Cash,	$500	00
Oct.	15	" " " 30 "		342	75	Nov.	20	" "	300	00
Nov.	18	" " " 60 "		212	13	"	30	" "	250	00
Dec.	1	" " " 30 "		175	50					

ANS. Nov. 19, 1877.

4. Average the following account :—

Dr.   GEO. BROWN *in account with* G. C. HOLTON & Co.   Cr.

1877						1877				
Jan.	1	To Mdse., 30 days,		$586	40	Feb.	1	By Cash,	$460	00
Feb.	15	" " 30 "		322	10	March	15	" "	280	00
March	3	" " 30 "		863	14	April	1	" Draft at 10 days,	400	00

ANS. March 14, 1877.

5. Find the equated time for the settlement of the following account :—

Dr.   JAMES HUGHES & CO.   Cr

1877						1877				
March	1	To Balance,		$325	00	March	16	By Cash,	$250	00
April	16	" Mdse., at 2 mos.,		623	47	May	20	" "	300	00
May	11	" " " 2 "		1722	30	July	30	" Note, 30 days,	1000	00
June	16	" " " 30 days,		975	12	Aug.	31	" Cash,	560	00
July	30	" " " 60 "		146	35					
Aug.	17	" " " 30 "		1650	25					

ANS. July 22, 1877.

6. When is the following account due per average ?

Dr.   H. C. WAMBERS.   Cr

1877						1877				
Oct.	13	To Mdse., at 3 mos.,		$275	16	Dec.	1	By Cash,	$150	00
Nov.	16	" " " 4 "		186	37	"	30	" "	300	00
Dec.	1	" " " 2 "		917	16	1878				
"	5	" " " 3 "		875	00	Feb.	18	" "	560	00
1878						March	1	" "	262	00
Jan.	10	" " " 2 "		327	16					
Feb.	16	" " " 3 "		186	70					

ANS. March 17, 1878.

The following account, illustrated by the interest method, if worked out by the preceding rule, will show the distinction between the two systems:

7. When will the balance of the following account become due ?

S. G. BEATTY *in account with* W. B. ROBINSON.

Dr.

Jan. 13 To Mdse., at 30 days, ... $300
Feb. 4 " Sundries   450
Apr. 15 " Real Estate   720
                                                                    $1470
                                                                   Cr.

Feb. 15 By Sundries, ...   750

```
May 20  By Cash,    ....  ....  ....        $300
June 10  "  Mdse.,  ....  ....  ....         120      1170
```

```
                Balance due,                          300
Int. on $300, from Feb. 12th to June 10th....   5.90
 "     450,   "      "   4th  "   "    "  ....  9.45
 "     720,   "    Apr. 15th "   "    "   ....  6.72

       Total debit interest to June 10th,        $22.07
Int. on $750, from Feb. 15th to June 10th....   14.38
 "      300,   "    May 20th  "   "    "  ....   1.05

       Total credit interest to June 10th,       $15.43
```

The difference between the debit and credit interest, $22.07—$15.43=$6.64, the balance of interest in favor of the debit side of the account.

Interest on the balance of the account for one day is 5 cents $6.64 ÷ 05= 133, the number of days to count backward from June 10th, giving January 27th as an equated date.

Dr.   W. A. FOSTER & Co., *in acct. with* A. M. SPAFFORD & Co.   *Cr.*

1877				Time of Credit	1877			
April	3	To Mdse.,	$220	3 months,	July	1	By Cash,	$200
May	1	" "	125	5 "	Oct.	3	" "	150
"	15	" "	200	6 "	Dec.	20	" "	300
June	24	" "	140	8 "				
July	1	" "	190	9 "				

By equating each side, the account will stand as follows:

Dr,   *Cr.*
Due, Nov. 21, 1877, $875.   Due, Oct. 10, 1877, $650.

It will be found, by the rule, that the balance of the account, thus equated, becomes due March 22, 1878. ANS.

       S. G. BATEMAN,
Dr.   In account with HENRY SMITH & Co.   *Cr.*

1877				Time of Cr.	When due.	1877			
Jan.	1	To Mdse.,	$1000	2 months,	March	1	April	1	By Cash,	$1000
Feb.	8	"	1500	3 "	May	8	May	1	"	1000
March	12	"	2000	3 "	June	12	June	1	"	1000
April	1	"	1000	4 "	Aug.	1	Aug.	1	"	1000
May	20	"	500	6 "	Nov.	20				

ANS. July 8.

AVERAGE OF ACCOUNT OF SALES.

In averaging an Account of Sales, the sales constitute the credits; the charges the debits, and the net proceeds the balance.

When sales are made on time, the consignee is entitled by custom to the same term of credit for the payment of the proceeds.

Expenses incurred in receiving the goods, and all charges paid in cash, are considered due the consignee when paid. Commissions and after-charges are, upon strict principle, due at the average maturity of the sales; yet this rule is not always observed.

The object of averaging an account of sales is to ascertain when the net proceeds become due. Except as regards the adjustment of the date of the commission and charges made on closing a consignment, the process is precisely the same as that of equating an account current.

In joint consignments, the consignee's share of the invoice may be considered due at the date of the receipt of the goods, or the date of shipment, or not until sales are effected; but this depends altogether upon the agreement between the parties. The consignee's share of the gain or loss takes date with the commissions and charges, being due at the average maturity of the sales.

EXAMPLE 1. Required the equated time for the payment of the net proceeds of the following:

ACCOUNT-SALES *Mdse. received from* J. B. WARNER, *to be sold on joint account of himself*, A. M. FOSTER, *and ourselves, each* $\frac{1}{3}$.

1877						
July	11	Sold on account, at 3 days, 100 bbls. petroleum, 4,000 gallons, at 48½ cts.	......	$1940	00	
"	11	Sold for cash, 250 bbls. do., 10,000 gallons, at 48 cts.	....	4800	00	
"	14	Sold on a note at 30 days, 50 bbls. do., 2,000 gallons, at 49 cts.		980	00	
						$7720 00
	16	100 bbls. on storage destroyed by fire; no insurance.				
		Charges.				
"	10	Paid cash for freight and drayage	$750 00			
"	16	Storage and cooperage, ...	25 50			
		Commission, 2½ per cent. on $7720	193 00			
				968	50	
		Less our ⅓ net loss	....	482	84	
						485 66
		Total net proceeds, ...		....	......	$7234 34
		Amount of invoice, ...	$8200 00			
		J. B. Warner and our ⅔, ...	5466 67			
		Less their ⅓ net loss, ...	482 83			
			$4983 84			
		Due by equation, July 17.				

Kingston, July 17, 1877.   W. R. BARBER & Co.

SOLUTION BY INTEREST METHOD.

Focal date, Aug. 16*th, latest maturity.*

SALES.	Due July 14	....	$1940 00	....	....	Interest, 33 days,	$10 67
	" " 11	....	4800 00	....	....	" 36 "	28 80
	" Aug.16	....	980 00	....	....	" 0 "	
LOSS.	" July 16	....	1448 50	....	....	" 31 "	7 48
6)9.168			$9168 50				$46 95

1.53 +)46.95(31—Average maturity of sales, 31 days prior
  459   to Aug. 16, or July 16.
  105

CHARGES,	Due July 10,	....	$ 750 00	....	Interest, 37 days,	$4 63
"	" 16,	....	218 50	....	" 31 "	1 13
Balance of Acct.,		....	8200 00	....	———	5 76
6)8.200		.	$9168 50			$41 19

1.37 +)41.19(30—Equated time for the payment of the Net Proceeds, 30 days prior to August 16th
   411   or July 17th.
    9

STORAGE.

STORAGE is a charge made by an individual who stores moveable property or goods for another. It is usually computed by the month of thirty days, at a certain price per bushel, cask, box, barrel, etc. The storage book contains the date when the goods are stored and the articles; also, the date when they are delivered. See Warehousing, page 181.

All goods stored are usually subject to one month's storage. In some places, if they remain any part of a month they are charged for a full month; in others, after the first month, if taken out within fifteen days, a half-month is charged; if after fifteen days, a whole month, and in other places they are charged only for the time they are in store. The owners of the goods pay for putting the goods in store, stowing away, and the expenses of delivery.

When goods are received and delivered at the pleasure of the consignor, the dues for storage are usually determined by an average.

To compute storage.

RULE.—*Multiply the number of barrels, or other articles, first entered, by the number of days between the time of entrance and the time of the first delivery, or second entrance. Then multiply each balance by the number of days it continues unchanged.*

The sum of all the products will be the number of articles in store for one day. To find the number stored for one month, divide the sum of the products by 30.

EXAMPLE.—What is the cost of storage at 1c. per bushel per month, of wheat received and delivered as per following account, closed Oct. 2d, 1877.

ACCOUNT OF STORAGE OF WHEAT RECEIVED AND DELIVERED FOR ACCOUNT OF
SANFORD, BAKER & CO., BELLEVILLE, ONT.

Date.		Received.	Delivered.	IN STORE.	Days.	Products.
1877.						
July	2	200		200	9	1800
"	11		150	50	5	250
"	16	350		400	5	2000
"	21		300	100	20	2000
August	10	400		500	5	2500
"	15		450	50	5	250
"	20		50	0	0	0000
September	5	200		200	5	1000
"	10	100		300	5	1500
"	15		200	100	17	1700
		1250	1150			30)13000
Bal. on hand Oct. 2,			100			433
		1250	1250			

433 x 1c. = $4.33, ANS.

ANOTHER FORM.

ACCOUNT OF STORAGE OF SALT FOR JAMES SMITH & CO., AT 3 CENTS PER BARREL PER MONTH.

Date.		Rec'd.	Delivr'd.	Bal. in Store.	Time.	Amount in store 1 day.
1877.						
May	1	1000		1000	22	22000
"	23	400		1400	5	7000
"	28		600	800	3	2400
"	31	1000		1800	6	10800
June	6		1000	800	10	8000
"	16		500	300	14	4200
"	30	500		800	4	3200
July	4	1000		1800	28	50400
Aug.	1		1600	200	31	6200
Sept.	1		200			
		3900	3900			3,0)11420,0
						3806⅔
						3
						$114.20 Ans.

HAY.

To ascertain the value of a quantity of hay, where the number of lbs. and price per ton are given.

RULE.—*Multiply the number of lbs. by one-half the price per ton, and point off three figures from the right of the product.*[*]

EXAMPLE 1.—What will be the cost of 2346 lbs. of hay, at $16 per ton; and 1874 lbs. at $17 per ton?

FIRST.   SECOND.
2346 No. lbs.   1874 No. lbs.
8 — ½ price per ton.   8½ — ½ price per ton.

$18.768 Ans. $15.929 Ans.

EXAMPLE 2.—What will a load of hay containing 2974 lbs. cost at $17.50 per ton?
ANS. $26.0225.

MEASUREMENT OF WOOD.

To find how many cords of wood a given pile contains.

RULE.—*Multiply the height, width and length of the pile in feet and fractions of a foot together, and divide the product by 128, the number of cubic feet in a cord.*

The following Rule for readily and accurately ascertaining the requisite length of a pile of wood of any height that will be required for a given number of cords, will be found useful.

RULE.—*Multiply together the two given sides, height and breadth, and by this product divide the cubical contents of the required quantity; the quotient will be the third side or length.*

---

[*] If the price per ton should contain cents, point off two extra figures, or remove the decimal point five places to the left instead of three.

EXAMPLE 1.—Suppose a pile of wood, 4 feet high and 4 feet wide; required the requisite length for one cord.

The two given sides, height and breadth, 4 × 4 = 16, and the cubical contents of 1 cord is 128 feet. Then 128 ÷ 16 = 8 feet, the third side or length.

Proof.—4 × 4 × 8 = 128.

EXAMPLE 2.—Suppose the wood piled 5 feet high, what length must we have for 10 cords? 128 × 10 = 1,280, the cubical contents, and 5 × 4 = 20, the product of the two given sides, and 1,280 ÷ 20 = 64 feet, the required length.

Proof.—64 × 5 × 4 = 1280.

EXAMPLE 3.—Suppose the wood piled 6 feet 3 inches high: required the length for 5 cords. 6.3 = 6.25 × 4 = 25, and 128 × 5 = 640 ÷ 25 = 25.6 feet the answer.

Proof.—6¼ × 25.6 × 4 = 640.

By the same rule, if we have any two sides and the cubical contents, we can find the other side.

EXAMPLE.—Suppose you have a space for piling wood 27 feet 3 inches long, how high must wood, cut 4 feet long, be piled to make 7 cords?

The given sides, length and breadth, *27.25 × 4 = 109.

The given quantity, 7 cords × 128 = 896, and 896 ÷ 109 = 8 feet $2\frac{78}{109}$ inches the Ans.

EXAMPLE.—Suppose the space be 25 feet long and 6½ feet high, how long must the wood be cut in order that the space may hold 25 cords.

If the pile is of various heights, take the measure at different places, and divide the sum of those heights by the number of them, thus: Suppose the pile you are measuring be the following heights:

```
      4 ft. 8 in.
      5 "  9
      3 "  6
      4 "  9
      ─────────
   4)18 "  8
      ─────────
      4 "  8 the mean height.
```

THE MILLERS' RULE FOR WEIGHING WHEAT.

Wheat weighing 58 pounds and upwards per bushel is considered merchantable wheat, and 60 pounds of merchantable wheat make a standard bushel. Hence, wheat weighing less than 60 lbs. per bushel will lose in making up; but, weighing more, it will gain.

When wheat weighs less than 58 pounds per bushel, it is customary, on account of the inferior yield of light wheat, to take two pounds for one in making up the weight; hence, it will take 63 pounds to make up a bushel, provided the wheat weighs but 57, and 64 if the wheat weighs but 56 pounds per bushel.

CASE I.—To change merchantable wheat to standard weight.

RULE.—*Bring the whole quantity of wheat to pounds, and divide by* 60.

---

* It is supposed that the student understands common and decimal fractions.

EXAMPLE 1.—How many standard bushels of wheat are in 150 bushels, each weighing 58 pounds?

```
   150           Or, each bushel lacks 2 lbs.;        150
    58                                                  2
  ----                                                ----
  1200                                              6,0)30,0
   750                                                ----
  ----           From 150 bush.   Deficiency,          5
6,0)870,0        Take   5
  ----
```

ANS. 145 b.   Leaves 145, the answer.

2. How many standard bushels of wheat are in 80 bushels, 45 pounds, weighing 63?

```
Bush.  lbs.
  80    45                Or, 80 bush.
  63                             3
 ----                          ----
 285                       6,0)24,0 excess of weight.
 480                           ----
 ----                          4 bush.
6,0)508,5                   80       45 lbs.
```

ANS. 84b. 45 lbs. == 84¾ b.   ANS. 84b. 45 lbs.

3. How many standard bushels of wheat are in 175 bushels, 37 pounds, weighing 59? ANS. 172 bush., 42 lbs.

4. How many standard bushels are in 100 bushels, 15 pounds, weighing 62 pounds per bushel? ANS. 103 bush., 35 lbs.

CASE II.—When wheat weighs less than 58.

RULE.—*Bring the whole quantity to pounds, and divide by as many pounds as make a standard bushel of such wheat.*

EXAMPLE 1.—How many bushels of good wheat are equal to 100 bushels weighing 57?

```
    100                Or, 6 lbs. per bush. = 600 lbs.
     57                63)600(9 bush. 33 lbs. defect.
   ----                 567
63)5700(90 bush. 30 lbs. ----
    567                from 100 bush. 33
   ----                Take    9 33
   30 lb.                    ----
       ANS.             90 27
```

2. How many standard bushels of merchantable wheat will be equal to 250 bushels, 18 lbs., weighing 56 lbs. per bush.? ANS. 219 bush., 2 lbs.

3. How much good wheat is equal to 1000 bushels, weighing 55? ANS. 846 bushels 10 lbs.

MEASUREMENT OF LUMBER.

The following practical methods of calculating the contents of lumber are generally employed by lumber dealers.

NOTE.—The odd pounds in the above and following results are also subject to a small drawback, viz., 1 lb. in every 21 when the wheat weighs 57; 1 in 16 when the wheat weighs 56, and so on; consequently, the above ought, in strictness, to be 90 bushels, and rather more than 28½ pounds, but millers seldom make this reduction.

A standard board is one which is 12 inches wide, one inch thick, and 12 feet long; hence, a standard board contains 12 square feet.

To find the superficial contents of boards, when the length is given in feet, and the breadth in inches.

RULE.—*Divide either dimension by 12, and multiply the quotient by the other; the product will be the contents in square feet.*

EXAMPLE.—How many square feet are there in a plank 15 feet long, 9 inches wide, and two inches thick?

$\dfrac{15 \times 9 \times 2}{12} = 22\tfrac{1}{2}$

$15 \times \tfrac{3}{4} \times 2 = 22\tfrac{1}{2}$

ANALYSIS.—The contents equal the length in feet multiplied by the breadth in inches, multiplied by the thickness in inches, and divided by 12; or since 9 inches equal $\tfrac{3}{4}$ of a foot.

Since the number of boards, the length and the breadth, are all factors of a product to be divided by 12, we may divide any one of them by 12, before multiplying.

EXAMPLE.—How much will the following lumber cost, at $15 per thousand square feet?

10 boards 13 feet long, 10 inches wide, 1 inch thick.
20 " 18 " 12 " 1 "
40 " 16 " 9 " 1½ "

$10 \times 13 \times \tfrac{5}{6} = 108\tfrac{1}{3}$
$20 \times 18 \times 1 = 360$
$40 \times 16 \times \tfrac{3}{4} \times 1\tfrac{1}{2} = 720$

1188⅓ square feet × 1½ price per foot = $17.825.

To obtain the price per foot it is only necessary to divide the price per thousand by 10. The same rule will answer for estimating plank and scantling of any description. Required the contents of the following:

40 pieces scantling 2 × 3, 18.
30 " joist 4 × 5, 16.
20 planks 2 × 9, 13.
4 pieces timber 6 × 8, 20.
2 " 8 × 12, 24.

The above is given in the form of the items of a bill. The sign of multiplication is placed between the side dimensions, and omitted before the length, as is customary in practice.

LOGS REDUCED TO BOARD MEASURE.

It is often necessary to ascertain the number of feet of boards which can be cut from a given log; or, in other words, to find how many logs will be necessary to make a given amount of boards.

A number of boards of various widths are first cut from the side of a log, in the operation of sawing. These boards have a wane edge which is afterwards sawed off, and as the waste in edging depends upon the quality of the logs and other circumstances, it is impossible to give a rule for finding the exact number of feet of SQUARE EDGED boards which can be cut from logs. Tables prepared from diagrams are used for this purpose; but the following rule may be adopted in the absence of tables.*

---

* Scribner's Tables are adopted as a standard for measuring lumber.

RULE.—*From the diameter of the log in inches subtract four for the slabs; then multiply the remainder by half itself, and the product by the length of the log in feet, and divide the result by eight; the quotient will be the number of square feet that can be cut from the log.*

A standard log is 12 feet long and 20 inches in diameter. Logs are usually required to be cut 13 feet long in order that the boards may trim 12 feet.

EXAMPLE.—How many feet of square-edged boards can be cut from a log 12 feet long and 24 inches in diameter.

If we saw off, say two inches from each side, the log will be reduced to a square 20 inches on a side. Now, since a standard board is one inch in thickness, and since the saw cuts about one quarter of an inch each time it goes through, it follows that one-fourth of the log will be consumed by the saw. Hence we shall have $20 \times \frac{3}{4} =$ the number of boards cut from the log. Now, if the width of a board in inches be divided by 12, and the quotient be multiplied by the length in feet, the product will be the number of square feet in the board. Hence $\frac{20}{12} \times$ length of log in feet=the square feet in each board. Therefore $20 \times \frac{3}{4} \times \frac{10}{12}$ length of log=the square feet in all the boards=$20 \times 10 \times \frac{3}{4} \times \frac{10}{12} \times$ length of log=$20 \times 10 \times \frac{1}{8} \times$ length. And the same may be shown for a log of any length.

Diameter,	24 inches.
For slabs,	4
Remainder,	20
Half Remainder,	10
	200
Length of log,	12
	8)2400
	300 = the number of feet.

2. How many feet can be cut from a log 12 inches in diameter and 12 feet long? ANS. 48.

3. How many feet can be cut from a log 20 inches in diameter and 16 feet long? ANS. 256.

4. How many feet can be cut from a log 24 inches in diameter and 16 feet long? ANS. 400.

5. How many feet can be cut from a log 28 inches in diameter and 14 feet long? ANS. 504.

TO FIND THE CUBICAL CONTENTS OF SQUARE TIMBER.

RULE.—*Multiply the area of one end in inches by the length in feet and divide the product by 144.*

EXAMPLES.

1. Find the cubical contents of a stick of square timber 24 feet long and 16 inches square.

SOLUTION. $\dfrac{16 \times 16 \times 24}{144} = 42\frac{2}{3}$ feet. ANS.

2. Required the cubical contents of a stick of square timber 26 feet long, and 17 by 15, side dimensions. ANS. $46\frac{1}{24}$ cu. ft.

3. What are the cubical contents of stick of timber 14 inches square and 20 feet long? Ans. 27⅞ cu. ft.

4. Find the cubical contents of a stick of timber, 16 × 18, and 23 feet long. Ans. 56 cu. ft.

ROUND TIMBER.

Round timber is now very generally bought and sold by its cubical measurement, when reduced to square timber.

The following rule for finding the contents is extensively used, and is considered practically just to both buyer and seller.

RULE.—*Deduct from the mean diameter in inches one-third of itself; multiply the square of the remainder by the length of the log in feet, and divide the product by 144.*

EXAMPLE 1.—Find the cubical contents, in square timber, of a stick of round timber, 14 inches in diameter at the smaller end, 20 inches at the larger, 26 feet long.

SOLUTION. $20 + 14 = 34 \div 2 = 17$ mean diameter.

$17 - 5\frac{2}{3} = 11\frac{1}{3}$; and $11\frac{1}{3} \times 11\frac{1}{3} = 128\frac{4}{9}$.

$128\frac{4}{9} \times 26 \div 144 = 23\frac{69}{124}$.*   Ans. 23+feet.

EXAMPLE 2.—Find the measurement, as square timber, of a stick of round timber 30 feet long, and of an average diameter of 15 inches.   Ans. 20⅝ cu. ft.

EXAMPLE 3.—Required the cubical contents, as square timber, of a stick of round timber, 25 feet long, and 20 inches as diameter at one end, and 28 inches at the other?   Ans. 44⅜ cu. ft.

EXAMPLE 4.—Required the cubical contents, as square timber, of a stick of round timber, 32 feet long, and averaging 23 inches in diameter.   Ans. 52 cu. ft.

When logs of various sizes are bought by the standard, lumbermen adopt the following rule to ascertain the number of standard logs in a given quantity.

RULE.—*Multiply the square of the diameter in inches, at the small end, by the number of logs of the same diameter, and divide the product by 400.*

EXAMPLE.—How many standard logs are contained in the following:

10 logs 13 ft. long, 23 in. in diameter.
20 " 13 " 18 " "
30 " 13 " 21 " "   Ans. 62½.

NOTE.—When the length of logs is more or less than 13 feet they should be multiplied by the length and divided by 12.

MECHANICS' WORK.

CARPENTERS' WORK.

Roofing, flooring, etc., are usually measured and computed by the 100 square feet.

In boarded flooring, the dimensions must be taken to the extreme parts, and the number of squares of 100 feet must be calculated from these dimensions. Deductions should be made for staircases, chimneys, etc.

NOTE.—The mean diameter is found by taking one-half of the sum of the diameters of the two ends.

* A fraction of ½ a foot or less is disregarded, and a fraction over ½ is called a foot.

EXAMPLE.—How many squares of flooring are there in a floor 57 feet 3 inches long, and 28 feet 6 inches broad?

OPERATION.

By Decimals.

57.25
28.5
―――
28625
45800
11450
―――
100)1631.625 feet.
―――
16.31625 squares

By Duodecimals.

ft. in.
57 " 3
28 " 6
―――
28 " 7 " 6
1603 " 0
―――
100)1631 " 7 " 6
―――
16.31 squares.

The mode of measuring roofing is given in the next exercise.

TILING OR SLATING.

Tiling and slating are measured by the square of 100 feet, as flooring, partitioning and roofing are in Carpenters' work; so that there is not much difference between the roofing and tiling; yet the tiling will be the most; for double measure is sometimes allowed for hips and valleys.

In this work the contents of the roof are found by multiplying the length of the ridge by the girt from eave to eave.

When gutters are allowed double measure, the way is to measure the length along the ridge-tile, and add it to the contents of the roof; this makes an allowance of one foot in breadth, the whole length of the hips or valleys. It is usual also to allow double measure at the eaves, so much as the projection is over the plate, which is commonly about 18 or 20 inches.

Skylights and chimney shafts are generally deducted, if they be large, otherwise they are not.

EXAMPLE 1.—There is a roof covered with tiles, whose depth on both sides (with the usual allowance at the eaves) is 37 feet 3 inches, and the length 45 feet; how many squares of tiling are contained therein?

By Duodecimals.

ft. in.
37 3
45 0
―――
185
148
11 3
―――
1676 3

By Decimals.

37.25
45
―――
18625
14900
―――
1676.25

EXAMPLE 2.— The length of a slated roof is 45 feet 9 inches, and its girt 34 feet 3 inches; what are its contents? ANS. 1566.9375 sq. ft.

3. What will the tiling of a barn cost at $3.40 per square of 100 feet, the length being 43 feet 10 inches, and breadth 27 feet 5 inches on the flat, the eave board projecting 16 inches on each side, and the roof being of the true pitch. ANS. $65.26.

PLASTERERS' WORK.

Plasterers' work is of two kinds, viz. : ceiling, which is plastering on laths; and rendering which is plastering on walls. These are measured separately.

The contents are estimated either by the square foot, the square yard, or the square of 100 feet.

Enriched mouldings, etc., are rated by the running or linear measure.

In estimating plastering, deductions are made for chimneys, doors, windows, etc.

EXAMPLE 1.—How many square yards are contained in a ceiling 43 feet 3 inches long and 25 feet 6 inches broad? ANS. $122\frac{1}{4}$ nearly.

2. What is the cost of ceiling a room 21 feet 8 inches by 14 feet 10 inches, at 18 cents per square yard? ANS. $6.42. +

3. The length of a room is 14 feet 5 inches, breadth 13 feet 2 inches, and height to the under side of the cornice 9 feet 3 inches. The cornice girts $8\frac{1}{2}$ inches, and projects 5 inches from the wall on the upper part next the ceiling, deducting only for one door 7 ft. by 4, what will be the amount of the plastering?

ANS. $\begin{cases} \text{53 yds. 5 ft. 3' 6'' of rendering.} \\ \text{18 yds 5 ft. 6' 4'' of ceiling.} \\ \text{37 ft. 10' 9'' of cornice.} \end{cases}$

The mean length of the cornice, both in length and breadth of the house, is found by taking the middle line of the cornice. Now, since the cornice projects 5 inches at the ceiling, it will project $2\frac{1}{2}$ inches at the middle line; and, therefore, the length of the middle line along the length of the room will be 14·feet, and across the room 12 feet 9 inches. Then multiply the double of each of these numbers by the girth, which is $8\frac{1}{2}$ inches, and the sum of the products will be the area of the cornice.

PAINTERS' WORK.

Painters' work is computed in square yards. Every part is measured where the color lies, and the measuring line is carried into all the mouldings and cornices.

Windows are generally done at so much apiece. It is usual to allow double measure for carved mouldings, etc.

EXAMPLE 1.—How many yards of painting in a room which is 65 feet 6 inches in perimeter, and 12 feet 4 inches in height? ANS. $89\frac{11}{24}$ sq. yds.

2. The length of a room is 20 feet, its breadth 14 feet 6 inches, and height 10 feet 4 inches; how many yards of painting are in it—deducting a fire-place of 4 feet by 4 feet 4 inches, and two windows, each 6 feet by 3 feet 2 inches? ANS. $73\frac{2}{7}$ sq yds.

MASONS' WORK.

The measure made use of in all sorts of stone work is either superficial or solid.

Walls, columns, blocks of stone or marble are measured by the cubic foot, and pavements, slabs, chimney pieces, etc., are measured by the square or superficial foot. Cubic or solid measure is always used for the material, and square measure is sometimes used for the workmanship.

EXAMPLE 1.—Required the solid contents of a wall 53 feet 6 inches long, 12 feet 3 inches high and 2 feet thick. ANS. $1310\frac{3}{4}$ ft.

2. What is the solid contents of a wall, the length of which is 24 feet 3 inches, height 10 feet 9 inches, and thickness 2 feet. ANS. 521.375 ft.

3. In a chimney-piece we find the following dimensions:

Length of the mantle and slab,	4 feet	2 inches.
Breadth of both together,	3 "	2 "
Length of each jam,	4 "	4 "
Breadth of both,	1 "	9 "

Required, the superficial contents.   ANS. 31 ft. 10 -.

Stone walls are measured by the solid foot, the superficial foot, and by the perch.*
Artificers' work in general is computed by three different measures, viz.:

1. The linear measure, or, as it is called by mechanics, running measure.
2. Superficial or square measure, in which the computation is made by the square foot, square yard, or by the square containing 100 square feet or yards.
3. By the cubic or solid measure, when it is estimated by the cubic foot or cubic yard.

The work, however, is often estimated in square measure, and the materials for construction in cubic measure.

Masons generally contract for foundations of buildings and other walls of that description at so much per perch ($16\frac{1}{2}$ feet) and in estimating their work adopt the following

RULE.—*Multiply the length, height and width of the wall together, and divide the product by* $16\frac{1}{2}$.

EXAMPLE.—How much will it cost to build a stone wall 60 ft. long, 8 ft. high and 3 ft. thick, at 70c. per perch?

OPERATION.

$$\frac{60 \times 8 \times 3}{16\frac{1}{2}} = 87\frac{3}{11} \text{ perches} \times 70c = \$61.09. \quad \text{ANS.}$$

BRICKLAYERS' WORK.

The dimensions of a brick generally bear the following proportions to each other, viz.:

Length=twice the width, and
Width=twice the thickness; and hence the length is equal to four times the thickness.

The common length of a brick is 8 inches, in which case the width is 4 inches, and thickness 2 inches. A brick of this size contains $8 \times 4 \times 2 = 64$ cubic inches; and since a cubic foot contains 1728 cubic inches, we have $1728 \div 64 = 27$, the number of bricks in a cubic foot.

If the brick is 9 inches long, then the width is $4\frac{1}{2}$ inches, and the thickness $2\frac{1}{4}$, and each brick will contain $9 \times 4\frac{1}{2} \times 2\frac{1}{4} = 91\frac{1}{8}$ cubic inches ; and $1728 \div 91\frac{1}{8} = 19$ nearly, the number of bricks in a cubic foot. In the examples which follow we shall suppose the brick to be 8 inches long, unless otherwise mentioned.

To find the number of bricks required to build a wall of given dimensions.

1. *Find the contents of a wall in cubic feet.*
2. *Multiply the number of cubic feet by the number of bricks in a cubic foot, and the result will be the number required.*

---

*Since different ways of measuring stone walls are adopted by different mechanics, it is necessary, when called upon to measure such work, to first ascertain which system is intended to be adopted.

EXAMPLE.—How many bricks of 8 inches in length will be required to build a wall 30 feet long, a brick and a half thick, and 15 feet in height? ANS. 12150.

2. How many bricks, of the usual size, will be required to build a wall 50 feet long, 2 bricks thick, and 36 ft. in height? ANS. 64800.

The thickness of mortar between the courses is nearly a quarter of an inch, so that four courses will give nearly one inch in height. The mortar, therefore, adds nearly one-eighth to the height. One-eighth is rather too large an allowance; but the mortar that goes to increase the length of the wall and to fill other spaces makes it about one-sixth. Mechanics in making estimates consider 5-6 of a wall solid brick.

3. How many bricks would be required in the first and second examples, if we make the proper allowance for mortar?

Bricklayers generally estimate their work at so much per thousand.

4. What is the cost of a wall 60 feet long, 20 feet high and $2\frac{1}{2}$ bricks thick at $7.50 per thousand—which price we supposed to include the cost of the mortar?

If we suppose the mortar to occupy a space equal to one-sixth the height of the wall, we must find the quantity of bricks under supposition that the wall is to be $16\frac{2}{3}$ feet in height.

In estimating bricks for a house, allowance must be made for the windows and doors.

To ascertain the number of bricks required to build 1 foot of a wall of any given thickness·

RULE.—*Multiply the thickness of the wall in inches by 144, and from the product deduct $\frac{1}{6}$ itself and divide the remainder by the solid contents of a brick.*

EXAMPLE.—How many bricks will it require to build 1 foot of a wall 1 brick or 8 inches thick.

SOLUTION.

8 × 144 = 1152—192 = 960.
8 × 4 × 2 = 64 solid contents of 1 brick.
960 ÷ 64 = 15. ANS.

NOTE.—The mode of working examples where the proper allowances for mortar, &c are taken into consideration, will be given in the following exercises.

EXAMPLE.—How many bricks will it require to build 1 foot of a wall 12 inches thick?

SOLUTION.

12 × 144 = 1728—288 = 1440.
8 × 4 × 2 = 64 solid contents of 1 brick.
1440 ÷ 64 = $22\frac{1}{2}$. ANS.

To ascertain the number of bricks required to build a wall.

RULE.—*Multiply the length and height of the wall in feet together; this product multiplied by the number of bricks required to build 1 foot of such wall will be the required result.*

EXAMPLE 1.—Find the number of bricks required for the erection of a building the walls of which are nine inches thick, the length 40 feet, width 32, and the height 18. Allowance to be made for 12 windows, 7 feet by $3\frac{1}{2}$, and 3 doors, $8\frac{1}{2}$ by 4 feet. (Bricks 9 inches long.)

301

SOLUTION.

40 + 40 + 30½ + 30½*=141, the length in a straight wall. 141 x 18, the height= 2538, the number of square feet. 7 × 3¼ × 12=294 feet, the space occupied by the windows; 8¼ × 4 × 3=102 feet, the space occupied by the doors—hence 294 + 102=396, the number to be deducted from the whole surface, 2538—396 = 2142 feet of wall; this multiplied by 12, the number of bricks required to lay one foot of such wall, gives 25704 for the total number of bricks.

EXAMPLE 2.—Required the number of bricks for building a wall 43 ft. long, 32 wide, 16 high and 8 inches thick, allowing for 14 windows, 8 by 4½ feet, 4 doors 9 by 4½ ft.

EXAMPLE 3.—Find the number of bricks required to built a house of the following dimensions: the main building to be 30 feet long, 24 wide, 15 high, and walls 8 inches thick: 2 doors, one 8½ by 6 ft., the other 7 by 3½ ft.; 8 windows 6½ by 4 ft. The kitchen to be 13 ft. long, 11 ft. wide, and side walls 10 ft. high, having a gable† 4½ ft. in altitude, 4 windows 4½ by 3 ft., and 2 doors, 7½ by 3½ ft.

2. How many bricks will be required to erect a wall 140 ft. long, 14 ft. high, and 1 t. thick; allowing for 2 doors 4 × 7 feet, and 12 windows, 3 × 5 ft.

3. How many bricks will be required to erect a house 26 × 36 ft., walls, 21 feet high and 1 ft. thick; allowing for 3 doors, one 4½×7 ft., two 3×6 ft., and 12 windows, two 5 by 7 ft., three 4×6 ft., and seven 3×5 ft.?

4. How many perches of stone-work are there in the foundation of the above building if the wall be 2 ft. thick and 4 ft. high, there being a cellar in one corner 18 ×20 ft. the walls of which are 7 feet high?

NOTE.—It is impossible, on account of the necessary waste and other modifying circumstances, to give the exact number of bricks required to built a wall, but the above system of calculation has been found by practical mechanics to be nearly right.

GLAZIERS' WORK.

Glaziers take their dimensions in feet, inches and eighths or tenths, or else in feet and hundredth parts of a foot, and estimate their work by the square foot.

Windows are sometimes measured by taking the dimensions of one pane and multiplying its superficies by the number of panes. But more generally they measure the length and breadth of the window over all the panes and their frames, for the length and breadth of the glazing.

Circular or oval windows, as fan lights, etc., are measured as if they were square, taking for the dimensions their greatest length and breadth, as a compensation for the waste of glass and labor in cutting it to the necessary forms.

EXAMPLE.—If a pane of glass be 4 feet 8¾ inches long, and 1 foot 4¼ inches broad, how many feet of glass are in that pane.

BY DUODECIMALS.	BY DECIMALS.
FT. IN. P.	4.729
4 8 9	1.354
1 4 3	
	18916
4 8 9	23645
1 6 11 0	14187
1 2 2 3	4729
	6.403066
6 4 10 2 3	ANS. 6 feet, 4 inche

* It will be observed that 1½ feet are deducted from each end to allow for the thickness of the wall.

† To find the contents of a gable, multiply the width of the building by the height of the gable, and divide the product by 2.

V

TO FIND DIVISORS FOR CIRCULAR FIGURES.

It has been found by experiment that the area of a circle, whose diameter is unity, will be .785398, &c.; but which, for the sake of convenience, is usually considered as, .7854 parts of an unit ; wherefore, by dividing the solid capacity of any figure by .7854, the quotient will be the proper divisors to the squared diameters of circular figures. To reduce the area, AT ONE INCH DEEP, into gallons, or if the contents of any vessel be first found in inches, by multiplying the area into the depth, &c., and then applying such divisors, the contents will be found in terms of the factor employed: hence

EXAMPLE.

.7854 $\begin{cases} 1 & (\ 1.273 \\ 144 & (\ 183.34 \\ 1728 & (\ 2200.16 \\ 282 & (\ 359.05 \\ 231 & (\ 294.13 \\ 2150.42 & (\ 2738 \\ 268.8 & (\ 342.25 \\ 277 & (\ 289 \\ 217.6 & (\ 277 \\ 326.4 & (\ 415.8 \end{cases}$ which are the divisors for circular figures, of which the dividends are the solid capacities in inches; and to each of which .7854 (as on the left thereof) is a divisor from whence such quotients result.

N. B.—Any divisor for a circular figure being multiplied by 1.5 gives the divisor for spheres.

To find multipliers answering the purpose of the foregoing divisors for circular figures.

RULE.—*Divide .7854 by the solid capacity of any figure, in inches, and the quotient is the corresponding multiplier to such divisors respectively.*

To find the solid contents of a cylindrical vessel.

RULE.—*Multiply area of bottom by height of vessel.*

EXAMPLE.—The inside diameter of a cylindrical vessel being 40 inches, and height of side 5 feet, find its cubical contents.

Area of bottom $=$ 40² × .7854 $=$ 1256.64.
1256.64 area ot bottom.
60 in height.

ANS. 75398.40 cubic inches.

To find the cubical contents of a vessel with rectangular base and vertical sides.

RULE.—*Multiply length of bottom by breadth, and the product by height of vessel.*

EXAMPLE.—How many cubic feet will a tank, measuring 8 feet long, 4 feet wide, and 4½ feet deep contain ?   ANS. 8 × 4 × 4½ or 144 cu. ft.

It frequently occurs that cisterns are to be so constructed as to hold given quantities o water, and it then becomes a useful and practical problem to calculate their exact dimensions.

If the height of a cistern be given, to find the diameter, so that the cistern shall contain a given number of hogsheads.

1st. Reduce the height of the cistern to inches, and the contents to cubic inches.
2nd. Multiply the height by the decimal .7854.
3rd. Divide the contents by the last result, and extract the square root of the quotient, which will be the diameter of the cistern in inches.

To find the solid contents of a vessel with circular top and bottom of unequal dimensions, and having straight sides; or to find the cubical contents of the frustrum of a cone.

NOTE.—The area of a circle is found by multiplying the square of the diameter by .7854.

RULE—*To the product of top and bottom diameters add the sum of their squares, multiply this sum by the perpendicular height and by constant .2618.*

EXAMPLE.—The top diameter of a circular vessel is 20 inches, the bottom diameter 11 inches, and the perpendicular height 18 inches; find its solid contents.

                To product of diameters,   20 × 11 = 220
                add sum of their squares,   400 + 121 = 521
                                                         741
                741 × 18 = 13338 × ·2618 = 3491.8884 cubic inches.

To find the capacity in gallons of a tank, cistern or vessel of any kind.

RULE.—*Divide the contents in cubic feet by 6.2321 and the result will be Imperial gallons; or multiply the contents in cubic inches by ·0036 for a like result.*

GAUGING CASKS.

RULE.—*Take the distance in inches from the centre of the bung inside, diagonally, to the chine; cube it, and divide by 370, and the quotient will express the gallons. Should there be a remainder, multiply by 4, and continue the division for quarts; by 2, for pints, etc.*

This standard number, 370, is derived from actual experiment. The measurement of a regular-shaped cask cubed as above, divided by the actual capacity of the English gallon pot, gave the standard 370.

EXAMPLES.

1. How many gallons will a hogshead hold measuring 37 inches from the centre of the bung inside to the chine?   Ans. 136 gals. 3 qts. 1 pt.

OPERATION.

        37 × 3737 = 50653 ÷ 370 = 136 gallons.
        1st remainder 333 × 4 = 1332 ÷ 370 = 3 quarts.
        2nd remainder 222 × 2 = 444 ÷ 370 = 1 pint.

2. A cask measures 16 inches from the centre of the bung, diagonally, to the chine; what is its capacity?   Ans. 11 gals., 2 gills.

3. A cask measures 18 inches, diagonally, to the chine inside, one way, and 19 ins. the other, what will it hold?   Ans. 17 gals. and 3 gills.

4. I have a small cask measuring 13 inches to the chine inside; what does it hold?   Ans. 5 gals., 3 qts., 1 pt., 2 gills.

TO MEASURE CORN IN THE CRIB.

Corn is generally put up in cribs made of rails, but the following rule will apply to a crib of any size or kind.

Two cubic feet of good, sound, dry corn in the ear will make a bushel of shelled corn. To get, then, the quantity of shelled corn in a crib of corn in the ear, measure the length, breadth and height of the crib, INSIDE OF THE RAIL; multiply the length by the breadth, and the product by the height; then divide the result by two, and you have the number of bushels of shelled corn in the crib.

In measuring the height, of course the height of the corn is intended. And there will be found to be a difference in measuring corn in this mode. between fall and spring, because it shrinks very much in the winter and spring, and settles down.

NOTE.—If the bung is not in the centre, measure both ways to chine; add the two results together, and take half the sum; then proceed as above.

MEASUREMENT OF GRAIN.

The standard unit of Dry Measure is the Imperial bushel, which is an upright cylinder, whose internal diameter is 18.789 inches, and depth 8 inches. It contains 2218.192 cubic inches or 80 lbs. Avoirdupoids of pure distilled water.

Grain is bought and sold by weight, allowing for a bushel as follows: Wheat, 60 lbs.; Indian corn, 56; rye, 56; peas, 60; barley, 48; oats, 34; beans, 60; clover seed, 60; timothy seed, 48; buckwheat, 48; flax seed, 50; hemp seed, 44; blue grass seed, 14; castor beans, 40; potatoes, turnips, carrots, parsnips, beets and onions, 60 lbs.; salt, 56; dried apples, 22; dried peaches, 33, and malt, 36 pounds.

TO MEASURE GRAIN ON THE FLOOR

RULE.—*Make the pile in the form of a pyramid or cone, and multiply the area of the base by one-third the height for the cubical contents.*

EXAMPLE.—A conical pile of grain is 8 feet in diameter, and 4 feet high, how many bushels does it contain?

SOLUTION.

The square of 8 is 64; and $64 \times .7854 \times 1\frac{1}{3} \times 1\frac{7\frac{1}{2}}{2\frac{1}{3}\frac{1}{8}} \cdot \frac{1}{192}$ the number of bushels=52.201.

TO ASCERTAIN THE WEIGHT OF CATTLE BY MEASUREMENT.

Multiply the girth in feet by the distance from the bone of the tail immediately over the hinder part of the buttock, to the fore part of the shoulder blade; and this product by 31 when the animal measures *more than 7 and less than 9 feet in girth;* by 23, when *less than 7 and more than 5;* by 16, when *less than 5 and more than 3,* and by 11, when *less than 3.*

EXAMPLE.—What is the weight of an ox whose measurements are as follows: girth, 7 feet 5 inches; length, 5 feet 6 inches?

SOLUTION.

$5\frac{1}{2} \times 7\frac{5}{12} = 40\frac{19}{24}$; $40\frac{19}{24} \times 31 = 1264 +$. ANS.

A deduction of one pound in 20 must be made for half-fatted cattle, and also for cows that have had calves. It is understood, of course, that such standard will at best give only the *approximate* weight.

MEASURING LAND.

To find the number of acres of land in a rectangular field, multiply the length by the breadth, and divide the product by 160, if the measurement is made in rods, or by 43560 if made in feet.

EXAMPLE.—How many acres in a field which is 100 rods in length by 75 rods in width.

SOLUTION.

$100 \times 75 = 7500 \div 160 = 46\frac{7}{8}$. ANS.

To find the contents of a triangular piece of land, having a rectangular corner, multiply the two shorter sides together, and take one-half the product.

DISCOUNTING BILLS AND INVOICES.

Price Lists are made out by manufacturers and dealers, as prices to be charged subject to the deductions of certain rates per cent., which fluctuate according to the cost of manufacturing, demand for goods, etc. By changing the rate of discount the prices are changed without altering the price lists.

In discounting Bills and Invoices, losses sometimes occur when they are not suspected. If an article is sold at a profit of 40 per cent., and 10 per cent. be deducted from the selling price, the gain is not 30 per cent. but 26 per cent., because the discount is calculated on the first cost and also on the profit, whereas the profit is calculated on the first cost only. So, also, if 40 per cent. be added, and then 30 per cent. deducted, the apparent profit is 10 per cent., but the REAL LOSS is 2 per cent.

Cost,	$200		Cost,	$1.00
40 per cent.,	80		40 per cent.,	40
Advanced price,	280		Advanced price,	1.40
Less 10 per cent.,	28		Less 30 per cent.,	42
Cash price,	252		Cash price,	98
26 per cent. profit.			2 per cent. loss	
10 per cent. of $200 (cost)	= $20		30 per cent. of $1.00 (cost) =	30
10 per cent. of 80 (profit)	= 8		30 per cent. of. 40 (profit) =	12
	$28			$.42
= 14 per cent. of cost.			or 42 per cent. of cost.	

3. What is the difference between discounting a bill of $1200 at 40 per cent., and then taking a discount off the remainder of 5 per cent. for cash payment, and discounting the whole bill at 45 per cent.? Ans. $24.

4. If a merchant buys a book at a discount of 20 per cent. on the retail price, and sells it at the retail price, what per cent. on the purchase price does he gain ? What per cent. does he gain if he buys at 33⅓ per cent. discount, and sells it at the retail price ?
Ans. to first 25 per cent. Second, 50 per cent.

To find the selling price from which a certain per cent. may be deducted and the goods sold at cost, or a given per cent. above or below cost.

Rule.—To sell at cost.

Multiply the cost by 100, *and divide the product by* 100, *diminished by the rate per cent. to be deducted.*

To sell at a given rate per cent., above or below cost.

Multiply 100 *increased by the per cent. to be gained or diminished by the per cent. to be lost by the cost ; and divide the product by* 100, *diminished by the rate to be deducted from the selling price.*

EXAMPLES.

1. Bought goods for $100 ; for how much must I sell them that I may deduct 20 per cent. and yet obtain what they cost ?
$$100 \times 100 = 10000$$
$$10000 \div 80 = 125.$$ Ans. 125.

2. For what must I sell goods worth $100, so that I may deduct 45 per cent. and yet gain 30 per cent ?
$$100 + 30 = 130 \qquad 100 \times 130 = 13000$$
$$13000 \div 55 = 236.36.$$ Ans. $236.36

NOTE.—236.36=136.36 per cent. advance on 100. When a long list is to be made out at a uniform rate of profit, labor may be saved by adding the total advance at once.

3. If I buy cloth for $1.90 per yard, at what price must I mark it that I may deduct 5 per cent. for my cash customers from the marked price, and yet gain 20 per cent.
ANS. $2.40.

4. A merchant marked a piece of goods 25 per cent. more than it cost him, but being anxious to effect a sale, and supposing he should still gain 5 per cent., sold it at a discount of 20 per cent. from his marked price. Did he gain or lose? ANS. Neither.

5. My retail price for cloth is $3.75 per yard, by which I make a profit of $33\frac{1}{3}$ per cent. I sell to a wholesale customer at 20 per cent. discount from the retail price. How much per cent. do I gain or lose and what do I receive per yard? ANS. $3; gain $6\frac{2}{3}$ per cent.

6. My retail price for broadcloth is $4.75 per yard, by which I make a profit of $33\frac{1}{3}$ per cent. I sell a wholesale customer 100 yards at a discount of 30 per cent. from the retail price. What per cent. do I gain or lose, and what do I receive per yard? ANS. Lose $6\frac{2}{3}$ per cent. Recd. $3.325 per yard.

7. I bought a quantity of tea at $1 per lb. Allowing that the tea will fall short 10 per cent. in weighing it out, and that 15 per cent. of the sales will be in bad debts, for how much per lb. must I sell it to make a clear gain of 20 per cent. on cost? ANS. $1.568.

8. Sold lumber on commission at 5 per cent. Invested net proceeds in dry goods at two per cent. commission. My whole commission was $70. What was the value of the lumber and dry goods? ANS. Lumber, $1020; Dry Goods, $950.

SUGGESTION.—Net proceeds of lumber equal $\frac{95}{100}$ or 95 per cent. Commission on dry goods equals $\frac{2}{100}$ of 95 per cent.$=1\frac{44}{11}$ per cent. $1\frac{44}{11}+5=6\frac{44}{11}$. Then, if $6\frac{44}{11}$ per cent. equals $70, 5 per cent. equals $51.

9. Sold flour on commission of 4 per cent. and invested the net-proceeds, less my commission at 3 per cent. in salt. My whole commission was $250. What was the value of the flour and the salt? ANS. $3678.57 flour; $3428.57 salt.

10. I invested in wheat the proceeds of a consignment of flour, less my commission on both, at 3 per cent., which was $60. What did I sell the flour for? and what did I pay for the wheat? ANS. Flour, $1030; wheat $970.

Belleville, Jan. 2, 1877.

MR. J. H BROWN,

Bought of S. G. BEATTY & Co.

240 gross College pens at $1.20.	$288	00
Less 5 per cent. for cash,	14	40
Express charges and duties.	$273 21	60 80
Rec'd payment, S. G BEATTY & CO.	$295	49

At what must I sell the pens per gross to gain 20 per cent., and allow a discount of 10 per cent. from selling price?

SOLUTION.

5 per cent. of $1.20=6c. 1.20—6=1.14, net cash price per gross in Belleville. Charges, 21.89=8 per cent. of total cost in Belleville. 8 per cent. of 1.14=9. +1.14 +9= $1.23, advanced cost per gross.

PROOF.

240 gross at $1.23=$295.20, which, allowing for fractions, is the cost of the invoice. 20 per cent. of $1.23=25c. nearly; adding this to the cost, we have $1.48 as amount to be received. Then, to obtain the selling price, 100—10=90. 148 ÷ 90=164 +

ANS. $1.64 per gross.

PROOF.

10 per cent. of $1.64=16 + $1.64—16=$1.48.

12. A merchant bought an invoice of grain, which, including $1\frac{1}{8}$ per cent. commission, cost $5050.62¼, and paid $15.25 for freight. He sold the grain at a profit of 15 per cent. on its first cost, and invested the proceeds in sugar, which he sold at 5 per cent. profit, receiving a note due in 48 days, including grace. This note he has discounted at 6 per cent. at bank. What was the cost of the grain, and how much were his profits? ANS. Cost of grain, $4994.43; total profits, $916.66.

The following transaction actually occurred in a commission house :

13. A commission merchant received an order to purchase merchandise worth $1000, on which he paid $50 for drayage. He was to effect insurance at the rate of 1 per cent. on 10 per cent. advance to total cost of merchandise, drayage, commission for buying of cost of insurance, and was to receive 3 per cent. commission on total cost of merchandise, drayage and insurance. What was the amount insured, and how much did he receive for commission and how much for insurance? ANS. $1203.28: Com., 31.86; Ins., 12.03

SUGGESTION.—1 per cent. of 3 per cent.=.0003, which added to 1 per cent.=.0103, which increased by ten per cent. of itself equals .01133, the rate of insurance on $1. $1050 increased by 3 per cent. of itself equals $1081.50, which increased 10 per cent. equals $1189.65. Then, to find the amount to be insured to cover $1189.65, and the insurance, or .01133 of itself, we divide $1189.65 by $1, less .01133, which gives us $1203.28.

PARTNERSHIP.

It is unnecessary to enter into an explanation of the terms Partnership, Firm, Capital, Net Insolvency, &c., as the student has already become familiar with them in working out the foregoing sets.

There are two kinds of Partnership, viz.: Simple and Compound.

SIMPLE PARTNERSHIP applies when the several shares of capital have been invested for the same length of time, and the gains or losses are to be divided proportionately to the investments.

COMPOUND PARTNERSHIP applies when the shares of capital have been invested for different periods of time, and the gains and losses are to be divided according to the average investments; that is, in proportion to the several amounts and times for which they have been employed.

SIMPLE PARTNERSHIP.

To divide gains and losses between co-partners in proportion to their investments when employed for the same period of time.

RULE.—*As the whole capital is to each man's capital, so is the whole gain or loss to each man's share of the gain or loss.*

EXAMPLE 1.—H. W. Barton and William Woods engaged in business as partners, and agreed to share the gains and losses in proportion to their investments. Barton invested $9000; Woods, $7000. They gained $2245.62; what was each one's share?

SOLUTION.

$9000
7000

$16000 whole capital.

$\frac{9000}{16000} = \frac{9}{16}$ B's fractional part of the capital.

$\frac{7000}{16000} = \frac{7}{16}$ W's fractional part of the capital.

$\frac{9}{16}$ of $2245.62 = $1263.16—B's share of gain.

$\frac{7}{16}$ of $2245.62 = $982.46—W's share of gain.

Or, *by proportion:*

$16000 : $9000 : : $2245.62 : $1263.16, B's share.
16000 : $7000 : : 2245.62 : $982.46, W's share.

ANALYSIS.—The whole capital being $16000, B's share is $\frac{9000}{16000} = \frac{9}{16}$; and W's share is $\frac{7000}{16000} = \frac{7}{16}$. And since the gain is to be divided in proportion to the investments, B is entitled to $\frac{9}{16}$ and W to $\frac{7}{16}$ of $2245.62, the whole gain.

By proportion, $16000 : $9000 expresses the ratio of the whole capital to B's investment; and $16000 : $7000 the ratio of the whole to W's share; and, making the whole gain $2245.62, the third term of a proportion in each case, and finding the fourth term, we have the same result as before.

2. Two merchants enter into partnership with a stock of $4300, of which A contributes $3000. They gain $1117; how should this be divided between them?

ANS. A's share = $779.302.
B's share = $337.697.

3. Three persons, A, B and C, agree to form a company, for the manufacture of woollen cloths. A puts in $6470, B $3780, and C $9860. By the end of the year they find they have gained $7890. What portion of this profit belongs to each?

ANS. A's share=$2538.453.
B's share=$1483.053.
C's share=$3868.493.

4. A, B and C entered into partnership with a capital of $7500, of which A put in $2500, B put in $3000, and C put in the remainder; at the end of the year their gain was $3000; what is each one's share of it? ANS. A's share=$1000.
B's share=$1200.
C's share=$ 800.

5. A and B have a joint stock of $4200, of which A owns $3600 and B $600; they gain, in one year, $2000; what is each one's share of the profit? ANS. A's share=$1714.29.
B's share=$ 285.71.

COMPOUND PARTNERSHIP.

To divide gains and losses between co-partners, in proportion to their investments, when their shares of capital have been employed for different periods of time.

When the partners employ their capital for *unequal times*, the profits of each will depend on two circumstances:

1st. On the amount of capital he puts in; and

2ndly. On the length of time it is continued in business:

Therefore, the profit of each will depend on the product of these two elements. The whole profit will be proportional to the sum of these products. Hence, the following

RULE. *Multiply each man's capital by the time he continued it in the firm; then say as the sum of the products is to each product, so is the whole gain or loss to each man's share.*

EXAMPLE 1.—A put in trade $500 for 4 months, and B $600 for 5 months. They gained $240; what was the share of each?

OPERATION.

A's capital, 500 × 4 = 2000
B's capital, 600 × 5 = 3000

Sum of products 5000 : 2000 : : 240 : 96, A's.
5000 : 3000 : : 240 : 144, B's.

EXAMPLE 2.—W. Parker, Samuel Warren and Milton Davis commenced business July 1, 1877, under an agreement to share the accruing gains and losses in proportion to their investments. Parker invested, July 1, $20,000; July 19, $5,000; and July 25 he withdrew $230. Warren invested, July 1, $10,000. Davis invested, July 1, $10,000. Their net gain, August 31, is found to be $1441.94. What is each partner's share, reckoning the exact time by days?

SOLUTION.

The time from July 1st to August 31 is 61 days.
Parker's investment, July 1, $20,000, for 61 days = $1,220,000 for 1 day.
" " " 20, 5,000, " 42 " = 210,000 "

Total. 1,430,000 "
Amount withdrawn July 25, $230, for 37 days= 8,510 "

His average investment 1,421,490 "
Warren's investment, July 1, $10,000, for 61 days= 610,000 "
Davis' " " 10,000, " " = 610,000 "

Total average investment. 2,641,490 "
And by proportion,
$2641490 : $1421490 : : $1441.94 : $775.96, Parker's share
2641490 : 610000 : : 1441.94 : 332.99, Warren's "
2641490 : 610000 : : 1441.94 : 332.99, Davis' "

EXAMPLE 3.—A commenced business with a capital of $10,000. Four months afterwards B entered into partnership with him, and put in 1500 barrels of flour. At the close of the year their profits were $5100, of which B was entitled to $2100; what was the value of the flour per barrel? ANS. $7.

EXAMPLE 4.—On the first of January, 1867, A commenced business with a capital of $23,000; two months afterwards he drew out $1800; on the first of April B entered into partnership with him, and put in $13,500; four months afterwards he drew out $10,000; at the end of the year the profits were $8400; how much should each receive? ANS. A, $6577.24; B, $1822.76.

EXAMPLE 5.—A and B enter into partnership, agreeing to share gains and losses according to capital invested. A invests $6500, B $5400. At the end of five months A withdrew $700, and B invested $400. At the end of the year they have gained $4200. How should it be divided? ANS. A., $2182.09; B, $2017.91.

PARTNERSHIP SETTLEMENTS.

When a partnership is dissolved, either by mutual consent or by limitation of contract, the adjustment of the proceeds between the members is called a partnership settlement. If in making a settlement, the Resources are found to exceed the liabilities, the difference is termed Net Capital; if the Liabilities exceed the Resources, the difference is Net Insolvency. The net capital at commencing is the investment of partners. If the net capital at closing exceeds the net capital at commencing, the difference is the Net Gain; if the opposite, the Net Loss. After having ascertained the net gain or net loss, the next step is to divide this gain or loss among the partners, in accordance with the original agreement between them. This division is frequently not made in exact proportion to the amount invested; sometimes the skill of one partner is considered equal to the capital of another; sometimes a stated salary is allowed each partner, according to his ability or reputation; and sometimes, where unequal amounts are invested, interest is allowed each partner on his investment; but, whether a salary or interest is allowed, such allowance must be classed as a liability of the concern, and go to reduce the gain.

NOTE.—See page 80 for remarks on distribution of gains and losses in partnership.

In order to easily acquire an understanding of this subject, it will be treated under several cases, and a variety of problems will be given in each case, with examples illustrating the best mode of solving them.

We have seen, in the different sets worked out, that the complete double entry ledger is reducible to three distinct parts—Resource and Liability, Ownership or Capital, and Loss and Gain; and that these, as a whole, are in a state of balance as to debit and credit, when the result of business is ascertained, as shown in second Trial Balance, page 44.

The terms Resource and Liability, as here employed, do not include the partners' accounts. They mean the outside property and debts of the partnership. They have no reference to the owing and being owed as between partners, which may be treated as a resource and liability, as between themselves. It is a grave mistake to confound resource and liability, springing from relations between partners and those that arise from relations between the partnership and outside persons and things. If a creditor wishes to know the financial standing of a firm, he little cares how much one partner may owe another. He wants to know what and how much are the resources and liabilities of the partnership; since it is the difference between these alone that gives the true status. For if the amounts with which partners are charged are to be included among the resources, the firm may make a large show of net capital, while, in fact, it is insolvent. So the partners' accounts, either as to the debit or credit, can never be included among the resources and liabilities, when the real solvency or insolvency of a firm is sought.

Therefore, in solving partnership problems, RESOURCE and LIABILITY will be treated exclusive of the OWNERSHIP accounts.

The ownership accounts seem to be the measure of successive services of the owners for given periods of time. They represent, in fact, their past labors, whether before or after they entered into the partnership.

The terms Loss and Gain represent the results of the firm's services or business during a definite period of time.

Having shown that Resources and Liabilities properly belong to one class of accounts, and Ownership and Loss and Gain to another class, it will be readily seen in the light of the double-entry principle, how, when any TWO PARTS of the ledger are given, the third, as to its NET, can be found. For we have only to contrast the excesses of the TWO PARTS given, and supply the THIRD to be found, with an amount which will produce an equilibrium between the two classes.

NOTICE OF DISSOLUTION OF PARTNERSHIP FOR PUBLICATION.

The partnership heretofore existing between Samual F. Jones and John S. White, wholesale grocers, in the city of Belleville, under the firm name and style of Jones & White, is this day dissolved by mutual consent. Samuel F. Jones has retired from the business. The assets and liabilities of the firm have been assumed by John S. White, to whom all debts must be paid.

Dated at Belleville, Ontario, the tenth day of February, 1877.

JOHN S. HALL, witness.

(Signed,) SAMUEL F. JONES.
" JOHN S. WHITE.

Referring to the above I beg to announce that I have formed a partnership with James Caldwell, and we shall continue the business under the firm name and style of White, Caldwell & Co.

JOHN S. WHITE.

By such a notice as the above being published and sent to each creditor, the outgoing partner would be relieved from any responsibility for debts contracted by the new firm. He cannot, however, be relieved of the debts contracted by the old firm until they are discharged.

PROBLEMS.

We will now give examples and exercises illustrating the application of the DOUBLE ENTRY PRINCIPLE in the solution of partnership problems. We will present them under three cases:

CASE 1.—RESOURCE AND LIABILITY AND INVESTMENT OR OWNERSHIP BEING GIVEN, TO FIND NET GAIN OR NET LOSS, AND THE STANDING OF EACH PARTNER AT CLOSING.

EXAMPLE.—A and B are partners. Having conducted business for a time, they close with the following property and debts. They have Cash, $3240; Mdse., $2575; Bills Receivable, $860; Jno. Brown owes an account, $375. They owe on Bills Payable, $1250; and James Jones on account, $370. A invested at commencing, $2500, and drew out, during business, $560. B invested $2500, and drew out, during business, $280. They agreed to share equally in gains and losses. What is the net gain, during business? What is the net capital of each at closing?

OPERATION.

Resources and Liabilities.			*Ownership.*	
Dr.	*Cr.*	*Dr.*		*Cr.*
$3240	$1250	$560 A withdrew		$2500
2575	370	280 B "		2500
860				
375	1620	840	Total investment	5000
			" withdrawn	840
7050 Resources at closing.				
1620 Liabilities "			Firms net investment	4160
5430 *Present worth of firm.*				
4160 Credit excess of ownership.				
1270 Net gain during business.				
635 A's ½ net gain during business.				
635 B's " " " " "				

PROOF.

A's investment	......	......	$2500	B's investment	......	.. ...	......	$2500
" withdrawal	......	... ..	560	" withdrawal	......	......	......	280
" net investment		......	1940	" net investment		......	......	2220
" ½ net gain	......	......	635	" ½ net gain	......	......	......	635
" net capital at closing	......		2575	" net capital at closing			......	2855
				Add A's net capital			......	2575
				Present worth of firm			......	5430

The difference of resource and liability values gives us an excess of debit, $5430, which is the present worth at closing. The difference of the ownership value gives us an excess of credit, $4160, which is the net investment. The difference of these excesses gives us a final excess of debit, $1270, which shows a net gain to that amount. The final excess of $1270, being a debit, shows just so much more resource at closing than the firm had at starting; consequently, this amount must have been gained during the continuance of business.

2.—A and B having conducted business one year as partners, close with the following resources and liabilities. They have Cash in bank, $3456; Mdse., per inventory, $2120; Bills Receivable, $1874. E. A. Corby owes $630. They owe on Bills Payable $3250; W. G. Smith, on account, $346. A invested, at commencing, $1500, and drew out $175. B invested $1500, and drew out $315. What is the net gain and the net capital of each at closing? Ans. Net gain, $1974. A's net capital, $2312. B's, $2172.

3.—A and B are partners, equal in investments and in losses and gains, and close with the following resources and liabilities: They have cash in bank, $3675; Mdse., per inventory, $1824; Bills Receivable, $1256; Real Estate, $2000; Bank Stock, $1884. They owe on Bills Payable, $2570; on Mortgages Payable, $1278; Accounts Payable, $3275. A invested $5000, and drew out $5486. B invested $5000 and drew out $6250. What is the net gain, and also net capital of each at closing?

OPERATION.

Resources and Liabilities.				*Ownership.*	
Dr.	Cr.	Dr.			Cr.
$3675	$2570	$ 5486			$5000
1824	1278	6250			5000
1256	3275	——			——
2000	——	11736 amt. withdrawn.			10000
1884	7123	10000 " invested.			
——					
10639 Resources at closing.		1736			
7123 Liabilities "					
3516 *Present worth of firm.*					
1736 Debit excess of ownership.					
5252 Net gain, at closing.					
2626 A's ½ net gain.					
2626 B' " "					

PROOF.

A's investment			$5000	B's investment		$5000
" withdrawal			5486	" withdrawal		6250
" overdraw			486	" overdraw		1250
" ½ net gain			2626	" ½ net gain		2626
" net capital at closing			2140	" net capital at closing		1376
				Add A's net capital		2140
				Present worth of firm		3516

4.—A and B close business as follows: They have Cash, $1424; Mdse., $1562; Fixtures, $383; Mortgages Receivable, $3485; Bills Receivable, $826. They owe on Bills Payable, $2450; on Accounts, $1240. A invested $6000, and a debt of his to the amount of $1000 was assumed by the firm at commencing, and paid during business. He also drew out, at different times, $685; and is allowed interest on capital invested, $420. B invested $4000, and drew out, during business, $1860, and is allowed interest on capital, $280. A is to share 3-5 and B 2-5 of gains and losses. What is the net loss? What is the net capital of each?

OPERATION.

Resources and Liabilities.				Ownership.			
Dr.		Cr.		Dr.			Cr.
$1424		$2450		$ 1000			$6000
1562		1240		685			420
383		—		1860			4000
3485		$3690		—			280
826				3545			
				Investment	......	......	10700
7680 Resources at closing.				Withdrawal	......	......	3545
3690 Liabilities.				Net investment	......		7155
				Debit excess of R & L.		......	3990
3990 Present worth of firm.				Net loss during business		......	3165
				A's 3-5 of net loss		......	1899
				B's 2-5 " "		......	1266

PROOF.

A's investment	......	......	.....	$6420	B's investment	......	......	$4280
" withdrawal	......	......	......	1685	" withdrawal	......	......	1860
" net investment		......	.....	4735	" net investment			2420
" 3-5 net loss	......	......	......	1899	" 2-5 net loss	......		1266
" present interest		......	......	2836	" present interest		......	1154
					Add A's interest		......	2836
					Present worth of firm	......	......	3990

5.—Jones and Brown close business with the following results: They have Cash on deposit, $3421; Mdse., $5789; G.T.R. Stock, $4321; Bonds and Mortgages, $6452; Montreal Bank Stock, $3689; Real Estate, $1724; Notes and Acceptances, $432; Accounts Receivable, $321. They owe on Notes and Acceptances, $8924; on Accounts Payable, $3479. Jones invested $12000. The firm assumed a debt for him of $1500. He drew out, during business, $600, and is allowed interest, at closing, $1000. Brown invested $6000. The firm assumed a debt for him of $750. He drew out during business $300, and is allowed interest, $500. Jones is to share ⅗ and Brown ⅖ of the gains and losses. What is the net loss? What is the net capital of each at closing? Ans. Net loss $2604; Jones' net capital is $9164; Brown's, $4582.

6.—A and B close business, and wish to know the financial standing of each. They have Cash on hand, $2263; and Real Estate worth $5000. They owe on Mortgages Payable, $3846; on Notes, $4462; and on Personal Account, $675. A invested $6000, and withdrew during business, $2860. B invested $4000, drew out, during business, $5560, and is allowed for extra services, $250. A shares 3-5 and B 2-5 of gains and losses. What is the net loss? What is the financial standing of each at closing?

OPERATION.

Resources and Liabilities.			Ownership.			
Dr.		Cr.	Dr.			Cr.
$2263		$3846	$2860			$6000
5000		4462	5560			4000
		675	—			250
7263		—	8420			—
Liabilities at closing	......	8983	Investment		......	10250
Resources "	......	7263	Withdrawal	......	......	8420
		—	Net investment	......	......	1830
Insolvency of firm	......	1720	Credit excess of R. & L.	......	......	1720
			Net loss during business		......	3550
			A's 3-5 of net loss	......	......	2130
			B's 2-5 " "	......	......	1420

PROOF.

A's investment	$6000	B's investment			$4250
" withdrawal	2860	" withdrawal			5560
" net investment	3140	" overdraw			1310
" 3-5 net loss	2130	" 2-5 net loss			1420
" net capital	1010	" net insolvency			2730
		Deduct A's net capital			1010
		Insolvency of firm			1720

7.—A and B dissolved partnership, and wish to know the financial standing of each. They have Cash, $2653.26; Bills Receivable, $1258.16; and amounts due on Personal account, $2831. They owe on Notes outstanding, $4428.50; John West, on account, $1234.60; Wm. East, on account, $1380.40; George South, on account, $1290.77. A invested $3000, and drew out $550. B invested $2000, drew out $3525, and is allowed for extra services, $175. A shares 3-5 and B 2-5 of the losses and gains. What is the net loss? What is the financial standing of each at closing? ANS. Net loss, $2691.85; A's net capital, $834.89; B's net insolvency, $2426.74.

CASE 2.—RESOURCE AND LIABILITY, LOSS AND GAIN, AND AMOUNTS ADDED OR WITHDRAWN BY PARTNERS GIVEN, TO FIND NET CAPITAL OR NET INSOLVENCY AT COMMENCING.

EXAMPLE 1.—A and B close business and wish to ascertain results. A invested $\frac{2}{3}$ and B $\frac{1}{3}$ of the capital, and they agree to share losses and gains in the same proportion. They have at closing, the following resources: Cash, $5474.50; Mdse., $2584.23; Notes $946.30; Fixtures worth $314.80. They owe on Notes, $875.75; and on Account, $364.12. They have lost $2345.62, and gained $4526.23. What was the net capital at commencing? What is the net capital of each at closing?

OPERATION.

Resources and Liabilities.			*Ownership.*	
Dr.	Cr.	Dr.		Cr.
$5474.50	$875.75	$2345.62		$4526.23
2584.23	364.12			2345.62
946 30				
314.80	1239.87	Net gain in business		2180.61
9319.83 Resource at closing.		A's $\frac{2}{3}$ net gain		1453.74
1239.87 Liability "		B's $\frac{1}{3}$ " "		726.87
8079.96 *Present worth of firm.*				
2180.61 Credit excess of ownership.				
5899.35 N. C. at commencing.				
3932.90 A's $\frac{2}{3}$ "				
1966.45 B's $\frac{1}{3}$ "				

PROOF.

A's $\frac{2}{3}$ investment		$3932.90	B's $\frac{1}{3}$ investment	$1966.45
" $\frac{2}{3}$ net gain		1453.74	B's $\frac{1}{3}$ net gain	726.87
" present interest		5386.64	" present interest	2693.32
			Add A's interest	5386.64
			Present worth of firm	8079.96

NOTE.—The excess of debit of resource and liability values is $8079.96. The excess of credit of the ownership values is $2180.61. The difference of these excesses is a final debit of $5899.35. Therefore, this is the amount of net capital at commencing, because it will make the excesses in the two classes equal. This is proved by the adjustment of the partners' accounts, since the capital of the two equals the present worth, as shown by the difference between the resources and liabilities.

2.—A and B have conducted business one year, and wish to know the present interest of each. The former invested ⅔ and the latter ⅓ of the capital, and they agreed to share gains and losses in same proportion. They have, at closing, the following resources: Cash, $3724.15; Real Estate, $2356.14; Notes and Drafts, $1762.18; Fixtures and unexpired Rent, $942.12. They owe on Notes, $1426.22; and on Book Accounts, $519 33. Their losses have been $1345.71, and gains, $4625.55. What was the net capital invested by the firm? What is the net capital of each at closing? ANS. Net capital invested, $3559.20. A's net capital, at closing, is $4559.36; and B's $2279.68.

3.—A and B, wishing to know their present interests, give the following data: They invested equally, and share in the same proportion the losses and gains. They have money on deposit, $1875.35; Lumber, $1532.50; Notes and Personal Accounts, in their favor, $684.41. They owe on Notes outstanding, $784.24; and on Personal Accounts, $365.40. Their losses have been $3464.12; and gains, $1639.46. A drew out, during business, $2232.50; and B lent the firm, $1764.50. What is the net capital or insolvency of each?

OPERATION.

Resources and Liabilities.			Ownership.		
Dr.		Cr.	Dr.		Cr.
$1875.35		$784.24	$3464.12		$1639.46
1532.50		365.40	2232.50		1764.50
684.41					
		1149.64	5696.62		3403.96
4092.26	Resources at closing.		3403.96		
1149.64	Liabilities "				
			2292.66		
2942.62	Present worth of firm.		Losses during business	......	3464.12
2292.66	Debit excess of ownership.		Gains " "	......	1 639.46
5235.28	Net investment of firm.		Net loss of firm		1824.66
2617.64	A's ½ net investment,		A's ½ net loss	......	912.33
2617.64	B's " "		B's ½ "	......	912.33

PROOF.

A's ½ investment at commencing	......	$2617.64	B' ½ investment at commencing	......	$2617.64
" withdrawal	....	2232.50	" loan to the firm	....	1764.50
" net investment	......	385.14	" net investment	....	4382.14
" ½ net loss	......	912.33	" ½ net loss	....	912.33
" insolvency at closing	......	527.19	" capital at closing	......	3469.81
			Deduct A's insolvency	......	527.19
			Present worth of firm	......	2942.62

NOTE.—Here the difference of resource and liability values is a *debit* of $2042.62; and the difference of the ownership is a *debit* of $2292.66; consequently, they are added, giving us $5235.28, as the net amount invested by the firm. Such an amount must have been invested for the reason that it, with the other ownership values, is required to make the excess of credit among the ownership class equal to the excess of debit among the resource and liability class. This is abundantly proved in making up the partners' accounts. A turns out insolvent, $527.19, and B has a net capital of $3469.81, the difference of which just equals their present worth, as shown by the resource and liability values. In final settlement, therefore, it will take the net amount of property owned by the firm and A's indebtedness to pay off B.

4.—A and B close business, giving the following data for the adjustment of their accounts: They invested equally, to share in like proportion. They have Cash, $2425.12; Furniture and Fixtures, $1832.14; Notes and Acceptances, $1756.17; and Verbal

Promises, $354.50. They owe on Notes and Acceptances, $2865.50; and on Verbal Promises, $842.75. Their losses have been $3426.39, and gains $1864.69. A drew out $2564.24, and B lent the firm $375.20. What was the net capital of the firm at commencing? What is the present financial standing of each at closing? Ans. Net capital at beginning, $6410.42; A's net insolvency, at closing, $139.88; B's net capital is $2799.56.

5.—A, B, and C, wishing to know the financial standing of each partner, give the following data: They have Cash, $3464.50; Bills Receivable, $1325.80; Accounts Receivable, $275.36, and Interest Receivable, $126.38. They owe on Notes, $2538.60; on Accounts Payable, $734.40; and on Interest Payable, $135.26. Their losses have been $1375.37, and gains, $6364.90. A drew out $850; B drew $620; and C lent the firm $1250. What was the net insolvency of the firm at commencing? What is the financial standing of each at closing?—it being understood that they were equal in their insolvency at beginning, and that they agreed to share equally the losses and gains.

OPERATION.

Resources and Liabilities.			Ownership and Gains and Losses.	
Dr.		Cr.	Dr.	Cr.
$3464.50		$2538.60	$1375.37	$6364.90
1325.80		734.40	850.00	1250.00
275.36		135.26	620.00	
126.38				$7614.90
		3408.26	2845.37	2845.37
5192.04	Resources at closing.			
3408.26	Liabilities "			4769.53
			Debit excess of R. and L.	1783.78
1783.78	Present worth of firm.			
			Net insolvency at commencing	2985.75
			A's ⅓ N. I. " "	995.25
			B's ⅓ " " "	995.25
			C's ⅓ " " "	995.25
			Gains during business	6364.90
			Losses " "	1375.37
			Net gain "	4989.53
			A's ⅓ net gain	1663.17
			B's ⅓ " "	1663.18
			C's ⅓ " "	1663.18

PROOF.

A's net insolvency at commencing ...	$995.25	C's net insolvency at commencing...		$ 995.25
" withdrawal	850.00	" loan to the firm	.....	1250.00
" insolvency without the gains......	1845.25	" net investment	.....	254.75
" ⅓ net gain	1663.17	" ⅓ net gain	.....	1663.18
" insolvency at closing	182.08	" net capital at closing	.....	1917.93
B's net insolvency at commencing....	995.25	Add B's capital	.....	47.93
" withdrawal	620.00	C and B's capital	.....	1965.86
" insolvency without the gains......	1615.25	Deduct A's insolvency	.....	182.08
" ⅓ net gain	1663.18	Present worth of firm	.....	1783.78
" net capital at closing	47.93			

6.—A, B, and C, at the end of one year's business, wish to know the financial standing of each partner. They have, at closing, Cash, $2375.15; Bills Receivable, $1246.82;

W

Accounts Receivable, $385.46 ; and Interest Receivable, $138.50. They owe on Bills Payable, $1872.50 ; on Accounts Payable, $634.80 ; and on Interest Payable, $125.70. Their losses have been $1482.27, and gains, $6836.80. A drew out $1650, B drew $450, and C loaned the firm $1475. What was the firm's net insolvency at commencing, and what is the financial standing of each at closing?—the partners being equal in their insolvency at starting, and sharing equally in losses and gains at closing. ANS. Net insolvency at commencing, $3216.60 ; A's insolvency at closing, $937.36 ; B's net capital, $262.64 ; C's net capital, $2187.65.

7.—A and B give the following data for adjustment : They were equally insolvent at starting, and agreed to share equally in the losses and gains. At closing they have only the following property : Cash, $1365.50 ; and Notes and Personal Accounts amounting to $2326. They owe on Notes, $3570.75 ; A.W. Parker, on account, $835.25 ; and E. A. Kyle, on account, $545.25. Their losses have been $2264.25, and gains, $3628.50. A drew out $1150.75, and B lent the firm $550.75. What was the firm's insolvency at commencing ? What is the financial standing of each partner at closing ?

In this case the resource and liability values have an excess of credit, $1259.75, and the ownership values an excess of credit, $764.25. Both excesses being *credits* they have to be added to effect a corresponding debit, and thus throw the two classes of values into opposite and equal excesses. The sum, therefore, of the two, which is $2024, is the amount of insolvency with which the firm began, since all the other values, except those which show the state of the ownership at commencing, are given in the problem. That the $2024 was the insolvency of the firm at commencing is proved by making up their accounts on this basis.

OPERATION.

Resources and Liabilities.				*Ownership.*		
Dr.		Cr.		Dr.		Cr.
$1365.50		$3570.75		$2264.25		$3628.50
2326.00		835.25		1150.75		550.75
		545.25				
3691.50				3415.00		4179.25
Liabilities at closing		4951.25				3415.00
Resources "		3691.50				764.25
				Credit excess of R. & L.		1259.75
Insolvency of firm at closing		1259.75		Insolvency at commencing		2024.00
				A's ½ of insolvency		1012.00
				B's ½ "		1012.00
				Gains during business		3628.50
				Losses " "		2264.25
				Net Gain "		1364.25
				A's ½ net gain		682.12
				B's ½ " "		682 13

PROOF.

A's ½ N. I. at commencing	$1012.00	B's ½ N. I. at commencing	$1012.00
" withdrawal	1150.75	" loan to the firm	550.75
" insolvency, without the gains......	2162.75	" insolv., without the gains	461.25
" ½ net gain	682.12	" ½ net gain	682.13
N. I. at closing	1480.63	" net capital at closing	220.88
		A's net insolvency "	1420.63
		Insolvency of firm at closing	1259.75

8.—A and B wishing to adjust their affairs give the following data : They have Cash on hand $6023.50. They owe on Notes and Acceptances, $4680.50 ; and on various Personal Accounts, $3490.75. Their losses in business have been $3375.75, and their gains $5874.75. A drew out, during business, $2260.25, and B lent the firm $660.50. They set out equally insolvent, and agreed to share equally in losses and gains. What was the net insolvency at commencing? What the financial status of each at closing? ANS. Insolvency of firm at commencing, $3047 ; A's net insolvency at closing is $2534.25 ; B's net capital is $386.50.

CASE 3.—*Ownership and loss and gain being given to find net resource or net liability*.

It will hardly be necessary to give examples and exercises under this case, for the reason that, when Ownership and Loss and Gain are given, we know, on the principal of equality of excesses between the two classes of values, that the difference of the values of Ownership and Loss and Gain always corresponds with the difference of the resource and liability values. And if all the Ownership and Loss and Gain values have an excess of credit, it pre-supposes an excess of debit among the resource and liability values, and that such excess of debit is a *net resource* ; while if there be an excess of debit among the Ownership values, there will be a corresponding excess of credit among the other values, and that excess will be a *net liability*.

It will be seen, therefore, that to find the financial status of a firm, whether constituted of one or more parties, it is only necessary to consult the capital and loss and gain accounts, which, as compared with the resource and liability accounts in most kinds of business, are very few in number. The proprietor's or proprietors' accounts show investments and withdrawals of property ; while the loss and gain accounts represent the increase and decrease of property by means of services during given periods of time.

There is another point coming appropriately under this head. It sometimes occurs that the only accounts given are the partners'—all the real accounts being cancelled. Suppose, then, two or more partners have got their business, all wound up, save the adjustment of their own account. They have divided up the property, and been charged with it. They have either paid off all their debts, or each are assumed to pay certain amounts, and thus cancelled the partnership debts. This being done, how shall the partners settle as between themselves ?

They have only to find the difference of all the values constituting the ownership, and if that difference be a *debit* it shows the *net gain* of the firm ; if a *credit* a *net* loss. This net gain or net loss is the amount wanting to restore the balance of co-equal exchange of values. Then if this net gain or loss be divided between the partners according to agreement, the difference of each partner's account will be each one's financial status. Then if the partner's accounts are not all equal as to debit and credit, the owing partner or partners must pay over to the partner or partners owed, when all will be adjusted.

ANOTHER FORM OF WORKING PARTNERSHIP SETTLEMENTS.

We will now give a few examples worked out by another method, which may also be solved by the form already illustrated.

EXAMPLE 1.—A and B, having been in business 1 year, dissolve partnership. B retires, leaving A to continue the business and liquidate the debts of the firm. A invested $12,000, B $10,000. Each is to receive interest on his investment, and share the gains and losses equally. How much did each gain ? what is A's capital at closing, and how much should be paid B on retiring, the resources and liabilities being as follows :

Resources.			Liabilities.	
Cash on hand,		$5,000	Personal debts firm owe per Ledger	$8,170
Personal debts due firm per			Bills payable,	4,200
Ledger	$12,000		Interest on notes and drafts,	130
Less 25 per cent. for bad debts,	3,000	9,000		
			Total Liabilities.	12,500
Mdse. as per inventory,		16,530		
Bills Receivable,		3,500		
Mortgage Rec.,		4,000		
Accrued interest on above,		120		
Real Estate (store and lot),		6,500		
Store Fixtures,		350		
Total Resources,		45,000		

OPERATION.

Total resources,			$45,000
" liabilities,			12,500
Firm's net capital at closing,			$32,500
Interest on A's investment $12,000 for 1 year,		=	$ 720
" B's " 10,000 "		=	600
Firm's net capital at closing,			$32,500
A's investment,	$12,000		
Interest for 1 year,	720		
		$12,720	
B's investment,	$10,000		
Interest for 1 year,	600		
		$10,600	
			$23,320
Firm's net gains in business,			$9,180
A's investment, $12,000	B's investment,	10,000	
Interest for 1 year, 720	Interest for 1 year,	600	
His ½ net gains, 4,590	His ½ net gains,	4,590	
A's net capital, $17,310	B,s net capital,	$15,190	
A's net capital, $17,310			
B's " 15,190			
Firm's net capital, as before,	$32,500		

—D and E are partners: each invested $3000, and agreed to share the gains and losses equally. During the year, D drew out $600, and E $500. What were their gains at the end of the year, their resources and liabilities being as follows:

Resources.		
Cash on hand,		$3,500
Mdse., as per inventory,		3,600
Bills Receivable,		1,200
Debts due firm, as per Ledger,		2,500
Total Resources,		$10,800
Liabilities.		
Debts firm owe, as per Ledger,		$1,500
Bills Payable,		800
Total Liabilities,		2,300
Firm's net capital at closing,		$8,500
D invested,	$3,000	
Less amount withdrawn,	600	
D's credit balance,		$2,400
E invested	3,000	
Less amount withdrawn,	500	
E's credit balance,		$2,500
Balance of investments,		4,900
Firm's net gains,		$3,600

PROOF.

D invested	$3,000	E invested	$3,000
Withdrew	600	Withdrew	500
	2,400		2,500
½ net gains,	1,800	½ net gains,	1,800
D's net capital at closing,	$4,200	E's net capital at closing,	$4,300

D's net capital,	$4,200
E's net capital,	4,300
Firm's net capital as above,	$8,500

3.—A, B, and C form a partnership; A invests $15,000, B $12,000, and C, nothing. They share the gains and losses as follows, viz.; A½, B ⅓, C ⅙. A draws out during the year $800, B $900, and C $400. What is each partner's capital, and what are the gains at the end of the year, when their resources amount to $40,000, and their liabilities to $44,000.

OPERATION.

Liabilities,	$44,000	A's investment,	$15,000	
Less resources,	40,000	Less amt. withdrawn,	800	$14,200
Firm's net insolvency,	$4,000	B's investment,	$12,000	
		Less amt. withdrawn,	900	11,100
				25,300
		Less amt. withdrawn by C,		400
A's ½ loss,	$14,450.00			
B's ⅓ "	9,633.33	Firm's net investment,		24,900
C's ⅙ "	4,816.67	Add Firm's insolvency,		4,000
Total losses,	$28,900.00	Firm's net loss,		$28,900
A's investment,	15,000.00	A's ½ loss,		14,450
Less amount withdrawn,	800.00	Net Investment,		14,200
	$14,200.00	A's net insolvency,		250
B's investment,	$12,000.00	C's ⅙ loss,		$4,816.67
Less amount withdrawn,	900.00	Add amount withdrawn,		400.00
	11,100.00	C's net insolvency,		5,216.67
Less his ⅓ loss,	9,633.33			
B's net capital,	$1,466.67			
		A's insolvency,	$ 250.00	
		C's "	5,216.67	
			5,466.67	
		Deduct B's net capital,	1,466.67	
		Firm's net insolvency,	$4,000.00	

In which a salary is allowed each partner. No interest account kept.

4.—A, B, and C entered into partnership, January 1st, 1876. A and B each invested $7000, C invested $14000. A's share of the gains or losses was ¼, B's ¼, and C's ½. A was to receive a salary of $1000 per year, B $1500 and C $500 for services. A drew out $650, B $450, and C $900. What was each partner's interest in the firm, January 1st, 1877, when their resources were $54,500, and their liabilities $13,500?

OPERATION.

Resources,		$54,500
Liabilities,		13,500
	Firm's net capital,	$41,000
A's investment,	$7,000	
Add salary,	1,000	
	8,000	
Less amount withdrawn,	650	
A's credit balance,		7,350
B's investment,	$7,000	
Add salary,	1,500	
	8,500	
Less amount withdrawn,	450	
B's credit balance,		8,050
C's investment,	14,000	
Add Salary	500	
	14,500	
Less amount withdrawn,	900	
C's credit balance,		13,600 29,000
Firm's net gains,		$12,000

A's credit balance,	$7,350	B's credit balance,	$8,050	C's credit balance,	$13,600
" ⅓ gain,	3,000	" ⅓ gain,	3,000	" ½ gain,	6,000
Net capital,	$10,350	Net capital,	$11,050	Net capital,	$19,600

PROOF.—A's net capital, $10,350
          B's   "   11,050
          C's   "   19,600

Firm's net capital, as above, $41,000

In which amounts withdrawn are averaged, and interest is charged and allowed.

5.—A and B entered into partnership January 1st, 1876. A invested $12,000, and B $14,500, the gains and losses to be shared equally ; each partner to be allowed 6 per cent. on his investment, and to be charged at the same rate on sums drawn out. A drew as follows : March 1st, $300 ; July 9th, $250 ; September 10th, $200; December 16th, $150. B drew April 7th, $100 ; August 4th, $400 ; November 23rd, $250. What was each partner's interest January 1st, 1877, their resources and liabilities being as follows :

Resources.		*Liabilities.*	
Cash,	$ 3,600	Personal debts firm owe,	$11,500
Personal debts due firm,	16,000	Bills Payable,	500
Bills Receivable,	1,400		
Mdse., as per inventory,	26,000	Total liabilities,	$12,000
G.T.R. R. Stock,	6,000	*Firm's net capital,*	41,000
Total resources,	$53,000		$53,000

Average date of amount withdrawn by A, July 6th.
    "   "   "   "   B, Aug. 26th.

A's investment,	$12,000			B's investment,	$14,500.00	
Less amt. withdrawn,	900	$11,100		Less amt. withdrawn,	750.00	$13,750.00
Interest on investment,				Interest on investment		
$12000 for 1 year,	720.00			$14,500, for 1 year,	870.00	
Less interest on $900 withdrawn, from average date, July 6th to Jan. 1st (178 days).	26.70	693.30		Less interest on $750 withdrawn, from average date, Aug. 26 to Jan. 1 (127 days).	15.87	854.13
A's credit bal.,		$11,793.30		B's credit balance,		$14,604.13
Firm's net capital,		$41,000.00				
A's credit balance,		$11,793.30				
B's "		14,604.13			26,397.43	
Firm's net gains.					$14,602.57	
A's investment, less amount withdrawn,		$11,100.00		B's investment, less amount withdrawn,		$13,750.00
Credit balance of interest,		693.30		Credit balance of interest,		854.13
His ⅔ gains,		7,301.29		His ½ gains,		7,301.28
A's net capital,		$19,094.59		B's net capital,		$21,905.41
Firm's net capital, as above, $41,000.						

6.—A and B commenced business as partners. A invested $20,000, and B $10,000, A sharing ⅔ and B ⅓ of the gains and losses. No interest account was kept. A drew out $1700, and B $2150. Their assets at the close of the year consisted of—Cash, $4200; Bills Receivable $8800; Mdse., $26,000; and Personal Debts, $16,000. 10 per cent. of the personal debts are considered bad. Their liabilities are—Bills Payable, $3250; Personal Accounts, $11,250. If B should retire from the firm, how much ought he to receive?

Assets.			*Liabilities.*	
Cash,	$4,200		Bills Payable,	$3,250
Bills Receivable,	8,800		Personal accounts,	11,250
Mdse.,	26,000			
Personal accts., less 10 per cent.,	14,400			14,500
			Capital invested,	30,000
	53,400			
				44,500
Add amount drawn out,	3,850		*Firm's net gain,*	12,750
	$57,250			$57,250

Dr.			*Cr.*	
A's acct. Drawn out,	1,700		Capital,	20,000
Balance,	26,800		⅔ net gain,	8,500
	28,500			28,500
B's acct. Drawn out,	2,150		Capital,	10,000
Balance,	12,100		⅓ net gain,	4,250
	$14,250			$14,250

TO REDUCE DOLLARS AND CENTS TO STERLING MONEY.

RULE.—*Divide the given sum by the value of £1 sterling (4.8674) the quotient will be pounds sterling and decimals of a pound.*

Reduce the decimal part to shillings and pence.

EXAMPLE.—Reduce $749.83 to sterling money.

OPERATION.

749.83 ÷ 4.867 =£154.0641 =£154 1s. 3¼d.   ANS.

EXERCISES.

1. Reduce $1006.90 to sterling money.   ANS. £206 17s. 7¾d.
2. Reduce $916.87 to sterling money.   ANS. £188 7s. 8¼d.
3. Reduce $2114.81 to sterling money.   ANS. £434 10s. 4¾d.

TO REDUCE STERLING MONEY TO DOLLARS AND CENTS.

RULE.—*Express the given sum decimally, and multiply by the par value of £1 sterling (4.867).*

EXAMPLE.—Reduce £78 11s. 4¾d. to dollars and cents.

OPERATION.

£78 11s. 4¾d.=£78.5697916 and £78.5697916 × 4.867=$382.399.   ANS.

EXERCISES.

1. Reduce £2043 11s. 3d. sterling to dollars and cents.   ANS. $9946.01868.
2. Reduce £777.7s. 7d. sterling to dollars and cents.   ANS. $3783.50437.
3. Reduce £557.19s. 5½d. sterling to dollars and cents.   ANS. $2715.65418.

www.ingramcontent.com/pod-product-compliance
Lightning Source LLC
Chambersburg PA
CBHW030742230426
43667CB00007B/811